THE GAA

COUNTY BY COUNTY

THE GAA

COUNTY BY COUNTY

Mike Cronin, Mark Duncan
and Paul Rouse

The Collins Press

First published in 2011 by
The Collins Press
West Link Park
Doughcloyne
Wilton
Cork

British Library Cataloguing in Publication data
Cronin, Mike.
  The GAA : county by county.
  1. Gaelic Athletic Association--History. 2. Gaelic
Athletic Association--Influence.
  I. Title II. Duncan, Mark. III. Rouse, Paul.
  796'.06'09415-dc22

ISBN: 978-184889-1289

Design and typesetting by Anú Design, Tara
Typeset in Garamond
Printed in Italy by Printer Trento

Prelim Photographs

p. ii: Against the spectacular backdrop of Scalp Mountain, the under-14 footballers from the Burt GAA club receive instruction in the finer points of the game from Danny Dowds at half-time in a match against Urris in 1988. *(Dónal Campbell)*

p. vi: On 29 September 2003, the Sam Maguire was brought to Tyrone. The homecoming in Omagh was one of the great emotional occasions in the history of the GAA. Local musicians, including Philomena Begley, entertained the crowds before the players were introduced to the vast crowd who turned out. *(Inpho)*

Jacket Photographs

Front and spine: (clockwise from top left) a hurling match in Loughinisland, County Down *c.* 1915 (Loughinisland GAC); a member of the Tulla Pipe Band, playing before a hurling match in County Clare, *c.* 1954 (Dorothea Lange Collection, the Oakland Museum of California, City of Oakland. Gift of Paul S. Taylor); Hugh, Joe and Liam McCabe (on bike) from Clonad, County Laois. Between them, Joe and Liam won fifteen county hurling championships. (GAA Oral History Project/Joe McCabe); in 1957, at a match in Tuam between Galway and Louth, the crossbar broke in two in the second half (Paddy Cotter/Aidan Claffey); young boys kick a football on Achill island in the early 1990s (Corbis).
Back: (top) under-14 football Burt v. Urris, 1988. Danny Dowds talks to the Burt players at half-time. (Dónal Campbell); (bottom) Wexford supporters on Dublin's O'Connell Street as they make their way to Croke Park for the 1965 All-Ireland hurling final (*Fáilte Ireland*).
Front flap: victory celebrations with the Mostrim team after the 1974 Longford County Championship. (GAA Oral History Project/John Mc Gerr).
Back flap: Laois v. Kerry in a National Hurling League game, 16 October 1955 (Kennelly Archive).

Contents

450   258   127   324   410

Acknowledgements

The GAA Oral History Project began in 2008 with the aim of recording and documenting the memories and experiences of GAA people across the world. The ongoing realisation of the project has been a pleasure: the creation of a disparate and fascinating collection of oral recordings, written questionnaires, original documents and photographs. Taken together, these recordings provide a unique resource for academics, journalists and broadcasters, or, indeed, for anyone seeking to understand or explain the place that the GAA has occupied in Irish life. This book is the second publication to emerge from the project and follows *The GAA: A People's History*, which appeared in 2009 on the occasion of the 125th anniversary of the Association. Neither book would have been possible without the project, which itself would never have happened without the generous support of the GAA, who saw its potential and provided its funding from the beginning. It is necessary to acknowledge the assistance we have been given at every step by three people within Croke Park, namely GAA President Christy Cooney, Lisa Clancy in Communications and Tom Ryan in Finance. We would also like to offer our thanks to former President Nickey Brennan, the Director General Páraic Duffy and the Chair of the GAA's 125 committee, Jarlath Burns, all of whom were instrumental in supporting the very idea of the project in its early stages. Alan Milton joined the GAA communications department along the way and, whenever called upon, was willing to put his extensive knowledge of the Association at the service of the project. While many other people are named in these acknowledgements and throughout the text, the simple fact is that this project would not work without the infectious enthusiasm of GAA members throughout Ireland and beyond. We have been lucky in the manner in which people have supported the project, and have given freely of their time and introduced us to a network of contacts that cover the complex map of GAA parishes and counties.

This book, like the project from which it is born, has been necessarily a collaborative endeavour. It is underpinned by an extraordinary volume of work by an exceptional group of people. Chief among them are Arlene Crampsie and Regina Fitzpatrick who, more than anybody else, have been drivers of the GAA

Oral History Project. Week in, week out, they have driven across the island through rain, sun and snow to record interviews in far-flung places. They have worked long and unsociable hours, but have always believed in the project and its potential value. If the size of the archive is a testament to their indefatigable commitment to the project, the quality of the thousands of hours of interviews they have recorded is a measure of their remarkable intelligence and integrity. Indeed, the professional standards they have brought to bear on the project, as well as their humour and humanity, means that future generations will always be able to access the lives of their GAA forefathers. Alongside Arlene and Regina at the beginning of the project was Ann-Marie Smith, who worked with us for the first year as we established ourselves, and we will always be grateful for the work she did for us. Since her departure, her seat has been filled by Ben Shorten, who has quietly worked away at the Herculean task of liaising with schools and volunteers, as well as logging interviews into our system. Ben has been the rock in our office. He has done an outstanding job and this book would never have been completed without his efforts.

The project is housed at Boston College – Ireland, and here the daily support of Thea Gilien and Claire McGowan is vital for keeping everything going, providing a daily diet of good humour and for indulging all of us when we have made them sit through another GAA story. Likewise, the insight of our colleague Roisin Higgins has been invaluable, especially given her intimate knowledge of Ireland's sporting landscape. Eoghan Clear and his staff are always on hand to assist us with a plethora of questions about complex matters relating to the project, and Ann Molloy and her colleagues at Kieran Ryan & Co. have always ensured, with good humour, that the necessary paperwork gets done on time. Across the Atlantic at Boston College, the support of colleagues in the Center for Irish Programs is always appreciated, and especially important, throughout the life of this project, has been the assistance with all things technological of Rita Owens and her team in Instructional Design. The work that they do for us is of the first order, and the fruits of their labours, and the scope of the project can be found at www.gaahistory.com.

Of course, the scale of the GAA Oral History's Project undertaking has been such as to require the assistance of a wide circle of volunteers and interns and that it has been advanced as far as it has is due in no small part to this diverse and talented cohort. Through their generous efforts, they have added greatly to the effectiveness of the project and the enjoyment of the permanent team at Boston College – Ireland. Among this group special mention must go to Aidan O'Donoghue, Anne Finn, Brian Becker, Mark Farrelly, Adrian Roche, Anna Rosenblatt, Aoife Doherty, Brendan O'Sullivan, Carmel Gilbride, Claire Finlay, Dan Black, Eileen Kennedy, Thérèse McIntyre, Tommy McCann, Eileen McCallion, George Cartwright, Laura Kelly, Megan Dolan, Noel Byrne, Padraic O'Connor, Seamus Donnelly, Caoimhe O'Connor, Philip Knox, Joshua Turner, Renaud Hutin and Nigel Fallon. In addition to the above, we are grateful to those volunteers who have been nominated by county boards across the country. Not alone have they done much to publicise the project within their counties, their ongoing endeavours will ensure that each county is properly represented in the final archive that will ultimately pass to the GAA Museum.

This book draws extensively from that archive and the quotes that fill each chapter were all taken from the project's recorded interviews and written questionnaires. How oral history quotes are used is no straightforward matter, however, and we are indebted to the recently established Oral History Network of Ireland – of which, we are proud to say, Regina Fitzpatrick of this parish is a founder member – for their advice in working with such material. As well as the GAA Oral History Project, this book has drawn from the voluminous literature, academic and otherwise, which has built up around the subject of GAA in recent times and which has reached deep into the experiences of all counties and many clubs. Irial Glynn and Eamonn Óg McGrattan were of immense help in locating many of the more obscure titles. Further, their wise counsel and extensive support work determined lines of enquiry and of writing that would otherwise have been neglected. Seán Kearns, Wexford's finest, did likewise. A detailed bibliographical note is included at the end of this book, but Dónal McAnallen and Tom Hunt deserve to be credited up front. As well as contributing to the transformation of the study of the GAA, they have been unflagging friends of this project. For his work with Sports History Ireland, amongst many other things, William Murphy at the Mater Dei Institute of Education, is also deserving of special mention.

The use of photographs and documents has also brought us into contact with a vast array of repositories and individuals whose willingness to make material available has been crucial to making this the book it is. We would like to thank Mark Reynolds at the GAA Museum and Archive; Catríona Crowe and the National Archives of Ireland; Gerry Kavanagh, Fran Carroll, Sara Smyth, Mary Broderick, Sandra McDermott and Bernie Metcalfe at the National Library of Ireland; David and Edwin Davison, Irish Picture Library; Nicholas Furlong; Gráinne Doran, Wexford County Archives Service; Leo McGough; Luke Morrissey; Derek Cullen, Fáilte Ireland; Sinéad O'Connor, Cumann Camógaíóchta na nGael; Tom Lyons; Joe Jordan; John Deveney; Dermot O'Brien, London; Tommy Murphy; David O'Brien; John Joe Conwell; Richard McElligott; Ross O'Carroll; Bernie Daly; Steven Miller, *Leinster Express*; Mick Carroll; Paddy Fenning; Bernadine McGauren; P. J. Maxwell; Martin Bourke; Eddie Nangle; Dominic Williams; Pat Murphy; Jack Napier; Enda McEvoy; Alan Clynch, www.hoganstand.com; Brendan Rice and family; the Fitzpatrick family, Galmoy; Pat Nolan, *The Irish Mirror*; Rónán O'Brien; Tom Butler; Mary E. Daly; John O'Regan; Mick O'Keeffe; Margaret Ó hÓgartaigh; Pádraig Conway; Seán Crosson; Barbara Duncan and family; Andrew and Mikey Duncan; Harry Hughes; Seán Cleary; Kilmacud Crokes GAA Club; Diarmaid Ferriter; Cian Ferriter; Stephen Cullinane; Martin Walsh; Greg Prendergast; Pat Leahy, *Sunday Business Post*; the Pozzey family, Brisbane; Dara Ó Briain; Willie Reilly; Michael Laffan; John McCafferty; Mike Liffey; Tom O'Donoghue; the Egan family in Gledswood; Tullamore GAA Club; Meadbh, Eoin, Caoileann, Shane and Lauren; the Rouse family in Offaly and further afield; Mick Rouse; Simona Stefanakova; Joe and Samantha Hughes; Noel Cooney; Tadhg Ó hAnnracháin; Colm Toibín; Dessie Donnelly; Roddy Hegarty; the staff at the Cardinal Ó Fiaich Memorial Library; Gerard Rushe; Liam McNiffe, St Patrick's College; Raymond Dunne; J. J. Reilly; Cavan County Museum; Robin Doolin, Rights and Reproductions, Oakland Museum of California; Maureen Comber, Clare County Library; Tom Lyons; Anne Kearney, *Irish Examiner*; Susan Kennedy, Lensmen; Conor Nicholl; Eoin Kinsella; Joe McLaughlin, University of Ulster; Damian Dowds; Michael Madine; Jim and Monica McGivern; Barry McConville; Prof. William Nolan; Ray Bourke; Bill Martin, Collins 22 Society; Liam McLaughlin; Michael Farrell; Damien Burke, Irish Jesuit Archives; David Hickey, *Connacht Tribune*; Cyril Helnwein; Michael Minoge; Daragh Ó Conchúir; Mick Gorman; John Rosling, British Pathé; Barry Purcell; Kieran Hoare and Vera

Orschell, James Hardiman Library, NUIG; Bray Public Library; Lucy Francis, Getty Images; Tommy Moran; Reamonn MacBrian; Seán Ó Súilleabháin and Mary Conefrey, Leitrim County Library; Jim Burns; Brian Walsh and Anita Barrett, County Museum, Dundalk; Alan Hand, Reference and Local History Library, Dundalk; Michael Gallagher, *The Western People*; Terry Reilly; Peter McDermott; Michael O'Brien; Gerry Dillon; Alan Clynch, Lynn Publications; Joe McMahon; Joe Kelly; Peter Dooley; Eithne and Catherine McAviney; Paddy Fenning; Eileen Fallon; Liam Byrne; Cathal Skeffington; Damian Cahalan; Oliver McVeigh; Michael Fitzgerald and William Fraher, Waterford County Museum; Kevin Lonergan; Eilís Ryan and John FitzSimons, *Westmeath Examiner*; Anita and Mary, P.J. Browne Photography, New Ross; Dave Barrett; Jimmy Dunne; Tom Coyner; Nikki Braunton, Museum of London; Megan Young, Sportsfile; Norman McCloskey, Inpho; Joe Lavery; Sean McGettigan; George Coulter; Martin Nevin; Frank Archbold; Tommy Kirwan; Moling Morrissey; Hugh Dempsey; George Cartwright; *The Anglo-Celt*; Seamus O'Reilly; Jim McKeever; Niall Muldoon; Eugene Gallagher; Dónal Campbell; Fred Reilly; Mark Pearce; Eamon Greene; Jimmy Mulrone; Selwyn Johnston, Headhunters Museum; Margaret Grehan; Dessie Boland; Ray Donlon; Delaney Family; Joe McCabe; John McGerr; Paddy Egan; Cathal Henry; Rose O'Rourke and Family; Emmett Flanagan; John McAviney; Paddy Cotter; Aidan Claffey; John Murray; Thomas Lennon; Christina Murphy; Paddy Williams; Oliver Corr; Anthony and Clare Daly; Dick Roche; Terry O'Dowd; Thomas Grennan.

It was a pleasure to work with The Collins Press once again, as it was to witness the professionalism of Karen Carty and Terry Foley at Anú Design. At home, no less than at work, we are fortunate to be surrounded by talented and wonderful people and, in spite of all the absences, we are grateful for the love and support of our families – Moynagh, Ellen and Samson; Sophie and Olivia; Nuala, Cáit, Éilis and Joe.

Finally, this book is dedicated to everyone who has participated in, or helped in anyway, with the GAA Oral History Project. Many thanks.

Mike Cronin, Mark Duncan, Paul Rouse
Dublin, 2011

Preface

It is often and quite rightly stated that our clubs form the bedrock of our Association, the anchor on which our very existence is founded and the source from which our talent springs. However, if our club network provides a foundation, the inter-county scene has served as the shop window for our activities, helping to enthral the masses and popularise our games far beyond our own shores. While the lines that dissect the map of Ireland creating counties and provinces existed long before the establishment of the GAA, it is not difficult to make an argument that it was our games that saw them bed down in the country's psyche.

Next to being asked one's name, county affiliation follows closely in the pecking order of importance when it comes to the all-important badge of identity. This practice has been forged on the back of age-old rivalries and titanic battles, epic encounters that have enticed the biggest crowds in Irish sport to flock time and time again to the hallowed playing grounds that stand as cathedrals of sport in their communities.

Our county scene has the uncanny ability to appeal to a wide spectrum of the population – even those outside the remit of our organisation – and the crescendo that are our finals in September emphasise this point. These are not just games. They are national occasions.

This handsome book takes the county system which underpins these occasions and examines it in all its splendour and complexity.

It is the second publication to emerge from the team at Boston College – Ireland, who previously produced *The GAA: A People's History*, which appeared in 2009 on the occasion of our Association's 125th anniversary. Like that critically acclaimed book, *The GAA: County by County* is a product of the GAA Oral History Project, a hugely significant undertaking, commissioned by the GAA to ensure that the memories and experiences of our members are recorded and preserved for future generations.

The archive that results from this vital project will, in time, pass to the GAA Museum at Croke Park; but for now, we have yet another beautiful book to add the GAA's growing library. It is a book to treasure and one that I'm sure readers will return to again and again.

Criostóir Ó Cuana, Uachtarán Chumann Lúthchleas Gael

Réamhrá

Is minic ráite é agus is fíor gur iad na clubanna buncharraig ár n-eagraíochta, an pointe daingnithe ar a bhfuil muid tógtha agus an foinse as a dtagann ár mbuannna. Ag an am céanna más iad na clubanna an bunsraith, is iad na cluichí idirchontae atá i bhfuinneog an tsiopa: na sluaite faoi dhraíocht acu agus daoine i bhfad i gcéin ag cur dúile iontu. Cé go raibh na teorainneacha a dhéanann deighilt ar chontaethe agus ar chuígí na hÉireann ann i bhfad sular bunaíodh CLG, ní deacair aragóint a chur chun cinn gur iad cluichí an chumainn a d'fhág gur leabaigh na teorainneacha sin in intinn an phobail.

Ní túisce a cuirtear an chéist faoin ainm atá ar dhuine ná a fhiafraítear dóibh cén contae ar as iad. Eascraíonn sin as iomaíochtaí atá linn leis na céadta bliain, as coimhlintí nach bhfuil a sárú le fáil agus as cluichí a mhairfidh go deo i gcuimhne na ndaoine. Is iad sin a mheallann na sluaite is mó lucht féachana i spórt na hÉireann chuig na páirceanna breátha atá againn.

Tá de bhua ag na cluichí idirchontae go gcuireann réimse leathan den daonra suim iontu – fiú daoine taobh amuigh den eagraíocht – agus is í an tsuim a chuirtear i gCluichí Ceannais na hÉireann i mí Meán Fómhair is fearr a léiríonn sin. Ní amháin gur cluichí iad siúd. Is ócáidí náisiúnta iad. Tarraingíonn an leabhar breá seo chuige féin bunús na n-ócáidí sin – an córas idirchontae – agus déantar scrúdú ar sin agus ar an taibhseacht agus an t-aimhréiteacht a bhaineann leis.

Seo an dara foilseachán atá tagtha ón bhfoireann i Boston College – Ireland, a chuir ar fáil freisin *The GAA: A People's History* sa bhliain 2009, tráth a raibh muid ag ceiliúradh 125 bliain ár mbunaithe. Dála an leabhair sin, a thuill ardmholadh, is as Tionscnamh Stair Bhéil CLG a tháinig *The GAA: County by County*. Fiontar thar a bheith tábhachtach é siúd a ndearna CLG coimisiúnú air chun a chinntiú go mbeadh fáil ag na glúine atá le teacht ar na cuimhní cinn atá ag ár mbaill. In imeacht ama, beidh fáil sa Mhúsaem i bPáirc an Chrócaigh ar an gcartlann a thiocfaidh as an tionscnamh ríthábhachtach seo; ach go dtí sin tá leabhar breá eile againn le cur le leabharlann CLG, atá ag dul i méid i gconaí. Seod de leabhar é seo, ceann a ndéanfaidh daoine é a léamh arís agus arís eile, tá mé cinnte.

Críostóir Ó Cuana, Uachtarán Chumann Lúthchleas Gael

Introduction

The boundaries between counties are sacred lines in Irish life. Each county – in its own way – is a place apart, with its own traditions and its own history. You may be born just a field or a street away from your neighbour, but if a county boundary runs through that field or street, your neighbour is somehow different. You might learn to love that neighbour, but you would never wish to trade places with them. Most often, this neighbourly rivalry is manifested and sustained through Gaelic games, where no contest is as intense as that between border rivals. People who might agree on everything else fall out over football and hurling. And from this sporting rivalry flows all manner of other differences. Typically, of course, these differences are imagined rather than real; they are things invented to sustain a tradition. Real, invented or imagined, they are important nonetheless.

There are many indicators of this importance; one such indicator is the notion and meaning of 'home'. When people from counties across Ireland move to live in a place beyond their native county, they usually (though, of course, there are exceptions) maintain an overriding allegiance to the county of their birth. Even when people have lived and worked for decades in a new county, when they talk of 'home' they mean two places: the house in which they now live and the place in the county where they were reared. There is no such ambiguity when the question is asked: where are you from? It is in the answer to this question that the enduring sense of overwhelming allegiance to a native county becomes apparent.

For those who leave Ireland and who set up home overseas, there are further aspects to this allegiance. In cities of Britain and America – most notably in London and New York – people from various Irish counties have long gathered in 'county associations'. These have usually been people who have mixed city life with a close relationship to their home county through involvement in a formal organisation. The county associations have offered a diverse range of social outings for men and women who have wished to socialise with people from their own county. It has also allowed for the children and grandchildren of these émigrés to be imbued with a connection to 'home' (whether such a connection was wished for, or otherwise). The county associations have offered more than sport and drink and dancing, however. They have also operated as a vital source of welfare, care and support for those arriving in an alien city – or for those who have fallen on difficult times. Apart altogether from money, basic personal relationships have helped people settle, survive and then prosper in times of hardship, not least in helping to overcome loneliness and isolation. Country people living in Dublin also replicated this process in the years after the Second World War but the ease with which people now travel back to their home counties – as well as the extraordinary expansion of the city through vast suburban estates – has left just a few county associations functioning. Essentially, through their endeavours, the county associations have been a way for people to look after their own, and a way to express an identity that is rooted in a sense of 'home'.

How have counties come to hold such relevance for Irish people and what part has the GAA played in this process? It was initially the Normans who began the evolution of the county system. By translating an English system of shires and counties to the Irish landscape, boundaries (although remaining fluid for a long time) were introduced and counties began to emerge. The initial boundaries of many counties were fixed under the rule of King John (1166–1216), but not all of them were under the control of a royally appointed sheriff, demonstrating how limited the extent of crown controlled land was. By 1200 the process of fixing boundaries was formalising the map of Ireland, and counties such as Cork, Kerry, Louth, Tipperary and Waterford (amongst others) had come into being. The lengthy period of time it took to establish all thirty-two counties (Wicklow being the last in 1606) demonstrates how incomplete and contested the British settlement of Ireland remained. This process was a mixture of military conquest and also a process of negotiating 'a number of frontiers, real and imagined, throughout the island along a contact zone with both Gaelic Irish and Old English cultural worlds'.

The county functioned mainly as an administrative unit for British colonisers through to the nineteenth century. Counties existed so that civil servants could more easily collect tax, formalise land ownership and control the country. For most Irish people, any sense of county identity prior to the nineteenth century was most likely quite weak. As Mary Daly has shown, 'the triumph of the county as the dominant badge of local identity and local government was by no means inevitable'. Indeed, in the years immediately preceding the Famine, the British administration in Ireland had effectively deemed that counties were *not* suitable administrative units for the modern state. Accordingly, they divided Ireland into Poor Law Unions. These Unions – which saw local taxpayers in an area become financially responsible for the paupers of that area – each had substantial towns as their centre, and readily ignored county boundaries. Enough of Irish life was organised around the county system, however, to overcome this move.

Changes in society assisted the growing relevance of the county. Literacy rates grew and people began to be more familiar, especially through the newspapers, with the importance of the county. The legal system was reformed and the use of county courts, for all but the most serious of crimes, became the norm. Bodies such as the Royal Irish Constabulary (although national) were organised around county units of organisation. The campaign for Catholic emancipation, the Land League and other movements were organised on a county basis. The census was collected on a county basis and during the nineteenth century various history books were written which chronicled the history of various counties. Crucially, a major shift in understanding county affiliations took place between 1833 and 1846, when Ireland was mapped by the Ordnance Survey. The act of mapping Ireland was immensely powerful, and boundaries between counties, which had previously only existed in the minds of a government administrator, became lines on a map. While the process of mapping was met by suspicion and violence in certain parts, the existence of the Ordnance Survey maps reinforced and cemented county identities. The reality of the maps was simple and powerful: people now knew in which county they lived, where the boundaries of that county were, and where next door began. This process was further reinforced when the counties began to be used as the unit of local government from 1898, and the passage of the Local Government (Ireland) Act.

It was around this time that the thirty-two counties of Ireland also became the basis upon which the GAA has rested so much of its structure. The county now sits beside the parish as the basic organisational unit of the GAA. These, in turn, sit into provinces and, ultimately, into a national organisation. And yet it was not the intention of the men who established the GAA to use the county structure of Ireland as a foundation on which to develop the GAA. In the beginning, it was simply decided to establish clubs across Ireland and these clubs were asked to affiliate to the central committee of the GAA. All correspondence was to flow through the general secretaries of the Association; the devolution of power was not imagined. This is not because of any particular opposition to such devolution, rather that no one predicted the speed with which the GAA would grow in its first three years. The extraordinary and immediate growth in the number of clubs left it impossible for the GAA to regulate matters at central level. The fact is that within just a couple of years there were more than 1,000 GAA clubs in the country.

There was already a precedent within sporting organisations for responding to a rapid increase in the number of affiliated clubs. In England, the Football Association had been established in 1863, but only really made progress after it instituted a national knockout competition between its clubs in 1871. Through the 1870s, an explosion in interest in soccer revolved around the FA Cup and led to the establishment of local Football Associations across England. It happened in Birmingham in 1875, in Staffordshire and in Surrey in 1877, in Lancashire in 1878, and so on across England. These local FAs ran their own challenge cups, which were seen as an ideal way of preparing for the national competitions. All of these associations affiliated to a central FA council with an elected membership. A similar process was undertaken by the Rugby Football Union. In cricket, the most prestigious competition in England was the county championship. This was not officially organised until 1890, but matches between English counties had been organised since the early eighteenth century and by the 1870s there was an unofficial county championship in play.

None of these routes was precisely followed by the GAA, but the similarities are obvious. It is, of course, impossible to prove that the GAA consciously followed the model laid down by sporting bodies in England. Anyway, the demands of organisation represent only one aspect of the emergence of the county in GAA terms. There were other dynamics at play. The first involved the simple fact that across the country local clubs were already thinking of themselves in county terms. This can be seen in a range of different places. In August 1886, for example, hurling teams from Tipperary travelled to Cork to play local club teams in a series of matches on a Sunday afternoon. It was a remarkable occasion, full of pageantry and music, and the newspapers estimated that up to 20,000 spectators attended. The Cork teams were generally victorious but even the local Cork papers were drawn to admit that the partisan behaviour of the local referees and the continuous interference of local spectators affected the chances of the Tipperary men. Despite this, those same papers preened at the defeat of Tipperary teams and lauded the superior skill of the Cork men. All along the line, the success of the county was celebrated.

In football, too, inter-county rivalries were beginning to appear. A series of inter-county challenge matches were played between clubs from Wexford and Wicklow on Charles Stewart Parnell's land at Avondale on 31 October 1886. Six teams of Wexford footballers travelled by train to play the matches and such was the level of preparation that a match programme was printed, which displayed the names of the players on every team. Also printed were the names of the referees, umpires and timekeepers, the colours that each team would wear and the times of the matches. The day was considered a huge success, drawing huge crowds, including Parnell's mother, sisters and brother.

The second critical factor in determining that the GAA should organise on county lines was the decision to establish All-Ireland hurling and football championships. This decision was taken at the second Annual Convention of the GAA, which was held in Thurles in November 1886. The rules upon which this championship was based continue to identify the club as the primary unit of the GAA, but they also clearly laid the basis upon which the future primacy of the county was founded. These rules stated that the All-Ireland championship was open to all affiliated clubs of the GAA; that clubs in each county would first play off a championship between themselves on a knockout basis; and that then the winning club in each county would proceed to play off, again on a knockout basis, against the winning teams from the other counties until an All-Ireland champion emerged. Critically, to facilitate the running of the championship, it was decided that county committees (the forerunners of modern county boards) should be established in each county. It was to these county committees that so much power ultimately devolved within the GAA.

If the establishment of county boards was vital to the future, so too was the manner in which GAA people observed the rules – or, perhaps, failed to observe them. From that very first championship a practice was established whereby the winning club in each county pulled in the best hurlers from other clubs in the county upon entering the All-Ireland championship. So it was that when Thurles played Meelick in the first ever All-Ireland hurling final in April 1888 the

Thurles team contained men from Moyne and Borris and other parishes around Thurles, while the Meelick team included men from Killimor and Eyrecourt and Mullagh. By the rules, they were illegal. Quickly, it became apparent that the only way to police such a tendency towards illegality was to legislate for its acceptance. So it came about that the winning club in each county would have the right to choose whichever hurlers it wished to field during the All-Ireland championships. Over time, more and more players were brought in to supplement the county champions. Steadily, too, the selection of county teams became the preserve of the county committee, rather than the champion club. This was a preserve entirely devoid of uniformity: in some counties it was established shortly after 1900, in others it took several more decades.

And, as the club loyalty of the players who represented a county broadened, so the jerseys they wore were refined. For the first twenty-five years of the GAA, the representatives of a county usually wore the colours of their champion club. The extent to which teams representing counties became genuinely representative of the county as a whole can be gauged by the gradual adoption of distinctive county colours. Kilkenny won seven All-Ireland hurling titles between 1904 and 1913. Photographs show that the first four of these were won in the colours of the various champion clubs – Tullaroan or Mooncoin – in any given year. The last All-Ireland winning Kilkenny team to be photographed in a club strip was that of 1909. When the combined Mooncoin and Tullaroan clubs returned to win a further three All-Ireland titles in a row between 1911 and 1913 they did so as a united county team, with 'Kilkenny' sewn across each player's jersey. It was the most obvious way for players from different clubs to accept the idea of a unity of equals. All of this underlined the idea of a county identity and, in turn, helped lend momentum to the creation of that identity.

The process by which the GAA shored up county allegiance was by no means smooth or clear cut, however. Even as many counties took to adopting distinctive county strips and to fielding county teams that were more truly representative, the very integrity of the county system remained a matter of open debate. In 1912, *The Gaelic Athlete* newspaper saw fit to question the appropriateness of boundaries that tended to hinder more than help the organisation of Gaelic games. There was, the newspaper insisted, 'no historical reason why Irishmen should desire to hold the present division of the country into counties of varied sizes and most irregular and absurd shapes'. For reasons of sheer pragmatism, the newspaper urged a radical redrawing of the Irish map so that areas that were linked – either by virtue of their geographic proximity or by the service of a suitable transport network – might be brought into closer cooperation for the purposes of arranging games and administrative ease. The argument was bolstered by the power of example: it was pointed out, for instance, that though Birr and Shinrone were geographically part of Offaly, the development of railways had effectively identified them with areas of north Tipperary. From Leitrim and Donegal in the northwest to Cork and Kerry in the south, incongruities like this abounded.

Perhaps understandably, the GAA showed little interest in dismantling structures that, on the weight of all available evidence, had begun to command significant loyalty. The inclination therefore was to build on what had already been established, not to undermine it. Consequently, developments across the twentieth century served only to copper-fasten the place of the county in the life of the GAA and the wider popular imagination. The expansion of inter-county competition – from the introduction of National Leagues in the 1920s to the revamp of the All-Ireland championships in the 1990s – added lustre to the county brand and provided the GAA with a financial engine to drive its various activities, including the promotion of games and the development of grounds. While the pull of the county team has certainly proved extraordinary, the growth of the inter-county game has not been without problems. Tensions between club and county, ever-present in the GAA, have in recent times been exacerbated by the skewing of playing schedules in a manner that favours county teams at the further expense of clubs.

Of course, the striking of a proper balance between club and county activity requires only a shift in priorities. It does not impinge on structures, which remain deeply rooted. The security of the county inheritance does not mean that any of its inherent contradictions have been resolved, however. For the modern GAA, the county system continues as a source of immense strength and mild frustration. What is overwhelmingly cherished for the contribution it makes to instilling a sense of place, nurturing identity and fostering loyalty is occasionally cursed for its arbitrariness, its inflexibility, the constraints it imposes on innovation and the progress it stifles. Interviewed as part of the GAA Oral History Project, John Henderson, a former Kilkenny hurler now resident in

Wicklow, reflected on these very issues: 'What makes the Association great is the line; the border line, the county line. That's what makes it … But you know, it's that line that keeps the lesser counties down. I was lucky to be born in Johnstown. If I was born the other side of Galmoy, in Laois or in Tipperary, and my sons born in Wicklow, instead of being across the line in Dublin … so it's the border line, everything's on the border line. And that's the restriction … a good player can't progress, he's hemmed in by that same border line.'

It is an acknowledgment of the immutable importance of the county within the GAA that the project – the GAA Oral History Project – upon which this book is based is organised on a county basis. The GAA Oral History Project began in September 2008. Commissioned by the GAA and carried out at Boston College – Ireland, it was envisioned to run for four years and to 'record the fullest possible picture of what the GAA has meant to Irish people, in their own words'. County by county, project members and volunteers have conducted oral history interviews with people involved in the GAA in Ireland and across the globe. The interviews provide a window on the often extraordinary lives of people and how their experiences are interwoven with their involvement in Gaelic games. These personal testimonies contribute to our understanding not only of the GAA, but also of the wider Irish experience, culturally, socially and politically.

The use of oral history to record the story of the GAA is a natural fit. In an Association bound by democracy, oral history embodies a democratic form of history where everyone's experience and story are valued equally. Its great strength lies in its ability to reach the stories hidden from history and to record not only well-known personalities, but also 'ordinary' people and everyday experiences. And so, within this collection, along with stories of epic matches and great players, more personal stories can be found, including for example, the impact of GAA involvement on people's family, work and social life. First-hand accounts are given of going to matches by horse and cart; making knicks out of flour bags; gathering around the window of a neighbour's house to listen to Michael O'Hehir; waiting three weeks for a letter to get from Ireland to Boston to find out the result of a match. As well as being a valuable historical source in this regard, what these interviews uniquely contribute to the story of the GAA are people's attitudes and beliefs; the nuances of tone and atmosphere and the power of what can be understood from a silence or hesitation. It is the human story of the grass roots of the GAA in all of its life, colour and its wide spectrum of emotion and wit in the voices of those who have lived it. The interviews document changes that both the GAA and Irish society have undergone and add layers of understanding and meaning to this history. In essence, this is a substantial and unprecedented public history archive that will act as a permanent resource on the history of the GAA and life in Ireland since 1884.

Most immediately, it has provided the stories which – county by county, chapter by chapter – lie at the heart of this book. Inevitably, of course, the book will give only a sense of the life of the GAA in any given county – and will only give that sense from a particular perspective. People will lament the failure to include a whole range of different issues in every chapter and in this lament they will be right. Equally, though, it is a simple fact that the demands of space and time are restrictive on the scope of any book, not least on one that covers a subject that has meant so much to so many people in so many different ways. Allowing for that, this is the story of the GAA told through the words of its membership. Underpinning this oral history are the written words of several generations of GAA journalists and historians. Each chapter draws from local histories of club and county. Without these works this book could never have been written. Individually, they are testament to the love and respect with which the authors hold the GAA in their localities. Collectively, they represent an extraordinary body of work, documenting the life and passion of people and communities across Ireland. Within their pages there is a vital understanding of what binds the GAA together, the shared commitment to the games of the Association and what it embodies. There is evidence of more than mere unity, however. What is apparent in every corner is distinction: things that mean that the GAA in each area is unique unto itself. This is a distinction that lies in individual personalities and in their communal acts in support of a particular jersey. It is these people – generations of them – whose relationship with the GAA has defined the development of the Association. And it is to all of them that this book is dedicated.

The O'Neill hurlers from Glenarm lead the procession to the first Feis na nGleann by marching from Cushendall to Waterfoot in 1904. Feis na nGleann was an extraordinary festival established in the Glens of Antrim as a celebration of Irish cultural traditions, from the Irish language to music, song and dance. Part of this festival saw the playing of 'shinny' matches, a stick-and-ball game which might be considered a forerunner of hurling. *(McQuillan's GAC)*

Westmeath Mayo Offaly
Limerick Laois Waterford
Carlow Longford Leitrim
Tipperary Kilkenny Derry
Kerry Cork Wicklow
Kildare **Antrim** Meath
Tyrone Dublin Galway
Armagh Fermanagh
Donegal Sligo Roscommon
Clare Cavan Monaghan
Louth Wexford Down

Antrim

On 15 August 1969 soldiers from the British Army regiment, the Queen's Regiment, were deployed on the streets of Belfast. The deployment of troops was given the code name 'Operation Banner'. For more than a year there had been sporadic violence in Belfast and Derry. Mostly, this involved rioting where nationalists fought, alternately with loyalists and with the police. In April 1969, the *Irish News* described the rioting in Belfast and Derry as being 'the most devastating wave of violence and strife' for half a century. A slow but perceptible increase in the intensity and the viciousness of the violence had continued month after month. The outbreak of the 'Battle of the Bogside' on 12 August 1969 had been attended with scenes of riot which soon spread to Belfast and which led to that deployment of troops on 15 August 1969. The police had been unable – or unwilling – to stop loyalist rioters burning hundreds of homes in the city, not least many on Bombay Street, which was reduced to ruin. One of the houses burned was that of Michael Culbert, who later recalled rooting through the rubble of the house to retrieve pots and pans. Two weeks later Culbert played for the Antrim Under-21 footballers in the 1969 All-Ireland under-21 football semi-final.

Antrim's opponents in that semi-final were Cork. An Aer Lingus plane, chartered by the Irish government, brought the players to Cork. In a thrilling match, Antrim left behind the turmoil of the emergence of the Troubles and won a classic match by 3-7 to 1-12. Facing Roscommon in the All-Ireland final, they again produced a great display to win once more by one point, 1-8 to 0-10. Antrim had started that final in devastating form but by the end were barely holding on. The victory brought scenes of pure emotion. As captain Liam Doyle accepted the cup, the Antrim supporters sang the great civil rights song: 'We shall overcome'. Later, when they made their way back to Belfast, the GAA people of the city and beyond gathered for a céilí at St Theresa's Hall. The following year Antrim made it to the Ulster senior football final. There they played Derry who had won the 1968 All-Ireland Under-21 football championship. The two teams looked set to be the powers of Ulster football for the 1970s. Derry won that Ulster final but, as the Troubles worsened, Antrim football collapsed. In the twenty-five years that followed Antrim won just four championship matches. While many of the players who played on those teams did not become embroiled in the Troubles, others did and spent long periods in prison; others lost their lives and some simply left. The ultimate impact, in sporting terms, was a loss of momentum which destroyed the potential shown in the summers of 1969 and 1970 as Antrim returned to the footballing wilderness.

The Antrim team were actually the first great power of Ulster football. They won Ulster senior titles in 1900 and 1901, and, most impressively, then won six titles in a row between 1908 and 1913. In their organisation and in their style, Antrim set a new standard in Ulster, one that was not always welcomed. Bitter comment followed their 1910 Ulster championship semi-final victory over Monaghan, with the *Dundalk Democrat* severely criticising the Antrim team for their 'soccer tactics' in overcoming the 'grand old Gaelic tactics' of their opponents. Before the rise of Antrim, Ulster teams were usually soundly beaten in All-Ireland semi-finals. Antrim, however, almost beat Louth in the 1909 semi-final and did eventually reach a final when they defeated Kilkenny in 1911. It was Kilkenny's last time to appear in an All-Ireland senior football semi-final, while the victory for Antrim marked the first occasion that a team from Ulster had reached an All-Ireland final. The 1911 final against Cork was eventually played on 14 January 1912 at Jones's Road. Cork won easily by 6-6 to 1-2, but even reaching the final was portrayed as a victory for Antrim. They were congratulated by the President of the Ulster GAA Council, Patrick Whelan, who said: 'Antrim have the determination and unity to cut down the barriers of West Britainism, so strongly erected in Belfast, to impede the Gael. The Gaels of Belfast have cut through the Shoneen lines and their banners proudly wave over all Ireland.'

As if buoyed by reaching the final, the Antrim footballers returned invigorated to the All-Ireland stage the following year where they were drawn to play Kerry. Despite being underdogs, Kerry were easily defeated by 3-5 to 0-2. There were stories that the Kerry team had been enthusiastic guests at a wedding on the day previous to the match, but the true story of Antrim's semi-final victory lay in Antrim's combination play and the training they had obviously put in. Pitted against Louth in the All-Ireland final, Antrim took the lead when they scored a goal as the game entered the last quarter. A first All-Ireland for an Ulster county was not to be, however, as Louth rallied and won out by five points. It was as close as Antrim were to come to an All-Ireland title for more than thirty years. Antrim retained the Ulster title in 1913, but were annihilated in the All-Ireland semi-final by Wexford, who were themselves the coming force in Gaelic football and on the cusp of winning an unprecedented four All-Ireland senior titles in a row.

By contrast, it was not until 1946 that Antrim footballers again made it out of Ulster. When they finally did so, the Antrim players travelled south to Croke Park filled with optimism. And with good reason: their dazzling, free-flowing forward play – based around short hand-passing and solo running – had cut a glorious swathe through Ulster in 1946. With Kevin Armstrong in extraordinary form at centre-forward, Cavan had been defeated in a classic Ulster final before 15,000 spectators in Clones. Cavan had been seeking an eighth Ulster title in a row; Antrim had been seeking to become the first county to take the Ulster title across the border into Northern Ireland. Now, 30,000 people travelled to Croke Park for the All-Ireland semi-final against Kerry. Those who came supporting the northerners were about to be dismayed. From the start Kerry adopted a physical approach, determined to stop men who ran in support as well as those who carried the ball. It was, wrote one journalist, 'warfare'. Michael O'Hehir's commentary was transmitted against the backdrop of a gathering chorus of boos. Kerry eventually won through a late Batt Garvey goal and Antrim returned devastated. Even getting out of Ulster to seek revenge proved a huge difficulty. Cavan had produced the finest team of a generation and won the next two All-Ireland football finals. When Antrim did finally emerge from Ulster again in 1951, they started slowly against Meath in the All-Ireland semi-final and trailed by ten points early in the second half. A brilliant comeback fell short by two points. In the end, Antrim had no All-Ireland to their name, though the style of their play was credited with dramatically shifting the techniques of Gaelic football. Ultimately, though, football in Antrim fell away and the county has not managed to win an Ulster senior football championship since.

By contrast, Antrim remains the great power of Ulster hurling. By 2011 Antrim had won 50 Ulster senior titles, 26 Under-21 titles and 52 minor titles. No other county in Ulster comes anywhere near that number of titles (Down and Derry come next with just four senior titles apiece) and there are whole swathes of decades in which Antrim has simply won title after title. There is a logic to this. Antrim is home to more hurling clubs than any other county in Ulster. In those clubs the game is promoted with a zeal which is potent and which ensures the primacy of hurling. In the Glens and Ballycastle and Loughgiel and Cushendall and Dunloy, hurling is *the* game. Indeed, across the hurling heartlands of Antrim, the game of hurling is cherished by GAA people with a passion similar to that of any stronghold on the island. Similarly, hurling has enjoyed great support in clubs in Belfast city such as Mitchel's, O'Connell's, O'Donovan Rossa, St John's and St Gall's.

This passion is a reflection of a tradition that extends back past the foundation of the GAA in 1884. As Dónal McAnallen has shown, stick-and-ball games, essentially early forms of hurling for which the words cammon/commons/camán, hurling and shinny are used apparently interchangeably, can be seen being played in Antrim throughout the nineteenth century. The incidence of the playing of those games certainly declined after the Famine of the 1840s, but did not disappear. Indeed, even after the founding of the GAA, the games survived. A famous game in the 1880s between Cushendall and Ballyeamon at Legge Green saw a hundred players in each team attempt to strike the small wooden ball between goals made from heaps of stones. It would appear that it was only after 1900 – and particularly with the establishment of the annual Feis na nGleann – that hurling as designed by the GAA impacted on Antrim. The Feis was established in 1904 in the Glens of Antrim as a celebration of Irish cultural traditions. It was the brainchild of Francis Joseph Bigger, a Gaelic League member, who developed the proposal in tandem with fellow language enthusiasts such as Sam Waddel, Fred Hughes, Dennis McCullough and Joseph Campbell. Part of the Feis was the playing of shinny matches, which evolved into hurling matches in time.

By then hurling was also being played in Belfast. Dónal McAnallen has revealed the extensive endeavours by Michael Cusack to promote hurling in Belfast, long after he had been removed as secretary of the GAA. He travelled to the city, for which he retained an enduring affection, in the 1890s and 1900s in support of the revival of hurling. The establishment of various clubs and the organisation of hurling leagues in the city after 1900 – led by men such as Bulmer Hobson – saw hurling make great advances. By the end of 1901 there were seven clubs promoting the game in the city. The ambition was clear: 'It will not be long now till the old game will be a potent factor in making Belfast as Irish as in the past it has been English.' The truth was that it proved impossible to sustain the momentum that had driven the early development of hurling. In the decades that followed, Antrim remained the strongest county in Ulster, but was equally unable to prosper at All-Ireland level.

While the 1940s are remembered for Antrim's progress in Gaelic football, it was in hurling the county came closest to success. In 1940 the county's minor team had created something of a shock by defeating Laois in an All-Ireland minor hurling semi-final before losing narrowly to Limerick in the final. Several of this minor team made the 1943 Antrim team that made dramatic inroads on the senior championship. Firstly, Galway travelled to Belfast and played Antrim in the All-Ireland quarter-final. The result was a three-point win for Antrim and a semi-final match against Kilkenny. Again, the match was played in

Corrigan Park in Belfast. Amidst appalling weather conditions, Antrim shocked the visitors and progressed to the All-Ireland hurling final. It was the first time that a team from Ulster had reached an All-Ireland hurling final. A star-studded Cork team – with Jack Lynch at midfield and Christy Ring at centre-forward – provided the formidable opposition in the final. Nonetheless, 48,843 turned up to Croke Park – the third highest then on record – with talk that Belfast had been 'evacuated' for the day. A huge cheer rent the air when Antrim took to the field. At the coin-toss before the game, the two teams exchanged gifts of butter and tea – a reflection of the privations of the 'Emergency' era – and a great spectacle seemed certain. What ensued was a rout. Antrim's hurlers were overwhelmed by the occasion. By half-time Cork led by 3-11 to 0-2, and by the end by 5-16 to 0-4. It was, remembered one observer, 'the greatest blow to hurling in Antrim and Ulster ... Had Antrim been left with a bit of pride, they might have come back.'

In some respects, the nightmare of 1943 was re-enacted in 1989. In that year, Antrim had defeated Down in the Ulster final and Kildare in the All-Ireland quarter-final before meeting Offaly in the All-Ireland semi-final. The Offaly team contained veterans who had won two senior All-Irelands earlier in the decade and newcomers who had just emerged from a minor team that won three All-Irelands in four years. In a significant shock, Antrim pulled away in the second half to win by three goals. The end of the match provided one of the iconic images of hurling history: as the Antrim players walked from the field the Offaly hurlers provided a guard of honour to congratulate their conquerors. The final against Tipperary brought devastating defeat, however, on a scoreline of 4-24 to 3-9 with the great Tipperary forward, Nicky English, scoring 2-12. Antrim have produced many fine hurling teams since then, but none have come close to making the breakthrough at All-Ireland level.

Although Antrim continues to wait for that All-Ireland victory, it is a credit to the quality of the club game in the county that it has claimed titles in both football and hurling. Indeed, West Belfast club side, St John's, was vital to the very establishment of the All-Ireland club championship. In the 1960s they initiated a tournament, which quickly evolved into a sort of unofficial Ulster club championship. Motions were put to the Ulster Council and the GAA Annual Convention which eventually resulted in an All-Ireland club championship being run from 1971. In 1983 Loughiel Shamrocks became the only club from Ulster to win the hurling championship when they defeated St Rynagh's from Offaly in a replay. Through the 1990s and into the 2000s, Dunloy were extremely unlucky not to repeat the achievement. As it was, it was left to the footballers of St Gall's to bring home All-Ireland honours. After defeat in the 2006 final, St Gall's defeated Clare champions Kilmurray-Ibrickane in the 2010 All-Ireland final. St Gall's victory was further confirmation of their status as the dominant force in football in Antrim. While their near neighbours, St John's, still head the table with twenty-four senior football titles, St Gall's had, by 2010, amassed fifteen – with fourteen of these won since 1982. For all that the GAA is strong in Belfast, the challenge for the Association remains the difficulties in competing with soccer, especially in working-class areas. Winning that battle will be key to the ambition of reclaiming a place at the top table at All-Ireland level.

By 1910, the GAA's rules for hurling had displaced local forms of the game. This photograph from Cushendun, north Antrim, is a wonderful illustration of hurling in the early years of the twentieth century. The old-style goalposts, the uneven field, the longish grass, and the crowd pressing in on the play created a scene that was replicated in the heartlands of hurling across Ireland at that time. *(McQuillan's GAC)*

The Ardoyne camogie team from Belfast takes a trip out of the city in the summer of 1910. Camogie has traditionally been strong in Antrim. Indeed, Antrim's camogie players have made it to sixteen All-Ireland finals, winning on six occasions, including a three-in-a-row from 1945 to 1947. *(Joe Lavery)*

The Most Reverend Dr Mageean, the Bishop of Down and Connor, meets the hurlers of Cork and Antrim, before the 1943 All-Ireland hurling final. *(McQuillan's GAC)*

A team of relay runners carried an urn with soil from Thurles Sportsfield and from Croke Park to celebrate the opening of Casement Park in Belfast in 1953. This is Brian O'Gara finishing the final leg of the relay. Sean McGettigan remembered the building of the stadium: 'It was the time after the Blitz, that was when Belfast was destroyed by the Germans and there was a lot of filling to be had and the Corporation were only too keen to get a place to put the fill so they filled the banks, made the banks around Casement Park and the banks are the same today as they were whenever they put them in … There were aeroplane hangars or seaplane hangars outside Enniskillen and they were owned by the Americans and they were put up for sale and Eastwoods, who were contractors, they decided that we should buy these and that we'd make a stand, and the steel in the Casement Park stand at the present time came from the American hangars.' *(GAA Oral History Project/Sean McGettigan)*

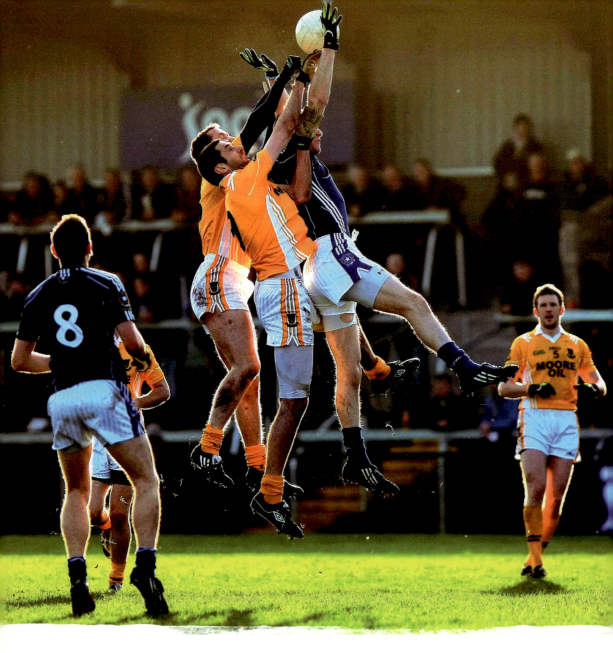

High fielding from the St Gall's v Clontibret Ulster senior football semi-final in 2009. Although the Antrim senior footballers have failed to make significant inroads on championship football for several decades, club football is fiercely contested. In 2010, the Belfast club, St Gall's, were crowned All-Ireland senior club football champions. *(Inpho)*

'Two games to which I travelled stand out in my memory. The first was in 1951 when Antrim beat Cavan in the Ulster final. My friend and myself were still students and short of money so we hitchhiked down to Clones on the Saturday evening, located an abandoned railway van on a siding outside the town, stripped half a haycock of hay to provide our bedding and had a great night's sleep before going to see Antrim triumph the following day.'

Michael McKeown, b. 1933.

'Nineteen forty-seven was the year I was on, but Antrim won it in 1945, '46, and '47 ... really, I do not recollect it being powerful ... I can remember us coming off the train and Brendan Barry's father was there and one other man, you know. I remember people saying there should have been more there.'

Lily Spence, b. 1924.

'Any of the women I was involved with in the Camogie Association throughout my time as a player or a spectator were all very strong women and they got things done.'

Marion Mc Fetridge, b. 1939.

'I would be very passionate about West Belfast. You see an awful lot of negative things about joyriding and about this, that and the other thing. That's 2 per cent of the population. Now, I could spend the next ten hours telling you about everything positive – not only about what the GAA is doing, but about other things that's going on positive in the community. You take us now, we're now involved in suicide prevention. We're now involved in work in alcohol and drug abuse. We're the hub of the community. With me, working with young people, you find that young people who have tendencies to take their life or have those feelings – a feeling of loss and no identity – what does the GAA give you? Your identity. What's this about? This is about the jersey. This is about our community. This is about the club colours.'

Gerry McClory, b. 1949.

'The greatest dream, I would say, we all had in those days, was to win a championship; to beat Loughgiel and win a championship. I would say that was the greatest dream that could ever come true for any Dunloy man.'

Jim McClements, b. 1926.

The Armagh team training for the 1953 All-Ireland football championship. Armagh lost to Kerry in the final before 86,155 spectators. A further 5,000 were estimated to have been locked outside the ground and listened to the match on radio. *(Cardinal Ó Fiaich Memorial Library)*

Westmeath Mayo Offaly
Limerick Laois Waterford
Carlow Longford Leitrim
Tipperary Kilkenny Derry
Kerry Cork Wicklow
Kildare Antrim Meath
Tyrone Dublin Galway
Armagh Fermanagh
Donegal Sligo Roscommon
Clare Cavan Monaghan
Louth Wexford Down

Armagh

The grass of Croke Park turned orange. Down from the stands and the terraces swarmed thousands of Armagh supporters. They danced and sang and hugged each other. As Kieran McGeeney lifted the Sam Maguire, tears flowed down the faces of players and spectators, alike. On that September Sunday in 2002, the broken dreams of previous visits to Croke Park disappeared into the Dublin air. The fact that it was Kerry who had been vanquished made the victory all the more valued. This first All-Ireland senior football title was Armagh's deliverance.

And yet the tradition of Gaelic football in Armagh was not one that was always celebrated. Despite the fact that football matches had been played under GAA rules in the county from 1886 and that the Armagh county board had been established at a meeting on 24 March 1889, there was considerable opposition to the development of the sport. Much of this early opposition came from the Catholic clergy, partly because of concern over Sunday play and partly because of fears of the presence within the GAA of Irish republican separatists. Cardinal Logue, for example, warned of the 'demoralising effect' of the GAA, while a local priest told an April 1889 meeting of the Holy Family Fraternity at the Catholic Cathedral in Armagh that there had been a falling-off in attendance at Sunday Mass because of the 'vile system of football playing that had come into vogue on Sundays'. The priest lamented the drunkenness and quarrelling which, he claimed, usually attended such matches, and continued: 'The devil had been at the bottom of secret societies such as Fenianism and Ribbonism; and when he found those detestable secret societies condemned and stamped out by the Catholic Church, the devil then invented this Sunday kicking, which he knew was doing so much harm.' There was, indeed, an apparent truth to the claims of the clergy. After all, the first president of the Armagh county board was Charles Cowan who was also the Head Centre for Ulster in the Irish Republican Brotherhood and a member of the Supreme Council of that organisation.

If politics mattered to the members of the newly established GAA in Armagh, it did not overshadow the importance of the games. In 1890 Armagh won its first Ulster senior football championship – Antrim and Tyrone were the only other counties to enter the competition – when the county was represented by its champion team, Armagh Harps. The Harps easily defeated their opponents in Ulster and were duly fixed to meet the Cork champions, Midleton, in the All-Ireland semi-final at Clonturk Park in Dublin on 16 November 1890. More than 250 supporters took the train to Dublin to support their champions. They were accompanied along the way by the music of the William O'Brien Fife and Drum band. The sense of carnival ended when the ball was thrown in, however, as the Armagh men were soundly beaten, losing by 1-14 to 0-0. Not alone did Armagh Harps fail to score, reports suggest they failed even to move the ball beyond their own half of the field. Failure in Dublin proved a recurrent theme for several generations of Armagh footballers.

Like most other counties across Ireland, GAA activity in Armagh in the 1890s fell steeply and there were several years when it appeared to have disappeared entirely.

This was, of course, partly the consequence of the impact on the GAA of the Parnell split and the manner in which the operation of the GAA was rendered all but impossible by internal political divides. It was also the consequence of economic stagnation and the impact of emigration on the county. Between 1881 and 1901 the population of Armagh fell by 39,391. By any standards this was a precipitate fall which denuded the county of the men of such an age as were most usually associated with the playing of games. It was only after the GAA was rejuvenated at central level that Gaelic games once again began to prosper in Armagh. After a gap of around a dozen years the Armagh county board was re-established and began to promote games within the county.

That formal re-establishment of the county board had actually been preceded by a team representing Armagh competing in the Ulster football championship of 1901 and 1902. After defeat the first year, Armagh won the Ulster championship for the second time in 1902. On this occasion, more than 400 supporters, including three bands, travelled to Drogheda for an All-Ireland semi-final against Dublin, the champions of Leinster. Again, the Armagh men were soundly beaten. The defeat was attributed, at least in part, to the fact that the grass on the field was longer than it should have been and Armagh's style of dribbling the ball and playing it soccer-style along the ground was significantly hampered. Reliance on playing the ball along the ground was retained by Armagh footballers for longer than seemed the case in many other counties; another distinctive feature of the game in the county was 'dandle ball', whereby players ran while bouncing the ball on the back of their hand. According to Con Short, the historian of the GAA in Armagh, this tradition persisted at least until the 1920s.

By then Armagh footballers were enduring one of the most dispiriting losing streaks in the history of Gaelic games. In 1903 they lost the Ulster final to Cavan in a second replay. By 1950, they had lost twelve more Ulster senior football finals – including eight to Cavan, alone – and had not a single victory to celebrate. Against the backdrop of persistent disappointment, there was a thriving club scene. Teams such as Killeavy, Tír na nÓg from Armagh town and Shane O'Neill's from Camlough won Armagh senior titles, but the two great heavyweights were Armagh Harps and Crossmaglen Rangers. Harps won the first seven senior football championships played in Armagh, while Rangers won their first three-in-a-row between 1911 and 1913. And then they just kept on winning the William

McKillop cup, the trophy which ultimately was presented to the winners of the Armagh county championship, having first been donated to the county board by McKillop, the Nationalist MP for South Armagh, in 1906.

Political and sectarian tensions in Armagh remained to the fore. In 1910, for example, the Lurgan Davitts club were given permission to play their football in Antrim or Down, because of the 'hostile areas' they would be required to pass through if they played matches in Armagh. Travel to matches presented a genuine risk. In October 1910, Castleblayney Faughs were passing the Armagh town of Newtownhamilton, having played a match against Camlough Shane O'Neill's, when they were attacked with rocks. The identification of the GAA with nationalist politics in Armagh was obvious at various levels. The War of Independence revolutionary and later Fianna Fáil government minister, Frank Aiken, played football with Camlough and enjoyed great support in GAA circles. Many years later, in 1967, when Éamon de Valera told the British ambassador to Ireland, Sir Andrew Gilchrist, that he much preferred rugby to Gaelic football which he agreed was 'a made-up sort of game, not really native', Aiken was having none of it. He interjected: 'That is not right, Mr. Ambassador. Gaelic football is not a made-up game; it was played here a thousand years ago and more. It is a splendid game.'

For footballers in Armagh, the establishment of the border brought a new complication to organising their games, particularly for clubs such as Crossmaglen in the south of the county. The natural hinterland for such clubs ran down to Dundalk and Castleblayney, but the establishment of customs and security positions along border roads impeded travel to such places. There were further problems occasioned by economic decline in the county, leading to a further growth in emigration and a decline in the number of affiliated GAA clubs in the county. Previously prosperous businesses collapsed. In Crossmaglen, for instance, McConville's mill and bakery closed down. Despite this, Crossmaglen Rangers enjoyed remarkable success, winning five-in-a-row senior championships in the 1920s. The rise of a new club, Armagh Young Irelands, broke the hegemony of the Rangers, winning five championships in seven years. Young Irelands were largely drawn from the old Harps club in the town and provided one of the great stars of the era, 'Big' Jim McCullough. McCullough won seven Armagh county championships and played inter-provincial football for Ulster for more than a decade, starring in three Railway Cup winning teams in the 1940s. However, he never managed to win an Ulster senior football medal. Throughout the long losing streak on the inter-county scene, possibly the most galling defeat was in 1938. In that year, Armagh had dramatically defeated their long-time nemesis, Cavan, in the Ulster semi-final, before losing the final to Monaghan by three points. The match ended in some controversy with the referee, Hughie O'Reilly, himself a great Cavan footballer, having to be escorted from the field.

There was success at national level, however. St Patrick's College, Armagh, defeated St Jarlath's of Tuam, County Galway, to win the Hogan Cup in the first year (1946) that the All-Ireland inter-colleges competition was held. That first Hogan Cup experiment was abandoned after three years, before being resurrected in 1957 and going on to become a central part of the GAA calendar. Armagh also made it to the 1948 All-Ireland junior football final. A narrow defeat to Dublin was disappointing, but suggested a new dawn. That dawn broke the following year when Armagh claimed a stunning victory in the All-Ireland minor football final against Kerry. The highlight of the game was a wondrous goal struck by the team captain, Seán Blayney, who slalomed through the Kerry defence from midfield before shooting to the net from 21 yards. The victory was enough to propel Armagh to overcome their hoodoo in senior football in Ulster. More than 30,000 spectators turned out to see Armagh's young team take on Cavan's established stars in the 1950 Ulster final. A marvellous match led the *Anglo-Celt* newspaper to note that 'if Gaelic football was played regularly like this, there is no field game in the world to touch it'. Armagh won by four points and, amidst tumultuous scenes, every player was carried shoulder-high to the dressing room.

The great promise of the Ulster campaign was swiftly followed by huge disappointment in Croke Park when Armagh were swept aside by Mayo. It took three years to recover sufficiently from that defeat to make it back to Croke Park as Ulster champions and, on this occasion, Armagh qualified to play Kerry in their first ever All-Ireland senior football final. A massive 86,155 spectators attended the match, with a further 5,000 estimated to have been locked outside the ground and restricted to gathering around loudspeakers to listen to Michael O'Hehir's radio broadcast. What ensued was a narrow defeat to Kerry and a whole host of regrets.

There were to be more regrets over the years that followed. The 1960s were stained by infighting between clubs and the outbreak of the Troubles brought a further tragic dimension to the story of the GAA in Armagh through the 1970s and beyond. The greatest physical symbol was the commandeering of the GAA pitch in Crossmaglen; in time this became a totem of the wider struggle within the north and the militarisation of ordinary life. It spoke, too, of the reputation of south Armagh as 'Bandit Country' (a term used in 1975 by Merlyn Rees, the then Secretary of State for Northern Ireland, to describe the area) as a stronghold of the IRA.

In a footballing sense, the nadir was reached in November 1973, when Armagh arrived in Carrick-on-Shannon to play Leitrim in a league match with just fourteen players, two of whom were goalkeepers. While a fifteenth player was found to allow Armagh to compete, it seems remarkable that within four years the county had regrouped to the point of reaching an All-Ireland final. If the late 1970s are remembered as the era dominated by Dublin and Kerry, the arrival of Armagh in the 1977 All-Ireland football final was a triumph of determination, even if it was to end in defeat. An extraordinarily colourful match ended with Dublin beating Armagh by 5-12 to 3-6; Armagh could still end 1977 reflecting on a fifth Ulster championship.

In the end, it was to be the 1990s when the greatest era of success came to the county. The success began with the rise of Crossmaglen Rangers who, under the management of Joe Kernan, were transformed from a successful local club to one of the most decorated clubs in the history of Gaelic games. Between 1996 and 2010, Crossmaglen Rangers won fourteen Armagh senior football championships, including thirteen championships in a row. Their total (by then) of thirty-eight Armagh championships sets them down as the club that has won more senior football championships than any other club in any county. Still greater success came at inter-provincial level with the winning of an unprecedented eight Ulster titles. And the greatest success of all came at All-Ireland club level. The brilliant Lurgan-based Clan na Gael team of the 1970s had made it to an All-Ireland club final in 1974, only to lose in a replay to UCD. Crossmaglen Rangers overcame obstacles year after year and have won five All-Ireland club championships.

And from that brilliant team Armagh constructed a county team that finally fulfilled the promise shown by generations of footballers throughout the county.

With a sprinkling of players from Crossmaglen and led eventually by Joe Kernan, Armagh won seven Ulster championships between 1999 and 2008. This was a phenomenal achievement in the context of the most competitive era of Ulster championship football in history. The Holy Grail of All-Ireland success finally came, of course, in 2002 when a second-half surge took Armagh past Kerry. That more All-Irelands did not follow was a significant disappointment, but the place of that team in the lore of Gaelic football was well established. So, too, was Armagh's reputation as a county in thrall to football.

Ball Alleys St Patrick's College Armagh.

The handball alleys at St Patrick's College in Armagh were filled by generations of schoolboys. This photograph was taken in the 1920s. All across Ireland, handball was a hugely popular game with ball alleys built in a range of institutions – including educational and medical ones. Alleys were also built in cities, towns, villages and out in the countryside. *(Cardinal Ó Fiaich Memorial Library)*

In 1950, Armagh won the Ulster football championship and qualified to meet Mayo in the All-Ireland semi-final in Croke Park. Legions of Armagh supporters travelled south for the match. Here, Armagh man George Coulter strolls down O'Connell Street with a friend, en route to the match. *(GAA Oral History Project/George Coulter)*

Croke Park in the 1950s drew immense crowds to All-Ireland finals. The pageantry of the 1953 final involved a pre-match parade in front of cheering supporters wearing paper hats and rosettes, and waving flags. On the tops of the stands, some of the more courageous spectators have set up station, from where they will see Armagh lose narrowly to Kerry. *(Fáilte Ireland)*

The commandeering of the Crossmaglen GAA grounds by the British Army in the 1970s was bitterly resented by the GAA. *(Crossmaglen Rangers GFC)*

The manager of the victorious Armagh senior football team, Joe Kernan, is overcome with emotion as the final whistle blows in the 2002 All-Ireland football final. *(Inpho)*

'There were certain houses in the country where a lot of people would have gathered around and one such place would've been Peter Woods' shop at Middletown, out in the country at Middletown. I remember being along with the same Jim Loughern at the shop on a summer Sunday and the men would've been sitting out on mineral crates – the crates the mineral bottles used to come in them times – and the radio going full blast could be heard all over the place.'

Joe Jordan, b. 1945.

'I like the GAA because everyone can do it, boys and girls and it is Irish.'

Rachel, b. 1998, St Brigid's P.S., Crossmaglen.

'In the early 1970s, West Armagh, where we are now, where I lived was a no-go area. There were barricades practically at every road ... I actually climbed over barricades and dodged rubber bullets and CS gas to get to training out in the Gaelic field, as we knew it. So the Cú Chulainn Hurling Club, the Pearse Ógs, St Brigid's Camogie Club and Armagh Harps, what they gave in social capital to people like me who were very vulnerable at the time, thirteen and fourteen, is immeasurable and I don't ever want to forget that. They gave tremendous social capital and they really held us together. Because we were a community like many many other communities, struggling, – struggling against all kinds of things.'

Paul Duggan, b. 1960.

'Washing kits for seven boys, consoling when matches were lost and rejoicing when matches were won, dealing with injuries.'

Ann Clarke, b. 1940.

'Crawling under the fence at the Athletic Grounds to go in and play camogie with two wonderful old stalwarts, Ellie Carson and Pat Toner. Both had to walk the long way round, Ellie too big, Pat too old, to get under fence.'

Fionnuala McGrath (née O'Connor), b. 1962.

'The biggest one and the most, you know, emotive one would be Armagh winning the All-Ireland final ... going back to my granny's house listening to the radio to Michael O'Hehir in that 1953 All-Ireland final – to think that one day I'd be sitting in the best seat in one of the best stadiums in the world watching my beloved county doing what they had failed to do for 150 years and that moment – I remember sitting in the seat and the final whistle went and Kieren McGeaney was on his knees. I just got up and I looked into the Cusack and I said "Sam, Sam, Sam".'

Joe McManus, b. 1945.

A view of Dr Cullen Park in Carlow town, 1990.
The ground was purchased in 1935 and opened in 1936.
No Carlow team participated in the games organised for
the opening day; instead Laois played Kildare in football
and Dicksboro of Kilkenny played Eoghan Ruadh
of Dublin in hurling. *(Hugh Dempsey/2c)*

Westmeath Mayo Offaly
Limerick Laois Waterford
Carlow Longford Leitrim
Tipperary Kilkenny Derry
Kerry Cork Wicklow
Kildare Antrim Meath
Tyrone Dublin Galway
Armagh Fermanagh
Donegal Sligo Roscommon
Clare Cavan Monaghan
Louth Wexford Down

Carlow

It was a distance of less than fifty miles, but it took more than a day to travel. The group set off from Carlow at midday on a Saturday afternoon in August and pointed their bicycles in the direction of Dublin. They followed the road through Tullow, Rathvilly and Blessington. It was only on reaching Tallaght on the outskirts of Dublin that they stopped, pulling up at a pub where the bicycles of fellow Carlow travellers were piled deep outside. It was eight o'clock in the evening by then and the men, exhausted and hungry, opted to rest for the night. The following morning, once Mass was said, the group, its ranks now swollen, completed the final leg of the journey. 'The ride into the city did us good', one of the travelling party later recalled. 'It took the stiffness out of our bones from the journey the day before, and left us in right form to cheer on Carlow.' Where Gaelic football was concerned, opportunities to cheer Carlow at this time of year and at this level of competition were not only rare – they were unprecedented. This was 1944 and the county had qualified for its first ever All-Ireland semi-final.

The game was one that Carlow lost in the end, but history had already been made. A mere matter of weeks before, the Carlow footballers had defeated Dublin in a Leinster final in Athy, a victory that loosed a tidal wave of emotion across the county. When news of the result reached Carlow town, for example, several large bonfires were lit and jubilant locals gathered around them. The atmosphere was one of exuberance and celebration. 'Gramophones, accordions and musical instruments of every description were brought out to enliven the festivities, and dancing took place around the fires until late in the night,' the *Nationalist and Leinster Times* reported.

A degree of delirium attends most sporting breakthroughs, yet the Leinster success of 1944, while certainly a novelty, was not unexpected. By the mid 1940s Carlow had established themselves as a serious force in Gaelic football. Against the backdrop of a national emergency, manifest in the enforcement of food and fuel rationing, the county contested three Leinster finals in four years. The two that were lost were coloured by misfortune and controversy. After reaching a first senior provincial decider in 1941, Carlow found itself, by a scourge of nature, unable to field a team. An outbreak of foot-and-mouth disease confined the team to home and led to the nomination of Dublin to represent the province in that year's All-Ireland competition. But, if the crisis in agriculture took precedence over sporting ambition, so too did the demands of local industry. When the Leinster final was eventually rescheduled for November, the preparations of a number of the Carlow players were again interrupted, this time by the drive to harvest beet for the local sugar factory, a major source of employment since its opening in 1926. Carlow recovered from the disappointment of 1941 by returning to another Leinster final in 1942. Once again Dublin provided the opposition and Dublin won. However, in the wake of that game, Carlow questioned the eligibility of some of their opponents' players, citing breaches of the ban on attendance at foreign games. The objection ultimately fell on the intervention of the GAA President, Seamus Gardiner, who dismissed the evidence of a witness (who alleged to have seen a Dublin player entering a rugby ground) on the basis that he was not a member of the Association's Vigilance Committee – a secretive class of GAA member charged with informing on how fellow members spent their hours of recreation.

If there was an obvious self-interest in seeking the invocation of the ban rule in this case, it should be said that the Carlow GAA authorities, mindless of the damage it might do to small clubs struggling to field teams, were not averse to its strict enforcement on home turf. For some, the rule drew a clear line of distinction between Gaelic sports and others. In 1941, for instance, the chairman of the Carlow county board, Thomas Ryan, asserted that the 'code of the GAA aimed at moral justice between man and man, right for right's sake, irrespective of the consequences. Hence the complete difference with "foreign" games played for gain or to obtain a "cap" and means of living; hence the ban.' Attitudes towards the ban evolved at different speeds in different counties, but the pace of change was perhaps greatest in Carlow: almost a decade before the abolition of the ban in 1971, Carlow was the only county to call for its outright removal from the GAA's official guide. 'It did not serve any useful purpose, at least not in this county', one delegate stated simply.

To an extent, the stance adopted by Carlow spoke of a confidence about the place that Gaelic games had attained in the local sporting culture. This was no slight achievement given that in Carlow, as elsewhere, the GAA were relative latecomers to sporting organisation. Indeed, the emergence of modern sports clubs in Carlow occurred before the GAA was founded and at a time when the entire structure of the county's largely agrarian society was subject to major upheaval. In the second half of the nineteenth century, the aftershock of the Great Famine was everywhere apparent. To begin with, the population of the county – the second smallest in the country – had gone into freefall: between 1841 and 1881, death and emigration combined to reduce the number of inhabitants by almost half: the population fell from 86,228 to 46,588. Among those who survived and stayed was Colonel Horace Rochfort of Glogrennane, owner of vast tracts of the county and the pre-eminent figure in its early sporting development. Rochfort's sporting passions were eclectic and his talent for organisation phenomenal: he founded not only the Carlow Cricket Club, but the Carlow Polo Club and the County Carlow Rugby Football Club. The origin of each of these clubs pre-dated the GAA and they all appealed to the same large Protestant farmer and Protestant merchant class. As the century progressed, they also appealed to more Catholics.

This was the context into which the GAA in Carlow had emerged. The Association offered something different from these pre-established clubs. It opened up sport to a new social cohort, to the small farmers and nationalist working class. Despite this, the Association's early development was less spectacular than that of many other counties. A first county convention was not held until October 1888 and the following year, in March 1889, the first county championship match was played between teams from Carlow and Donore at Ballybar, on the site of a well-known racecourse. Across the decades that followed, the progress of Gaelic games was hampered by the fallout from the Parnell split and poor local administration, a truth underlined by the holding of only nine county conventions in the twenty-one years between 1898 and 1919. These administrative frailties notwithstanding, new clubs were still formed and games played. The Graiguecullen club was an exception: it was not founded in Carlow, but absorbed into it. Established as Graigue Young in 1886, the club competed in Laois until 1904 when, in the wake of a boundary change the year before, it successfully applied for affiliation to Carlow. The club, which became known as Carlow Graigue, dominated Gaelic games in the county until the mid 1920s when a row involving players and spectators at a county final led to the suspension of the club by the Carlow county board and its subsequent return to Laois.

Graigue's departure deprived Carlow of its most powerful club, yet there is little evidence that Gaelic games in the county suffered. In fact, the 1930s saw significant progress. Carlow's senior footballers returned to the Leinster senior championship in 1934, a new county ground named in honour of Dr Matthew Cullen, a recently deceased bishop and GAA enthusiast, was opened in 1936, the same year that a league for rural primary schools was initiated. Taken together, these developments point to improvements on and off the field of play and they suggest that the exploits of the Carlow senior footballers in the 1940s did not emerge in a vacuum, but were consistent with a wider pattern of development.

The run of Leinster final appearances in the 1940s maintained momentum and engendered huge excitement among the community. They also highlighted the ascendancy of football in Carlow. Hurling did exist, but it was slower to emerge and more difficult to spread. The sport prospered most in the south of the county, in those areas closest to the borders of Kilkenny and Wexford. In many ways, however, hurling in Carlow has had to make do with the worst of all worlds given that it was both overshadowed by football and severed from hurling's strongholds by the sheer arbitrariness of Irish county boundaries. That the sport survived at all was largely due to the passion of the few. The game was sustained by the efforts of a small number of clubs – there were seven senior hurling clubs in 2011 – aided, in recent times, by better organisation and the availability of coaching expertise to back up the voluntary effort. By the early twenty-first century, the careful husbandry of scarce resources had begun to yield a dividend. From the underage to senior levels, the indicators pointed to steady improvements in the quality of hurling played within the county: the Carlow minor hurlers reached a provincial final in 2006, while the seniors were twice winners of the Christy Ring cup, a competition established for middle-ranking hurling counties, the prize for which was entry into the All-Ireland senior championship. Coming from such a modest base, these were substantial achievements and the effect was as much psychological as sporting. As one county board official and underage mentor optimistically remarked in 2010: 'They [the players] are starting to know and to believe that it is an honour, a matter of pride, to be wearing the county jersey, that wearing Carlow's colours is as meaningful as wearing the colours of any other place. It is huge.'

Ultimately, the push to extend the base of hurling will necessitate a greater concentration of effort on building playing numbers among urban-based youth. The reason for this is straightforward: despite its rural aspect, Carlow has developed into an ever more urban society, its population increasingly concentrated around its principal town. Indeed, as a result of rapid population expansion from the mid 1990s to the mid 2000s, Carlow town and its hinterland came to account for over 40 per cent of the population of the county. This movement of people has raised serious questions for the GAA in Carlow, not least in relation to participation rates, infrastructure and the geography of club development. As for the games themselves, the expansion of Carlow town is more likely to accelerate further the gap in support for Gaelic football over hurling. The town is already a football stronghold and home to two clubs – Éire Óg and O'Hanrahan's – which have effectively dominated the local football scene since the late 1950s and which, through their performances in the All-Ireland club championships in recent decades, have built a profile for Carlow football that the county team has struggled to equal. In the 1990s, in particular, Éire Óg developed a formidable reputation, not only in Carlow, but in Leinster, where they won all five club finals that they appeared in. In Carlow town, hurling has never acquired anything like this status. The challenges that confront the GAA in Carlow are therefore many and profound. How it deals with them will determine whether the GAA plays as important a part in the lives of the people of the county in the future as it has in the past.

Members of the O'Hanrahan's club from Carlow town, popularly known as the 'Blues', make their way through the long grass to the field at Bagenalstown, *c.* 1920s. Established in 1919, the club was named in honour of Michael O'Hanrahan, a founder of the Carlow Gaelic League who was executed for his involvement in the 1916 Rising. *(Frank Archbold)*

Carlow and Kerry players parade around Croke Park prior to the All-Ireland semi-final, July 1944. Carlow would lose by 3-3 to 0-10 in a game that attracted a record attendance. Just weeks before, the same Carlow team, trained by Dubliner Jack Dundon, won their first and only Leinster senior title in Athy. *(Martin Nevin)*

A hurlers' homecoming: the scene at the Carlow/Kilkenny border as the county's hurlers returned after defeating Cork to win the All-Ireland junior 'home' title in 1960. Three years before, in 1957, when Carlow defeated Wicklow in the junior hurling championship, it was the first game the county had won in twenty-two years. In 1962, the county added an All-Ireland intermediate hurling title. *(Tommy Kirwan)*

Éire Óg's Brendan Hayden releases the ball to his teammate Jody Morrissey in the 1998 Leinster club final against Dublin champions, Kilmacud Crokes. The Carlow club dominated the provincial club championships in the 1990s, winning five titles. *(Sportsfile)*

'It's a community centre. There's christenings to first communions, confirmations, twenty-firsts, weddings, funerals. Everything is centred around the club. And then the weekends, there's football training, hurling training, the juveniles are training. It's rented out to different other clubs. It's a massive community and even a lot of the committees that are in Ballinabranna at the moment and back through the years, they all have stemmed from the football, from the football committee.'

Pat Amond, b. 1964.

'Carlow had their best team — their best season was in '42. And I remember going with my father up across the hill, going to Rice's with a couple of cows and we went over the top of the hill and we could see lads digging holes over in Colliers'. The foot-and-mouth thing was there and that was the first we had heard of it you know. At this stage, all the stock had been condemned and they all had to be slaughtered and buried and quick lime put on them, you know … Carlow, that was their best time ever and they were in the Leinster final and weren't allowed to play; they weren't let travel on account of the foot-and-mouth.'

Andy Redmond, b. 1930.

'At that time, people had no money. People were very poor; their parents hadn't got it. And it was the only thing they had to do that wasn't going to cost them big money. If they had a pair of boots, they got a second-hand pair off somebody. They got a bad oul' football; they actually made up paper footballs when they hadn't the money for a proper football to kick around. And it was every night in the summer time.'

Liam Byrne, b. 1947.

'When I was hurling with Bagenalstown, I used to have to ride a bike to the town and it wouldn't be a case of just getting up and dilly-dallying along — you'd be going flat out, thinking that you'd be late. And you'd go train for an hour, maybe two hours and you'd be up on the bike and come back home again. So it was seven, eight miles every day and that was the kind of fitness we had.'

John Foley, b. 1943.

'I remember my young days when I wouldn't be going to the matches and see them going off to the matches. The whole town would be dead, everyone gone. There'd be no one around only a couple of women that might not be interested.'

Martin Nevin, b. 1939.

In 1956, boys on retreat at St Patrick's College in Cavan town are pictured strolling around the football pitch. Originally a seminary, St Patrick's College was a hotbed of Gaelic games after it first fielded a team in 1913. The college won the MacRory Cup for the first time in 1935 and have subsequently won another eleven Ulster titles. *(St Patrick's College)*

Westmeath Mayo Offaly
Limerick Laois Waterford
Carlow Longford Leitrim
Tipperary Kilkenny Derry
Kerry Cork Wicklow
Kildare Antrim Meath
Tyrone Dublin Galway
Armagh Fermanagh
Donegal Sligo Roscommon
Clare **Cavan** Monaghan
Louth Wexford Down

Cavan

It was in Cavan that the GAA first took root in Ulster. And it is Cavan that has proved the most successful of all the counties in Ulster, even if the great flourish of that success has now receded into history. The first official GAA event to be staged in Ulster was organised by the newly formed Ballyconnell Joe Biggars. Biggar was actually a Belfast man, who was elected as a nationalist MP for Cavan in December 1885. His election seemed to offer local proof that the prospect of Home Rule being secured for Ireland under the leadership of Charles Stewart Parnell was a very real one and, reflecting the political mood of the times, the Ballyconnell men were proud to be associated with Biggar. The exact date of the foundation of the club is unclear, but it had affiliated to the GAA by March 1886 and in April 1886 it staged a sports meeting in Ballyconnell. That the Ballyconnell men should call their club after a nationalist MP was a significant statement, of course – and one typical of the times – but this was not a matter of undying principle. Later, when other clubs attempted to claim the title of being the oldest club in Ulster, Biggar's name was considered expendable and Ballyconnell simply changed their title to Ballyconnell First Ulsters.

Athletics meetings were central to the sporting life of GAA members in those first years and the sense of popular excitement in the newspaper reports of these meetings is palpable. For many people, the GAA thrived precisely because it offered a day out, a social occasion at which every class was welcome. Eventually, of course, the GAA would abandon its engagement with athletics, but its function in building the early prosperity of the GAA is readily apparent. Critically, though, even as athletics was displaying its early dominance, the rise of Gaelic football in Cavan was under way. Hurling did not enjoy anything more than a spectral presence in the county, but football was soon dominant in every corner. The passion for football was manifest, for example, when Ballyconnell played Bailieborough in a field near Cavan town in late 1886. The Bailieborough men brought the goalposts with them by horse and cart and the match was played despite warnings from the police that they were breaking the Lord's Day Observance Act, 1695, which decreed that no person should play 'hurling, communing, football, playing cudgels, wrestling or any other games, past-times or sports, on the Lord's Day'. The warnings were ignored and the match was played.

No Cavan clubs competed in the first year of the All-Ireland championships in 1887, but by 1888 the county was sufficiently organised to play a first county championship. The final was played between Ballyconnell First Ulsters and Maghera MacFinns on 30 April 1888 and, again, a field near Cavan town was the venue. The Ballyconnell men were strong favourites and were commended in the local press for the quality and style of their playing gear. The appearance of the Maghera MacFinns was remembered for other reasons. Many years later, the famed editor of the *Anglo-Celt* newspaper, John F. Hanlon, recalled being at the match as a young boy: 'I vividly remember the Maghera team, twenty-one of fine stature, almost all of them wearing long beards. Beards were fashionable in those days, but worn with football togs they gave a team a fearsome appearance.'

Ferocity won the day: led by men such as John Duffy, Tom Clarke and Andy Cumiskey, Maghera won the first Cavan championship by 1-4 to 0-1. Victory in Cavan did not launch the MacFinns on a successful campaign in Ulster; they were defeated in the Ulster final by Inishkeen Grattans who were considered to be too 'scientific and skilfull' for the more powerful Maghera men.

In his excellent history of the GAA in Cavan, Rev. Daniel Gallogly notes that, by the end of 1888, GAA clubs were thriving all across Cavan to the point where there were actually thirty-eight of them in existence. Police reports from the area suggested that the great majority of GAA officials were active IRB men. This seems possible, though unlikely. Police intelligence on the IRB and the GAA across Ireland was usually patchy and often filled with fanciful conjecture. Police reports also suggested that in Cavan during the 1890s, Ribbonmen (an agrarian secret society active in violent land agitation) were also prominent and their activities – possibly in dispute with members of the IRB – saw GAA matches used as cover for faction fights. Indeed, it was claimed by the police that the activities of Ribbonmen went 'a long way in explaining why there was so much fighting at games in 1888 and 1889 and how it was virtually impossible to control them'. And impossible it was. The *Anglo-Celt* from those years contains numerous articles outlining the fighting in Gaelic football matches in Cavan and expressing its horror at events, all of which it naturally felt obliged to record in detail and with relish.

Inability to control such fighting – and, indeed, to control the GAA itself – led the Catholic Church to withdraw its support for the Association. In Cavan, the county board fell asunder in the winter of 1889–1890, the county championship was not played and Cavan withdrew from inter-county competition. Remarkably, it was against this backdrop that, the following year, Cavan actually won their first ever Ulster title. A leading IRB man in the county, Terence Fitzpatrick, who was also a vital official of the Cavan Slashers club, attempted to reorganise the county board and arranged for his team to play against Ballyconnell First Ulsters in a reformed county championship. In the course of the match Ballyconnell walked from the field. Cavan Slashers claimed victory and it says much for the collapse of the GAA in Cavan that this outing was enough to see them crowned county champions. As if to prove that the title was merited, Slashers (representing Cavan) went on to beat Armagh Harps at Smithborough in the

Ulster final. To underline the sense that these truly were formative years for the GAA in Ulster, when the Slashers arrived at the ground they had to erect the goalposts and sling a rope between them to serve as a crossbar.

It was not until the early years of the twentieth century that the GAA properly reconstituted itself in Cavan. Former Slashers' players such as Andy McEntee were to the fore in this endeavour. The role of McEntee, a reporter with the *Anglo-Celt* newspaper who served as chairman of the Cavan county board from 1912 to 1920, was recalled in a wonderful collection of articles entitled *Memories of the Lifetime in Journalism in Cavan of A. F. McEntee*. The 1905 Ulster championship in which Antrim were Cavan's opponents at a match played at the grounds of the County Cavan Agricultural Show Society offers a vivid illustration of some of the almost farcical aspects of football at the time. Cavan beat Antrim by 0-5 to 0-2 but Antrim subsequently lodged an objection in which it was complained (amongst many other things) that a hawker had stood in front of the Antrim goalkeeper and tried to sell him an orange in the course of the match. Ultimately, Cavan went on to win that championship, before losing by 0-8 to 0-0 to Kildare in the All-Ireland semi-final. Victory in that Ulster championship was part of a three-in-a-row of titles that Cavan landed between 1903 and 1905.

That spell of dominance in Ulster was merely a prelude to an extraordinary period of success, which saw Cavan bestride the province for five decades from the 1920s to the 1960s. The earliest decades were particularly rewarding with Cavan winning seven Ulster titles in the 1920s, eight in the 1930s and nine in the 1940s. Indeed, from the beginning of the First World War to the end of the Second World War, the only other team to win the Ulster senior football championship was Monaghan. There was a decline thereafter with just three titles harvested in the 1950s and four in the 1960s, but that decline was relative only to the unprecedented scale of the success that had come before. Central to the emergence of this tradition of success was the vibrant club scene in the county which saw Cornafean and Mullahoran emerge as the strongest clubs in a county noted for competitive clubs. Both of these clubs produced legends of Gaelic games. Amongst the extraordinary men who played for Cornafean, for example, was Packie Masterson, who played for the club from 1910 to 1947. It says much for the power of Cornafean that, although they have not won a senior championship since 1956, they remain easily the most successful club in the county with a record twenty senior titles.

Of further importance was the construction of Breffni Park as the home of Cavan football. The planning that underpinned this venture – the purchase of land, the fund-raising, the management of the project – epitomised the approach to football that ultimately rendered the county so successful. Victory in Ulster did not quickly translate into victory at All-Ireland level, however. Instead, there flowed a series of heartbreaking defeats. There was a galling loss to Kerry in the 1925 semi-final, played in Tralee. The *Anglo-Celt* recalled that several car-loads of supporters made the long journey south: 'One Model T which left Cavan at 5am on Sunday arrived an hour before the match ... Lindberg's solo flight across the Atlantic was a cake walk compared with the experience of some of those who travelled to Tralee.' A one-point loss ended in objection and counter-objection – and, ultimately, defeat. More galling still was another one-point loss in 1928, this time to Kildare in the All-Ireland final played in Croke Park in what was the first match played for the Sam Maguire trophy. The Kildare victory was rooted in a goal scored by Paddy Loughlin, of which the journalist 'Carbery' (P. D. Mehigan) simply said: 'Let it be written quickly: P. Loughlin threw the ball in the Cavan net.'

Controversy, of course, has a way of quickly swinging around and favouring those who have previously suffered. And so it swung for Cavan. In 1933 Kerry travelled to Breffni Park with what was then the greatest team in their history, studded with men such as Dan O'Keefe and the Landers brothers, who were in search of an unprecedented five-in-a-row of All-Ireland titles. When the Kerry players arrived the night before the game they were met by a parade of bands and stayed at the Farnham Hotel. Stephen Walsh remembered the event as a young boy: 'If the Fianna of old had arrived in Cavan that August evening we could not have been more excited.' As the game reached its climax with the teams level, the excitement grew still further. Against all the odds, Vincent McGovern punched a goal and Kerry were beaten. The final against Galway was almost an anticlimax, although at half-time a number of men are said to have seized the microphone of the 2RN commentator, Éamonn de Barra, and called for the release of Republican prisoners who were on hunger strike. For the team's star player, Jim Smith, the victory over Galway marked a joyous vindication of his efforts: 'My life's ambition is now realised, for after fourteen years of struggle I have what I want at last.'

Winning the All-Ireland set the scene for more success. That Cavan were so dominant in Ulster allowed them to contest at All-Ireland level almost two years in every three. Further All-Ireland senior titles followed in 1935, 1947, 1948 and 1952. By then Cavan were acknowledged as one of the great powers in Gaelic football and, in the middle years of the twentieth century, were considered second only to Kerry. That this success was achieved was in many respects something of a minor miracle. After all, the population of Cavan was low – fewer than 80,000 people lived there by the time of the first All-Ireland success – and falling still lower throughout the decades of greatest triumph. Decade after decade, people flowed from the land of this predominantly agricultural county, to the point where, from a population of more than 240,000 on the eve of the Famine, just 54,000 people lived in Cavan in 1966. The presence of the border further undercut economic development in a county that had lost all its railways by the end of the 1950s. Across Irish emigrant communities, the men and women of Cavan were always well represented. It was no wonder that the *Anglo-Celt* deemed Cavan's All-Ireland success 'an event of international importance.'

It was this sense of Cavan's diaspora which made it so appropriate that Cavan should have emerged victorious when the All-Ireland football final was played in New York in 1947. Cavan's team of the 1940s – which won nine Ulster titles and played in four All-Ireland finals – was feted for the style of their forward play, their sharp hand-passing and the talent of men such as Peter Donohoe, the O'Reilly brothers, 'Gunner' Brady and Mick Higgins. Even without winning the 1947 final they would have been remembered with fondness, but the romance of that final victory – conveyed by the voice of Michael O'Hehir across the Atlantic on a crackling, atmospheric line to clusters of Cavan people gathered around radios – ensured a glorious place in history. When victory in New York was declared, 'every door was thrown open and the people hurried onto the streets. Bonfires were alighted and children and parents joined in singing local ballads and cheering.'

In the years after Cavan's fifth All-Ireland success in 1952, the county slipped slowly towards decline. Initially, success in Ulster continued to come their way but by the 1970s the great traditional power of Ulster football was entirely impotent.

Why did this decline happen? Gallogly notes that the refusal to admit that there was a decline at all, while at the same time hankering after the past, was disastrous. Crucially, Cavan were bypassed by other counties who had powerful schools' teams and a coherent underage structure. Cavan had neither. And then there was the enduring population decline. Even when counties around Cavan began to increase in population after 1961, Cavan's still fell. With negligible industrial development and little in the way of investment, a hugely agricultural county enjoyed little economic advancement.

Clubs from the county – who had once set a high benchmark – made limited progress and no Cavan club has won the Ulster club championship since its inauguration in 1968. And then, from 1970 to 1996 Cavan did not win a single Ulster senior football championship. There was a brief rebirth in the mid 1990s. A narrow defeat in the 1995 Ulster final to Tyrone was followed two years later by dramatic victory over Derry in the provincial decider courtesy of a late Jason Reilly goal. The All-Ireland semi-final threw up a nostalgic meeting with Kerry to mark the fiftieth anniversary of their tussle in New York. There was no romance about the result, however, as Kerry strolled to a seven-point victory. Subsequent to that defeat, the decline of Cavan was put into sharp perspective by the rise and rise of Tyrone and Armagh, but when the stock of Ulster football was at an all-time high in the 2000s, Cavan's footballers remained at low ebb. The appearance of the Under-21s in an All-Ireland final in 2011 signalled the prospect of a brighter future, but the scale of work needed to bring a return to the glory days remains daunting.

For Cavan's star player, Jim Smith, the victory over Galway in the 1933 All-Ireland football final marked a joyous vindication of his efforts: 'My life's ambition is now realised, for after fourteen years of struggle I have what I want at last.' *(Cavan County Museum)*

In Cavan, as in every other county, the GAA has been built on the labour of generations of volunteers. Here, eight local men – Jimmy Donohoe, Benny Cassidy, Tommy Brady, John McKiernan, Michael Donohoe, Tommy Duignan, Peader McSeain and Frank McGee – are making blocks to lay at the new park in Cornafean. *(George Cartwright)*

In a county where Gaelic football dominates, camogie makes its presence felt. On the occasion of National Camogie Day in 1987, the camogie clubs of Cavan marched from the main town's Cathedral (following Mass) to Breffni Park. *(The Anglo-Celt)*

The 1997 National Football League began with a match between Cavan and Kerry. The game was played in Downing Stadium, Randall's Island, New York, on Saturday, 18 October. The venue was chosen to mark the fiftieth anniversary of the playing of the 1947 All-Ireland football final between the same counties in the Polo Grounds in New York. *(Sportsfile)*

'I'll just tell a funny incident that happened the day that we were going to play our first match in March of 1963. We were going to Belturbet, it was our first game, and we had ordered jerseys and the jerseys were to be collected at Ballyconnell on the way up to Belturbet. And there were two men coming in a car, and cars weren't too plentiful that time now, but anyway there were two boys coming to collect the jerseys ... We met this particular fella in the street in Ballyconnell and he said "I'm after getting the jerseys"; I said "that's great". "Well," he said, 'I don't know, on the way down here, we killed a duck and I always heard it was unlucky to kill a duck and not stop.'

Hugh McGovern, b. 1940.

'It's probably an old-age story, ladies don't always have as much attendance as the men, unless you're getting in finals and you're winning in county finals, they just don't always have as much attendance. And I mean, sometimes it was just a case that our games clashed with the lads' games or if it was a case that it was at the other end of the county, it might have been just a bit of a hindrance ... but the lads might have had part-time jobs, and you know that kind of thing ... Obviously parents who were there with their kids and other supporters, they were brilliant but it would have been ... you would always find the time to go to the lads' game and the lads mightn't always find the time to go to yours.'

Fiona McConnell, b. 1984.

'I was speaking myself at a reception in Northern Ireland recently and I had to explain what kind of a place Ballymachugh was, so I said that it was a place mainly of Catholics, of 85 per cent, 15 per cent Protestants but the religion was the GAA.'

Peter Brady, b. 1935.

'It is all money today with the GAA. Manager gets a wage at the end of the year win or not and players have to put in a lot more effort than we did.'

David Cassidy, b.1965.

'The day after I got married I went to the Ulster final in 1997 when Cavan beat Derry.'

Kevin Reilly, b. 1976.

Brian Lohan contests a ball in the 1997 All-Ireland hurling final against Tipperary. This was the first ever all Munster All-Ireland final and it resulted in Clare's second All-Ireland success in three years. The county's previous hurling All-Ireland had been won in 1914. *(Inpho)*

Clare

In 2006, at a special ceremony in Carron, the sod was turned on a new €1 million visitor centre to celebrate the life and legacy of Michael Cusack, and the splendour of the surrounding countryside. The building was once a humble homestead into which, in 1847, the founder of the GAA was born. It was not the first local memorial to the county's most famous sporting son. Seventy years before, in 1936, new GAA grounds were officially opened in Ennis and named in Cusack's honour. In an occasion marked by speeches, music, pageantry and games, one newspaper trumpeted that, at last, the 'Gaels of Clare' had a pitch 'in keeping with their strength'. If Cusack, the son of native Irish speakers, spent much of his working life – as educator, journalist, sportsman and organiser – at a remove from his native county, his extraordinary legacy was as apparent in Clare as anywhere else. The GAA had been born of Cusack's sporting vision and restless energy and, in Clare, it quickly took root. It is a measure of the early vitality of the Association in the county that on a single Sunday in August 1887, a field laid out for hurling in Barefield played host to five matches and over 200 players, their teams drawn from ten parishes.

Hurling tournaments were by then 'the order of the day' and what took place in Barefield on one weekend could be routinely found in Ennis, Crusheen or Ruan on the next. Playing and attending Gaelic games quickly became established as a Sunday ritual. Alongside regular tournament games, 1887 saw the hosting of the first county championships and Clare's involvement in the inaugural All-Ireland inter-county championships. Newmarket represented the county in the football and the Smith O'Brien GAA club, backboned by a team of farming men in their mid twenties, played in the hurling.

There was nothing inexorable about the rise of the GAA in Clare, however. While the Tulla club reached the All-Ireland hurling final in 1889, the closing decade of the nineteenth century saw the GAA in Clare not so much stagnant as in retreat. Between 1891 and 1895 Gaelic games ground to an effective halt as a result of divisions caused by the Parnell split, as well as the brutal impact of emigration. It was not until the early twentieth century that the Association regained momentum and over the course of the decade that followed Cusack's death in 1906, the county achieved unprecedented success in All-Ireland competitions.

The year 1914 marked the high point. It was then that Clare completed an extraordinary double of All-Ireland senior and junior hurling championships. The success enjoyed was no accident. It was planned. A special committee had been established to raise funds from the general public, as well as to engage the services of a trainer: Jim O'Hehir, father of the legendary broadcaster, Michael. In the build-up to the final against Laois, the local newspaper, the *Clare Champion*, attempted to meet public interest with match previews and pen pictures of players. The team was taken away for special training, which involved early morning walks from Lisdoonvarna to Liscannor and back each day before breakfast. This, or at least something in the preparations, worked.

Clare defeated Laois and their success and the efforts behind it – the fund-raising and special training – were indicative of the changing culture of Gaelic games and a growing professionalisation of approach.

What the hurlers of Clare achieved in 1914, their footballers came close to matching in 1917 when they reached the All-Ireland football final only to come up short against the Kickhams club from Dublin. Throughout that campaign, the circumstances around the games proved as compelling as the games themselves. The 1917 championship took place in a charged political atmosphere, which spilled into the sporting sphere. When a by-election for East Clare was held in July of that year and recently released prisoner Éamon de Valera stood as a Sinn Féin candidate, the Gaelic footballers of Clare affixed their colours firmly to his political mast. Prior to each of their championship games, they marched onto the field behind a banner bearing the slogan: 'Up de Valera.'

Over the years that followed, the intersection of politics and sport worked to the detriment of the Association in Clare. When the unity of rebellious nationalism gave way to the division of Civil War, the fallout did not simply intrude on how Gaelic games were administered – it split them. The GAA in the county sundered in a row over its response to the execution of two anti-treaty republicans and GAA activists, player Con Mac Mahon and county secretary Paddy Hennessy. For a time, the county board divided into two rival factions, which set about organising separate competitions. Although the board soon reunited and the GAA came to be credited with helping restore harmony within the county, stories survive which suggest that certain resentments lingered.

Throughout the decades that followed, the one personality who dominated Clare GAA affairs more than any other – serving as president and chairman of the county board – was Canon Michael Hamilton. A man of multiple roles and talents – teacher, pastor, broadcaster and advocate of Irish language and culture – his influence in GAA terms extended far beyond Clare's boundaries. It was Hamilton, for instance, who drove the GAA's decision to play the 1947 All-Ireland football final in New York, believing it a necessary show of solidarity with Irish emigrants. But if Hamilton's vision was broad, his nationalism was narrow and, after initially opposing it, he was among the staunchest supporters of the Association's ban on foreign games.

This ban itself was by no means universally popular within the broad GAA community. St Flannan's, the college which Canon Hamilton attended as a pupil and at which he later taught, opted out of the Munster colleges hurling competition, the Harty Cup, from 1928 to 1943 in opposition to the extension of the ban rule to colleges. In defending its abstention, Canon O'Kennedy, the College President, derided the broadening of the ban as 'a violation of the principle of liberty in athletics and the rights of the heads of schools'. When St Flannan's eventually re-entered the Munster colleges competition, they met with immediate success, winning four titles in a row between 1944 and 1947. Jimmy Smyth from Ruan was a member of three of these teams and became one of Clare's best ever players. After learning his hurling in the open fields surrounding his family's homestead, using a stick cut from hazel and ball improvised from sponge, his arrival at St Flannan's constituted something of a culture shock. It was, Smyth later recalled, 'a tough, bleak, and strange place compared with the friendliness of the parish.' Yet it was at St Flannan's that Smyth, and many like him, learned and developed the essential skills of hurling, honing them through a regimen of practice and training and under the guidance of informed and enthusiastic teachers.

The schools and colleges of Clare stood in complement to a club structure that served at once to bolster and epitomise the strong communal ties in many parts of the county. Indeed, so striking a feature of Clare society was this sense of community that visitors to the county felt compelled to document it in word and image: the American anthropologists Conrad Arensberg and Solon Kimball produced a groundbreaking sociological profile of the county in the 1930s and, two decades later, inspired by their work, the great American photographer of the depression era, Dorothea Lange, arrived in Clare. Lange's Clare photographs touch on similar subject matter to that of Arensberg and Kimball and included among them were photographs of hurling and the people and pageantry that went with the game.

These visitors captured a county on the cusp of significant change. It was change that was visible in the skies and on the ground. What drove it was the development of Shannon Airport, itself a product of local traditions of aviation (a seaplane base operated from nearby Foynes in the 1930s) and the growing commercialisation of air travel. The steady expansion of the airport – it became a vital hub for transatlantic flights – transformed the region, acting as a driver for industrial development, employment and increased urbanisation. Out of it grew an entirely new town – Shannon – which was built on reclaimed marshland in the 1960s and which, in an Irish context, was distinctive for the planning that went into its design. Shannon was a town established to cater for those who came to work in the airport and the industries that built up around it. It was hardly a surprise that these new residents were as anxious to play as to work, and clubs – sporting and otherwise – soon sprang up to meet their recreational needs. One such club was the Shannon Airport and Athletic Club (it evolved into Wolfe Tones, Shannon), which was founded in 1967 and which, over time, acted as an important focus of community for people migrating into the area who wished to play Gaelic games.

For all that the developments at Shannon emphasised a county in a state of flux, one constant appeared to be the geographic divide between football and hurling. The former predominated in the west of the county, the latter in the east. If the line that separated one from the other was not always clear – it ran with the 'limestone', according to one writer – it was no less real for that. By the mid 1960s, indeed, the west of the county was so bereft of hurling that the county board was compelled to launch a plan of sporting plantation with five parishes identified as pilot areas where the game might be introduced. There was little to suggest it met with much success; while shifting demographic trends led in the late 1990s and early 2000s to some blurring of traditional loyalties, there was no great bridging of the divide between east and west.

In many ways, for much of the second half of the twentieth century, the one point of convergence between hurling and football in the county was the absence of inter-county achievement. Despite a vibrant club scene, which gave rise to intense – at times excessive – rivalries, Clare struggled to assert itself at provincial and national levels. Indeed, the gap between local passion and national reward began to close only in the 1970s, when the county's hurlers, led by local priest Fr Harry Bohan, managed to win back-to-back National league titles. The progression from winter to summer success proved a steep climb, and it was not until the 1990s that Clare's big championship breakthroughs came. The footballers were first up: in 1992, building on All-Ireland 'B' success the previous year, they defeated Kerry in a Munster final to claim their first provincial title since 1917, a victory that sparked wild celebrations across west Clare. Then came the hurlers' turn: in 1995, managed by ex-player Ger Loughnane from Feakle, they not only survived the furnace of a Munster championship summer, but went on to claim their first All-Ireland title since 1914. It was a victory that left an indelible imprint on hurling. Stories of the physical preparations of the Clare hurlers achieved near-mythical status within the sport and the characteristics that defined that team – elemental passion, extraordinary strength and stamina – proved hugely significant in shaping how others thought about, and trained for, the game in the years that followed.

Clare's 1995 victory, which was followed by another in 1997 (a first in the GAA's newly introduced back-door championship system) temporarily turned the hurling world on its head. But the deepest impression was made on the county itself. Jimmy Smyth captured perfectly its local importance when he wrote: 'It was more than the preservation of honour, glory and reputations; more than self-fulfilment, more than the joy of mastering an art, more than the satisfaction of beating an opponent, more than the thrill of seeing the net shaking, and more than the exuberance of fitness and health. It was on a plane far higher than this. It was a totality, the merging of the collective spirit, a unification of minds that included every man, woman and child of a county unit at home and abroad. It brought life into the people and it was good to be alive.'

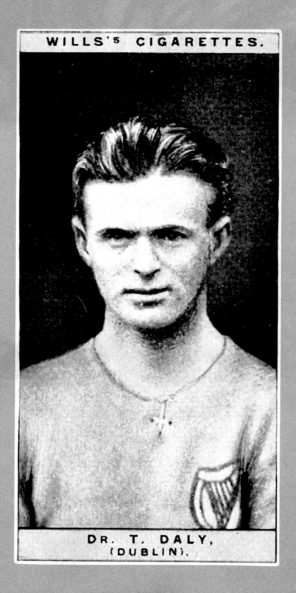

WILLS'S CIGARETTES.

DR. T. DALY,
(DUBLIN).

A cigarette card from the 1920s bears the image of Clare and Dublin hurler, Dr Tommy Daly. One of the greatest goalkeepers of the early twentieth century, Daly won a junior All-Ireland for Clare in 1914, before moving to Dublin and adding four senior titles between 1917 and 1927. He later returned to play for Tulla and Clare. The Listowel writer Bryan McMahon penned a poem in his honour: 'On the windswept Hill of Tulla/Where the Claremen place their dead/Four solemn yews stand sentinel/Above a hurler's head/And from the broken north lands/From Burren bleak and bare/The dirge of Thomas Daly/Goes surging on through Clare. *(National Library of Ireland)*

A hurling match in County Clare in the early 1950s, taken by the great documentary photographer Dorothea Lange. The Californian was drawn to Clare by the work of anthropologists Conrad Arensberg and Solon Kimball, who undertook a major study of the county in the 1930s. In choosing Clare, they believed it offered a 'microcosm' of Ireland as a whole – it was a county where there was 'a blending of older Gaelic and modern British influences, and one that was neither entirely Gaelic nor entirely English in speech'. *(Dorothea Lange Collection, the Oakland Museum of California, City of Oakland. Gift of Paul S. Taylor)*

The Tulla Pipe Band performs before a local hurling match in the early 1950s. From the very beginning of the GAA music was part of the entertainment laid on for spectators attending games. The Tulla Pipe Band continues to perform at GAA events in Clare. *(Dorothea Lange Collection, the Oakland Museum of California, City of Oakland. Gift of Paul S. Taylor)*

'My two brothers moved to Dublin. Their families are in Dublin now and their boys – they will never play for Naomh Eoin again because their friends are in Dublin and that's it. The next generation is completely lost.'

John Bonfil, b. 1962.

'I find in east Clare, as I said to one particular club, "You promote soccer and hurling but you don't promote football". That didn't go down too well, but that's the way I saw it. Thriving soccer club and a thriving hurling club and anti-football, very anti-football. And they always had good footballers if they gave them a chance.'

Gus Lohan, b. 1941.

'There's a peculiarity about west Clare. West Clare is not west Clare; west Clare is a series of parishes – each an independent unit. And when they play against one another, there's rather a serious situation.'

John Hanly, b. 1928.

'It being in that season of the year
      when nature's yield in store,
When fields are green and trees were
      bare and the harvest almost o'er,
A few of Erin's gallant sons whose
      courage was often tried
With bands did meet with hearts elite
      down by the Shannon side.'

– Extract from 'The Hurlers of O'Gonnelloe', recited by Michael McNamara, b. 1947.

'Well, we didn't play on the roads but we played in fields that might have a nice cover of rushes on them … We played with sponge balls and sliotars, whatever came our way. And we played with hurleys made from bits of sallies, they were usually home-made hurleys anyway – anything that had a little twist in it at all was used as a hurley. One old neighbour said one time, "If all the balls that are in there start to sprout, there'll be a great crop!"'

Tom Burke, b. 1943.

'My late mother was a saint. She did all the washing of togs. No electricity, no washing machine, no running water, always had them washed and ironed. When I got older I helped, I never minded, sport is a great tonic for anyone. We always looked forward to their return that no one was minus a tooth or a swollen lip. It often happened but there was still talk of where the next match would be played.'

Cecilia Collins (née Arthur), b. 1929.

Christy Ring (far right) in action for his club Glen Rovers against University College Cork in a Cork county championship match in April 1955. A winner of eight All-Ireland medals with Cork in a career spanning four decades, Ring is widely recognised as hurling's greatest ever player. The journalist P. D. Mehigan described his fellow county-man as a 'pocket Hercules, beautifully built with a powerful frame. And those hands? I have never seen a man with such perfect hands. He had tremendous wrists packed with dynamite.' *(Irish Examiner)*

Westmeath Mayo Offaly
Limerick Laois Waterford
Carlow Longford Leitrim
Tipperary Kilkenny Derry
Kerry **Cork** Wicklow
Kildare Antrim Meath
Tyrone Dublin Galway
Armagh Fermanagh
Donegal Sligo Roscommon
Clare Cavan Monaghan
Louth Wexford Down

Cork

On 3 November 1884 the first report on the founding of the GAA appeared in an Irish newspaper. It was published in the *Cork Examiner* and was written by John McKay. The Downpatrick-raised journalist had been invited to attend the Thurles gathering, which took place on 1 November, and emerged from it as one of the newly formed Association's honorary secretaries. Securing the support of McKay constituted a significant triumph for Michael Cusack and Maurice Davin, the GAA's principal instigators. McKay was a prominent personality in Cork and Munster athletics and through his work as a reporter he offered the prospect of a flow of positive publicity for the sporting start-up. This he certainly delivered, but his influence extended beyond the powers of his written word. McKay not only helped ensure backing for the GAA from the renowned Cork Athletic Club, he also proved active in opposing the rival Irish Amateur Athletic Association (IAAA). If McKay's status in the local athletics scene helped secure a certain receptiveness to the GAA, the early Cork connection to the new sporting body was by no means limited to any one individual. A mere eleven days after its foundation, the first athletics meeting under GAA rules was held near Macroom and a just over a month later, on 27 December 1884, the Association met for only the second time at the Victoria Hotel in Cork city.

McKay, of course, was in attendance, but so too was Paul Madden, the Mayor-elect of Cork city, as well as other prominent local Home Rulers. This marriage of sport and nationalist politics was among the most striking features of the GAA's early workings, yet growing tensions between rival strands within nationalism resulted ultimately in division and a weakened GAA. It was a Midleton native, Patrick N. Fitzgerald, who chaired the controversial Annual Convention of the GAA of November 1887, at which clerical opponents of increased Fenian control over the Association were essentially evicted. Fitzgerald, an IRB veteran, expressed gratitude to God 'that there were men in Ireland who would not stand for clerical dictation'. Back in Cork, his actions and those of his Fenian colleagues were by no means universally popular. Fitzgerald was denounced at a convention of the Mitchelstown club, while another in Blackrock expressed its abhorrence at the insult caused to the priests at the Thurles convention.

As it happened, the schisms in the GAA at national level were not merely mirrored in Cork; they were accentuated. The Cork county board, which had been established in December 1886, split not in two, but three. The rupture came at the County Convention in October 1888 when Fr O'Connor from the Blackrock club started a breakaway board (known variously as the 'Cork Board' and the 'O'Connor Board') in opposition to the official IRB-dominated board led by Alderman Eugene Crean (known as the 'Crean Board'). A third board, also under clerical control and soon allied to that of Fr O'Connor, sprang up in Mallow under the presidency of Fr J. Carver of Castletownroche. This 'North Cork Board' was essentially concerned with enabling clubs in that part of the county to play games within a reasonable distance from each other.

This concern with travel pointed up problems of geography, which in many ways were as big as those of politics. From the beginning, the sheer size of Cork raised questions over how it might be administered or the feasibility of running competitions on a county-wide basis. Despite the dense local network of railways, which made possible the transport of teams and spectators, these concerns were slow to dissolve. In 1903, for instance, a secession request was made to the GAA Central Council by west Cork; later, in 1912, *The Gaelic Athlete* newspaper advocated, on pragmatic grounds, that the county be divided into three or four units. No such scenario was countenanced: by then, the GAA in many counties was already well on the way to becoming a focus for county identity and in Cork it would bring a sense of cohesion to a vast and geographically diverse territory.

None of this meant that distinctive regional personalities were magically obliterated. On the contrary, when the county board divisions were resolved in the early 1890s and the emphasis returned to the games, it became clear that inclinations towards hurling and Gaelic football – now overshadowing athletics – were often geographically determined. As the historian John A. Murphy has observed, 'hurling flourished in the fertile plains and river valleys, while football thrived in the hillier and rugged parts – "ash" and "rush" in the neat shorthand.' In both, the county's first All-Ireland titles came in 1890, with the Aghabullogue club winning the hurling and the Midleton club taking the football, a double that would be repeated only once more and not until a century later. The 1890s, in fact, was the decade in which Cork, for all its difficulties, effectively established itself as the premier dual county, its representative clubs winning four national hurling titles and contesting six football finals. Five of the latter were lost, but none as controversially as that in 1894 when the city-based Nil Desperandum club, which had been born as a rugby team known as Berwick Rangers, were deemed to have lost to Dublin when failing to agree to a replay after the metropolitans walked off the pitch when two points down. Unwilling to recognise anyone but their own as the rightful winners, the Cork county board presented medals to their players bearing the inscription: 'GAA, All-Ireland Football Championship, won by Nils, 1894.'

As the level of GAA activity increased, so too did the pressure to secure grounds where games might be played. The availability of enclosed grounds enabled gates receipts to be collected, but the use of them involved substantial cost. In 1896, lands owned by Lord Midleton in east Cork were leased to the GAA and used for over fifty years until members of the Midleton club, with the help of emigrant subscriptions, finally bought the site. But it was in Cork city that the demand for playing fields was perhaps greatest and it was here, on the banks of the River Lee, that the GAA-supported private company, Cork Athletic Grounds Committee Limited, took steps to develop a proper stadium. The facility was intended to be run on a commercial basis and to be open to all, but with the exception of a few games of hockey and Association football, it was, from 1906 onwards, used exclusively for Gaelic games.

The story of the GAA in Cork evidences some of the ambiguities of pre-1916 Irish nationalism. It suggests a more nuanced picture than that usually presented of the political leanings of the Cork GAA in the pre-independence period. It is known, for example, that GAA members were among those who joined the British war effort in the Great War, yet for the most part, it has been those linked with the separatist tradition who have been most identified with the local Association, an inevitable consequence of the charismatic personalities involved. Cork men like Liam MacCarthy, Sam Maguire and Michael Collins combined IRB and GAA activity when working in London in the early 1900s, while closer to home, Bandon-born businessman and politician J. J. Walsh saw the GAA as a potential training ground for physical force nationalism. Walsh, above all, left an indelible mark on the GAA in Cork. In 1907, while still in his twenties, he became president of the county board and set about professionalising the way it conducted its affairs: football and hurling leagues were organised in city streets and across the county, and the board's finances, boosted by the installation of turnstiles at all major venues, were overhauled by more efficient accounting. As a result of its improved financial standing, the board was even in a position to purchase shares in the Great Southern Railway, a move designed to exert influence when it came to securing travel facilities for teams and spectators.

For all the improvements he helped bring about, Walsh's engagement with the GAA diminished as his commitment to separatist nationalist politics deepened. His was not an isolated case. Across Cork, the sidelining of GAA activity by politics became widespread. With the War of Independence being fought with particular intensity in the county, the effects on the GAA were severe: railways were disrupted, grounds were occupied, leading administrators imprisoned and games abandoned. The Civil War only prolonged such difficulties, though the Cork county board did propose that the Association be used as a force for mediation between two nationalist factions. The idea of a 'national convention for peace' was, however, rejected by the Central Council on the basis that it might possibly exacerbate rather than narrow divisions within the GAA community. As it turned out, the GAA's post-independence decades were shaped by men who were prominent on either side of the Civil War divide. J. J. Walsh re-emerged as a minister in the first Irish Free State government in the 1920s, where he spearheaded the revival of the ancient Tailteann Games with an upgraded Croke Park as its focal point. Elsewhere, the former county board chairman, IRA leader and anti-treaty republican Seán McCarthy rose to the position of GAA President in the 1930s, where he served alongside Pádraig Ó Caoimh, another ex-prisoner from Cork, who filled the role of GAA General Secretary from 1929 to 1964, his influence earning him widespread recognition as the 'architect of the modern GAA'.

On the field as off it, the influence of Cork was everywhere apparent. In the mid to late 1920s, the Cork hurlers, with a backbone of players from the then dominant Blackrock club, won four All-Irelands in six years, the most memorable coming in 1931 when the men in blood-red jerseys – which had been adopted by the county in 1919 – defeated Kilkenny after three titanic encounters. That victory signalled the end of a particular era, however. Soon after, Cork captain Eudie Coughlan, a fisherman from Blackrock whose father had won two All-Irelands in the 1890s, announced his retirement in opposition to a decision to remove the selection of the county team from the county champions. If Coughlan's departure coincided with the ending of Blackrock's local hegemony, the dominance of urban clubs remained a feature of the Cork hurling scene for much of the century. St Finbarr's were a vital presence on the south side of the city, while their great rivals, Glen Rovers, drew from the working-class estates of Ballyvolane and Blackpool on the industrial north side. The rise of Glen Rovers was rooted in the cultivation of young talent, but it was more obviously bound up with the brilliant career of Christy Ring. Balding and somewhat stout of frame, he assumed a stature far above that of his peers. He devoted himself to hurling and helped Cork to win eight All-Ireland titles over a quarter of a century.

There was much more to Ring than All-Ireland medals, however. In the perfection of his game, honed during hours of practice, Ring raised hurling to a living art form, winning admirers far beyond his home place and his sport. On Ring's death in 1979, it fell to the then Taoiseach, Jack Lynch, a club-mate of Ring's and himself a multiple All-Ireland medal winner for Cork, to give the graveside oration. Speaking to, and for, the thousands of mourners, he said: 'As long as young men will match their hurling skills against each other on Ireland's green fields, as long as young boys swing their camáns for the sheer thrill of the feel and the tingle in their fingers of the impact of ash on leather, as long as hurling is played the story of Christy Ring will be told. And that will be forever.'

Christy Ring, in death, remained the presence that Lynch foresaw. Not only is his genius frequently replayed on television in the form of Louis Marcus's brilliant filmic study from the early 1960s, but in Cork, specifically, his memory is routinely invoked in verse or witnessed in the bronze of prominently placed public monuments. That a hurler should be accorded such status is symptomatic of the centrality of sport to Cork's social and cultural life. And though the GAA is merely one part of a crowded sporting landscape, it alone acts as a unifier of city and county and the authentic expression of Cork identity.

However, the relationship that has existed between city and county, urban and rural, has not been static. The closing decades of the twentieth century saw a movement towards urban living, a trend evident in the expansion of many towns and villages throughout the county, as well as the suburbs of Cork city. Douglas was one of the latter, its population growth coinciding with the growing success of the local Nemo Rangers club, which broke the monopoly of rural teams on the club football championship and enjoyed remarkable success in the All-Ireland club football championships, winning the competition on seven occasions between 1973 and 2003. Across all codes – football and hurling, camogie and ladies' football – the success enjoyed by Cork teams at club and county levels was impressive. Every decade brought All-Ireland titles, but more and more went into their winning. Greater commitment of time and effort was required of players and greater professionalism demanded of team managements and county boards.

In Cork, tensions between these various parties ignited in conflict. And not just once: the 2000s were blighted by a series of disputes between players and managements, and between players and administrators. These clashes, only in part a product of growing 'player power' in the Association, were deeply divisive and their often personalised nature reflected poorly on those involved. And yet the passions they aroused spoke volumes for the seriousness with which the games are treated by GAA people in the county. Ultimately, it is these very passions and this seriousness that has given the GAA its firm foothold in Cork. By 2010 the county was home to 263 clubs and host to 16,500 games every year. This level of activity and participation bestows an importance on the GAA that transcends sport. Writing against a backdrop of national economic crisis and as part of Cork GAA's Strategic Vision and Action Plan up to 2015, the historian John A. Murphy acknowledged as much: 'With so many organs of our society broken or dysfunctional, the Association stands out not only as a vital sector of the national community but in a real sense it can claim to be the community itself.'

Two teams line up before a football match at the Cork Athletic Grounds in 1905. The previous September, the official opening of the newly reconstructed grounds was marked by the hosting of the delayed 1902 All-Ireland football and hurling finals. *(Irish Examiner)*

Supporters pictured at the Cork schools camogie final between St Aloysius and the School of Commerce at the Mardyke, Cork, 29 May 1946. At the time, the popularity of camogie in Cork was greatly helped by the prior success of the county team – in the eight years between 1934 and 1941, Cork won six All-Ireland camogie championships. The next title was not won by the county until the 1970s. *(Irish Examiner)*

Club activities regularly extended beyond the training of teams and the playing of games. This photograph shows a fun day at the Mayfield Hurling and Football Carnival, May 1967. *(Irish Examiner)*

Cork football training at Páirc Uí Chaoimh, previously the site of the Athletic Grounds, April 1990. The following September Cork completed a remarkable All-Ireland double in football and hurling. *(Inpho)*

Cork's Ben O'Connor celebrates after scoring a goal late in the 2006 All-Ireland hurling final against Kilkenny. It was not enough. The Cork men, then chasing a three-in-a-row, were defeated by 1-16 to 1-13. As Kilkenny's hurling fortunes continued to rise over subsequent years, Cork's collapsed amid disputes involving players, team management and county board officials. *(Sportsfile)*

'I've been twelve months in the county board and I've learned more about the internal politics in the GAA than I did in the twenty-five years that I was involved before because, there are fellas in 'high station' we'll call it and they know where every fella is from — not political but because that club wouldn't be good to the county board in selling tickets or because they wouldn't be supportive of it, and maybe they were supporting even the strike, on the wrong side or whatever it is ... I suppose 'tis all politics even though 'tisn't Fianna Fáil/Fine Gael/Labour politics or 'tisn't government politics but, it all comes down to the political mind of a person.'

Denis Keohane, b. 1948.

'Listening to matches you had a wet and dry battery for the radio. And you turned on no news in case you'd run down the wet battery for the match on Sunday. Sparing the battery, 'twould go very low, and you'd be trying to keep it strong for Sunday for the match. And then you turned on the match and hopefully, it might finish out the match and you'd know who won it.'

John-Joe McCarthy, b. 1926.

'We had a camogie club here in Valley Rovers, they were called the Shamrock Maids ... One time they played this camogie game, they were playing in a final and they were short a couple of players, so they dressed up two men to play.'

Marie O'Brien, b. 1961.

'The balance in it is fierce important — the balance in the hurley when you catch it. That must be right and it must feel right down along the handle.'

Michael Fitzgerald, b. 1952.

'The downside of ladies' football as against the gents — or boys — is the amount of travelling they do around the county to compete, you know, because you wouldn't have as many locally, d'you know, to form a division as such. They travel the length and breadth of the county. And Cork is a big county, fair play to them and they're quite successful at that.'

Noel O'Neill, b. 1957.

When Derry beat Cork in the 1993 All-Ireland senior football final it became the third Ulster county to win the championship in as many years. This 1993 success remains Derry's only All-Ireland senior title. *(Inpho)*

Westmeath Mayo Offaly
Limerick Laois Waterford
Carlow Longford Leitrim
Tipperary Kilkenny **Derry**
Kerry Cork Wicklow
Kildare Antrim Meath
Tyrone Dublin Galway
Armagh Fermanagh
Donegal Sligo Roscommon
Clare Cavan Monaghan
Louth Wexford Down

Derry

In 2008 Martin O'Neill, the former soccer international and the then manager of Aston Villa Football Club in the Premier League in England, was invited to Áras an Uachtaráin to give a lecture on the meaning of being Irish. In a charming, wide-ranging address, he spoke of the great anomalies, ironies, paradoxes and even downright contradictions that characterised his life. He remembered his upbringing in an Irish working-class family in County Derry and recounted how his family – like most nationalist families in rural Derry – paraded their strong GAA background like a banner, all the while frowning on soccer. Involvement in the GAA was a badge of Irishness and a matter of considerable pride.

His father was a founder member of Kilrea Pearses GAA club and O'Neill himself loved to play the game. His older brothers played football for Derry and this was something to which he too aspired.

Many of his earliest memories revolved around travelling to GAA matches, most notably to the 1958 All-Ireland football final. He was just six years old and was brought to the game by his mother. The fact that his brothers, Gerry and Leo, were part of the Derry team only added to the lustre of the occasion. The journey to Croke Park in Dublin was, he remembered, their Holy Grail. And what a journey it was. The family left at 5.30 a.m. to drive the six hours to Dublin. The journey was shortened (despite the fact that they stopped to take Mass on the way) by giving a lift to two young women who were hitching to Dublin for the match. The women were marvellous singers who sang the county song of each county they passed through. They began with the 'Mountains of Pomeroy' when they reached Tyrone and continued in a similar vein as they rolled across Armagh, Down, Louth and, finally, into Dublin. More even than the disappointment of losing the match, O'Neill recalled the occasion as an extension of his Irishness, a celebration of family and place and belonging.

In time, of course, O'Neill's dream of playing for Derry was displaced by dreams of soccer and of playing in the great soccer stadiums of England, which were beamed into Irish homes with the spread of television through the 1960s. He continued to play Gaelic football through his schooldays and was a star of the St Malachy's college team for whom he played after the family moved to Belfast. He was, equally, a brilliant soccer player who was making a name for himself with Distillery soccer club. With the ban on GAA members playing soccer then in place, O'Neill's profile made controversy somewhat inevitable. When St Malachy's were due to play a colleges' match in Casement Park, the GAA deemed that the match should not be played there, apparently because of O'Neill's soccer activities. O'Neill saw it as a challenge to his Irishness and it left a foul taste in his mouth (and in his father's). Ultimately, O'Neill pursued a career in professional soccer in England and became the first Catholic to captain Northern Ireland, helping Northern Ireland reach the quarter-final of the 1982 World Cup in Spain. Nonetheless, he retained vivid memories of his Gaelic past.

The GAA in Derry has always existed side by side with a strong tradition of soccer; this is particularly true of Derry city. The establishment of the GAA occurred in tandem with dramatic expansion of the population in the city. Between 1881 and 1911 the population of Derry doubled to more than 40,000, making it the fourth largest city in the country. The expansion was driven by the development of the shirt-making industry. This was an industry that was low-wage and was dominated by women, many of whom were outworkers working in rural Derry and Donegal. The economic expansion of Derry created a Catholic majority in city and county, and it was this majority who embraced Gaelic games after 1884 with the establishment of GAA clubs.

The divided politics of Derry coloured the early development of the GAA and lent a certain tension to events staged by the new Association. When the Emmets club from Dundalk travelled to play the Derry Hibernians in June 1888, 3,000 spectators turned up to watch the football match. The Sarsfields Flute Band provided the music, but when they defied an order that they play music only at the playing field, they were baton-charged by the police. The ensuing disorder saw eighteen people jailed for periods of up to six months. That the GAA was identified with nationalists was emphasised by a police report of a GAA excursion to Dundalk in January 1889. While it was agreed that no meeting of the IRB had taken place under cover of the match, nationalist songs such as 'The Wearing of the Green' were sung and three cheers were dedicated to the Phoenix Park Invincibles, who in May 1882 had murdered the two most senior British officials in Ireland.

In the early years of the twentieth century the GAA in Derry was part of a broad range of nationalist organisations such as the Gaelic League, the United Irish League and the Ancient Order of Hibernians. This was a world of football matches and feiseanna, Irish language and literature classes. As Eoghan Corry has shown, the Gaelic League was particularly potent in starting hurling clubs and was influential in arranging for the playing of a hurling league between teams from the counties of Derry, Donegal and Tyrone in the early 1900s. Hurling progressed to a point that enabled Derry to win the Ulster hurling championship by defeating Antrim by two points in the 1902 Ulster final, played at Celtic Park, Belfast, on 11 October 1903. The All-Ireland semi-final was not played until 5 June 1904. The Derry hurlers travelled overnight to Drogheda where they took to the field wearing white jerseys embroidered with green shamrocks and were accompanied every step of the way by the music provided by the 'formidable contingent of pipers' who had travelled with them. The game proved an anticlimax. The long grass on the pitch was not merely unsuitable for hurling, but 'absolutely dangerous'. The Derry hurlers were considered to be particularly disadvantaged because they usually played the ball along the ground. The *Freeman's Journal* reported that 'their aerial play was defective and their dribbling a complete failure,' and they were duly defeated.

For all that there was passion for Gaelic games in Derry, the reality was that the GAA struggled to establish itself with the same level of organisation as elsewhere in Ireland. For example, county championships in football and hurling were only sporadically played up until the mid 1930s. No hurling championship was played between 1906 and 1930, and only nine football championships were played between 1914 and 1932. During this period, soccer was thriving in Derry city and by 1929 the GAA was 'all but dead in the city'. The great problem was that the establishment of an enduring structure centred on a county board proved impossible. Several times boards were brought into existence only to wither away within a couple of years. Only in 1933 was the Derry county board permanently constituted. Almost immediately the GAA flourished in south Derry with the formal establishment of clubs in Ballinascreen, Desertmartin, Lavey and Magherafelt in 1933 and 1934. Against that, the GAA essentially collapsed in Derry city. The immediate explanation for this collapse and the long-term difficulties that the GAA experienced in establishing itself in the city is a matter of considerable debate. One factor was certainly the GAA ban rules. Interestingly, counties in Ulster had initially opposed the introduction of these rules, imagining that their enforcement would impede the development of the GAA in areas where soccer and rugby were strong. The story of Gaelic games in Derry city in the 1920s seemed to offer at least partial proof of this. The foundation of Derry City Football Club in 1928 and its entry in the Irish League in 1929 offered a sporting counterpoint to the nationalist majority who lived in Derry city. Based at the Brandywell Stadium, Derry City enjoyed extensive, enduring support from the very people who would most usually have been expected to involve themselves with the GAA.

Attempts to spread the GAA in the city were driven by the purchase in October 1943 of Celtic Park as a venue for Gaelic games. A remarkable surge of interest saw the establishment of up to seventeen clubs in the city. Many of these clubs folded almost as quickly as they had emerged and the GAA retained a limited presence, with only one urban club winning a senior football championship in the decades that followed: Éire Óg in 1952. The GAA in Derry remained dominated by rural clubs. These clubs had expanded in number during the Second World War. Clubs were founded in Bellaghy, Castledawson and Ballymaguigan, while the establishment of clubs in Dungiven and Ballerin spread the GAA beyond the dominant southern parishes of the county. Evidence of progress was found in Derry's capture of the National Football League in 1947. That League was truncated by appalling weather conditions and led to Derry defeating Clare in Croke Park. Eoghan Corry records how one of their players, Francie Niblock, had three teeth knocked out, but scored a wonderful goal on the half-volley, with the ball flying into the back of the net off a post from a 20-yard shot.

In 1950, led by the burgeoning talents of men such as Jim McKeever, Derry claimed the Ulster junior title. An innovative approach to training saw the county board recruit Frank McGreevy, whose expertise lay in training Newry Town Football Club, to take training sessions. Jim McKeever remembered: 'He was an endearing man, approaching sixty years of age at that time, who knew very little about Gaelic football, indeed scarcely enough to referee a practice match. His specialism was doing drill exercises. But his presence focused us for the match.' The sense that momentum was building in Derry football was enhanced by victory in the 1954 McKenna Cup and by reaching the final of the 1954 Ulster championship. There was to be no immediate breakthrough, however. Cavan were still a powerful force and Armagh had emerged as a vital presence in the early 1950s. Finding a way past these two was complicated by the rise of Tyrone who broke a cycle of defeat to win the Ulster championship in 1956 and 1957.

Seeing their neighbours win championships pushed Derry to greater heights. Derry had been trained in 1957 by Paul Russell, the great Kerry footballer who introduced the methods used by the legendary Eamonn O'Sullivan to bring decades of success to Kerry. Now, in 1958, the *de facto* trainer and manager of the team was their injured star, Roddy Gribben. Gribben was assisted by Jim McKeever, a PE instructor who was one of the new generation of northern footballers who had reaped the benefits of the expansion of second- and third-level education in the years after the Second World War. A narrow first-round win over Antrim was followed by a breathtaking defeat of Cavan in which Derry scored four goals. The final against Down – themselves seeking a first ever All-Ireland title – was played in front of 22,000 people and, although the match was disappointing, it resulted in a four-point win for Derry. Next stop was Croke Park for a meeting with Kerry on a famously wet day. So brutal was the rain that the pre-match parade was abandoned. Kerry missed a succession of chances and were shocked by Derry who claimed a one-point victory, with Sean O'Connell outstanding.

More than 70,000 people turned up for the final against Dublin – including Martin O'Neill, his family and the female singers. Derry recovered from a sluggish start to draw level in the second half, but the game fell away from them when Paddy Farnan scored a goal for Dublin. One of the Derry players, Patsy Breen, recalled: 'I still thought we were going to win after we drew level in the second half, but I suppose the euphoria of it all and the loss of a bit of concentration let us down in the end. Even though we lost to Dublin, it was very special to play in an All-Ireland final.' Equally, though, that Derry team were never able to recapture the heights of 1958 and, in the 1960s, Derry made no impact on the Ulster senior football championship.

Through all of this, club football in Derry was ferociously competitive; it also had its lighter moments. Jim McKeever remembered playing in a match for Ballymaguigan against Coleraine: 'The pitch wasn't very well marked. The crossbar was only a rope, and there weren't any nets. The ball was bobbing around and somebody pulled on it. One umpire gave a goal, the other a point. Our umpire gave the decision against his own team. Likewise with the other. The referee split the difference and awarded two points. The really comic part of the story was that one of our best players, the late Michael Young, did not want to play as he had hay ready for baling and the weather forecast was not very good. However, he was persuaded to play. When the controversy emerged, Young went up to the referee and told him to hurry up and make the decision, as he had to be home to bale the hay!' The strength of club football in Derry was epitomised by the Bellaghy Club who won twelve county championships in sixteen years, in a run which climaxed in the winning of the 1972 All-Ireland club championship.

At county level, development in the schools and at underage level saw St

Columb's win the All-Ireland colleges' title in 1965, and Derry minors also won the All-Ireland championship that year. The promise of those players seemed to be confirmed in 1968 when Derry won the All-Ireland Under-21 championship. Again, the transition to senior status seemed to have been successfully made when Derry won their second Ulster title in 1970. Further Ulster championship success came in 1975 and 1976 but on no occasion could Derry make the step and secure an All-Ireland senior title. Through the 1970s the violence of the Troubles was a constant presence. The place of the GAA – with its expanding network of social centres – within the wider nationalist community dictated that the organisation and its people would be drawn into the conflict. Bellaghy was a particular flashpoint, while the death of former Derry hurler, Kevin Lynch, on hunger strike in 1981 led to the hurling section of his Dungiven club being renamed Kevin Lynch's hurling club. There were further reminders of the impact of the Troubles, notably arson attacks and the sectarian murder of Seán Brown, the central figure in the running of Bellaghy Wolfe Tones club, in 1997.

It was through the voluntary work of men such as Brown that the GAA in Derry had grown to the point where there were more than forty clubs active in the county in the 1990s. The strength of club football was confirmed with the emergence of Lavey, who won the 1991 All-Ireland club title, by Ballerin, who reached an All-Ireland final, and by Ballinderry who won the Ulster club championship. This strength finally payed dividends on the inter-county stage when a National Football League was won in 1992 and the All-Ireland championship was claimed in 1993. An outstanding team delivered on earlier promise and, even if no further All-Ireland success has followed, four further National League titles have been claimed, the most recent in 2008. Across the county, the GAA retains huge support in rural areas; the traditional strongholds remain steadfast. Crucially, the games are also making progress in Derry city.

The relationship between the GAA and Irish nationalism varied from club to club and from county to county. In Derry, the Irish Volunteers – including members of the GAA – used Celtic Park to drill. Celtic Park was then used for soccer, but was later purchased by the GAA and became the county grounds of the GAA in Derry.
(University of Ulster Archives)

Camogie was fostered at the Dominican Convent in Portstewart. This shot of the game being played at the school comes from the 1920s. Camogie has retained a vital presence in Derry across the decades and in 2011 Derry won the Ulster Under-16 camogie championship. *(Cardinal Ó Fiaich Memorial Library)*

On the weekend of the 1958 All-Ireland senior football semi-final against Kerry, the Derry contingent relaxed with the newspapers in a Dublin hotel: (l–r) Willie Cassidy, Barney McNicholl, Tom Scullion, Jim McKeever, Teresa McKeever, Harry Cassidy, Hugh A. McGurk, Gerry McCann and Liam Mulholland. *(Jim McKeever)*

More than 70,000 spectators turned out to see Derry play Dublin in the 1958 All-Ireland football final at Croke Park. Derry had beaten Kerry in the semi-final, but could not repeat the feat against Dublin and lost by six points. Midway through the second half the teams were level, but Derry fell away in the latter stages of the game. *(Lensmen)*

The new grounds of the St Mary's, Faughanvale GAA Club – John McLaughlin Park – were opened in 2009. Amongst the events at the official opening were underage blitzes and a masters' match between Derry and Tyrone. The centrepiece of the day's events was a men's senior football league fixture between St Mary's, Faughanvale and their parish rivals, Slaughtmanus. The souvenir programme for the day noted that games between the two clubs were 'typically competitive, with no quarter asked, none given'. *(St Mary's, Faughanvale GAA Club)*

'We have to reach the other half of the population. That's going to be very tough because I mean we're sort of looked at as "the IRA at play", and this is very bad ... I think the GAA could do a lot in reconciliation in the North, because as it is even today – despite all their talks about peace and all – there's a big divide between how we perceive of one another ... I'd hope to think that the GAA would help in the process of reconciliation to prove that we, we who believe in the Irish language and the Irish culture, and it's part of us and part of our country, that that should be accepted as it is instead of being blown up into something that it's not, and I think the GAA could do well by getting across our message that we are a sporting organisation, involved culturally – and culturally only. And involve them. Because I think it's rather sad that my fellow people in the North here, this wonderful gift we have of a beautiful language and tremendous tradition with it, that part of us speak every day, with our townlands and all the traditions, that this is being denied to them. I think it's terrible ... All patriotism starts at the village pump and we should all start there, at this level, spread our wings and bring in.'

Paddy MacFlynn, b. 1918.

'We were brought up in what I would term a very strong GAA family. My father played football for the local club, Michael Davitts in Swatragh, for numerous years. I can recall us growing up that there would be an excursion every Sunday morning to a football match that my da would have been playing.'

Sean Gunning, b. 1968.

'Students [in St Columb's] also used crystal sets – home made radios – to pick up the results. Sometimes big matches were relayed to us in the college hall. Day boys also carried reports of matches for us on Monday mornings.

Seán Beattie, b. 1943.

'I am the oldest man to win an All–Ireland medal at any level, while representing the Ulster Council Inter Firms team in 2006 at the grand old age of fifty-five years!'

Terence McWilliams, b. 1951.

'At club level it was worse, because you hadn't the big fancy fields you've got today. Wee tight pitches, no fencing, spectators standing on top of you, it was good atmosphere all right, but I mean you had to be fast and clever to avoid these fellas, and your spectator would even come in from time to time.

Willie Cassidy, b. 1935.

Against the spectacular backdrop of Scalp Mountain, the Under-14 footballers from the Burt GAA club receive instruction in the finer points of the game from Danny Dowds at half-time in a match against Urris in 1988. *(Dónal Campbell)*

Westmeath Mayo Offaly
Limerick Laois Waterford
Carlow Longford Leitrim
Tipperary Kilkenny Derry
Kerry Cork Wicklow
Kildare Antrim Meath
Tyrone Dublin Galway
Armagh Fermanagh
Donegal Sligo Roscommon
Clare Cavan Monaghan
Louth Wexford Down

Donegal

A most remarkable headstone stands against the ruins of a church at Clonca, near Malin Head on the Inishowen Peninsula in Donegal. An intricate floral design down one side stands in sharp contrast to the other which depicts an old claymore sword alongside a hurley and ball. The headstone marks the grave of Magnus MacOrristin, reputed to be from the islands of Scotland. It was rediscovered in 1890 by William James Doherty, having been lost from public sight at some point after the church fell into disuse in the 1820s. The precise date of MacOrristin's death has been lost. The church was built on an ancient Christian site – one which possibly once housed a monastery – and the headstone is dated as being from the fifteenth century.

What it vividly illustrates is a tradition of stick-and-ball games in Donegal that extends back centuries before the establishment of the GAA, ultimately shaping the development of the Association after 1884. This is a tradition that might rightly be considered an ancestor of hurling, even if it cannot of course be considered precisely the same game as modern hurling. The game was often referred to as camán (anglicised as 'commons') and does not seem to have embraced handling of the ball; rather this was driven goalwards along the ground by men swinging long and narrow sticks. Games were played in south Donegal as well as in the north of the county, and varied from one region to the next. Reports of matches from Burt in the Inishowen Peninsula tell of players taking to the field in their bare feet, using sticks cut from hawthorn, whin-root or sallies, and playing from one field to the next. Later, and certainly by the 1880s, the form of camán played in Burt had evolved and was played from ditch to ditch. Matches were infrequent and usually scheduled for Christmas Day or St Stephen's Day. Up to forty players played for each team, in a game for which no written rules have been found, but which should not be considered unsophisticated for that.

The foundation of the GAA and the construction by Maurice Davin of a set of rules for hurling, published in January 1885, did not bring the men of Burt to discard their traditional game. Although Burt Hibernians GAA Club was founded on 5 February 1888, they did not simply fall into step with the new movement. The GAA club in Burt had been founded with the assistance of a visiting team from Derry, St Patrick's. The two clubs then proceeded to play a match, the first half of which was played according to GAA rules and the second according to the traditional rules of play in Burt. This did not prove a launch pad for the proper organisation of the GAA in Donegal. Such GAA clubs as wished to, affiliated to the Derry county board and played in the Derry county championships, but a formal GAA structure was not established in Donegal. Almost all of these clubs – Buncrana Emmets, Cahir O's Buncrana, Burt Hibernians, Newtowncunningham Harps, Portlough Harps and Killea Hibernians – were in the northeastern corner of the county, close to Derry city. The great exception was the Bundoran Irish Hearts club, which was established to play Gaelic football in 1889. Crucially, though, these clubs never united to form a county board and the early initiative was lost. Widespread poverty, a dispersed rural population, an inadequate educational system and an underdeveloped transport system contributed to the failure of the GAA to establish itself in Donegal. So, too, did the diversity of sporting engagement in the county. Soccer, in particular, enjoyed great popularity in the county, something borne out by the establishment of the Donegal Football Association in 1894. Historical links with Scotland – later manifested through a connection with Glasgow Celtic – and the presence of extensive British army and navy bases in the area – provided an impetus to the growth of soccer, which certainly hampered the development of the GAA.

The failure to develop the GAA in Donegal was also related to fidelity to the past. While hurlers in other counties abandoned their traditional stick-and-ball games in favour of hurling, as Conor Curran has demonstrated, the men of Donegal were less easily swayed. Glengesh Pass was the venue for a cross-country hurling match played over 5 miles of ground between teams from Glengesh and Scadaman, as late as 1906. The old traditions of play were about to be lost, however: it was in that year that the first Donegal senior hurling championship was played. A county board, charged with the organisation of such a championship, had finally been established at a meeting held in Cassie Mac's Hotel in Mountcharles on 22 October 1905.

The driving force behind this development was Seumas MacManus, who was the leading activist in the Gaelic Revival in Donegal and a renowned writer. On 1 March 1905, MacManus wrote to the *Derry Journal* saying: 'it is a great pity that while the other counties of Ireland have awakened to the fact that they are Irish, and have adopted again their own Irish games in preference to games introduced by the foreigner, Donegal, alone, one of the most Gaelic counties in Ireland, should not realise its duty.' MacManus had attended meetings of the Derry county board where he encouraged members to speak Irish and to read patriotic literature such as the works of John Mitchel and Thomas Davis. Now, driving the establishment of Donegal's own county board, he became its first chairman. To facilitate the spread of the GAA, the county was divided into two divisions, east and west. Through the activities of cultural nationalist activists and Catholic priests, clubs were established in parishes across Donegal. The plan was to spread Gaelic games and crush soccer. Canon James McFadden – who had previously been involved with soccer through Derrybeg Celtic – now described those who played soccer as 'Anglo-Saxons' who 'loved the foreign game as they do their king and if they must play the game of their country, England, they should be sent to play at the back of the Croach in Airgid, where no Irishmen would see them.'

To give evidence of their progress in promoting Gaelic games, Donegal men entered the Ulster championship. The footballers were soundly defeated by Derry but, represented by Burt as county champions, Donegal played Antrim in the Ulster hurling final. The match was an entirely one-sided affair with Burt winning by 5-21 to 0-1. The Burt men, the newspapers reported, were much too physically strong for their opponents who were 'useless in checking the rushes of Donegal who added point after point till full-time.' The physique of the Burt men, as Conor Curran has suggested, was rooted in their work on the land. Most were agricultural labourers or farm servants, one worked on the railways, another was a postman and one more was a blacksmith. This was not the start of a glorious tradition of inter-county success for Donegal. The rebirth of the GAA in Donegal in 1906 had been driven by Gaelic revivalists but this was not enough to sustain the development of the Association. The organisation of the GAA in the county suffered through emigration and by the fact that Seumas MacManus was spending more and more time lecturing in America.

A further attempt was made to promote Gaelic games in Donegal when the county board was re-established in April 1919 and affiliated to the Ulster Council of the GAA. Through the 1920s the number of clubs grew steadily and the county championships were now held on a regular basis. Ardara, Dungloe, Gaoth Dobhair and Ballyshannon emerged as the most successful clubs in the football championship. And it was now football, rather than hurling, which emerged as the most popular game in the county. Some of the players who now played GAA – such as those from Ardara – had previously played soccer. That game remained strong in Donegal and this contributed to the fact that Donegal made no impact on the inter-county scene in Ulster. Donegal did win Ulster junior titles. In 1933, they also defeated Cork in the All-Ireland semi-final, but were then hammered by Mayo in the final. The minor footballers also played in an All-Ireland minor semi-final in 1935 despite having lost to Tyrone in the Ulster final. They had been awarded that title, having placed an objection, before having it taken back off them through a counter-objection.

Throughout the 1940s and the 1950s, emigration destroyed the playing base of Donegal. In 1951, for example, when Ardara played Gaoth Dobhair in the first round of the Donegal senior football league, both teams fielded without many of their best footballers who had moved to work in England and America. In fact, Ardara had actually lost eight players who had been on their team the previous year. Year after year through the 1950s, the minutes of club AGMs and of county board meetings record the dismay over the exile of players. The drain of people was undercutting progressive moves at underage level in the county. St Eunan's College in Letterkenny had made a significant impact in reaching the final of the MacRory cup for colleges football and ten players from that school made the Donegal minor team, which won the Ulster minor football championship in 1956. Again, though, many of the players from that team emigrated, including the wing-forward, Hugh O'Donnell, who moved to Birmingham where he played football for the John Mitchel's club for fourteen years. At the end of the 1950s just 4,300 people were employed in manufacturing in Donegal; for all that tourism was developing, the small-scale of manufacturing and the decline of agriculture placed inevitable limits on the number of Donegal people who could find work in their own county.

And yet, in the 1960s, Donegal began to emerge from the abyss. Before that decade Donegal had never even reached an Ulster final. It was enough to lead Brian McEniff to remark: 'When I began playing football for Donegal, even the cows in the field would turn their backs when Donegal came to play.' Work in the clubs and the schools at underage level began to pay dividends, however, when Donegal won three of the first four Ulster under-21 championships staged in the years between 1963 and 1966. This was immediately translated to progress at senior level with Donegal reaching the Ulster finals of 1963 and 1966. The 1963 final against Down proved disastrous with Donegal failing to score in the first half, but the 1966 final seemed set to see revenge exacted as Donegal led by a point with the game nearing a conclusion. This match was the first Ulster final to be televised live on the BBC and viewers saw a scrappy, free-ridden match which ended in heartbreak for Donegal when Sean O'Neill drove a last-minute penalty into the net to give Down a two-point victory. That Donegal team is remembered as being filled with brilliant footballers who simply could not quite overcome the psychological barrier of generations of defeat.

Club football in Donegal gathered strength through the 1960s. Gaoth Dobhair, a powerhouse of previous decades, won their last championship of the era in 1961. Sean MacCumhaills of Ballybofey then came to the fore, before the St Joseph's team – an amalgamated team drawn from Bundoran and Ballyshannon – came through to win seven senior football championships, six senior leagues and three Ulster championships in their fourteen years of existence between 1963 and 1976. Players from all these clubs came together to win Donegal's first Ulster senior football championship in 1972 and then a second in 1974. The team was in the charge of player-manager Brian McEniff: 'I'd say we had a better quality of player in 1966, but we hadn't the total commitment to win it from all the players. There was no outstandingly good player among the 1972 team in comparison to the mid 1960s team. There was a great commitment and a great feeling of being a Donegal man, instead of being a St Joseph's man, or a Gweedore man, or a Letterkenny man. We were as one.'

The place of the GAA in the life of the county and the failure to establish a strong base in the Inishowen Peninsula was of regular concern to GAA people. The *Donegal GAA Yearbook* of 1980, for example, laments the failure to develop more clubs in Inishowen and also lamented the notion that the GAA was a mere games-playing association: 'Our games, our language, other aspects of cultural distinctiveness make people better and fuller people, and make communities better and fuller communities ... Industrialisation and affluence have proved to be mixed blessings, not only as far as CLG [Cumann Lúthchleas Gael] is concerned, but for the Irish language as well. These and other modern phenomena such as materialism, the lounge bar society, the media and so on are forcing the Association to fight for its life in various parts of the county.'

So successful was that fight that within a dozen years Donegal were crowned All-Ireland senior football champions. A boom in club football saw more than thirty-four clubs field teams in the county. Players came together to win the 1983 Ulster football championship and several of these – including Anthony Molloy, Matt Gallagher, Donal Reid and Martin McHugh – were still there a decade later when Donegal staged a major surprise in winning the All-Ireland football championship under the management of Brian McEniff. The 1992 final victory over Dublin by 0-18 to 0-14 drew incredible scenes of jubilation. A long and emotional journey home saw crowds gather at train-stops in Kildare, Meath,

Westmeath, Longford, Leitrim and Sligo to salute the champions. At Sligo train station, 9,000 people were waiting to welcome the team. Later, when the team bus approached the Drowes River, the players disembarked to carry the Sam Maguire across into the county. It was something that for many decades had seemed unlikely to the point of being impossible. Donegal may have belatedly taken to Gaelic games, but the arrival of Sam confirmed what the GAA now meant to the people of the county.

Players and supporters of the Four Masters GAA club celebrate success in the Democrat Cup in the late 1940s, with their captain, Anthony McBrearty, held shoulder-high. Also in the photo are Mary Mullin, Hugh Cassidy, Jim Carr, Fr Deeney, Noel Mulhaire, Paddy McGowan, Michael Williamson, Jim Harvey, Jack Diver, Mrs McBrearty, Lily McIntyre, Danny Meehan, Jim 'The Natch' Gallagher, Jimmy McGranaghan, Susie McBrearty, Michael McIntyre and Dill Harvey. *(GAA Oral History Project/Niall Muldoon)*

In 1971 Sean MacCumhaill's defeated Clanna Gael in the Donegal senior football final in Ballyshannon. That evening the victorious players were paraded through the streets of Ballybofey when they arrived home with the Dr Maguire cup. *(GAA Oral History Project/Eugene Gallagher)*

There were extraordinary scenes when Donegal people celebrated the capture of the Sam Maguire cup in 1992. *(Inpho)*

Karen Guthrie leads the celebrations of the Donegal team who defeated Waterford by 2-12 to 0-16 in the All-Ireland ladies' football intermediate championship final at Croke Park in September 2010. The full-forward on the team, Yvonne McMonagle, scored 2-5 from play in the final. The development of ladies' football in Donegal undercut the popularity of camogie, though that game has now been reorganised and is again making strides in the county. *(Inpho)*

The Kilcar GAA club pitch juts out into Tawny Bay. The club dominated football in Donegal in the 1980s and is home to players such as Martin and James McHugh. *(Fred Reilly)*

'The year we played in the county minor final, we're talking about early in 1945, we travelled to Letterkenny that day, and us playing in the final on the back of a lorry, the whole team ... you weren't allowed to take people in a lorry you know ... we went out through Churchill and came in by O'Donnell Park and we came off the lorry, maybe a quarter of a mile outside of the town, I suppose at the time the town wasn't that big, and we walked up to the dressing room. We got beat anyway, but that's how we got to it.'

Jimmy Gallagher, b. 1928.

'From '52 until 1973, my late father, Hugh Daly, was county secretary, so we had all that sort of activity going on around the house in relation to his organisational work, people going and coming in relation to teams, players going and coming and the county jerseys were always at the house, so we would have been very conscious, I suppose, of the whole thing about Donegal football in particular. We were obviously intrigued by the jerseys, which my mother used to wash by hand and used to repair. In fact, I even remember my late grandmother helping her to make numbers when the set would be put together and there was the usual one missing.'

Tom Daly, b. 1954.

'My father never played in his life ... he played a game called camán which was the forerunner of hurling, I suppose, in this area, even though the hurling never took off. But he often talked about playing it on the strand, on Sundays maybe or maybe during school days when the tide was out; the school was just beside the sea.'

John Michael O'Donnell, b. 1951.

'My sister and I, we started this camogie team and we got all the girls from around the place and we brought them down to the town ... We met Letterkenny and we, oh we were all very smart. We got our white jumpers and our navy blue tunics; Letterkenny came down and they were dressed in yellow and a big stripe like this and they wore frocks, but we were more in a uniform thing. And my God, the first shot they drove off, they hit out the ball and this Eileen Kearns, she was head of the Letterkenny team and she could hit from one end of the field to the other! We were looking up at the ball going way up over us and passing us out! I was a full-back and my sister was a full-forward and oh, we never got anywhere as regards winning anything because we just were only beginners and they could play around us, you know; they could pass the ball in the air and it would go from one to the other and we never saw the ball at all, but we kept on and we kept on.'

Nora McCarthy Walsh, b. 1914.

Before the 2010 All-Ireland football final between
Down and Cork, Down supporters erected a
massive flag on top of the Mourne Mountains,
imitating Joe Rosenthal's famous photograph taken
of American marines raising the Stars and Stripes
on Mount Suribachi during the Battle of Iwo Jima
in the Second World War. The American press
said of Rosenthal's photograph: 'In that moment,
Rosenthal's camera recorded the soul of a nation.'
(Mark Pearce)

Westmeath Mayo Offaly
Limerick Laois Waterford
Carlow Longford Leitrim
Tipperary Kilkenny Derry
Kerry Cork Wicklow
Kildare Antrim Meath
Tyrone Dublin Galway
Armagh Fermanagh
Donegal Sligo Roscommon
Clare Cavan Monaghan
Louth Wexford **Down**

Down

'**I grew up in Belfast** but I was the child of a Down mother and a Roscommon father. That set my GAA allegiances in stone. I remember the 1960s as a sea of red and black, of soaring, mad rip-roaring pride in the accomplishments of those men whose names I could never forget, who came to Croke Park, took on the princes and kings of Kerry and brought the Sam Maguire cup north. How could we ever fully evaluate the influence of those giants of the 1960s for those growing up in the divided Northern Ireland of the time? … These men changed the mood, infused us with a fierce self-belief, a vision of ourselves as winners and as serious shapers of the GAA,' said Mary McAleese, as President of Ireland, speaking to a history conference at the Cardinal Tomás Ó Fiaich Memorial Library in 2009.

Sometimes teams transcend the boundaries of their own counties and the boundaries even of their own eras to achieve a place in the history of a sport that is entirely new. Sometimes they transcend sport itself and leave an indelible mark on wider society. So it is with the Down team that won three All-Ireland senior football titles between 1960 and 1969. From the 1880s through to the 1950s no team from the six counties that ultimately comprised Northern Ireland won an All-Ireland title. Indeed, the only Ulster county to manage the feat at all was Cavan. On several occasions teams from the North came close and could – even should – have won the All-Ireland championship; the Armagh team of 1953 can be considered a case in point. That they consistently fell short weighed heavily on those who sought to make the breakthrough.

Through the 1950s Down sought to find a way to demolish the barrier. Maurice Hayes, once a key administrator in the Down county board and later (amongst many other things) a senator and journalist, described the project to win an All-Ireland with Down: 'We wanted to build on the natural skills and abilities of what was a talented group of footballers, and to allow them to express themselves in what would be recognised as a distinctive, flowing, exciting brand of football. All the time, however, it was almost more about building self-confidence and team spirit than success in football. We were, unashamedly, creating a unique set, a group that players would be glad to be part of, and others anxious to join: no need to threaten them with suspension. They were standard-bearers for the game in the county, and role models for the young ... We took the view that the main barrier to a Northern team winning a senior All-Ireland title in football was psychological.'

And when Down's meticulous planning came to fruition with victory over Kerry in the 1960 All-Ireland football final, it was the psychological impact that was of greatest importance. Hayes: 'We broke the spell which released the other counties to achieve similar success later. I thought at the time it was a bit like the four-minute mile: until Bannister did it, everybody said it could not be done, and then everybody started doing it.' The reality, of course, was that it was to take until the 1990s before another county took Sam across the border, but by then Down had become established as the standard-bearers for the province of Ulster.

Such was the level of interest in the 1960 final that almost 88,000 people paid in to watch it. When the championship was retained with a dramatic, thrilling win over Offaly in 1961, the numbers who paid in had grown to almost 91,000. And these official attendances tell only part of the story. Many more are thought to have made it into the grounds unofficially to watch these historic matches. The brilliance of that Down team led them to reach twelve Ulster finals in a row between 1958 and 1969; they won seven of these finals. If anything, it was something of a surprise that it was not until 1968 that a third All-Ireland championship was claimed, with the peerless Sean O'Neill as captain. In the course of a decade, they had dramatically shifted the landscape of Gaelic football; Down football would evermore be associated with style and confidence.

Never was this more obvious than in the 1990s when Down emerged seemingly from nowhere to win the All-Ireland senior football championship in 1991. Indeed, in the previous league campaign Down had won just one of seven matches and even in May 1991 attendances at training were not of the required standard. With Peter Whitnell at full-forward, however, Down went on an extraordinary run which saw them eventually beat Meath in the All-Ireland final and reclaim the Sam Maguire. Of course, Down had not reappeared from the wilderness by accident. The quality of their underage and schools teams had delivered players of the very highest quality. These players had been good enough to win All-Irelands as minors and 1991 saw them deliver on that potential at senior level. The crucial thing about the 1991 victory was not how it was achieved, rather its impact. In this it served as an extraordinary dam-burst. In the two years that followed, Donegal and Derry won successive All-Irelands. Finally, in 1994, as if to underline the belief that they were indeed the true footballing giants of Ulster, Down beat Dublin in the All-Ireland final by two points. It was their fifth All-Ireland final victory from five final appearances. Their manager, Pete McGrath, paid homage to this new tradition of success: 'The players weren't conditioned by me ... They were conditioned by what they were told when they were younger, by their parents or their uncles or people who knew.'

While the tradition of victory was something that had grown from the 1960s, the tradition of GAA involvement in Down was rich and extended back into the nineteenth century. Indeed, even before he had founded the GAA, Michael Cusack had worked as a schoolteacher at St Colman's College in Newry in the

1870s and in 1876 he married a woman from Dromore, Margaret Woods. The couple had six children (several others died in infancy), who ranged in age from six to thirteen years, before Margaret died from TB on 16 September 1890. A month after the death of his wife, Cusack also suffered the loss of his eight-year-old daughter, Mary, also from TB, and the remaining children were dispersed to orphanages and to live with family members. Cusack's life was shattered by the death of his wife, whom he described as a 'Betsy Gray type of girl', and the woman who counselled him in everything he did, including the setting up of the GAA.

Cusack had other associations with Down. When he was involved with the establishment of the Dublin Hurling Club in 1882 – almost two years before the foundation of the GAA – amongst the men who played the game in the Phoenix Park were Rev. Samuel Holmes, and the brothers Frank and Robert Patterson, all from Down. Indeed, one of the students who graduated from Cusack's Civil Service Academy, which he ran on Gardiner Street in Dublin in the late 1870s and the 1880s, was J. L. Savage from Backaderry, Castlewellan. Savage went on to become a founder member of the Leitrim Fontenoys GAA club, which was one of the first clubs established in Down. In truth, the GAA in Down did not make significant progress through the 1880s and 1890s. There were, of course, clubs and matches between clubs, but the 'prairie-fire' which Michael Cusack used to describe the early spread of the GAA left Down relatively unscorched.

It was only after 1900, with the rebirth of the Association nationally, that the GAA truly began to prosper in Down. The county board was established and county championships were run in football and hurling from 1903. The role of the language revivalists of the Gaelic League was vital in all of this. Crucially, it was the Gaelic League that ensured hurling would now be a part of the GAA in Down, where once football had been the only game played. More than that, the Gaelic League in Newry was instrumental in setting up a camogie club in 1903. This club – the Newry Faugh-a-ballaghs – was claimed as the second ever club established in the country, after the Keating club in Dublin, which essentially designed the game of camogie. Camogie did not flourish in Down, but the GAA did. By 1906 – as Sighle Nic an Ultaigh relates in *An Dún: The GAA Story* – there were eight affiliated clubs active in the county and in the following year they were joined by others, including Downpatrick, Newcastle, Loughlinisland and

Annsborough. These clubs were in competition with soccer, which had flourished in the county in the 1890s, and the GAA did not enjoy a stellar rise in Down. Indeed, the county did not field a team in the Ulster championship between 1908 and 1916.

The 1920s brought progress, but this progress was tempered by failure. Only once in the 1920s did Down win an Ulster senior football championship match: they surprised Antrim in 1920. Against that, they failed even to field teams in the football championship in 1923 and 1925. Then, in the 1930s, Down did not usually enter a team in the Ulster senior football championship, preferring to concentrate on junior level. This brought victory in that championship in 1932 and 1934. There was also success in hurling. Abbey CBS was a hurling stronghold and, wearing the jerseys of that school, Down won the 1930 Ulster minor championship. They repeated that achievement in 1932 and 1934. In 1941 Down won the Ulster senior championship for the first time, but this was not the first flowering of a glorious period of success. Indeed, five decades passed before another Ulster championship was claimed. The 1990s marked the most sustained period of hurling success in the county's history. Ulster championships were won in 1992, 1995 and 1997, and these were followed by creditable performances in All-Ireland semi-finals. The reality of living in a county dominated by the pursuit of footballing success creates challenges that the hurlers of Down have often struggled to overcome, but the passion for the game in its heartlands – not least in the clubs of Ballygalget, Portaferry and Ballycran – cannot be dismissed.

In respect of football, in 1939 Down returned to senior level and actually reached the Ulster final twice in the 1940s, only to lose heavily to Cavan on both occasions. It was in the 1940s that the origins of the successes of the 1960s can be found. The work of Brother Rice at Abbey CBS laid the basis for future success in the MacRory Cup in the 1950s. And then, at Michael Cusack's old school, St Colman's College in Newry, Fr John Treanor made decisive inroads. Treanor joined the college in 1942 and under his endeavour, St Colman's progressed to win the MacRory Cup in 1949 – and then kept on winning it. In the years that followed, successive generations of footballers came through the schools of Newry imbued with a winning mentality. Indeed, by 2011 St Colman's had won the cup nineteen times and Abbey CBS had claimed it on five occasions. Abbey CBS had also once won the Hogan Cup, awarded to the school which wins the

All-Ireland colleges title, while St Colman's had won the same competition on eight occasions, leaving it second only to St Jarlath's of Tuam on the roll of honour.

If the success of the Down team of the 1960s owed much to the schools of the county and to the planning of the county board, and, ultimately, was of profound psychological importance, the outbreak of the Troubles was also hugely important in shaping the GAA in Down. The Troubles did not, of course, affect every county, or every part of every county, in precisely the same way. Down was perceived to be a more moderate county than others in Northern Ireland in the decades after 1969. Nonetheless, although the Troubles do not seem to have impacted as deeply on the GAA in Down as in, for example, Antrim, Derry or Tyrone, that impact was still profound. In part, this was a reflection of the relationship between the GAA and the nationalist community. In the 1880s, Gaelic football matches had actually enjoyed a certain amount of Protestant involvement, but by the twentieth century this had essentially disappeared. In 1903 the Newry hurlers were travelling to play a challenge match in Ballyvarley when 'they were attacked at Banbridge with a fusillade of stones and other missiles by an Orange mob'. Only the intervention of a police inspector saved the hurlers from riot and bloodshed on the way home.

By the time of the Troubles, relations with the police were tense. GAA members – subject to roadblocks, searches and much else – believed themselves to be routinely harassed by the security forces, some of whose members considered the GAA to be an adjunct of the IRA. This was certainly the view of loyalist paramilitaries who regularly targeted GAA members. The hurling clubs of the Ards Peninsula were particularly vulnerable. The clubhouse of the St Joseph's club in Ballycran was subjected to seven arson attacks in the twenty years before 1993. All of this spoke of a divided community. When Down won the All-Ireland senior football championship in 1994 their victory was noted by Belfast City Council but, under an Ulster unionist motion, they were not accorded a civic reception because it considered the GAA to be 'politically sectarian', not least because its prohibition on members of the security forces joining the GAA 'lent indirect support to the IRA'.

The Peace Process and the consequent easing of tension across the north was of great benefit to the GAA in Down. The club scene grew from strength to strength and a new generation of footballers brought Down to the 2010 All-

Ireland senior football final. This team was based around members of the All-Ireland winning 2005 minor football team. Although the team had hinted at considerable potential in previous years before being smothered beneath the weight of Tyrone and Armagh, when they eventually made it to an All-Ireland final it came as something of a surprise. Inevitably, such was the power of tradition that the belief was that once Down made it to a final they would win it. This was not to be. Cork proved too strong, but Down showed enough to demonstrate that a sixth All-Ireland title is now a genuine possibility.

Loughinisland v Saul 14th April 1913.

Two Down clubs, Loughinisland and Saul, play a football match in Loughinisland in 1913. *(Loughinisland GAC)*

Camogie has been a part of the Gaelic games scene in Down for more than 100 years. Here the women of the Clann na Banna club parade to play a match in 1949. There is also a strong tradition of hurling in Down, particularly on the Ards Peninsula. *(Clann na Banna)*

Victory over Kerry in the 1960 All-Ireland football final brought the Sam Maguire across the border into Down for the first time. It was an iconic moment in the history of Ulster football. *(Kennelly Archive)*

Joe Lennon won three All-Ireland senior football medals with Down in the 1960s. Throughout this period, he presented his ideas on the playing of Gaelic football in a book entitled *Coaching Gaelic Football for Champions*, which was published in 1964. A renowned scholar of Gaelic games, Lennon was later conferred with a doctorate for a 1,200-page thesis, entitled 'Towards a philosophy for legislation in Gaelic games'. *(Joe Lennon)*

Another Down homecoming. In 1991 Down brought the Sam Maguire cup north of the border for the fourth time. For players, officials and supporters, it was a joyous occasion. *(Loughinisland GAC)*

'This day we were travelling to the Ards ... and the craic was that good, I missed the turn and I ended up in this farmyard. And this old man was standing — God help him — he didn't know what happened to him. He had the cap on him and the pipe and one big tooth stuck here. And the girls all kept saying: "Gotta go to the toilet! Gotta go to the toilet!" So I opened the boot of the car and I went over to him and I says: "I'm awfully sorry. We've missed the turning in the road." And he kept saying "Uh?" ... But anyway after a few minutes, he stood there and he was mesmerised by these girls all running behind different things to spend a penny and Bernadette came over and she put her arms around him and she says: "Oh you handsome hunk! Don't you ever, ever die!"'

Belle O'Loughlin, b. 1942.

'It was the ordinary people of Rostrevor who involved themselves in the GAA to keep it going; no high-falutin, well-educated people, just ordinary salt of the earth. And they were part of my formation ...and I'm forever grateful.'

Val Murphy, b. 1939.

'The only reason I went to Queen's was to win a Sigerson Cup. I did manage one as well but certainly career was not my first choice when it came to university choice.'

Michael Madine, b. 1961.

'I was the secretary at the time and I recall a lot of tension — I don't know whether it was actually in the club or not — but in the area, just about the whole hunger strike and I did realise at the time that it was a tricky situation to manage for the club and I felt that Charlie [the chairman] probably managed it very well, having looked at the wider interests of the Association, and he realised that within the club there were lots of people with different political views and the GAA is supposed to be a non-political organisation, so I suppose he was conscious of that sort of thing. He was careful to tread a very middle course and while there was sympathy amongst club members for the hunger strikers, it didn't impinge on the activities of the club in any way, as far as I remember.'

Michael McCartan, b. 1955.

'Sports in Down ... were a very big thing in those days. Most of the clubs were ...Gaelic and athletic clubs and it was always a sports meeting and seven-a-side football afterwards.'

Dominic Fitzpatrick, b. 1935.

Dublin supporters on Hill 16, summer 2007. The rise of Dublin football in the 1970s attracted a new generation of urban youth to the GAA. Ever since, Dublin football teams have been both the focus of massive media attention and important drivers of attendance revenues for the Association. *(Inpho)*

Westmeath Mayo Offaly
Limerick Laois Waterford
Carlow Longford Leitrim
Tipperary Kilkenny Derry
Kerry Cork Wicklow
Kildare Antrim Meath
Tyrone **Dublin** Galway
Armagh Fermanagh
Donegal Sligo Roscommon
Clare Cavan Monaghan
Louth Wexford Down

Dublin

Does the GAA mean as much to the people of Dublin as it does to those of other counties? If anyone doubted that the answer to that question was 'yes', then the publication in 2002 of a major report on the GAA's structures and operations provided confirmation. The document ran to 264 pages and was necessarily wide ranging in scope. The immediate reaction to it focused almost exclusively on a single, headline-grabbing detail, however. This concerned the future of the GAA in Dublin. The report – by the Strategic Review Committee (SRC) – claimed that the capital had become too big, too populous and too important to be left as a single administrative unit. It recommended that the county be split in two for GAA purposes, with the River Liffey serving as a natural boundary between north and south. Divide Dublin? The idea struck at the very principle of county identity and, ultimately, proved much too radical to implement. What the SRC proposal and the reaction to it achieved, however, was to highlight two fundamental truths: firstly, that GAA people in the capital were possessed of a strong sense of their county as a single, unified entity; and secondly, that Dublin was a county like none other.

To assert Dublin's difference is, of course, to state the obvious. In sport, as in so much else, the capital city has always stood as a place apart. In the second half of the nineteenth century, with Ireland still part of the British Empire, Dublin began to import many features of the Victorian sporting revolution: bowling, tennis and golf clubs sprang up in the suburbs of the wealthy, while the grounds of the elite schools were laid out with pitches for cricket and rugby. The GAA was partly a reaction against the exclusivity of the Dublin sporting scene, encouraging Michael Cusack, its founder, to look south – to Munster – to establish his rival sporting body. Although Thurles became the birthplace of the GAA, Dublin was undoubtedly its place of conception. It was to the capital that Cusack had come to establish his own school and in 1883, prior to the foundation of the GAA, he established two hurling clubs: the first was the Metropolitans Club and the second was for pupils attending his school, known as Cusack's Academy. Cusack later asserted that it was out of the Metropolitan Hurling Club that the GAA 'sprang'. The Metropolitans, standard-bearers for hurling in the early years of the new Association, were a club built around countrymen who had moved to the city; in 1885, its membership included players from twelve counties and three provinces, with only a single Dubliner among them.

There was nothing exceptional in this. The development of GAA clubs in Dublin was driven by rural migrants, those who left the land to find employment in the city. Where they worked and at what would prove crucial to how they spent their hours of leisure. A striking feature of Dublin's early GAA clubs, for instance, was their concentration around institutions, trades and occupations. In 1886 the GAA had introduced a rule which stipulated that clubs should be based on the boundaries of Catholic parishes. In Dublin, however, the 'one parish, one club' rule was never enforced; the complexity of urban society rendered it impractical. Unlike other counties, where geography ruled, workplaces and social networks provided the impetus to club formation. And their numbers grew exponentially: by the end of 1888, there were approximately 120 clubs spread across the city and county. Among these were the Young Irelands, which had been founded by a group of Wexford employees of the Guinness Brewery and which, in 1891, delivered a first All-Ireland football title for Dublin. The Young Irelands team, led by John Kennedy, changed the way Gaelic football was played. Their 'catch and kick' style, with its emphasis on strict positional play, helped move the game beyond the cruder 'kick and rush' approach, whereby teams would look to use possession by sweeping it forward in packs. The Young Irelands pioneered a more open and attractive brand of football and they were rewarded with two more All-Irelands, won in 1892 and 1894. By the end of the decade, however, the club was no more. It had disbanded, its transience a characteristic it shared with many other Dublin clubs at this time.

By the early twentieth century, however, more clubs were being born than were dying away. A resurgence in nationalist culture added fresh impetus to GAA life. For instance, the Gaelic League, founded in 1893 to promote a range of Irish cultural activity, led directly to the emergence of an association for the promotion of camogie, a variant of hurling established by women, for women. It also led to an influx of new members into the Dublin GAA and it is these who dominated GAA involvement in the subsequent armed push for national independence. An analysis undertaken for a brilliant three-volume history of Dublin GAA, edited by William Nolan, concluded that a total of 302 players from 53 clubs participated in the Easter Rising of 1916. This is a sizeable number, but what it implies is that the great majority of the rebels (about 80 per cent, in fact) were not GAA members, evidence which disputes the claims of some the Association's earliest historians, who were keen to ascribe to the sporting body a principal role in the Irish revolution.

For all that, the story of the GAA in the capital is one inextricably bound up with revolutionary upheaval and the civil strife of the 1916-23 period. The county board did its best to maintain a semblance of normality – competitions were organised and matches scheduled – but its efforts were frequently derailed by wider political and military events. Dublin was effectively a city in the grip of war, a fact underlined by the introduction of a British ban on the holding of unapproved public meetings. On 4 August 1918 the GAA instructed its county boards across the country to stage matches in defiance of this injunction. Twenty-four matches were staged at venues in Dublin. At Croke Park, the GAA's recently acquired grounds in the capital, police and army blocked access to a group of camogie players, who reportedly staged a game on the street outside. Two years later, at the same venue, Dublin were playing Tipperary in an inter-county football match when armed British forces stormed into the ground and fired indiscriminately at players and spectators. The atrocity left fourteen dead, among them Tipperary player Michael Hogan. 'Bloody Sunday' had a lasting impact on the GAA. It cemented its identification with Irish nationalism and ensured that Croke Park would never be regarded as a mere place of play.

When the murder and mayhem ended and peace was restored, Croke Park developed into what the GAA had always intended it to be: a permanent headquarters for Gaelic games. Previously known as the Jones's Road sports ground, the site had been acquired by the GAA in 1913 and in the early years of the new Irish Free State it received a massive refurbishment to enable it to stage the Tailteann Games, an ancient Celtic festival that was revived as a cultural and sporting extravaganza. The importance of the stadium to Dublin was immense as it made the city a focal point for all major GAA occasions. On All-Ireland final days in particular, its pull was gravitational. Thousands of GAA people from across the country would arrive into the city by train, by car and bicycle and fill it with colour, noise and bustle. 'Nobody could walk through O'Connell Street and escape the infection of excitement,' the *Irish Independent* columnist Gertrude Gaffney wrote after attending a replayed All-Ireland hurling final in 1931. As the crowds moved from O'Connell Street towards Croke Park, Gaffney, later a prominent critic of Éamon de Valera's new Irish constitution, was borne along with them. 'It was impossible to stay behind,' she wrote, 'one had to be carried along with it'.

Dublin teams were no strangers to such occasions. By 1934, the GAA's silver jubilee year, the county had won fourteen football titles and five in hurling – six were won between 1916 and 1925. This impressive run of success was as much a commentary on the quality of the country players who had come to play for the county as it was on those who were Dublin-born. In 1925, however, a new 'declaration rule' was passed allowing players to play for their county of birth, rather than their county of residence. The effect on Dublin was dramatic. Fewer players became available for county teams and fewer All-Irelands were won. Over the next eighty-five years (1925-2010), the success rate of the county slowed considerably: as it fell back increasingly on its own resources, it added eight more football titles and just two more hurling titles, both of these recorded pre-1940.

The distribution of All-Ireland titles serves to underscore the divergent fortunes of Gaelic football and hurling. The pre-eminence of the former owed much to the rise of the St Vincents club, which had emerged in the 1930s and which, in time, assumed a position in the vanguard of the Dublin nativists, going so far as to apply a strict eligibility code to its own club membership. It did it no harm. By the 1950s, the club was dominant in the capital, supplying the majority of the players to a resurgent county team. Dublin won an All-Ireland title in 1958 but that team is perhaps best remembered for its final defeat in 1955, a day when Dublin supporters made Hill 16 their home and when Dublin's revolutionary style of play, based on the creation and use of open spaces, came up short against the more traditional catch-and-kick approach of their Kerry opponents. In the 1970s, Kevin Heffernan, the star corner-forward on that 1950s team, shaped a new county team in his own image – cerebral, tough, talented. Heffernan's Dublin struck up a classic rivalry with a brilliant young Kerry team trained by Mick O'Dwyer, another veteran of the 1955 final. The drama of the games between the two counties was enhanced by the sheer speed of play, which was rooted in high levels of fitness and the increased use of the hand pass, which allowed for the swift transfer of possession. In winning three All-Irelands in four years, the Dublin footballers reached out to a new audience of urban youth, capturing their imaginations at a time when fears about the counter-attractions of televised soccer were widespread. This was the essential feature of the triumphs of the 1970s. By creating a new support base for Gaelic games, Dublin teams became one of the biggest drivers of media profile and attendance revenues for the GAA.

The phenomenon of Dublin's summer support has concealed a more worrying reality, however. This was the continued undersupply of GAA clubs in the city. Across the post-independence decades, the pattern of club development had broadly tracked that of Dublin itself. In the 1920s and 1930s, as new housing estates were laid out, as Catholic parishes were established and schools were opened, clubs – among them St Vincents – were founded to cater to the sporting needs of their local youth . Later, in the 1960s and 1970s, when further population growth led to the rapid expansion of more outlying suburbs such as Kilmacud and Ballyboden on the city's south side, there was a further wave of club development. These clubs provided not only pitches, but large social centres offering a broad range of facilities and services, from table tennis to television, bar rooms to billiards. The purpose of it all, as the founders of the Kilmacud Crokes club made clear, was 'to serve as a means of bringing people together'. In doing so, GAA clubs helped fashion communities from the grey concrete of suburban sprawl. The problem, as the SRC report of 2002 pointed out, was that there were far too few of them. For all the progress that had been made, vast swathes of Dublin were still untouched by an Association that had become largely middle class in aspect. The upshot is that Dublin today is what it always has been – home to the GAA's biggest challenges and its greatest opportunities.

Revolutionary leaders Michael Collins and Harry Boland, on the left, with members of the Dublin hurling team in Croke Park, 1921. Less than a year before, on 21 November 1920, British forces entered the same venue on the occasion of a challenge match between Dublin and Tipperary, opening fire on players and spectators. 'Bloody Sunday' in Croke Park left fourteen people dead, among them Tipperary footballer, Michael Hogan. *(Collins 22 Society)*

Action from an Ashbourne Cup game between UCD and UCC in 1964. The game of camogie was founded in the early years of the twentieth century, with Dublin at its core. An Cumann Camógaíochta was formally established at 8 North Frederick Street in the city in February 1905. The first President of the new sporting body was Máire Ní Chinnéide, a Dublin-born Irish language activist. *(Cumann Camógaíochta na nGael)*

Marcus de Búrca, who would later author the first major history of the GAA, gets changed after a training session in the Phoenix Park, July 1944. The city centre park provided the early focus for Michael Cusack's sporting revolution as it was here, in the early 1880s, that his Metropolitan hurlers regularly met to practise and play. *(The Bourke family)*

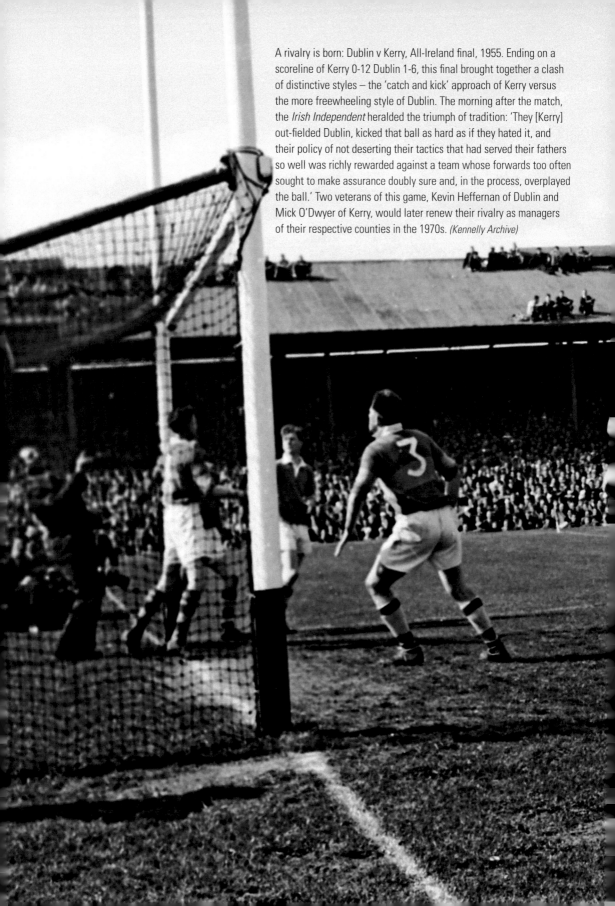

A rivalry is born: Dublin v Kerry, All-Ireland final, 1955. Ending on a scoreline of Kerry 0-12 Dublin 1-6, this final brought together a clash of distinctive styles – the 'catch and kick' approach of Kerry versus the more freewheeling style of Dublin. The morning after the match, the *Irish Independent* heralded the triumph of tradition: 'They [Kerry] out-fielded Dublin, kicked that ball as hard as if they hated it, and their policy of not deserting their tactics that had served their fathers so well was richly rewarded against a team whose forwards too often sought to make assurance doubly sure and, in the process, overplayed the ball.' Two veterans of this game, Kevin Heffernan of Dublin and Mick O'Dwyer of Kerry, would later renew their rivalry as managers of their respective counties in the 1970s. *(Kennelly Archive)*

A mini All-Ireland day at Kilmacud Crokes GAA club helps to sustain interest among a new generation of GAA members. Despite the strong presence the GAA has developed in many Dublin suburbs, the scale of population growth in the capital has outpaced its response. Speaking in 2009, the GAA's Director General Páraic Duffy acknowledged the Association's difficulties in extending its influence in many working class areas of Dublin. *(Fred Reilly)*

'I remember ... getting my first pair of camogie boots and that was just, I thought it was amazing to have them, camogie boots that were up around your ankles, the canvas ones, playing out in Phoenix Park in the rain, it was always raining, and the cow pats! You had to play around the cow pats!'

Bláithín Fitzgerald (née Ní Shíocháin), b. 1969.

'There was a lot of opposition to the GAA club starting at the time' (John). 'You just weren't accepted. I mean there was no doubt about it you weren't accepted. And go into a local establishment looking to sell a ticket and they'd laugh at you because you were GAA ... so it did take a long time to get established. But when you look at it now, GAA is sexy.' (Pat).

John Sheridan, b. 1937 and Pat Sheridan, b. 1939.

'I remember the ball coming in very low and heading it in to the back of the net. The Christian Brother carried out an unchristian act by thumping me on the back of the neck and telling the referee to cancel the score because that was a soccer score and he was the manager of my team.'

Ken McCue, b. 1954.

'Down through the years, all the kids from juvenile players and then up to adults that came through club — hundreds of them — never got into trouble with the law. And that's a great feat. It just shows you the work that the GAA clubs are doing, when you can say that — and say that with no hesitation.'

Paddy Delaney, b. 1941.

'The obvious change is the opening up of Croke Park and, in my mind, the social changes this has brought. People who before wouldn't even think of visiting Croke Park (seriously, they had to put maps to Croke Park on the south-side DARTs) have visited the stadium and seem to be a lot more open to Gaelic Games. The whole GAA/rugby/soccer divide seems to be eroding.'

Mark Reynolds, b. 1979.

'I love more than anything else when someone brings a girlfriend or child or nephew or niece who has never been to Croke Park for a big game and just watch them being cast under the same spell I was when I was ten in 1974.'

Matt Treacy, b. 1964.

In 2004, Armagh footballers were on a quest to win a second All-Ireland title. They faced Fermanagh in the All-Ireland football quarter-final at Croke Park on 7 August 2004. A victory for Armagh was considered a sporting certainty. That certainty crumbled as Fermanagh ran Armagh ragged all over the field to claim a deserved one-point victory. As the RTÉ commentator, Marty Morrissey, said on the day: 'Dreams do become a reality sometimes!' *(Inpho)*

Westmeath Mayo Offaly
Limerick Laois Waterford
Carlow Longford Leitrim
Tipperary Kilkenny Derry
Kerry Cork Wicklow
Kildare Antrim Meath
Tyrone Dublin Galway
Armagh **Fermanagh**
Donegal Sligo Roscommon
Clare Cavan Monaghan
Louth Wexford Down

Fermanagh

The landscape of Fermanagh is a vital reminder of the importance of geography to sport. The complex lakelands of Lough Erne rise to higher ground in a county that is predominantly rural, but which also contains the developing towns of Enniskillen, Lisnaskea and Irvinestown. The sheer scale of Lough Erne shapes the social, economic and cultural life of the county; its pre-Christian archaeology and early Irish Church heritage are potent reminders of the antiquity of life in the area. While Lough Erne separates Fermanagh from itself, the presence of the border between north and south has also been significant in disrupting the normal flows of life in a natural hinterland, which, for many

Fermanagh people, had always extended across to the counties of Donegal, Sligo, Leitrim, Monaghan and Cavan. Despite all of this – or possibly because of it – the people of the county retain 'a very strong sense of Fermanagh identity'. The story of the GAA in the county is woven into this identity.

While the geography of Fermanagh presents a unique challenge to its GAA members, so also does demography. The difficulties that Fermanagh GAA teams have long sought to overcome are related to population. In 1841, the population of Fermanagh stood at more than 150,000 but the ravages of famine and emigration saw this collapse to just over 60,000 by 1911. This collapse was twice the average in Ulster. The decline of the late nineteenth century continued into the twentieth century. By the early 1950s, the population actually fell to just above 50,000 before recovering in subsequent decades to around 60,000 by 2011. The GAA-playing population has been further reduced by the legacies of political divide, which has usually limited its membership to the Catholic community, comprising just under 60 per cent of the population of the county.

Although the GAA spread into Fermanagh in 1887 with the establishment of a club named the Newtownbutler First Fermanaghs, there was a long tradition of ball-play in the county. One such game was 'caman', which might be considered an older version of hurling. It was played in villages and between islanders on Lough Erne. The game is recorded on a tombstone erected in Enniskillen to the memory of a man who died in 1800. The tombstone is also dedicated to the memory of the man's son, Alexander, who had died at the age of thirteen, having had 'his head cut off playing caman on the ice at Killyhelvin'. Folk memory of football in Fermanagh recalls a game played by 'a parish against another, no rules, no bounds, except to kick the ball to blazes'. Such games in the county were 'apt to rouse mad, wild passions in the players'.

It was this passion for football – rather than for hurling – which manifested itself when the GAA began establishing itself in Fermanagh. The establishment of the Newtownbutler First Fermanaghs was quickly followed by clubs in Clonmaulin and Donagh (who later amalgamated as Sons of Erin), and other clubs on either side of Lough Erne such as Roslea Fag-a-bealaghs, Drumlone Lough Erne Leaguers and Derrylin Mitchels. Although a county board was not then formed, there were actually fifteen clubs active in the county in 1888.

Regrettably, this was to prove a high-water mark for the GAA in the county as it was a number not reached again for many years.

Just as in the rest of Ireland, the early 1890s proved difficult for Fermanagh – difficult to the point where just one club survived by 1892. The Association had, of course, been torn apart in the wake of the IRB gaining control, professing support for Charles Stewart Parnell and thereby incurring the wrath of the Catholic Church. The GAA in Fermanagh was also the focus of unionist disapproval. A letter to the *Fermanagh Times* in late 1888 accused what the letter-writer dubbed the 'Newtownbutler Sunday Desecration Football club' of misleading Protestants in the area by stating that a raffle it was organising was being supported by non-Catholics. It was further alleged that the proceeds from the GAA raffle were being donated to the Parnell Defence Fund.

The rebirth of the GAA in Fermanagh after 1900 was, in many respects, reflective of a social transformation in the lives and aspirations of the Catholic community. The 1898 Local Government Act gave nationalists control of several of the seven local councils in Fermanagh, including the county council. The growth of second level education – though still limited – enhanced the provision of primary education in a county, where the literacy rate had pushed beyond 85 per cent by 1911 – up from 64 per cent in 1891. The impact of a succession of land acts underpinned a social transformation that saw small farmers emerge as a vital presence. There was also cultural transformation – or, at least, an attempt at it. The spread of the Gaelic League into the county, led by the formidable nationalist politician Cahir Healy sought to reverse the decline in the Irish language; there were still native Irish speakers in Fermanagh at the beginning of the twentieth century. Indeed, in 1911 more than 1,500 people were recorded as Irish-speaking in the county.

This was the world into which the GAA fitted, and one which it also sought to shape. In his excellent book on the history of the GAA in Fermanagh, Gabriel Brock recounts how a letter-writer to the *Ulster Herald* newspaper called, in 1901, for the GAA to work in tandem with the Gaelic League: 'this district is fast becoming anglicized to the silent gratification of our West-British friends and to the disgrace, let it be said, of our national spirit.' The rejuvenation of the GAA saw clubs established across the county to the point where a county board was formed on 4 July 1904 and a football championship was run. That year

Fermanagh also entered the Ulster football and hurling championships. A match against Monaghan in the football championship was lost by 0-4 to 0-1, while the county's hurlers lost by a huge margin against Armagh. These results marked the beginning of a relationship with the Ulster championship which has been always passionate, occasionally joyous, but ultimately stained with disappointment. As if to emphasise the challenges facing the GAA in Fermanagh, the county's hurlers could muster only ten players for their first-round Ulster championship match against Tyrone in Omagh. As teams then were seventeen-strong, Fermanagh's ten men were routed.

Within the county, the club scene became increasingly vibrant. Club matches were important social occasions with teams and their supporters criss-crossing the county on foot, on bicycle and in wagons. Stories recall extended sing-songs backed by musicians and the occasional pause for refreshment. Men usually played matches in their working clothes and boots – with only iron toe-caps banned – and simply used sashes to distinguish one team from the next. The play was ferociously competitive and this extended even to disputes over the legality of teams, of pitches, of referees' decisions and, indeed, of anything that could be used to lodge an objection in respect of a lost match. The presence of a relatively strong soccer scene in parts of Fermanagh also brought controversy with clubs suspended for fielding soccer players in their teams. Equally, though, clubs were also prone to borrowing players from other clubs to help them win matches.

Through this period, the divisions within Fermanagh society became more clear cut. Previously, Catholics and Protestants had worked together for the Land League in the county, they had united to support a farmers' candidate in general elections until at least 1903, and a leading nationalist in the county, Jeremiah Jordan, was Protestant. The rising tensions of the 1912–23 period destroyed such unity as did exist. This period also saw a decline in activity in the GAA in Fermanagh. Political tensions, emigration, enlistment in the British army and other factors saw the disappearance of a number of clubs.

The 1920s did not bring immediate improvement. The GAA in Fermanagh was heavily dependent on small, rural clubs and it took several years for the Association to hit its stride after the turmoil of war. After all, this was a war that lasted longer in Fermanagh than in many other counties. After the Anglo-Irish Treaty had been supported by a majority of Dáil Éireann in January 1922, members of the IRA continued to fight against partition. The last major episode of the IRA offensive came near Pettigo and Belleek, a small area of land on the Fermanagh/Donegal border and near Lower Lough Erne. A stretch of land that was actually in Northern Ireland was held by the IRA until June 1922. Eventually, the IRA was driven out by a combination of the British army and the Ulster Special Constabulary.

The re-establishment of the Fermanagh county board in 1923 heralded a new era for the GAA in Fermanagh. The number of clubs in the county grew from eleven to twenty-six. The gathering sense of momentum in the club scene was reflected with progress at inter-county level. In 1930 Fermanagh won the Dr McKenna cup – the secondary competition after the Ulster championship, played for by the counties of Ulster – and then repeated that feat in 1933. In 1935 greater success came tantalisingly close. Fermanagh reached the finals of both the Ulster senior football final and the National Football League final. The Ulster final was lost by five points to Cavan, while the League final was lost to Mayo on a score line of Mayo 5-8, Fermanagh 0-2.

The defeats did not mask the progress being made and this progress was aided by the development of a minor football championship between the clubs of the county and entry into the Ulster minor championship. Players from these teams progressed to play junior and senior football for Fermanagh in the 1940s. Against the backdrop of world war, Fermanagh reached the 1943 Ulster junior football final where they played defending champions Antrim. The day ended with a memorable five-point victory. There was no opportunity to add an All-Ireland title, however, as travel restrictions led to the cancellation of the All-Ireland championship. The success at junior level facilitated progress at senior level. In 1945 Fermanagh progressed to their third Ulster senior final where they were well beaten by Cavan. This was no disappointing prelude to redemptive triumph. Fermanagh's footballers fell into a long slump which saw them fail to reach another Ulster final for thirty-seven years. In part this was a reflection of the economic decline of the county. Fermanagh remained dependent on an agricultural sector that was struggling to modernise. The travails of the farmers of the county is evidenced by research from the Inishmore area which showed that the majority of farmers owned only one horse and that just three tractors were owned across 123 farmers surveyed. This was emblematic of economic stagnation and led to rural areas being devastated by emigration. The GAA was inevitably affected and clubs collapsed across the county at the end of the 1940s and into the 1950s. By 1950, indeed, only four clubs were competing in the senior football league. A revitalisation in the mid 1950s was spearheaded by a new generation of officials, who focused on development at juvenile, minor and schools level. Clubs were rejuvenated and provided sufficient talent for Fermanagh to reach the All-Ireland junior football final of 1959, having defeated Dublin in a replayed semi-final in front of 7,000 spectators. The scenes of jubilation after that match were surpassed only by those after the final, which saw Kerry defeated by seven points. The players were carried shoulder-high from the field, but their work was not yet complete. The victory over Kerry was merely the 'Home' final; there remained the task of defeating London at their pitch in New Eltham. The match offered the opportunity for reunions of family and friends, as Fermanagh secured a tense victory. When the players arrived home on the following Tuesday, they were paraded through Newtownbutler aboard an open lorry and a celebratory night saw 10,000 people take to the streets of Enniskillen, while the evening was rounded off by a 'Monster Ceilí' in the town hall.

The victory gave a significant boost to the GAA in the county. The senior team enjoyed no success but Fermanagh reached the Ulster minor football final, won the Ulster minor league and won the All-Ireland vocational schools' title. The county Under-21 team won back-to-back Ulster titles in 1970 and 1971, only to be defeated in the All-Ireland final on both occasions by Cork. Players from these teams – notably Peter McGinnity – went on to star for Fermanagh for more than a decade. Senior success did not follow through the 1970s. In 1982 there was a glimmer of hope when Fermanagh reached their fourth Ulster senior final, only to lose to Armagh. If there was consolation, it was in McGinnity being awarded the county's first ever All-Star award.

Through the years of the Troubles more than 100 people lost their lives in Fermanagh and, with the county still ravaged by emigration, the GAA had many challenges to overcome. The club scene in Fermanagh was vibrant, led in the 1980s by the progress of Roslea Shamrocks. Later, clubs such as Devenish, Lisnaskea (restoring the glory days of the 1940s), Newtownbutler and Enniskillen Gaels came to the fore. Indeed, Enniskillen Gaels won six senior championships in a row between 1998 and 2003. The Fermanagh senior football team also made significant progress. In an era when Tyrone and Armagh were acknowledged as being amongst the top four teams in the country on an annual basis, Fermanagh came close to unprecedented success. Using the new Qualifiers format, Fermanagh broke free from the shackles of Ulster and went on a run that saw them reach the 2004 All-Ireland senior football semi-final. The end result was heartbreak following a narrow defeat to Mayo in a replay, but there was immense pride in the progress of the team. The prominence of Fermanagh was recognised through All-Star awards for Barry Owens (twice) and Marty McGrath, but still no cherished Ulster senior championship.

The search for that elusive senior championship goes on. The plans of the Fermanagh county board to develop the games in the county using clubs and schools (not least the St Michael's school in Enniskillen), to improve the playing facilities, and to enhance the organisation of the GAA, all of which underline the ambition of the county. This is not merely the narrow pursuit of championship success. The plans of the county board offer a strong commitment to bring the GAA to sections of the community where it has no presence and to use the games to improve the lives of people who face 'issues of isolation and disadvantage on a daily basis'. These same plans note the manner in which the county has changed and will continue to change. They also note the challenges of geography and demography that need to be overcome, and that the way to achieve this is 'to be particularly well organised and to overpunch our weight'.

A group of footballers from Ederney practising in the field they call 'The Moss' in the 1930s. The man taking the free kick is Johnny Monaghan. The men in the goals are Dinny Reid, Francie Murphy, Fr John Eves, Fred Curtis and Danny Monaghan. *(Dónal Monaghan)*

Sligo, Leitrim and Northern Counties Railway

G.A.A. FOOTBALL MATCH
MAYO V. DUBLIN
AT ENNISKILLEN
SUNDAY, 2ND OCTOBER, '32

A Special Passenger Train will run from
SLIGO
AS UNDER IN CONNECTION WITH ABOVE.

	(Winter Time)	Third Class Return Fares
SLIGO	dep. 11.10 a.m	
BALLYSODARE	,, 11.20 a.m	
COLLOONEY	,, 11.30 a.m	3s 6d
BALLINTOGHER	,, 11.40 a.m	
DROMAHAIR	,, 11.50 a.m	
MANORHAMILTON	,, 12.20 p.m	3s 0d
KILMAKERRILL	,, 12.32 p.m	2s 6d
GLENFARNE	,, 12.42 p.m	
BELCOO	,, 1.0 p.m	1s 6d
ABOHILL	,, 1.5 p.m	1s 0d
FLORENCECOURT	,, 1.15 p.m	9d
ENNISKILLEN	arr. 1.30 p.m	

These Tickets will be available for Return on day of issue only by
Special Train leaving Enniskillen at 7.30 p.m.

S. C. LITTLE, General Manager.

Enniskillen, September, 1932.   PRINTED AT THE "CHAMPION" PRINTING WORKS, WINE ST., SLIGO.

The partition of Ireland sundered Fermanagh from its natural hinterland running across counties Sligo, Leitrim and Cavan. The survival until the Second World War of a decent train network in the region offered the opportunity to draw in people from various counties, regardless of the new political dispensation. Throughout the middle decades of the twentieth century, challenge matches between counties proved a great draw all across Ireland. It was a chance to see in action players who were known only through the pages of the press and through the increasing use of radio. *(Selwyn Johnston, Headhunters Museum)*

Men from Derrygonnelly Harps – Henry Greene, Peter Burns, John Corrigan – working away in front of a lorry on the club field in the late 1950s. The club was founded in 1924 and draws its players from the parish of Botha, taking in the areas of Boho, Monea and Derrygonnelly itself. The club purchased Sandhill Fields, later named as Canon Maguire Park, in 1958. The new pitch was officially opened in 1962. Canon Maguire Park now comprises a main playing field, a full-size training pitch, a changing-room complex, a meeting room and a covered stand. *(Eamon Greene)*

Club football in Fermanagh has always been fiercely competitive. Jimmy Mulraine proudly shows off a cup won by Devenish at a tournament match in Castlederg, County Tyrone in 1962. *(GAA Oral History Project/ Jimmy Mulrone)*

On 20 July 2008 Fermanagh's supporters travelled to Clones in huge numbers to see if their team could break their losing streak in Ulster senior football finals. The match with Armagh ended in a draw but the replay was lost. It is the closest that Fermanagh have come to winning an Ulster senior football title. *(Sportsfile)*

'The first Ulster final that I went to ... we didn't cycle, we went in a pony and trap. That possibly had to have been around the mid-forties ... As we got older we cycled to local matches. We had no football club here of our own. We cycled to championship matches in Lisnaskea and Roslea and we cycled then to Clones to the Ulster finals and semi-finals. There was no other means. We hadn't got a car in those years ... Our football club was formed in 1953 and our first matches were played in 1954 ... Our first football field was beside our church, and during that period of the fifties and possibly long before, there were stables where the people came in the pony and traps to Mass and we used those stables for changing rooms for the football matches. After that then we changed our football field and we had no facilities at all and you stripped out at the back of the ditch or underneath the hedge ... you rolled your clothes up in a bundle and hoped it didn't rain on them. A few years later on we got a lease of the field and we built a tin hut which acted for changing rooms for quite a number of years.'

James McCaffrey, b. 1937.

'My earliest GAA memory was attending a football match as a child. This match has stuck in my mind as my father was playing in the match. I was watching the match with my mother and her friend when my father hit his head against a pillar which outlined the pitch. He had the ball and a player from the opposite team tackled him. My father sustained a head injury. As a child I remember my mother being worried and seeing lots of blood! However, much sympathy left us when he insisted on waiting until the end of the match to see if his team would win instead of going to the hospital. Enniskillen Gaels won the match with my father sitting in the dugouts with a huge bandage wrapped around his head.'

Laura Kelly, b. 1984.

'I dare ye. I'm the man that owns this field and if you're good enough to put me out of me own field, you've another thing coming.'

Joe O'Loughlin, b. 1932.

'That time, the footballs was different 'cos if they got wet they got very heavy. You couldn't have kicked her three metres to get rid of her. She'd get too heavy in the wet grass and it wouldn't have been cut too often either.

Anthony McGrath, b. 1941.

In the mid 1960s, Galway produced one of the greatest Gaelic football teams ever seen. Three All-Ireland senior football championships were won in consecutive years between 1964 and 1966. In the 1964 final, action from which is pictured here, Galway defeated Kerry by five points in front of 75,000 spectators at Croke Park. *(Fionnbar Callanan)*

Westmeath Mayo Offaly
Limerick Laois Waterford
Carlow Longford Leitrim
Tipperary Kilkenny Derry
Kerry Cork Wicklow
Kildare Antrim Meath
Tyrone Dublin **Galway**
Armagh Fermanagh
Donegal Sligo Roscommon
Clare Cavan Monaghan
Louth Wexford Down

Galway

In the lore of east Galway, it is in that area – and not in Thurles, County Tipperary – that Michael Cusack initially planned to establish the Gaelic Athletic Association. According to this version, on 15 August 1884, Michael Cusack was reputed to have taken the train to Galway and, in the early evening, joined a meeting of five local men in the home of leading IRB man John Sweeney in Loughrea. There, Cusack professed his desire to establish a Gaelic Athletic Association and his profession was supported by the other men in the room. Together, they walked 300 yards down the road to the residence of Dr Patrick Duggan, the Bishop of Clonfert. Duggan was renowned as a rather exceptional figure amongst the Irish Catholic hierarchy – he was nationalist, a man of the people, a man who had supported the tenants of his diocese in their campaigns for land reform. Cusack asked Duggan to become patron of his new association. Duggan declined. His health and advanced years (he was seventy-one) were not conducive, he said, to assuming the position. He advised Cusack to go to Thurles and to approach Dr Thomas Croke, the Archbishop of Cashel and Duggan's principal ally in the hierarchy, about becoming patron. This Cusack did and it was, of course, in Thurles that the GAA was founded under Croke's patronage.

Accepting this myth as historical truth involves making too many leaps of faith for it to be considered sound. Nonetheless, the very fact of the existence of the legend demonstrates the importance of Galway to the early development of the GAA. Indeed, it was to Galway that Michael Cusack looked to play a hurling match even before he established the GAA. On Easter Sunday 1884 Michael Cusack took his hurling club – the Metropolitans – down to Galway to play a match against the hurlers of Killimor on the Fair Green in Ballinasloe. A huge crowd turned out for the match, with the victors being promised a silver cup. The match was never finished. Indeed, it hardly even started. In the early minutes of the game, the Galway men scored a goal, but Cusack believed that their style of play was too rough and in contravention of the rules. A dispute arose and Cusack refused to allow his men finish the match. The cup was awarded to the Killimor men who returned to their home town, which was ablaze with celebratory bonfires. The dispute over rules laid bare the need to regulate the game of hurling on a national basis. Six months later Cusack founded the GAA in Thurles.

As if to emphasise the bond between Michael Cusack and Galway, when a convention was called in February 1887 to establish a Galway county committee, Cusack took the train from Dublin to Athenry to attend the meeting. Having booked in to the Railway Hotel, he headed straight to the home of P.C. Kelly. Kelly was the head of the Athenry hurling club, an ardent Fenian who had been elected to the Central Executive of the GAA at the Annual Convention of November 1886. It was Kelly who was organising the following day's GAA gathering. Cusack spent Saturday night in his kitchen, drinking whiskey and singing songs. He reported that the following day's convention was 'the most thoroughly Gaelic meeting I have ever seen'. All bar three of the delegates spoke

Irish and all could understand it. He wrote that the men who attended were 'Nature's Gentlemen', men whose 'manners came from their hearts, and not from ninepence worth of etiquette, which may be picked up in a second-hand book-shop. They reminded one of the time when the "Wild Geese" at the Court of Europe were regarded as the first gentlemen in Europe. They showed no trace of the sullenness and suspicion and fear and dread and crouching ruffianism which our English friends put on the stage to show what manner of men we are.'

Under the guidance of these men, the GAA began to thrive in Galway. Hurling tournaments were organised on a regular basis in the county and matches between its most celebrated teams drew huge crowds. The spread of hurling clubs in Galway was underlined by a tournament held in Clarinbridge on Sunday, 6 March 1887. Fourteen clubs played matches in front of an estimated 10,000 people. The Galway county committee also entered a team in the first All-Ireland championships. They did not run off a local championship to decide which club should represent the county; rather a team was selected, which played under the banner of Meelick and which comprised players from Meelick, Killimor, Eyrecourt and Mullagh. They reached the final of that All-Ireland championship, before losing to Thurles, the champions of Tipperary, in a match played in Parsontown in King's County (as Birr in County Offaly was then known). They have never received the losers' medals due to them.

In the end it was not until the 1920s that Galway produced another formidable representative team. In 1923 Galway hammered Kilkenny in an All-Ireland semi-final by 5-4 to 2-0, before progressing to meet Limerick in the final. An extraordinary match (not played until sixteen months after the semi-final ended with Galway winning by 7-6 to 4-5. The Galway team had engaged in collective training at an estate house near Craughwell to prepare them for that final. For the remainder of the decade Galway remained a serious force and reached three more finals; all were lost. Indeed, far from liberating Galway to further success, winning the All-Ireland instead heralded decades of defeat. Club hurling in Galway remained fiercely strong, but the county team languished in the wilderness, occasionally threatening to conquer all, only to deceive.

A Galway team emerged during the second half of the 1970s to change all that. Often the very best sporting moments are defined not so much by what happens on the pitch as by what happens off it. And so it is with Galway's All-Ireland hurling victory in 1980. The passage of more than five decades since the previous victory and the overwhelming sense of frustration at a catalogue of near misses, disappointments, spurned opportunities and moral victories had created a deep well of emotion in the county where hurling was cherished. That emotion was heightened by the enduring economic travails of the west of Ireland where the twin evils of unemployment and emigration were particularly acutely felt. When Limerick were defeated in the All-Ireland final by a goal, it served as a dam-burst that loosed a celebration only partially rooted in sport. The wildness of the celebrations on the field in Croke Park gave way, firstly, to Joe Connolly's iconic speech: 'A mhuintir na Gaillimhe, tar éis seacht mbliana is caoga, tá Craobh na hÉireann ar ais i nGaillimh. Is iontach an lá inniu le bheith mar Gaillimheach. Tá daoine ar ais i nGaillimh agus tá gliondar in a gcroí. Ach freisin caithfimid cuimhniú ar dhaoine i Sasana, i Meiriceá agus ar fud na tíre agus b'fheidir go bhfuil siad ag caoineadh faoi láthair.' And, then, another Galway player, Joe McDonagh, took the microphone and from the Presentation Box in the Hogan Stand, gave a memorable rendition of *The West's Awake*, modifying its chorus to fit the moment:

> 'And if, when all a vigil keep,
> The West's asleep! The West's asleep!
> Alas! And well may Erin weep
> That Galway lies in slumber deep.
> But, hark! A voice like Connolly spake,
> Galway's awake! Galway's awake!'

Galway almost retained the All-Ireland the following year, but lost the final to an emerging Offaly team. Indeed, over the ten years that followed, Galway lost three further All-Ireland finals, all by narrow margins. Against that, the brilliant Galway team of the late 1980s did win two All-Ireland finals, beating the traditional powers of Kilkenny and Tipperary in successive finals in 1987 and 1988. The brilliance of that team was rooted in a half-back line of Pete Finnerty, Tony Keady and Gerry McInerney. On top of that, the team were fiercely competitive and had an ability to close out tight matches with a toughness that evaded subsequent Galway teams. Given the passion for hurling in the county it is somewhat remarkable that, over the more than two decades that followed the 1988 victory, Galway did not win an All-Ireland senior hurling title. As if to emphasise the failure at inter-county level, Galway club sides have been prolific winners of the All-Ireland club hurling championship with Kiltormer, Sarsfields, Athenry, Clarinbridge, Castlegar and Portumna all claiming success.

Through all of this, Galway also developed as a potent footballing force. Initially, Galway had simply refused to enter a team in the All-Ireland football championship, considering hurling to be the only game worthy of recognition. This changed dramatically in the course of the twentieth century. The spread of Gaelic football in Galway has seen it emerge as the dominant game in huge swathes of the county. Indeed, it is largely in the east of the county that hurling can be considered the primary game. Such has been the quality of footballers produced that once Galway won the Connacht senior football championship in 1900, it then kept on winning to the point where forty such championships had been won by 2010.

As if to emphasise the quality of Galway footballers, they have managed to turn provincial success into All-Ireland glory nine times. To put that in context, the next most successful county in Connacht is Mayo who have won three All-Ireland senior titles, while the only other county in Connacht to have won an All-Ireland senior title is Roscommon, who won two titles in the 1940s. The first All-Ireland won by Galway was claimed in 1925; two more followed in the 1930s (1934 and 1938). The 1934 final was the first time that Galway wore the maroon-and-white colours that soon became synonymous with the county. It was possibly the most high-profile final of that era, marking the fiftieth anniversary of the founding of the GAA. The fact that Dublin were the opponents added lustre to the game. Before the game the Dubs trained in the Wicklow Mountains, while the Galway players set up camp for a couple of weeks in Tuam. In the end, Galway prevailed in a fantastic match by 3-5 to 1-9. A noted feature of that era was the manner in which the Galway players of the 1930s combined with their great rivals in Mayo to bring the Railway Cup back to Connacht. Four times in the five years between 1934 and 1938, Connacht won the Railway Cup.

Inspired by Sean Purcell, Galway returned to claim the 1956 All-Ireland championship. Indeed the presence on the Galway team of three men who had grown up together on Bishop Street in Tuam – Sean Purcell, Frank Stockwell and Jack Mangan – lay at the heart of Galway's success. The quality of that team of the 1950s was such that it seems rather disappointing that only a single All-Ireland was won. Either way, the achievement of the Galway team of the 1960s quickly overshadowed all that had passed before. This team grew into one of the greatest Gaelic football teams of all time, with brilliant players all over the field. They claimed three All-Ireland titles in a row between 1964 and 1966. In the course of these victories, the team drew from St Jarlath's College of Tuam – one of the great storied colleges in the world of Gaelic games. It also had a brilliant centre-forward in Mattie McDonagh who became the only man from Connacht to win four All-Ireland senior medals. On top of that McDonagh also became the only man to win ten Connacht senior football medals.

As well as their natural ability as footballers, the strength of that Galway team lay in their unity, determination and cohesiveness. It is a striking fact that twelve players played in all three finals between 1964 and 1966, while just nineteen players in all were used. This strength, however, ultimately proved to be a long-term weakness. When the three-in-a-row team faded from the scene, Galway struggled to find adequate replacements. For three decades there was regular success in Connacht, but it was only in 1998 when Galway reclaimed the Sam Maguire. Again, with a team feted for the style of their play, a further All-Ireland was added in 2001. In every decade the strength of the GAA in Galway leaves them marked down as potential contenders at All-Ireland level. Indeed – along with Cork, and particularly with the decline of Offaly – Galway must be considered a prime example of the possibilities of fostering both hurling and Gaelic football to the very highest level.

Two GAA officials – Paddy Ruane and Joe Grealy – count the takings at a match in Clarinbridge, County Galway, in 1943. *(Clarinbridge GAA Club)*

Mol an óige … The three boys pictured at Coláiste Iognáid in Galway in 1953 are D. Ó Don[ ], E. Ó Loinsigh and C. Ó Liodain. *(Irish Jesuit Archives)*

Galway captain, Joe Connolly, is mobbed by supporters after the county's historic 1980 victory in the All-Ireland senior hurling championship. Connolly's acceptance speech has passed into the lore of Gaelic games. He later said: 'I had nothing prepared, because I thought after 57 years it would be tempting fate.' That same year, Connolly also won an All-Ireland club hurling championship with Castlegar. *(Connacht Tribune)*

In the new millennium, Portumna emerged as one of the greatest club hurling teams in history. In winning the Tommy Moore Cup, the biggest prize in club hurling, Portumna became the fifth Galway club to lift the trophy. They won the cup for a second time in 2008, and for the third time in 2009. Since 2003, Portumna have also won five Galway senior hurling championships. *(Connacht Tribune)*

'If you knew there was a burying ground, or anyone buried in that particular area, you wouldn't take that tree out of that particular spot. There wouldn't be luck in the tree or there wouldn't be luck in the hurleys.' Tom Joe Larkin, b. 1942.

'I remember when a friend of mine got her first car, six of us squashed into a Fiesta to see Galway play Mayo in Castlebar. It was (surprisingly) a very warm day and the traffic was terrible. We didn't care because Galway won.'

Orlaith Mannion, b. 1975.

'I once watched an All-Ireland senior football final in a cinema in West Roxbury, Boston (Cork v Meath). It was a thrilling experience watching the crowd singing the National Anthem with ómós [respect] right to the end. It was also an insight into how precious the games are to the diaspora. I have also seen Irish people abroad reading local Irish newspapers avidly about their local parish or club or county.'

Tom Kenny, b. 1944.

'The great three-in-a-row Galway team of the sixties ... I remember going to a house up the road here, Kinsella's, where they had a black-and-white television — 'twas the only television around the area. And there'd be a big crowd in at the house ... And the man of the house — he was an old man — he used to sit in front of the fire, and he had a big mirror over the fire, and he used to look at the television through the mirror. That's the way he looked at the television; he wanted to face the fire.'

Tom Lowry, b. 1950.

'Being brought on crossbar of bicycle to see the great Paul Russell, Kerry, in local club match.'

John Ryan, b. 1934.

'Seán Duggan, Galway's greatest living hurling goalkeeper. Why? He still swims everyday in Blackrock (Salthill) — now at the age of eighty-five. He played hurling for Galway before the Second World War even started.'

Peadar O'Dowd, b. 1941.

Kerry supporters entertain themselves after travelling to Dublin by train for the 1955 All-Ireland final. The railways were central to the experience of GAA players and supporters from the very outset of the GAA and in Kerry, it was immortalised in verse. The all-night train journey from Cahersiveen to Dublin for big matches in the 1920s and 1930s was the subject of Sigerson Clifford's poem 'The Ghost Train to Croke Park':
'We all met at Keating's corner when 'twas midnight by the clock/Casey's mouth-organ made music like a lark/And we gave the Kerry war cry as we marched north two by two/ To lep aboard the Ghost Train to Croke Park.'
(Kennelly Archive)

Kerry

Westmeath Mayo Offaly
Limerick Laois Waterford
Carlow Longford Leitrim
Tipperary Kilkenny Derry
Kerry Cork Wicklow
Kildare Antrim Meath
Tyrone Dublin Galway
Armagh Fermanagh
Donegal Sligo Roscommon
Clare Cavan Monaghan
Louth Wexford Down

In February 1885, Ireland acquired its second new sporting organisation in four months. The Irish Amateur Athletics Association (IAAA), which largely adopted the rules of the British Amateur Athletic Association (AAA), had been established in opposition to the GAA and with a firm determination 'to quash the Gaelic Union'. Its emergence signalled the beginning of a battle for the control of Irish athletics. The bitterness of the rivalry that developed between the two sporting bodies was fuelled not simply by considerations of class, culture and politics; personality also played an important part. Michael Cusack was only too willing to use the pages of the local and national press to vent his fury and prejudice towards the new sporting arrival. In typically intemperate tones, the GAA founder described the IAAA as a 'ranting, impotent West British abortion'. The escalation of the dispute was as apparent on the playing fields as it was in the vitriol spilling from newspapers, with both sides deciding to ban from their own sports those athletes who participated in events run by the other.

According to Cusack, Irish men were faced with a stark choice 'between Irish and foreign laws'. The showdown between the two came in Kerry. On 17 June 1885, a mere matter of weeks after the establishment of its first Kerry branch (which emerged under the chairmanship of the Fenian William Moore Stack, following a gathering of the Irish National League), the GAA held a sports meeting in Tralee on the same day and in the same town as the County Kerry Amateur Athletic and Cricket Club (CKAACC) had organised its major, annual competition. People voted with their feet and their verdict was emphatic. Whereas only a few hundred attended the event championed by the CKAACC, a huge propaganda drive brought a crowd of 10,000 people out in support of the rival GAA sports. These events were a watershed. They asserted the pre-eminence of the GAA in the provinces and precipitated a retreat of the IAAA to its urban strongholds of Dublin and Belfast.

In Kerry itself, however, the face-off yielded little by way of a dividend for the GAA. Over the months that followed, more events may have been held under the Association's auspices, but the momentum was soon stalled by problems in the wider economy and society. Kerry was among the country's most underdeveloped counties and endured an escalation in agrarian disturbance in the mid to late 1880s. With passions elsewhere engaged, the GAA was slower to organise there than in many other places. A first county convention was not held until November 1888. Three years later, as if to emphasise the progress that had by then been made, Kerry were All-Ireland champions – in hurling. The impetus for this victory came from the fertile north of the county, then as now the local power base of the game. After defeating the Limerick Treaty Stones club in a replayed provincial final, the hurlers of Ballyduff, Kerry's representatives in the 1891 championship, travelled to Clonturk Park in Dublin to play Crossabeg from Wexford in the All-Ireland decider. Attired in their work trousers and bare feet, they won by 2-5 to 1-4. It was the county's first – and only – hurling All-Ireland. News of the victory sparked a wild night of celebration in Ballyduff, but the joy of the players in Dublin was soured by the manner of their treatment. A team of mostly farmers and farm labourers – men of modest incomes – they were aggrieved at having to bear the considerable cost of their own travel and board. In protest, the majority never played again.

Losing players was something the GAA in Kerry would become familiar with throughout the 1890s, however. Weakened by political division and clerical opposition – Dr Coffey, the Bishop of Kerry withdrew support for a major GAA tournament in 1895 on the grounds that it was a front for secret societies – the problems of the GAA in Kerry were compounded by a rise in emigration from depressed rural areas. It is perhaps significant that when the GAA in Kerry began to rejuvenate in the early twentieth century, it did so powered by clubs from Killarney and Tralee, towns that actually experienced a population growth. The Dr Crokes club from Killarney and Tralee Mitchells combined to provide the basis of the team which, following a celebrated trilogy of games against Kildare, secured a first All-Ireland football title for Kerry in 1903. Although widely recognised as the beginning of a soon-to-be famed footballing tradition, this was a breakthrough success built on deep-rooted local customs. Long before the GAA's inception, a form of folk football called 'Caid' was popular among the Kerry peasantry. Played cross-country over fields and hedges and with a makeshift ball (made from a pig's bladder stuffed with hay), games of Caid were often rough-and-tumble affairs, prone to ending in bouts of riotous brawling. Yet these traditions of play clearly informed the popularity of organised ball sports, especially rugby, in Kerry in the late nineteenth century. Killorglin was one of many towns to have a rugby team in the 1880s, but its club, Laune Rangers, converted to Gaelic football on the arrival into the town of two teachers from Dublin, Jack Murphy and Tom Cronin, both of them previously members of the Erin's Hope club in the capital. For the men from Laune Rangers, the transition from rugby to Gaelic was remarkably smooth. Led by J. P. O'Sullivan, also a renowned athlete, Laune Rangers came to dominate Kerry football in the early 1890s, contesting unsuccessfully the All-Ireland final of 1892.

By the early twentieth century, as pioneering research by Richard McElligott has shown, the eclipse of rugby across Kerry was well under way. Two reasons for this were the administrative reorganisation of the GAA within the county and the implementation of the ban on the playing of foreign games. Another was the great excitement and interest that accompanied the phenomenal success enjoyed by Kerry's footballers. As well as winning five All-Ireland titles between 1903 and 1914, Kerry participated in two remarkable series of games – against Kildare in the 1903 All-Ireland final (played in 1905) and against Louth in the 1913 Croke Memorial Cup – that acted as bookends for a period of rapid transformation in how Gaelic football was both played and perceived. Rule changes, including the reduction of team sizes, contributed to this process of change, as did the evolution of various styles of play. The effect, as the Dr Crokes and Kerry footballer Dick Fitzgerald observed, was to shift the emphasis of Gaelic football away from 'strength and endurance' and towards 'skill'. Fitzgerald himself both personified and encouraged this change. In 1914, he wrote *How to Play Gaelic Football*, the game's first instructional manual, offering practical advice on the proper practice and execution of essential skills such as catching, kicking and tackling. The book was both a paean to the virtues of Gaelic football and a warning shot about the perils of professionalism. Fitzgerald was adamant that GAA players should remain true to the traditions of their own sports. He wrote: 'We have, we trust, all been playing the game for its own sake, because it is OUR OWN GAME, and we should be loth to copy the methods that prevail in many of the modern games.'

Fitzgerald was Gaelic football's first real celebrity, his reputation sufficient to transcend county lines. Away from the field of play, however, he found himself drawn into the maelstrom of political events that would soon convulse his native county. Fitzgerald joined the Irish Volunteers in 1914, but was arrested and interned in the aftermath of the 1916 Rising. In the overlapping of sporting and political interests, there was, however, nothing exceptional about Fitzgerald's story. In Kerry, it was commonplace. So much so that, in October 1914, the Kerry county board put forward a motion to the GAA's national convention recommending the inclusion of rifle shooting in the range of activities offered by clubs. In the end, the motion was never actually debated, yet Kerry was among the most deeply scarred of counties by the political violence that followed. And when the nationalist unity of the independence struggle was replaced by the division of the Civil War, there were Kerry GAA people – county footballers among them – stranded on either side of a bitter divide. In 1924, however, a remarkable match between pro- and anti-treaty players was organised to select a team to represent the county. Political grievances certainly lingered – Kerry opted out of competitions as late as 1935 when demands to release republican political prisoners were refused – yet there is no denying the symbolic significance of John Joe Sheehy, a leading anti-treaty republican, and Con Brosnan, an army captain in the pro-treaty forces, burying their differences for the cause of the county. What resulted was a sixth All-Ireland football title in 1924.

The 1924 Kerry team was, of course, memorable for more than the extraordinary manner of its selection. It was also the first county side to be trained by Dr Eamonn O'Sullivan who, more than any other individual, would shape the development of modern Kerry football. In doing so, he brought spectacular success to the county. Across five decades, O'Sullivan, a son of the great Laune Rangers captain of the 1890s, was the architect of eight All-Ireland winning campaigns, his Kerry teams all adhering to a simple, immutable, football philosophy. This was ultimately set out in *The Art and Science of Gaelic Football*, a book written by O'Sullivan and published in 1958, the first such volume since Dick Fitzgerald's more than four decades earlier. O'Sullivan wrote of his belief that players should, as far as possible, stick to their own sector of the field rather than indulge in 'indiscriminate wandering', which inclined towards 'bunching' and 'disorganised effort', particularly by forwards. This tactical rigidity was coupled with a coaching model that stressed the importance of habit formation in the development of skills. For this reason, amongst others, O'Sullivan was a firm advocate of the system of whole-time collective training where, in the fortnight leading up to an important game, players and subs would enter a training camp and subject themselves to 'a daily 24 hour schedule of alternating exercise, tuition, rest and play'. It was a practice that came to an end in 1954, when it was outlawed by a vote of the GAA's national convention.

Although concerns over costs and an incipient professionalism swayed the case for prohibition, Kerry were among the minority to argue for its retention. Their stance had as much to do with the complex geography of the county as it had with the success the system had undoubtedly delivered to them. The expansion of the railway network in the late nineteenth century had been crucial in bringing previously isolated parts of the county into a closer relationship with each other, yet there were still players who were required to cover large distances and circuitous routes just to train for the county side. The example of Mick O'Connell, the great footballing stylist from Valentia, provided a case in point. Much of his training was done alone in the fields around his island home, but when he was compelled to attend collective sessions or games with his Kerry teammates, his journey began with a row across to the mainland. From there onwards, O'Connell would often be joined in the journey by Mick O'Dwyer. 'Being the only two team members from South Kerry, most of the time at any rate, meant more miles travelling for us for games and training,' O'Connell later recalled. The conversation that flowed between the two men revolved around football and little else. 'At all hours of the night as we drove homeward we debated and re-debated the game, expounding our theories openly ... I doubt if any two sportsmen in Ireland knew each other's game and thoughts on the game as well as we did.'

O'Connell and O'Dwyer's playing careers ran in parallel. They were both schooled in the catch-and-kick tradition that Dr Eamonn O'Sullivan had done so much to foster but which, by the early 1960s, appeared ill-equipped to deal with the more fluid, interchangeable style as pioneered by Down. How Kerry football responded to this and later challenges has proved an essential feature of the development of Gaelic football over the course of the last half century. For what Down did in the 1960s, Armagh and Tyrone would do again in the 2000s – they gave rise to the need for reinvention. It fell to Mick O'Dwyer as Kerry manager in the 1970s and 1980s to jettison the simplicities of the catch-and-kick tradition he himself had been brought up with. Alongside a Kevin Heffernan-inspired Dublin, O'Dwyer's Kerry – an extraordinary crop of players – set new standards for the physical preparation of teams, their style of play built upon movement, pace and the use of the hand pass to transfer the ball quickly. It was certainly different and at times thrilling, but it was also remarkably productive. Kerry achieved a dominance previously unknown in the sport: over the course of twelve summers, they won eight All-Irelands, including a four-in-a-row (1978–81) and a three-in-a-row (1984–86).

It could be said that the finest achievement of this Kerry team was the effect they had on others. Their hegemony was such that they forced other counties to think deeper about their own game and to take strides to improve standards. The result has been a more competitive football scene and a greater democratisation of success. And yet, for all the changes that have swept through Gaelic football, Kerry have remained the benchmark against which all teams have ultimately been measured. It is a tribute to the county's standing in the game that it was they who brought the best out of the Armagh and Tyrone teams that won All-Irelands in the early 2000s, a decade during which a new generation of gifted Kerry players still contested seven All-Ireland finals and won five.

In Kerry, Gaelic football has become a self-sustaining tradition. Success has bred success. More than that, however, it has helped establish the GAA as a vital marker of county identity, as central to the image of Kerry as its spectacular scenery or its thriving culture of music, song and literature. Of course, all of these facets of culture and identity ultimately become enmeshed, each one drawing on and building upon the other. The writer Gabriel Fitzmaurice realised as much when, in a poem of praise to Mikey Sheehy, one of the more elegant stars of Kerry's great team of the 1970s and 1980s, he described him as being 'flesh of tribal soil'. As Fitzmaurice saw it, the footballer was no longer a representative of Kerry; he was the embodiment of Kerry. It's hard to argue.

Fielding the Ball and keeping an Opponent off.

Dick Fitzgerald demonstrates the art of fielding with Kerry teammate Johnny Mahony. The photograph was published in Fitzgerald's seminal book, *How to Play Gaelic Football*, in 1914. In lauding the evolution of Gaelic football as a 'scientific' sport, Fitzgerald expressed himself keen that it 'will always remain as natural a game as it is today' and that it should 'never become the possession of the professional player'. *(GAA Oral History Project)*

Islandman: Mick O'Connell arrives on the mainland en route to county training before the 1968 All-Ireland final. A supreme stylist, O'Connell was selected at midfield on the GAA's Team of the Century in 1984. Over a decade before, in 1974, he published *A Kerry Footballer*, a memoir in which he outlined his 'obsession' with training. From his home on Valentia Island, O'Connell would devise his own training programme for speed and endurance, but for ball work, he would routinely 'enlist the help of local schoolchildren, farmers, County Council workers, whoever was available'. *(Fionnbar Callanan)*

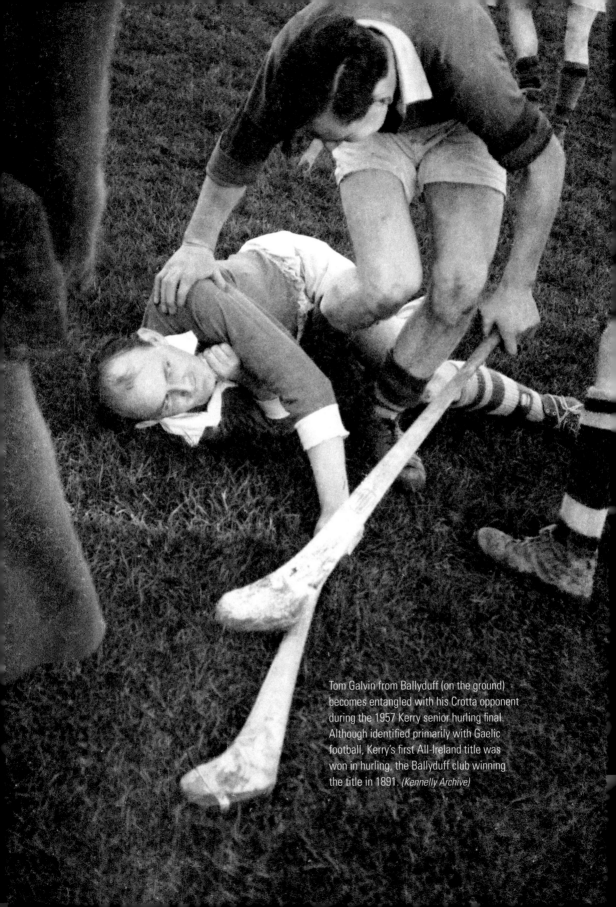

Tom Galvin from Ballyduff (on the ground) becomes entangled with his Crotta opponent during the 1957 Kerry senior hurling final. Although identified primarily with Gaelic football, Kerry's first All-Ireland title was won in hurling, the Ballyduff club winning the title in 1891. *(Kennelly Archive)*

From the field to the dance floor, GAA life was all-encompassing. This photograph shows Denis (Massey) Moran and his niece, Nora O'Connor, enjoying a Kerins O'Rahillys GAA club social night at the Moadowlands Hotel, Tralee, in February 1954. The event was held to celebrate the club's 1953 senior county championship win against Shannon Rangers, played the previous September. *(Kennelly Archive)*

Mick O'Dwyer urges on his players in the dying moments of the 1985 All-Ireland final against Dublin. The rivalry between these two counties was more than a clash between urban and rural, city and country: it defined Gaelic football over the course of a decade. With O'Dwyer as a manager, Kerry would contest ten All-Ireland finals between 1975 and 1986, winning eight of them. In 1982, they came within minutes of winning a record fifth All-Ireland in a row. *(Inpho)*

'There were many memories of the atrocities that took place in Kerry, especially in the final months of the Civil War, in the spring of 1923, and some clubs and some families were strongly associated with the Republican tradition in North Kerry, whereas other clubs were not; you had great tension.'

Seán Seosamh Ó Conchubhair, b. 1935.

'I stood at the door and I was in awe, really; these were people, usually at that time I wouldn't have seen any of them, ever, and I probably would have had an exaggerated opinion of how high they could jump and everything like that because of hearing my father talk about them.'

John Stephen O'Sullivan, b. 1940.

'Being from a small rural area, the Gaeltacht probably will suffer from emigration again like in previous years.'

John King, b. 1950.

'After Mass on Sunday, you would head straight to the matches, club or county, and then head back to the pub to discuss the results. When I was young there were very little county colours. For training and home matches, I would cycle when I was young, up to six or seven miles. For away matches a bus would be put on. One of the neighbours might take turns going to matches, the cars would be full, even people in the boot. My next-door neighbour would go, he had a Ford pickup with eight-foot-high rails on the back. He could fit twenty people into the back.'

Patrick Murphy, b. 1968.

'It wasn't my cup of tea ever to be celebrating … the football game was the thing that was important to me … I got as much satisfaction playing for the club team as I did for the county team in that regard. Some people might find that hard to understand, but to me it was any game you go out, the challenge is against yourself, whether it's a big game, small game or any other game. So if you did well for your team, well and good; if you failed not so good, that was it.'

Mick O'Connell, b. 1937.

'A lot of family life revolved around the club, such as looking after underage teams, attending the club lotto draw every week, attending bingo sessions, meeting people through the club.'

Brendan O'Regan, b. 1953.

A big crowd gathers at St Conleth's Park in Newbridge on county football final day in the mid 1950s. Despite the lack of success at inter-county level during the middle decades of the century, the Kildare club scene continued to excite local enthusiasm.
(Dessie Boland Photography)

Kildare

They were games that changed Gaelic football. There were three of them in all, played over a period of four months and combining endless controversy, excitement and skill. The clash of Kildare and Kerry in the 1903 All-Ireland final, delayed until 1905, brought together two counties that had yet to win football's ultimate honour. It also brought together a clash of two distinctive styles. Where the Munster men opted for a direct catch-and-kick approach, the 'men from the short grass', their boots bleached white to match the colour of their shirts and shorts, favoured innovations like the hand pass and 'picking the ball up with the toe'. In the end, orthodoxy won out. After two replays, which saw attendances and gate receipts swell, Kildare were defeated but their contribution did not go unrewarded. When the Central Council of the GAA met soon after, it decided to present the Kildare players with a set of gold medals 'in recognition of their services to the Association'.

The 1903 trilogy impacted upon the GAA at various levels. Most obviously, it affirmed the popular and commercial appeal of Gaelic football, but it was also credited with setting a new standard of Gaelic football, drawing a line between what became recognised as the modern game and its somewhat chaotic rough-and-tumble origins. In Kildare, too, the effect of the games was profound: for a start, it provided a very public demonstration of the resuscitation in the Association's fortunes after a decade of disruption and decline. The extent of the GAA retreat in the county during the 1890s, a consequence of the Parnell split, had to a large extent been a measure of the great progress that had preceded it. The initial development of the Association had been helped by the adoption of its rules by established athletics clubs in places such as Maynooth, Clane and Monasterevin, but it was a passion for football, and the intensity of local rivalries engendered by the introduction of county championships in 1888, that really drove the growth of the early GAA in Kildare. If that growth was rapid – club numbers reached thirty-eight by late 1890 – the decline was precipitous. By early 1901, the number of clubs had fallen to just twelve. It was at this point the recovery began.

In April of that year, a meeting was called in the village of Sallins to consider ways of lifting what one contemporary writer called the 'pall of lethargy' that hung over the GAA in Kildare. It resulted in two key outcomes: firstly, a new committee was formed with Jim Archer of Clane appointed chairman and Dick Radley, a Cork-born teacher in Prosperous, elected as honorary secretary; secondly, it agreed to re-establish the county championship which had lapsed for five of the previous eight years. Radley, in particular, came to be seen as a vital influence on the county's revival, while the county championship brought to the fore two clubs – Clane and Roseberry – who provided the backbone of the Kildare teams of the mid 1900s, their players among the first to come together for organised county team training.

The uniting of these local rivals may not have been enough to overcome Kerry in the 1903 All-Ireland final, but redemption was not long in coming. Kildare and Kerry met again in the 1905 final, played in June 1907, and on this occasion only one game was required to decide an outcome. Kildare won on a 1-7 to 0-5 scoreline. In Thurles, where the game was staged and into which thousands of Kildare supporters had poured, the victory was met with scenes of near hysteria. The *Leinster Leader*, the newspaper of which John Wyse Power, who had attended the GAA's founding meeting in 1884, was a former editor, described how the crowd's roar 'that thundered from Archbishop Croke's town and woke echoes over the Slieve Bloom Mountains announced the victory of Kildare Gaels in the All-Ireland championship ... The ladies waved their handkerchiefs, and hats and caps were tossed in the air. The tooting of motor cars, the blowing of brass instruments and the beating of drums swelled the pandemonium.'

Kildare's victory came freighted with symbolism. For a county in the heart of the Pale with a large garrison and strong traditions of sports such as cricket, hockey, rugby and soccer, the winning of an All-Ireland title in Gaelic football was considered by some as deserving of celebration for wider cultural and political reasons. One such person was 'Thigeen Roe', the pseudonym used by Fr Ramsbottom, the influential and frequently hyperbolic columnist with the *Leinster Leader*. For his work covering the GAA, Roe was himself lauded by the *Gaelic Athletic Annual* for having helped to consign 'to the Limbo of the past in Kildare, the fantastic field sport of the coquettish Anti-Irishman'.

Vivid rhetoric like this masked a reality that the GAA in Kildare was anything but a hotbed of radical nationalism. Unlike the experience in some other counties, the Association was largely unscathed by the political and military tumult of the decade that ended in the Anglo-Irish settlement of 1922. It is also true that nationalist schisms were played out in a number of clubs and that the county rowed in behind 'Gaelic Sunday', when it organised seventeen games across Kildare in defiance of a British ban on public gatherings in 1918. It is also true that a fund-raising game was staged in aid of the Republican Prisoners Dependants' Fund in 1919. But it is equally true that the Kildare GAA gave the authorities little cause for concern. With only the odd exception – Jack Fitzgerald, chairman of the county board, was imprisoned in Wakefield Prison in 1916 for his role in the rebellion of that year – GAA officials in Kildare preferred to remain detached from politics. And so too did their players. It is striking, for instance, that none of the All-Ireland winning team of 1919 played any apparent role in the War of Independence.

That All-Ireland victory, Kildare's second, symbolised the local triumph of sport over politics, but it also brought to national prominence Caragh's Larry

Stanley, who despite appearing only seventeen times for his native county over a fifteen-year period, is recognised as one of their greatest ever Gaelic footballers. He was more than that, however. Stanley was a sporting prodigy, an all-rounder. A brilliant high jumper, who represented Ireland at both the Paris Olympics and the Tailteann Games in 1924, he also played soccer in the colours of Belfast Celtic and Gaelic football in the colours of Dublin, for whom he qualified when he became a member of the Dublin Metropolitan Police – later An Garda Síochána – and with whom he would win another All-Ireland. Stanley returned to Kildare in 1926, helping them to an All-Ireland final where Kerry, yet again, defeated them after a replay. On the morning of that replay, the *Sunday Independent* ran a profile of Stanley declaring him a 'star amongst stars ... he has a football style of his own, his novel methods of fielding and evading opponents as yet unmastered by others'. It is perhaps because of these very qualities that Stanley felt that he was subjected to rougher than usual treatment by his Kerry opponents in that game. It was enough to force him into retirement. Unfortunately for Stanley, the loss was entirely his as it meant missing out on Kildare's two All-Ireland victories in 1927 and 1928, the latter of which saw the county become the first recipients of a new trophy named in honour of Sam Maguire, the Cork-born IRB man who had served as chairman of the GAA's London county board.

The successes of the late 1920s bred an interest that was reflected in increased club numbers. In the year that followed Kildare's 1926 All-Ireland final appearance, for instance, the number of affiliated clubs climbed from thirty-three to forty-eight. Among the newcomers were teams that had emerged from the Curragh military camp, where the army of the new Irish Free State had taken up residence after the British departure. Military teams exerted a bigger influence on hurling than football in Kildare, their arrival providing a challenge to clubs in relative strongholds of the game such as Monasterevin, Clane and Celbridge. That said, hurling received nothing like the type of shake-up needed to enable it to challenge the position of football. Even as the performances of the county footballers began to wane – Kildare won only three Leinster titles (1931, 1935 and 1956) between 1930 and the late 1990s – the primacy of the big ball game was apparent from the intensity and excitement generated by inter-club competition. As if to underline the point, a crowd in excess of 10,000 attended the replayed senior club final to witness Ardclough defeat Curragh in 1949.

For all the passion and rivalry stirred up by the local club scene, Kildare's footballing trough proved deep and prolonged. Writing in 1984, Eoghan Corry, author of the county's centenary GAA history, observed how, since the 1930s, Kildare had produced little more than an 'average football team fulfilling fixtures, hoping, trying out new players, hoping, changing tactics. Hoping.' It was not until the 1990s that the hope appeared to have been replaced by belief. And it took an outsider to instil it. The appointment as Kildare senior football manager of Mick O'Dwyer, the legendary Kerry player and manager, had a galvanising effect on the county and was accompanied by immense fund-raising drives off the field and improved performances on it. Under O'Dwyer, Kildare won two Leinster titles – in 1998 and 2000 – and were beaten by Galway in the All-Ireland final of 1998, a day on which their supporters in their thousands created the impression of having thrown a white blanket over the Croke Park stadium.

In many ways, it was entirely appropriate that it should fall to an outsider to spearhead this resurgence. After all, by the end of the twentieth century, the county was home to more non-native Kildare people than native. This was the result of the extraordinary population growth that had taken place since the 1970s. It was a phenomenon that left no part of the county untouched, though the highest rates of increase were found, understandably, in the towns and villages of the north – areas which were more urban-based, which were geographically closer to Dublin and which saw the highest concentrations of industry. As if to underline the point, Leixlip, a town of less than 1,000 in 1961, ballooned to 15,016 in 2002.

How did all this affect the GAA? At one level, it sharpened pre-existing divides between clubs in the more transitory north and the more settled south of the county; at another, it forced the Association to confront the myriad difficulties associated with huge social change. In places like Leixlip, the GAA was not found wanting. Not only did the long-established Leixlip GAA club become a key focal point of the community – its bar membership grew to more than 3,000 – but a second club was also established specifically to serve those living in the rapidly expanding parish of Confey, on the edge of the town. Sociologists have since credited the creation of the Confey club with helping to create a greater 'sense of place' in that part of the sprawling town. The impact of all this has been to transform Kildare's social and sporting landscape and to widen the gulf between the county's GAA past and present.

A scene from the Kilcock Sports in 1911. The role of athletics was crucial to the early success of the GAA in Kildare as elsewhere. Pre-existing athletics clubs in Maynooth, Clane and Monasterevin joined the GAA soon after its inception. Although it was soon eclipsed by Gaelic football, the athletics tradition was maintained, most obviously by Larry Stanley, the great Kildare and Dublin footballer of the 1920s. Stanley would represent Ireland at both the Paris Olympics and the Tailteann Games in 1924. *(Margaret Grehan)*

A still-frame from a British Pathé newsreel of the 1927 All-Ireland final, when Kildare defeated Kerry. Prior to the creation of the National Film Institute in the late 1940s, it was left to foreign companies to produce a film record of Gaelic games. The archive is by no means comprehensive, however. Despite Kildare contesting three All-Ireland finals in a row (winning twice) between 1926 and 1928, the 1927 final is the only one for which film footage survives. *(British Pathé)*

Kildare's Tommy Carew shoots for a score despite the attention of two Galway defenders in the mid 1980s. Always the secondary GAA game in Kildare, it is believed that Paddy Molohan, a friend of Michael Cusack's and a member of his Metropolitans hurling club in the early 1880s, introduced the game to Monasterevin. Molohan was Kildare's sole representative on the GAA's so-called 'Invasion Tour' of the United States in 1888. *(Dessie Boland Photography)*

Kildare supporters spill onto the Croke Park pitch to celebrate their county's Leinster football final victory in 1998. It was Kildare's first senior title since 1956. *(Sportsfile)*

An aerial view of Leixlip from 2009 shows the GAA club grounds at the centre of extensive housing development. Although Leixlip, like most of north Kildare, has experienced massive population growth in recent decades – a result of the spill-over from Dublin suburban sprawl – the GAA has acted as a force for social cohesion and community identity. *(Dessie Boland Photography)*

'This thing they have now going on – putting them in green jerseys. I strongly object to it. We are the Lily Whites. There has to be some way around it – if another team has the same colour as we have, put a green armband or something like that or have Kildare or Cill Dara on the back of the jumper. Putting them in green jerseys! The Lily Whites, the Shortgrass and the Flower Bags – that's what we were called.'

Catherine Gannon, b. 1943.

'It was either stay at home, or get involved and I decided "Why should he have all the fun? I'm going too."'

Rosanna Curran, b. 1951.

'In this club here, we have people from a lot of different denominations – different religions and everything else. And they have this thing at Kildare county board level, at county board meetings and everything else; before they commence the meeting, they say a prayer. Outdated. Religion is a person's own business, but every county board meeting that's held, and the man that used to do them – he's not well at the moment – and he's a gentleman and he did it for years and years and when he got sick and left the county board and they carried on the tradition. And it doesn't have any place – it's not a prayer meeting, it's a meeting of clubs doing business about how the GAA in the county is run … . That's wrong. It shouldn't be happening.'

Michael Gorman, b. 1957.

'Confey is an unusual area because 95 per cent of the people here have come in from around the country. It's like the United Nations. Every county is represented here … And Leixlip would've been the same but Leixlip would've been fifteen or twenty years before us and when we moved in, in '79, again, we were all the same age coming in. We were all in our mid twenties, we were all from the country, we all had young children. So these kids started getting that bit older, people saw the need of maybe another club, 'cos Leixlip was big enough up there and it was a bit of a distance from here to St Mary's.'

Eamon Fennelly, b. 1954.

'Oh one night as we rambled down Kildangan way/We met with Tom Lennon, to us he did say/Oh we throw yous a challenge, we heard yous were good/But to prove it you may beat the lads from the stud.'

Kildangan Song, sung by Johnny Casey, b. 1940.

Eddie Keher strikes a score in Kilkenny's 1963 All-Ireland hurling final victory over Waterford. This was the first of six All-Ireland medals won by the Rower-Inistioge player in an inter-county career that ran from 1959 to 1977. A graduate of St Kieran's College, Keher once recalled his early years practising the skills of hurling in the village square in Inistioge: 'The older guys used to hurl there. Then, when they were gone, we'd come out and try to hurl. That was my first real introduction to hurling.' *(Fionnbar Callanan)*

Westmeath Mayo Offaly
Limerick Laois Waterford
Carlow Longford Leitrim
Tipperary Kilkenny Derry
Kerry Cork Wicklow
Kildare Antrim Meath
Tyrone Dublin Galway
Armagh Fermanagh
Donegal Sligo Roscommon
Clare Cavan Monaghan
Louth Wexford Down

Kilkenny

On an April morning in 1887, Michael Cusack stepped off a train in Kilkenny city. He had travelled from Dublin to check on the progress of the Association he had founded almost three years before. His spirits quickly sank. Strolling through the streets of the city, Cusack was aghast at the pitiful appearance of the men he saw. On the steps of the local bank, for instance, he spotted a 'crowd of persons, who probably call themselves men, slothfully reclining with their faces towards the sun', while the huge pillars of the town hall supported the 'dead weight of a lot of fellows' who, he suggested, would have been better out in the fields practising the games of their fathers. Yet Cusack formed no better impression of those who did take to those fields. Attending a poorly supported hurling match, he described how at one point, as the game continued about them, a half dozen players took to lying on the ground to take a rest. Disgusted, he raged that the scene was a 'contemptible perversion' of the ancient game, an abomination that would break the heart of more serious GAA people in Galway or Tipperary. Above all, though, Cusack felt the episode offered irrefutable evidence of the failure of the Association to take root properly in the county.

Damning as this assessment was, it was not entirely accurate. Kilkenny might not by then have emerged as a power base of Gaelic games, but nor was it a wasteland. Big crowds routinely turned out to watch GAA events, in many cases monster tournaments where Gaelic football provided the principal attraction. Indeed, Kilkenny enjoyed a pivotal place in the early evolution of Gaelic football as it was on a Fair Green in Callan in February 1885 that the first ever match under GAA rules was played, an encounter between Callan and Kilkenny that ended in a scoreless draw. The extent to which football rather than hurling provided the driving impetus for the early GAA in Kilkenny became glaringly obvious when a newly established county board organised its first county championships in 1887: nineteen clubs entered the football competition and four the hurling. The winners of the former were Kilmacow, a team of 'brawny countrymen' from the southern end of the county, who progressed to win the inaugural Leinster football championship, defeating the Blue and Whites from Wexford in a final played before a crowd of 12,000 people at New Ross. It was the first of three football titles won by Kilkenny clubs in the opening three decades of the Association, the second coming in 1900 through the efforts of the Slatequarry Miners, a team drawn from workers in the booming quarry industry on either side of the Kilkenny/Tipperary border, and the third coming eleven years later when the county was represented by players from Knocktopher and Ballyhale.

While football was undoubtedly the more successful and widely played of Gaelic games in Kilkenny's early GAA experience, the position of hurling was not necessarily as shambolic as Cusack had depicted it in 1887. In pockets, the sport was played with passion. One of these was Mooncoin, a parish encompassing a collection of largely prosperous farming villages in the south of the county. Another was Tullaroan, a more socially volatile village to the northwest where the founding of a hurling club in early 1887 came in the wake of years of significant

Land League activity in the area. Tullaroan would become the most successful of Kilkenny's early hurling clubs, but it was formed from men whose principal sporting interest lay with cricket, among them Henry J. Meagher, a farmer and Parnellite nationalist who was reputed (inaccurately) to have attended the founding meeting of the Association in Thurles in 1884. Tullaroan was not alone in having players who crossed back and forth between cricket and hurling and the dynamic between the games is an essential element in the story of the GAA's early development in the county. Cricket in Kilkenny enjoyed a broad-based appeal, which the emergence of the GAA did nothing to diminish. Whereas there were over thirty cricket clubs in the county in 1884; by the mid 1890s, with the GAA then weakened by Parnellite divisions, this had risen to fifty. In fact, such was the predominance of cricket that a letter writer to the *Kilkenny Journal* in 1895 implored clubs to help out the GAA by turning to hurling and football in the winter months.

The question that needs to be asked is what happened to change the relative strengths of cricket and hurling in the early twentieth century? In answering, it is necessary to acknowledge a confluence of factors: the impact of the GAA ban on foreign games, dropped in the 1890s and reinstated in 1902, which undermined the prospects of a harmonious co-existence between the different sports; the better organisation of local GAA competitions; and the boost that came from winning a first All-Ireland hurling title in 1904, a championship that was not run off until 1906. That success proved the first of many over the course of the decade that followed: in all, Kilkenny contested seven finals between 1904 and 1913, winning all of them. This period marked the effective birth of the county's modern hurling tradition, yet it was achieved against a backdrop of inter-club bickering and general discord. The effect of various disputes was enough to lead Tom Ryall, a historian of the GAA in Kilkenny, to speculate that Kilkenny might have won eleven All-Ireland titles in a row had a greater unity prevailed. Even so, the shaping of a particular county consciousness can be discerned throughout this period, perhaps most symbolically in the replacement of club strips for a distinctive county jersey, the black-and-amber shirts, with 'Kilkenny' embroidered across the players chests, being worn on the occasion of the All-Ireland victories in 1911, 1912 and 1913.

A shared loyalty to Kilkenny did not involve the sublimation of all difference, however. Over the following decade, issues of class and politics pointed up tensions in the local society. The parish of Thomastown, for example, acquired two hurling clubs, Mung (founded *c.* 1910) and Thomastown (founded in 1918), their very existence serving to both expose and exacerbate a local division between town and country, and between farmers and farm labourers. A more powerful local influence was nationalism, however. In January 1914, as momentum built behind the Irish Volunteer movement, James Nowlan, an alderman on Kilkenny Corporation and then GAA President, encouraged all members of the Association to join the Volunteers and to 'learn to shoot straight'. When the shooting did eventually start in Easter 1916, Nowlan, as an IRB member, found himself promptly arrested and interned for several months in Wakefield Prison in England. Nowlan, whose name would later adorn the first GAA-owned ground in Kilkenny, was imprisoned again in 1919, by which time the disruption to the GAA in his home county had become widespread. As military activity escalated, no senior county hurling championship was held in 1917, 1918, 1920, 1921 or 1922. What passed for normality was not easily restored. The onset of civil war in the aftermath of the Anglo-Irish conflict prolonged the disturbance to everyday social routines and in Kilkenny, for a time at least, the GAA offered an outlet for lingering political resentments. In November 1923, the failure of the county board to approve a motion to suspend matches until detained republican prisoners were released led to a walkout by delegates of the Clonmantagh club from the county board and the withdrawal of Callan from the then resumed county championships.

By the mid 1920s, however, politics had largely been obscured by more prosaic concerns, among them the running of competitions, the acquisition of a county ground and the proper preparation of county teams. Much of this involved heavy expense. The fact that most of Kilkenny's top hurlers earned their living on the land meant, for instance, that replacement workers had to be paid to cover for them when they were training in advance of big championship games. The money was raised from grants by county and provincial committees and by public subscriptions and, though there was an acceptance that genuine expenses must be covered, there was also recognition of the potential for abuse. That sensitivities around so-called 'broken-time' payments should be acute was understandable: after all, the continued belief in the essential purity of Gaelic sports was enmeshed in the commitment to amateur principles. Speaking in August 1928 at the official opening of Nowlan Park, towards which a levy had been imposed on all Kilkenny clubs, the Bishop of Ossory, Dr Collier, spoke of his wish that the park would remain the preserve of 'clean, manly, Irish games' and his hope that there would continue to be a shunning of the kind of 'commercialism and professionalism' which he considered ruinous to sport.

If the demonisation of professionalism was a consistent motif in GAA rhetoric, there was no disguising the reality that hurling and football, at the elite level, were becoming increasingly commercialised. The 1920s and 1930s witnessed an expansion of inter-county activity and a proliferation in media coverage, though these alone did not account for the great surge in the popularity of the games. Also important were the rising standards of play and the forging of fantastic rivalries, none more so than that which sprang up in the 1930s between the hurlers of Kilkenny and those of both Cork and Limerick. When the Noresiders met Cork in the 1931 All-Ireland final, for example, it ran to three games, setting a new attendance record for a hurling decider and a new standard in terms of the quality of play. The trilogy ended in defeat for Kilkenny, who were deprived of the services of an injured Lory Meagher, the team's captain and inspiration, in the third and decisive game. A son of Henry Meagher from Tullaroan, Lory, tall and thin, was one of the game's 'supreme stylists' and would prove a pivotal influence in making Kilkenny the dominant hurling county of the decade. From 1931 to 1939, Kilkenny contested seven All-Ireland finals, winning four of them. Meagher had retired to farming by the time the last of these was won in 1939, a victory achieved in an All-Ireland final against Cork, which was played amidst a thunder and lightning storm on the same September day that Britain and France declared war on Adolf Hitler's Germany.

As war came and went, Kilkenny's place in hurling's hierarchy remained constant. In the immediate post-war decades, the rate at which the county won All-Ireland titles slowed from the heady days of the 1930s, yet its hurling traditions remained continuously nourished and strengthened by a steady flow of talent from the underage to the senior ranks. In this, Kilkenny undoubtedly enjoyed benefits that many rival counties did not. Not alone was it served by the usual network of clubs, it could also rely upon the thriving hurling culture in its schools and colleges. Pre-eminent among them was St Kieran's. Founded as a Catholic college in the late eighteenth century, St Kieran's had replaced rugby with hurling as its sport of choice in 1906, the decision coming only after heated discussion within the college and following the intervention of the local bishop. The shift in emphasis would, it could be argued, exercise as big an influence on the future development of the GAA in Kilkenny as the winning of the county's first hurling All-Ireland in 1904. For what Kilkenny became to the inter-county hurling scene, St Kieran's became to the colleges' equivalent, the relationship between the two becoming increasingly interdependent. Even as access to secondary education opened up from the 1960s onwards and more and more students were drawn to other secondary and vocational schools in the county, St Kieran's remained the standard-bearer for colleges hurling. Its importance, however, resided less in the number of provincial and national titles it won – though these were many – than in the influence it would exercise in the formation of young hurlers. In short, St Kieran's provided an education in hurling excellence. So much so, indeed, that to trawl the list of past pupils is to run a thumb across many of the greatest names in modern hurling history, among them Wexford's Nicky Rackard and Kilkenny's Eddie Keher, D. J. Carey and Henry Shefflin.

For all that, perhaps the most influential hurling graduate of the St Kieran's school was not one of its more famed players, but the pupil-turned-teacher, Fr Tommy Maher. A college contemporary of Nicky Rackard, it ultimately fell to Maher to frame the Kilkenny response to the Rackard-inspired rise of Wexford hurling in the late 1950s. In doing so, he has been credited with revolutionising the coaching of hurling. Maher's impact on Kilkenny's fortunes was at once immediate and long-lasting. In his first year in charge of the county in 1957, he delivered a first All-Ireland in a decade and between then and 1978, when he eventually stepped down, he delivered a further thirteen Leinster and six All-Ireland titles. There was no mystery to Maher's hurling philosophy; only common sense. What he preached above all else was the intelligent use of possession. 'Every ball must be used to the advantage of your colleague', as Eddie Keher, himself a beneficiary of the credo, explained it.

The message was simplicity itself, but it worked. And it endured. Maher's influence survived his departure from coaching for the simple reason that the game continued to be shaped by those schooled in his hurling methods, either as pupils, players or attendees at the ground-breaking coaching workshops he ran at Gormanstown College in the early 1970s. One of these was Diarmuid Healy, whose application of his learning in the Offaly team helped break the duopoly of Kilkenny and Wexford in Leinster and deliver a first All-Ireland title for the midlanders in the early 1980s. Another was Brian Cody, the St Kieran's graduate and James Stephens' clubman, who reasserted the primacy of Kilkenny hurling in presiding over an extraordinary run of success in the opening decade of the twenty-first century, winning seven All-Ireland titles in ten years.

The success of Cody's Kilkenny owed much to a style of management that emphasised team over individuals, but it was also firmly rooted in a thriving local hurling culture. With Gaelic football barely tolerated, let alone encouraged, hurling came to dominate the county like nowhere else. And yet the more tightly stitched into the county identity the sport has become, the more urgent the need to secure its future. All-Ireland success certainly helps in the sustaining of tradition, but the challenge of growing urbanisation and a dwindling rural community raise genuine concerns around the future geography of the game and the preservation of the same sense of place that underpins its healthy club structure. More than anything else, it is this club scene that has shaped generations of Kilkenny hurlers. Brian Cody is only one example of this. 'The Village, the parish, the people, the hurling – they mean everything to me,' the James Stephens' man has remarked. 'They made me what I am as a hurling person and in many other ways too.'

Brothers Pat and John Fielding from Mooncoin set out on their journey to the 1906 All-Ireland hurling final. The Mooncoin club, based in the south of the county, was central to the forging of a great Kilkenny hurling tradition in the early twentieth century. *(Mooncoin GAA Club)*

'A Kilkenny hurler', photographed by W. D Hogan, *c.* 1923. The black-and-amber striped jersey shown here was worn by an All-Ireland winning Kilkenny team for the first time in 1911. The adoption of a distinctive county jersey – to replace that of the club champions – helped forge a greater unity of purpose at a time when inter-club feuding in the county was rife. *(National Library of Ireland, Hogan Collection)*

Schools hurling in St Kieran's College, Kilkenny, *c.* 1952. The college substituted the playing of rugby for Gaelic games in 1906 and would, in time, become one of the premier hurling academies in the country. In 1982, to celebrate the bicentennial of the college, the annual congress of the GAA was held on the college grounds. *(Pickow Collection, James Hardiman Library, NUIG)*

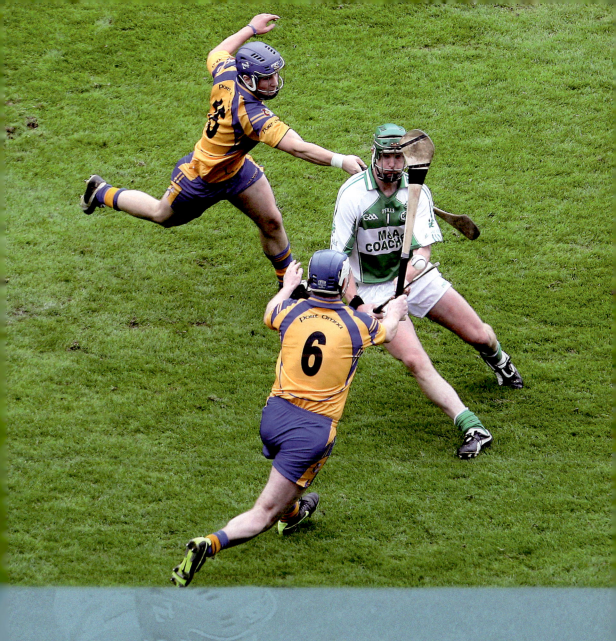

King Henry: the great Ballyhale Shamrocks and Kilkenny hurler, Henry Shefflin, eludes two Portumna players in the 2010 All-Ireland club final. Brian Cody, the Kilkenny manager during the 2000s, highlighted the role of clubs in the sustenance of Kilkenny's hurling tradition. Clubs were not there, he pointed out, 'to provide him with star players to slot into the county team, nor are they there for the honour and glorification of their star players or the county manager. Clubs love feeding talent into the county system as part of the natural process but, ultimately, their main responsibility is to cater for all their members, which they do extremely well.' *(Inpho)*

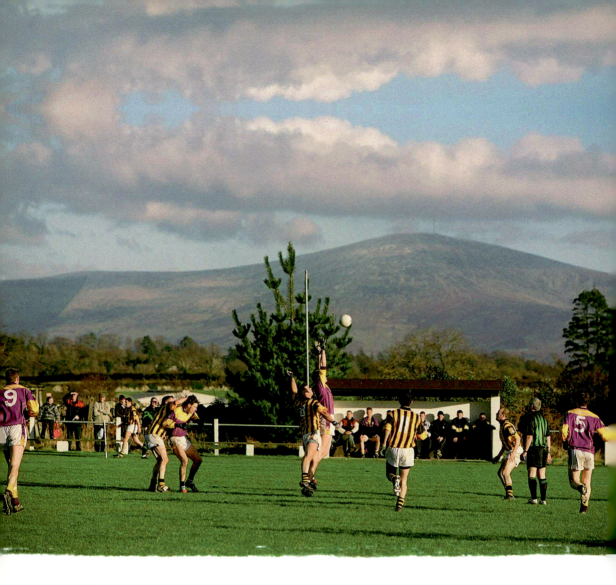

Kilkenny footballers in action against Wexford in an O'Byrne Cup match at Tom Walsh Park, Skeoughvosteen, County Kilkenny, in January 2003. Now overshadowed by hurling, it was in Gaelic football that Kilkenny enjoyed its earliest success, winning the inaugural Leinster football championship in 1887. The county no longer competes in the All-Ireland football championship (unlike New York and London), though the game continues to be played, free mostly from the glare of publicity or spectators. *(Sportsfile)*

'A lot of those chaps that were there [St Kieran's College], they went for the priesthood afterwards; on account of that they were lost to hurling then. Once they went across to the ecclesiastic side, they could hurl way over in the field but they didn't play for a team after then, that was kind of a strict rule at the time.'

Martin White, b. 1909.

'We are a most unusual county to be honest about it ... we're a small county with 85,000 people and it's part of the life of Kilkenny, hurling. I think it's in the blood. It's handed down from generation to generation ... there's a love of hurling in the people.'

Paddy Buggy, b. 1929.

'We had a bad night coming home but we were consoled by Lory Meagher. Lory came down through the train like and ... he talked to all of us: "you're only beginning" and "you're gonna win" ... Lory was a real gentleman, you know. Smoking a cigarette there in the corner and you would never think he was Lory Meagher. He wouldn't talk to you unless you said something but he was a real gentleman.'

Pat Hennessy, b. 1920.

'There'd be a lot of musicians too, playing melodeons and accordions and sure the morning of an All-Ireland, there'd be Mass at half six in the Friary and on to the station then and John's Street would be alive with excitement. Fellas selling badges, little tin boxes with little flags with a pin in it and there'd be another lad with a big board with rosettes and all that and shouting out the prices and ... it would be a hive of activity across and they'd be lads drinking too, that early, before they'd go up to the station ...'

Jim Cantwell, b. 1920.

'And that time, the Tipp supporters, ah they gave us hell. They said all we need do to the Kilkenny lads is shake the jersey, the Tipperary jersey. And they said that Pa Dillon from Freshford was the first man to put steel into the Kilkenny hurlers.'

Dan McEvoy, b. 1928.

'Unfortunately sometimes when some of the volunteers should step aside they don't, some of them believe they're indispensable ... there are times when people should move on and let the new ideas come in ... Nothing is better than experience, but as you get older there's time to move on and mature and let the new ones come in, but be available for advice.'

Honora Kavanagh Martin, b. 1944.

The parting: as Laois become the first football team from Leinster to tour the United States in 1938, the families of the players gather to see them off at Portlaoise train station. The team travelled by train to Cork, sailing from Cobh to New York on board the SS *Manhattan*. This photograph shows the crowds gathered at Portlaoise and features many members of the Delaney family from Stradbally. Included among them are (front row, l–r): Kathleen Carroll (née Wheeler); Marie Murphy (née Delaney); May Delaney (née Wheeler, the wife of team captain, Jack); infant Noel Delaney; Nell Delaney (Jack's aunt); Maria Delaney (Jack's mother) and Annie Delaney; (back row, l–r): Willie 'Bolshy' Wheeler; Michael Delaney (Jack's father); Margaret Barron (née Delaney – a sister of Jack); Annie Quinn (née Delaney – sister of Jack); Matt Delaney; Catherine McNally (née Delaney). *(GAA Oral History Project/The Delaney Family)*

Westmeath Mayo Offaly
Limerick **Laois** Waterford
Carlow Longford Leitrim
Tipperary Kilkenny Derry
Kerry Cork Wicklow
Kildare Antrim Meath
Tyrone Dublin Galway
Armagh Fermanagh
Donegal Sligo Roscommon
Clare Cavan Monaghan
Louth Wexford Down

Laois

The long-serving **GAA** journalist
with *The Irish Times*, Paddy Downey, once
recalled eavesdropping on a group of young
men in a pub in Abbeyleix. It was the mid
1980s and they were talking sport, Gaelic
sport. When their conversation ended, an
elderly man sitting nearby broke his silence to
declare that during his lifetime he had often
seen all the major trophies in Laois. 'But they
never stopped here', he added. 'They were
always passing down the road to the south.'
Downey's anecdote neatly encapsulated the
place of Ireland's most landlocked county in
the wider scheme of GAA affairs. In essence,
it told of a county where hurling and football
are enthusiastically played and passionately

debated, yet sustained without the rich nourishment of continuous success on the national stage. It would, of course, have been a surprise had it been otherwise: Laois is a small county with a modest population and the allegiances of its GAA community have always been split between football and hurling.

For all that, however, the passage of silverware through the midlands did not always go unchecked. Occasionally, as in 1986, it stopped. The moment that Paddy Downey chose to revive the overheard remark in Abbeyleix was the aftermath of Laois's National Football League final victory over Monaghan in May of that year. It was the county's first national title since winning the inaugural National League competition sixty years previously and the scenes that greeted the bridging of this historical gap were a measure of what it meant to the people of Laois. Fewer than 30,000 attended the League final, but when captain Colm Browne climbed the steps of the Hogan Stand to receive the cup, it appeared to those present that 'the whole population of the county thronged the pitch' in front of him.

Turning out in large numbers for Gaelic games is something that Laois people had been doing since the earliest days of the GAA. The story of the GAA in Queen's County (as Laois was then known) in the late nineteenth century was one of impressive rise, precipitous fall and gradual resurrection. The opening games of the inaugural Queen's County championships were held in a wintry, windswept field in Abbeyleix in February 1888 and by the time the competitions were concluded the hurling and football honours had been divided between Rathdowney and Ballinakill respectively. The championships certainly enhanced the profile of the GAA in the county and encouraged greater participation: by the following year, the GAA had grown to a point where it was said to boast 41 clubs and 1,692 members. The upward curve was not maintained. Club numbers soon stalled; then declined. The reasons for this are many, yet straightforward. The GAA was simply overwhelmed by the scale and range of the problems with which it had to contend: political infiltration by the IRB, police surveillance and clerical opposition brought on by reports of disorder and drunkenness at games. If each problem alone was enough to stultify a fledgling sporting body, together they threatened to cripple it. And they did. By the end of 1890, the year before the Parnell split, the number of clubs had fallen to thirty-three and, midway through the same decade, the county board itself had become effectively defunct. Although some clubs remained in existence and county board activity resumed in the late

1890s, it was not until the early years of the twentieth century that the GAA in Laois recovered anything like its early momentum. What changed? The triumph of sport over political distraction; the emergence of skilled administrators like Fr J. J. Kearney, who, amongst other things, established Leix and Ossory schools leagues and helped in the acquisition of O'Moore Park as a venue for hosting games; and the coming together of an exceptional group of hurlers, a mix of home-grown players and settlers from neighbouring counties.

The second decade of the twentieth century saw Laois contest two All-Ireland hurling finals in a row, winning their first – and only – senior title in 1915. At the time, Gaelic games were part of a diverse sporting culture that encompassed everything from gymnastics to golf, cricket to clay-pigeon shooting. What the All-Ireland championship victory did, however, was to underline the extent to which the GAA had been rehabilitated and to reassert its local primacy. The Laois hurlers pushed the boundaries of their sport, though not necessarily to everyone's satisfaction. Reservations were expressed that their preparations had strayed into the realm of professionalism. These concerns were given credence by the use of money from a training fund to pay in part for substitute workers so that players could concentrate their efforts in the run up to big games. The time afforded to physical training and the practice of skills was apparent from the team performances. In the aftermath of one championship victory in 1915, the *Cork Examiner* was moved to observe that it was as if 'a hurling ball had been thrown up between two teams, one side armed with stout ash camáns and the other side with frail tennis rackets. Laois were certainly not the side equipped with tennis rackets.' Ultimately, the success of Laois was a tribute to the dedication and determination of a group of men – players and administrators – who were united in the pursuit of success. In this, they represented the very best of sporting endeavour.

What were the lessons to be drawn from Laois's All-Ireland victory? According to one contemporary writer (from Cork), it was to demonstrate that success was 'not the sole priority of those who had been born into a hurling atmosphere'. The clear inference here was that Laois was virgin hurling territory, yet the reality was somewhat more complex. The historical record told of hurling in the county as early as the eighteenth century and it was fair to say that the game was as natural to parts of Laois as it was to areas regarded as its traditional heartlands. This has much to do with their proximity to those very heartlands. Portlaoise and Clonad aside, it is striking that the areas within the county where hurling has prospered most are those closest to the borders with Kilkenny and Tipperary and the hurling pockets of neighbouring Offaly and Carlow. A feature of the geography of Gaelic games in Laois is that, by and large, hurling's strongholds remain as they were in 1915. Up to the present, football in these areas is often more tolerated than indulged. The case of Castletown provides an arresting example: in 2009, the Shamrocks club was founded out of a need to provide an adult outlet for football that was not being met by either of two established local GAA clubs, whose interests lay mostly with hurling.

Not that football has had much cause for complaint. With the exception of one remarkable decade, it has been the dominant code and the most obvious standard-bearer for Laois GAA. The indisputable high point was the 1930s and 1940s. It was a remarkable era: Laois won three Leinster titles in a row between 1936 and 1938 and appeared in a further two provincial finals before adding another title in 1946. The rising fortunes of the county team coincided with the coming to prominence of the Stradbally and Graiguecullen clubs, the latter having previously been affiliated to the Carlow county board. In the end, the ultimate prize of an All-Ireland title eluded the county, but Laois made history in becoming the first football team from Leinster to tour the United States in 1938, the year before the outbreak of war brought the wanderlust of GAA champions to a temporary end.

The tour of the United States was a huge success and players found themselves feted at their points of departure and return and almost everywhere in between. Among the party of twenty players to set sail on the SS *Manhattan* was Bill Delaney who in 1939 became the only Laois man to captain a Railway Cup winning team. Another was Graiguecullen's Tommy Murphy, who by the time of his death in 1985 found himself the recipient of a slew of honours, the most notable of which was his inclusion in the GAA's Team of the Century. If the Laois team throughout this period relied on the remarkable Delaney family from Stradbally – described by the journalist P. D. Mehigan as 'the most uniform lot of footballers of high-class that I have ever known in any family' – it was equally the case that it looked to Murphy for its inspiration. Making his debut for the county senior team as a schoolboy in 1937, he was quickly dubbed 'The Boy Wonder', though his finest moment came a decade later when, in the 1946 Leinster final defeat of Kildare, he scored eight of his team's eleven points from centre-back. Murphy was then an iconic figure in the county but there were limits to how far he could leverage his sporting fame. In 1948, while still a player, he was courted by a number of political parties who were anxious to use his name to enhance their electoral appeal. Murphy declined the overtures of fellow Laois man Oliver J. Flanagan, then an Independent TD (though a long-time member of Fine Gael) who fought under the umbrella of the Monetary Reform Association. He did, however, stand as a candidate in the Laois–Offaly constituency for Seán MacBride's Clann na Poblachta party; he failed to take a seat, his chances no doubt damaged by the party's decision to stand three candidates.

Over the course of the decades that followed, success for Laois at inter-county level was more sporadic than constant. The county has fared worst at senior levels. Between 1950 and 2011, the Laois hurlers failed to win a single Provincial title, while the footballers added only one to their number in 2003. This victory came on the back of a wave of enthusiasm that accompanied the arrival of Kerry's Mick O'Dwyer as trainer; more significantly, though, it was built on an impressive record of underage achievement. Three All-Ireland minor football titles were won: 1996, 1997 and 2003. This emphasis on youth development underlined the progressive approach of Laois GAA administrators and signalled a willingness both to invest in their future and to adapt to the changing demands of the society in which it was rooted.

Catering for the sporting needs of women was perhaps the most conspicuous of these demands. In this context, the establishment of a county board for ladies' football in 1975 marked a watershed. The sport flourished. Not only did it surpass the more established game of camogie for popular appeal, it gave rise by the 1990s and early 2000s to a generation of women footballers whose achievements easily eclipsed those of the county's men. It is an undeniable truth that the women's game owed much to the infrastructure – physical and otherwise – that established GAA clubs already provided. However, as the twentieth century drew to a close and the population of the county continued to grow, many of these clubs sought to redevelop their facilities to serve their memberships better. Portlaoise was one. The town club, which was situated at the crossroads of a national transport network, had developed into the pre-eminent force in the county, but its achievements on the field were soon matched by its extraordinary misfortune off it. When the Irish property bubble burst in the early 2000s, the club was left saddled with enormous debts. In response, it has faced up to its problems and continued doing what it has always done: promoting and playing the games. 'We feel that we just have to plough on with our teams, win county championships, keep our teams going right along from Under-8, Under-10 level up and see how it'll work itself out,' Brian Delaney, a club member and son of the great Bill Delaney, the Stradbally and Laois star of the 1930s, told the GAA Oral History Project. 'In times of adversity the club has always come good and we feel that this will happen again.'

Gaelic Athletic Association.

———(o)———

Leix and Ossory Training Fund.

———(o)———

MARYBOROUGH,

AUGUST 29, 1914.

DEAR SIR,—

As you are, no doubt, aware, the Senior Hurling Team representing our County have, by their recent victory over the County Kilkeeny Team (All-Ireland Champions) become Champions of Leinster for 1914. They are accordingly in the All-Ireland Final.

It is, therefore, of the utmost importance that our men should be thoroughly trained for the All-Ireland contest, and to ensure this it has been decided by the County Committee of the G.A.A. to appeal to all lovers of our great National game for contributions in aid of a Training Fund.

The preparation of the team for the Leinster Championship was carried out at the personal expense of the members of the team. This has involved a serious drain on the means of the men, who, in many cases, had to provide substitutes to fill their places of employment during frequent special practices.

It would be too much to expect them to bear the expenses of the extra special course of training which it will be necessary for them to undergo for the playing of the All-Ireland Final. The team is mainly composed of working men to whom the loss of a day's wages is a serious matter, and they have, as stated, already sacrificed a considerable sum in this way.

Now that they are setting themselves out to win for our County the much-coveted honour of the Championship of All-Ireland, the County Committee appeal with confidence to the Gaels of Leix and Ossory and to all friends of the Gaelic Athletic movement to contribute to the Training Fund.

Subscriptions will be received by the undersigned, or by the Secretary of your local Gaelic Athletic Club, and, as our men will go into training about the 10th September, 1914, Subscribers would greatly help matters by handing in Subscriptions before that date. **UP LEIX !**

Yours faithfully,

Rev. J. J. KEARNEY, C.C., Maryborough, President.

JAMES MILLER, Mountrath, Trustee.

JOHN J. HIGGINS, Maryboro', and M. J. SHERIDAN, Maryboro', Hon. Secs. to Training Fund.

A special training fund was established to enable the Laois players to prepare properly for the 1914 All-Ireland hurling final. The fund was used, amongst other things, to pay substitute workers in order that players could take time off work to train with their teammates. Laois lost in 1914, but returned to win their one and only title in 1915. *(GAA Museum, GAA/Laois/2)*

Lar Brady, Jack Delaney, Dick Rankins and Josie Conway play a game of shuffleboard en route to America in 1938 on the SS *Manhattan*. The 1930s and 1940s were a high point for Gaelic football in Laois and it coincided with a coming to prominence of the Stradbally and Graiguecullen clubs.
(GAA Oral History Project/The Delaney Family)

The Laois hurlers in action against Kerry in a National Hurling League game, 16 October 1955. Despite the intensity of local club competition, the fortunes of Laois teams at senior inter-county level peaked in the early twentieth century. Since 1950, the county has failed to win a single provincial title in hurling and has added only one in football. *(Kennelly Archive)*

The growth of ladies' football has been one of the impressive developments in Gaelic games in Laois in recent decades. A county board for the sport was established in 1975 and, in 2001, Laois defeated Mayo to win their first ever All-Ireland title. That game achieved the highest ever rating for a TG4 programme at the time. *(Inpho)*

'There was a football tournament played up in Ballyfin one time to raise money for something, and the prize for the football tournament was a new football. So I think it finished up in dispute anyway, and someone — in Ballyfin there was a bit of a hill off from the field — someone, actually a priest was running the tournament, and the priest kicked the ball off down the field. And there was a scramble for the ball, but it finished up in a boxing match anyway, so I don't know who got the ball.'

Billy Phelan, b. 1946.

'In the sixties, when there were few cars, there was a man in Durrow had a bread van, and he used to bring us all to the matches. One night we were stopped in Abbeyleix and a guard made us all stand out in a line, and it turned out there was seventeen of us in the back, even though we only had five miles to go ... they were supporters in their own way as well like; only for them we wouldn't have been able to go.'

Matt Lawless, b. 1952.

'Phil Shanahan was training the team when I was involved ... I remember one of the sessions he asked Tommy Maher, who was in St Kieran's in Kilkenny, to come up for one evening and he spoke to us one evening in the Killeshin Hotel ... There's one thing I remember him always saying ... you wanted to be a good sportsman and that, and you wanted to be a tinker-gentleman. And it meant that, on the field you wanted to have a little bit of a blackguard about you but when you cross the line, you're a gentleman — the game is over and you shake hands.'

Mick Carroll, b. 1943.

'I noticed it with my father when he was hurling years ago. I noticed it especially when my father — I know there's six of us now in my family, I think there was four of us in it at that time — when my father broke his leg hurling, he was in a cast for I don't know how many months. He had to give up his job as a lorry driver and did not get anything from the GAA.'

Tina Cuddy, b. 1978.

'With the Celtic Tiger causing the developing of housing estates it has been seen to increase the number of members in the club — we have many underage teams on the go.'

Scott Conroy, b. 1987.

On 11 May 2008 Leitrim travelled to New York for a first round match in the Connacht senior football championship. The game was played at Gaelic Park in The Bronx. Many who attended the match were originally from Leitrim or were descendants of Leitrim emigrants. On the eve of the Great Famine, the population of Leitrim was 155,000. It is now less than 30,000. *(Sportsfile)*

Westmeath Mayo Offaly
Limerick Laois Waterford
Carlow Longford **Leitrim**
Tipperary Kilkenny Derry
Kerry Cork Wicklow
Kildare Antrim Meath
Tyrone Dublin Galway
Armagh Fermanagh
Donegal Sligo Roscommon
Clare Cavan Monaghan
Louth Wexford Down

Leitrim

In his brilliant *Memoir*, John McGahern wrote of how, in the rural communities of Leitrim, 'the local and the individual were more powerful than any national identity'. As if to illustrate this point, he recounts his memories of Eddie McIniff, who is described in *Memoir* as a good footballer, the man 'who took all the close-in frees for the Ballinamore team'. Eddie and McGahern picked potatoes together one autumn when McGahern was a boy. One evening, Eddie gave McGahern a lesson in free-taking, using the potatoes as footballs and the whitethorn hedge bordering the field as the goal. Under Eddie's expert instruction, McGahern started kicking the potatoes himself: 'I missed the first few kicks, but soon, with Eddie's help, was managing to send the occasional potato clear of the hedge'. While a seemingly innocent pastime, the practice session was observed by McGahern's father who was outraged. Because McIniff was a star footballer, a drinker and a casual labourer, the Sergeant, with his authority and local standing, had little time for him: 'The child is bad enough, but I don't even know how to begin to describe you.' Later, when Aughawillan played Ballinamore in a match the following spring, McGahern met McIniff again. Although McGahern was cheering on his own Aughawillan, it was Ballinamore, led by Eddie, who won the day. At the end of the match a crowd swirled round Eddie, but he saw young McGahern and lifted him into the air. McGahern was delighted at the attention and told him, in tears: 'You played great, Eddie.' He, in turn, was made to laugh when Eddie replied: 'We'll always have spuds and eejits.'

John McGahern is more usually remembered as a man who loved cricket. Declan Kiberd once wrote in *The Irish Times* of this love: 'At lunchtime in Belgrove, when other teachers talked of the GAA, McGahern often sat in a corner of the staff room and listened to John Arlott's cricket commentaries. After a few weeks of this, he removed the earplug from the transistor and soon half the colleagues had become Arlott addicts.' And yet the GAA – and especially Gaelic football – was a constant presence in his life. In writing about it, McGahern highlighted just how there was no escaping the GAA in Leitrim. He remembered as a young boy: 'I had watched enviously from the bank as the older boys played football, and my dream was to learn to play.' Later, in his last novel *That They May Face the Rising Sun*, a crowd returning from a football game enters a bar. After a discussion between those in the bar and the football crowd about who won and how bad the local team was, a comment is made about the team: 'They are not great but it's a day out. Only for football we might never get out of the house.' It was a statement that underscored the meaning the GAA holds for the lives of many.

Leitrim's formal involvement in the GAA began in 1886 when clubs were founded in Dromahair and Killanumery. The first championship was played in 1890; it ended with Mohill beating Ballinamore. As well as football matches, Leitrim's early clubs ran athletics meetings and in common with the prevailing enthusiasm across the rest of the country, these events drew huge crowds. Equally in keeping with the rest of the country was the decline of the GAA in the 1890s. Nationally, the GAA lost approximately 65 per cent of its membership in the early

1890s, and some 70 per cent of its clubs disappeared. Leitrim and other smaller and geographically marginalised counties were worst affected, with county and club structures evaporating. By the close of 1891 there was no organised GAA left in Leitrim, even though it appears that football continued to be played by groups of men throughout the remainder of the decade.

It was in 1904 that the modern structures of Leitrim GAA re-emerged. A county board was formed and the number of clubs in the county grew steadily. Over the century that followed these clubs expanded across all the territory of Leitrim and their names stand as a sporting and social map of the county. The rivalries that ensued between these clubs has been intense, not least because of the size of the county. Seán O'Heslins is the most successful club with twenty senior football titles, but it says much for the rivalries of the county that clubs such as Cloone, Aughawillan, Gortletteragh, Aughavas, Glencar/Manorhamilton, Melvin Gaels, Mohill, Fenagh and Allen Gaels have each won more than five senior titles apiece. Ten other clubs have also been successful in the senior football championship at some point. No other county can boast such democracy of success amongst its clubs.

While Leitrim has not enjoyed the success of other counties on a national level, the GAA is arguably more important to social and cultural life than in any other place in Ireland. There is proof of this importance. Although the county has the smallest population of any of Ireland's thirty-two counties, it has the highest number of GAA clubs and players per capita. Indeed, that in 2010 its total of twenty-four clubs could field more than forty adult teams is an extraordinary achievement in itself. Football dominates – of that there can be no doubt – but hurling has a presence and Leitrim is the leading county for Scór in Ireland. That simple fact alone illustrates the place of the GAA in the lives of the people. And yet it is undeniable that the GAA in Leitrim has suffered for its size; it has also been ravaged by emigration. The 1841 census recorded in the region of 155,000 people living in Leitrim. Just ten years later that had fallen by almost 28 per cent to 112,000. By 1901 Leitrim's population had fallen to 69,000 and the twentieth century saw further decline. By 1951 the population had fallen by a further 28,000 to 41,000. One of the people who went was John McGahern's friend Eddie McIniff, whose return every Christmas was memorable. His friends and others from the town band with whom he played the drums met him at the train station: 'After the handshakes, the slaps, the embraces, the jokes, the laughter, he was carried shoulder high from the platform. The band would lead the crowd through the town to whatever bar had been decided upon.' McIniff was but one of thousands who left, generation after generation. Leitrim's population reached its lowest number in the 1990s (at just over 25,000) before experiencing its first demographic growth in over a century and a half in the late 1990s and early 2000s.

Against this backdrop, it is not surprising that Leitrim is the least successful county in Connacht in terms of titles won. Nonetheless, there has been success and, when that success has come, it has been cherished all the more fervently for its rarity. The first great success came in 1927. In their opening game in the Connacht championship, Leitrim faced Roscommon at Laird's Field in Carrick-on-Shannon. The match was won with a goal from Willie Martin 'which sent hats and caps skyward'. Despite their four-point defeat, Roscommon lodged an objection on the grounds that the pitch at Carrick-on-Shannon was too small. This appeal was upheld and a replay was called for. The weather prevented many turning out for the replay at Ballinamore on 26 June 1927 and Roscommon were forced to start the game with some last-minute replacements from the sideline crowd as five of their team were stranded en route when their car broke down. In the end, Leitrim won comfortably and restricted Roscommon to just a single point. In preparation for the Connacht final, Leitrim enrolled the services of trainer James O'Hehir. Father of future GAA commentator Michael, he had trained Clare hurlers to win their only All-Ireland until then, back in 1914. More than 6,000 people came to see the Connacht final against Galway. In a match when tempers were occasionally lost, Leitrim ran out winners by 2-4 to 0-3. Their reward for that victory was an All-Ireland semi-final meeting with Kerry at Tuam. In preparation, the team went into intensive training with O'Hehir for the fortnight in advance. More than 10,000 turned out for the game, which proved another relatively physical affair. The referee on the day chose a discreet style: 'He stayed out of controversy, ironing over awkward situations by getting the two players involved to shake hands,' remembered one observer. Leitrim missed a string of chances and eventually lost by 0-4 to 0-2.

The Leitrim players later received their Connacht championship medals at a dance in Ballinamore in February 1928. That same month, their success was also acknowledged by the selection of five Leitrim players for the Connacht team to play in the Railway Cup. For all the genuine pride and delight at their success, there was also the lingering sense of what might have been. The 1927 team was the greatest in Leitrim's history, but it could have been still better. In 1926 key players Johnny McGoldrick, Willie Daly, Nipper Geelan and John McGuinness had been lost to emigration. All four of these players formed the backbone of the New York GAA football team of 1927 and McGoldrick's departure for New York was particularly mourned. In his fine book *Scéal Liatroma: Leitrim GAA story 1886–1984*, Seán Ó Súilleabháin describes him as 'probably one of the greatest Leitrim footballers of all time'. Indeed, McGoldrick went on to play for America in the 1928 Tailteann Games. The loss of key players had meant that Leitrim almost did not enter a team in the 1927 Connacht senior championship. The captain of that team, Tom Gannon, later recalled: 'By 1927 morale was so low that the county board wanted to regrade the team into the junior championship. It was a completely new team in 1927, we had only a handful of practice matches together.' The 1927 team, too, was destroyed by emigration. Tom Gannon recalled that the last he saw of some of his teammates was when they posed for a team photo after arriving back in Ballinamore following the defeat to Kerry. Against this backdrop, the scale of Leitrim's success is rendered all the more impressive.

For all the travails of economic stagnation, agricultural depression and limited industrial development, the club scene remained vibrant and there was limited success at inter-county level. Connacht junior titles were won in 1938, 1941, 1946, 1952 and 1962; minor titles were won in 1945 and 1956; and a first Under-21 title was won in 1977. These victories did not adequately reflect commitment to the cause, but they did at least bring some reward. There could have been more, however. Leitrim qualified for four Connacht finals in a row between 1957 and 1960, but lost out in all four finals to one of the great Galway teams of the age. The star of that team was Packie McGarty, who made his senior county debut at just sixteen in 1949; McGarty continued playing for Leitrim through to 1973 when he played his final game at the age of forty-one.

GAA secretary Seán Ó Síocháin said when addressing the Leitrim county board in 1967: 'We think too much in terms of victory and defeat and too little in terms of the social impact the games make – the pageantry, the excitement, the sense of pride and moral uplift which a sporting, manly game can engender in a whole community (and don't forget the disappointment, the distaste, amounting to disgust which the bad game, the rough and unsporting game can engender).' At the same meeting, Ó Síocháin's comments were echoed by Fr Bernie Doyle from Aughawillan who was county board chairman at the time. Given Leitrim's lack of success at county level, Fr Doyle nailed down why the GAA was still important in a county like Leitrim that was bereft of top honours: 'I want to avail of this opportunity to speak of the place which the parish holds in our Association and more importantly in our lives. While the country may get precedence at times, it is true to say that patriotism begins and ends for most of us with the parish.'

This should not be taken to mean that Leitrim GAA did not crave success as much as the people of other counties. The truth of that statement was obvious in the response to the events of 1994, when Leitrim won their second Connacht title. The roots of that success lay with the arrival of P. J. Carroll as manager in 1989. He arranged for the Leitrim-based and Dublin-based players to train together in Kells, County Meath, and the team went on a run which saw them win the All-Ireland 'B' title in 1990. The following year, Leitrim won the Connacht under-21 championship, defeating Mayo and Galway in the process. The next challenge was to improve at senior level. A key player on the team was 1990 All-Star winner, Mickey Quinn, who played for Leitrim for five years at underage level, for twenty years at senior level and then for another nine years at Over-40 level. Quinn recalled the arrival of John O'Mahony as manager in 1992 as another key moment: 'He drove us so hard. There were evenings that we would turn up for training in Kells that would be so wet that you wouldn't let your dog out in it ... We'd be thinking: "This guy is off his rocker," but he was setting an example ... He brought us to train on the biggest sand dunes in Sligo ... that toughened us up and then we were ready to move on to the next phase.' That next phase ended with a Declan Darcy-inspired win over Roscommon in the Connacht quarter-final and then a one-point victory over Galway in a replayed semi-final. More than 30,000 people turned up to see the Connacht final against Mayo. This ended in scenes of delirium following a one-point win. Next stop was an All-Ireland semi-final against Dublin in front of 50,000 people. Declan Darcy recalled: 'For Leitrim people just to be in Croke Park one day in their lives was such a proud moment for them. That's the magic of the GAA. It is so much more than football.'

Leitrim lost that match but the truth of Darcy's words were laid bare when tragedy struck the county in 2010. The Mohill footballer, Philip McGuinness, had made his senior county debut in 2003; such was his commitment and ability that he also played county hurling for Leitrim. More than simply his talent, McGuinness was loved in Leitrim for his attitude, for the spirit with which he played the game. Mickey Moran, the Leitrim manager, described him as 'the heart of our team'. When Philip McGuinness died following a freak accident in a club match in April 2010, the county went into mourning. He was just twenty-six. As his body was returned to Leitrim from Dublin, guards of honour were formed at every town and village the cortège passed through. The immense throng at the funeral confirmed the respect in which the McGuinness family were held and the importance of the GAA to the county. Mohill GAA club grounds have been redeveloped and named in his honour. It was an elegant gesture in the midst of tragedy, one which John McGahern – with his deep knowledge of the importance of place and tradition and football – would readily have understood.

Sligo, Leitrim & Northern Counties Railway

SPORTS
AT MANORHAMILTON

Wednesday, 29th June, 1932.

On above date, Tickets at SINGLE FARES (or Market Fares where available) will be issued from all Stations on this Company's line to MANORHAMILTON, available for return on day of issue only.

A Special Train will leave ENNISKILLEN at 11.20 a.m. for MANORHAMILTON, calling at all stations. Return Special Train will leave MANORHAMILTON for ENNIS-KILLEN at 8.30 p.m., calling at all stations.

SPORTS AT COLLOONEY
WEDNESDAY, 29th JUNE, 1932

A Special Train will leave SLIGO at 2.0 p.m. on this date for COLLOONEY, by which Excursion Tickets, as under, will be issued—

	Third Class Return Fare
SLIGO	1s 0d
BALLYSODARE	6d

available for return on day of issue only by 6.45 p.m. train ex Enniskillen

Enniskillen, June, 1932.

S. C. LITTLE, GENERAL MANAGER.

W. D. Perkins, "Independent" Works, Sligo.

Sports days – like this one at Manorhamilton – were run by GAA clubs and were vital social outlets for people who lived in rural Ireland. They were also an opportunity for rail companies to make money. Until the late 1940s, Ireland still had an extensive railway system, which was almost exclusively steam-operated. The Sligo, Leitrim and North Counties Railway continued to operate across the border along a single track, which connected Sligo on the west coast to Enniskillen in County Fermanagh. It closed in 1957. *(Selwyn Johnston, Headhunters Museum)*

Two young boys – Philip Murphy and Brendan Wisely – lie out on the grass, wearing crêpe hats in support of the Ballinamore team playing in a Leitrim county final. *(Leitrim County Library)*

Páirc Achadh Easa at Aughavas was officially opened by
Rev. Andy McGovern on 15 October 1978. The development of
the grounds was one of the main factors in Aughavas winning
'Club of the Year 1978'. The GAA has been a central presence
in the area for decades. A group of locals came together to enter
the first ever Leitrim championship, played in 1890, under
the name Aughavas Home Rulers. *(Aughavas GAA Club)*

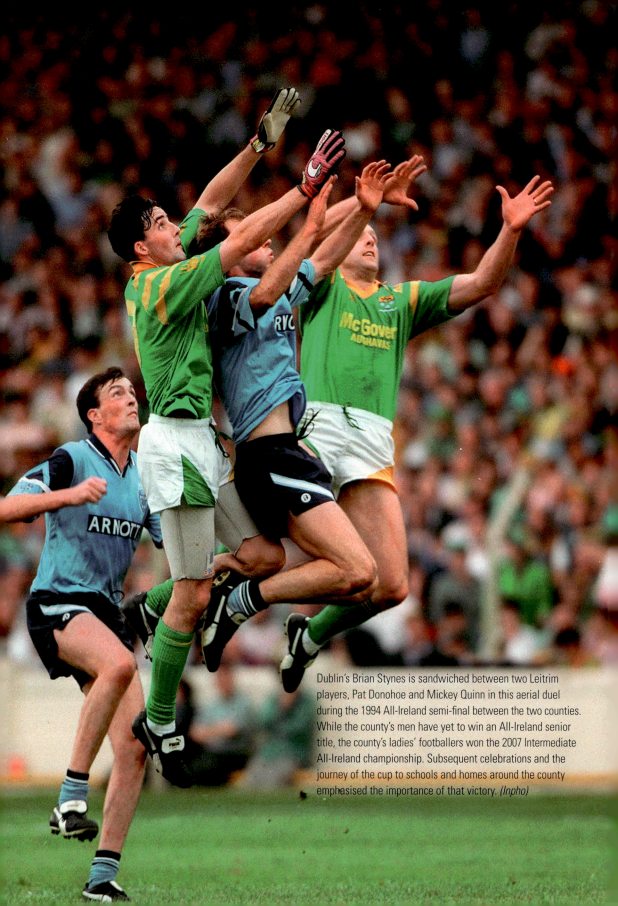

Dublin's Brian Stynes is sandwiched between two Leitrim players, Pat Donohoe and Mickey Quinn in this aerial duel during the 1994 All-Ireland semi-final between the two counties. While the county's men have yet to win an All-Ireland senior title, the county's ladies' footballers won the 2007 Intermediate All-Ireland championship. Subsequent celebrations and the journey of the cup to schools and homes around the county emphasised the importance of that victory. *(Inpho)*

'The first football I ever had, my father gave it to me, and it was two Leitrim Observers wrapped in twine ... We used to love to go to Ballinamore to play in Ballinamore because in that time, Ballinamore were after getting a new dressing room and it was beautiful. The old railway line had closed here in '59 and through a great feat of engineering, they managed to bring a full carriage down the road, nearly a mile down the road to the park and got it parked inside the gate, and that was the dressing rooms.'

Gerry Mahon, b. 1939.

'The amount of exposure referees and their families get, my God, it can be so hard on children, it can be so hard on wives, partners. To think that their loved one went out there on the particular Sunday, gave off their best and was crucified in the media ... tried by television. I don't think myself that any referee deserves that type of lambasting that indeed I got in '88. The people of Monaghan will, of course, tell you he deserved it.'

Seamus Prior, b. 1952.

'Packie McGarty was like Maradona to us.' Teddy Loughlin, b. 1942.

'If I won ten All-Irelands with another county, and if I won one Connacht Championship with Leitrim, I'd prefer it. Because you were born, you were reared, you went to school, you played with them lads.'

Packie McGarty, b. 1933.

'Leitrim's famous for its rushy fields. You can imagine what they were; little scruffy fellas that size. Fields were right ... there was humps on them, there was everything on it. But there was no such thing as a level playing pitch. That was non-existent. There might be one on the side of a hill, or deep in a valley. It was hard to know which was worse.'

Mick Kilkenny, b. 1918.

'It was an unpleasant job at times ... We had to collect money then at games. That wasn't an ideal job, because people hadn't money at the time. And people oftentimes went in back ways to matches; across the river in the Grange ... The people that were trying to organise funds had to deal with these difficulties.'

Michael Reynolds, b. 1921.

Guests attend a banquet to honour the Limerick hurling team in New York, May 1936. The event, hosted by the Limerick Men's Benevolent and Social Association, was organised as part of the Limerick team's American tour, in which they played — and defeated — teams from New York and Boston. *(Greg Mackey)*

Westmeath Mayo Offaly
Limerick Laois Waterford
Carlow Longford Leitrim
Tipperary Kilkenny Derry
Kerry Cork Wicklow
Kildare Antrim Meath
Tyrone Dublin Galway
Armagh Fermanagh
Donegal Sligo Roscommon
Clare Cavan Monaghan
Louth Wexford Down

Limerick

In 1912, a quarter of a century after they had won the inaugural All-Ireland football championship, members of the Limerick Commercials team were finally presented with their winners' medals. Not all the players were in attendance, their number having dwindled with the passage of time. Of the team of twenty-one who played in the 1887 final, five had died, three had emigrated – two to America and one to Australia – and three more had moved within Ireland, two to Dublin and one to Galway. Only ten of the team were still resident in Limerick and it was upon these that the county board belatedly conferred honours. *The Gaelic Athlete* newspaper took the view that 'tardy reparation [was] better than none at all', but the belief that an injustice had been perpetrated on the Commercials club, founded by and for businessmen and their employees in the city, left a clear residue of resentment. In a brief history of Limerick Commercials, written in 1910, P. J. Corbett, who combined the roles of player and club secretary in 1887, asked whether there was any other club in Ireland that had 'done so much for the GAA, and met with such bad treatment'. The sense of affront extended beyond the fiasco over medals. It also owed much to the non-payment of travel expenses, which the team had steadily amassed over the course of a championship campaign that culminated in their historic defeat of Dundalk's Young Irelands in a final played at a field in Clonskeagh on Dublin's south side.

The story of Limerick Commercials was much more complex and interesting than this series of dismal slights, however. It was intimately bound up with that of the wider GAA experience in the county. The club's remarkable run of success over the course of a quarter of a century – it dominated the local football scene and added a second All-Ireland title in 1896 (played in February 1898) – was achieved against a backdrop of occasionally bitter division. As it did at national level, the GAA in Limerick was no sooner founded than it tore itself apart. By the end of 1887, Limerick was served by two county boards. When the original board fell under the influence of a Fenian chairman in Pat O'Brien, a breakaway board of anti-IRB elements was established by Fr Eugene Sheehy, a Land League campaigner and parish priest in Bruree. Efforts to force unity floundered. In May 1888, on the advice of the GAA's Central Council, the winners of the separate championships run by the two boards played off against each other before a huge crowd at Croom. The two clubs that prevailed, Commercials in football and South Liberties in hurling, were both affiliated with the Fenian-controlled county board and at a subsequent meeting of the rival groupings, Fr Sheehy once more led a walkout of delegates. Sheehy developed quite a penchant for this grand gesture as he repeated it again at the GAA's National Convention the following year after IRB members subjected Maurice Davin, the Association's first President, to sustained criticism. This eventually drew Davin to resign and remove himself from official involvement with the Association he had been so instrumental in founding.

IRB infiltration, and the clerical opposition to it, weakened the GAA as a sporting body. So too did the political divisions that followed the revelations of Charles Stewart Parnell's affair with a married woman. While the GAA supported their patron Parnell, then the effective leader of Irish nationalism, many of its members took a different view. In Limerick, the Parnell split led to a collapse in the number of affiliated clubs, the abandonment of competitions and the demise of the county board. Similar disruption occurred in other counties, but the speed of its recovery in Limerick was quicker than most. By the end of 1894, a special convention at Limerick City Hall led to the establishment of a new county board and local competitions resumed shortly after. Within a matter of years, Limerick teams were back winning national honours: Commercials claimed the All-Ireland football title in 1896, while Kilfinane secured a first All-Ireland hurling title for Limerick in 1897, defeating Tullaroan of Kilkenny.

For all the internal acrimony with which it had to contend, Limerick was among the most thriving GAA units during its formative years. From the very beginning, club teams and athletes – Commercials among them – would travel to neighbouring counties to play matches and compete at tournaments. Across the full spectrum of early GAA activity, indeed, Limerick sportsmen excelled. At a GAA meeting in Limerick in 1888, for example, Dan Shanahan of Kilfinane became the first man ever to cover a distance of more than 50 ft for the hop, step and jump. Similarly, in 1895, at the first All-Round Athletic Championships held under GAA laws at Clonmel, John J. Flanagan from Kilmallock set a world record for throwing the hammer when he flung it a distance in excess of 145 ft. Flanagan would later extend this mark when he moved to the United States, a base from where he won gold medals in three successive Olympic Games. And as in athletics, so too in handball: in John Joe Bowles, Limerick had, by the turn of the twentieth century, produced a national champion of world class.

Despite the prowess of its athletes, handballers and Gaelic footballers, the sports with which the county would ultimately become identified were rugby and hurling. Unlike in other cities in Ireland, rugby transcended class in Limerick and offered stiff competition to the GAA. Nonetheless, the GAA developed a potent presence of its own in the city, while it also dominated rural life. The passion for the game of hurling was not in question, but it was not until 1910 that a Limerick club, Castleconnell, again contested an All-Ireland final and it was not until 1918 that the county eventually made its breakthrough. The Mackey family was central to the rise of Limerick hurling. John 'Tyler' Mackey, was the captain of the Limerick team that won the 1910 Munster championship. Tyler's style of play was euphemistically described in the newspapers as 'direct' and 'robust', and a noted referee of the period, Willie Walsh, described Tyler as being 'of impetuous nature'. In fairness to Tyler, it should be pointed out that he was not exactly out of place with his physical approach to the game. He himself said that the toughest man he ever played against was one Jim 'Spud' Murphy from the 'Barrs in Cork. Tyler said of Spud that he was 'never one to bother overmuch with rules'; the statement was not intended as an insult.

Tyler Mackey had actually retired by the time Limerick won that All-Ireland title in 1918 and there had been other changes, too. The years that spanned these two final appearances were characterised by major upheaval on and off the field. In a decade when Irish politics became increasingly militarised, GAA officials in Limerick were reluctant to become embroiled in these wider developments, refusing applications by the National Volunteers to use pitches for drilling exercises. The example of Limerick warns against simplistic assertions regarding the GAA's role in the separatist politics of this turbulent decade. Among the thousands of Irishmen who joined the British effort in the First World War, for instance, was Lawrence Roche, a former Limerick county chairman and Munster Council member. Roche led the Royal Munster Fusiliers in the capture of Guillemont in the Great War, an endeavour said to have been 'unequalled for bravery in the whole history of the War'. These years of crisis and war were equally years of sporting innovation. Within the GAA, an incipient professionalism was apparent in the ways that teams prepared for big games. Whereas in 1910, the majority of Limerick players were compelled to work up to the day before the All-Ireland final (which was lost to Wexford), by 1918 the county had adopted a similar template that had brought success to the likes of Clare and Laois. They set up a training fund, placed their players on a strict diet and a regime of physical fitness before taking them into camp in the run-up to major games. The approach proved a revelation. In the All-Ireland final of 1918, the Newcastle West selection representing Limerick crushed Wexford by a margin of 26 points.

Limerick added another All-Ireland title in 1921, but its hurling heyday came in the 1930s. Winning five National League titles in a row and two All-Ireland championships (a third followed in 1940), this was a hurling decade that the county came to define, if not quite dominate. Limerick changed the hurling landscape with a team whose personality was shaped by that of its greatest player.

From Ahane, Mick Mackey was born into a family of reputable Limerick hurlers: his grandfather Michael Mackey had played for Castleconnell in Limerick's first county championship in 1887 and his father, the aforementioned John 'Tyler' Mackey, had captained the county in the 1910 All-Ireland final. For achievement and talent, Mick surpassed them both: combining rare skill and a raw physicality, he was a devastating presence in Limerick's half-forward line. He was, as P. D. Mehigan, the leading GAA journalist of the time, memorably described: 'the greatest playboy and stunt artist in the game, dummying and swerving his way through, shooting goals and points with easy freedom.'

Mackey became an iconic figure in the sport of hurling, yet he played the game as much for the fun and camaraderie he derived from it as the honours and accolades that came his way. Alongside his brother John, indeed, he continued to play football and hurling for Ahane until the late 1940s, by which time the fortunes of Limerick hurling had well and truly waned. The retreat of Limerick GAA into relative national obscurity did nothing to diminish its social significance, however. A major survey undertaken in rural Limerick in the 1950s and 1960s not only underscored the importance of Gaelic games to the fostering of community consciousness and loyalty; it also highlighted the extent to which, in rural localities, proficiency at sport conferred a special status: to hurl well, it seemed, was often to attract the attention of women and the admiration and respect of men. But for many social groups, farm labourers in particular, there was no compensating for the lack of opportunities that rural Limerick had to offer and over the course of the middle decades of the century thousands left the land in search of better futures elsewhere. If the high levels of migration provided a damning commentary on rural Limerick society, the situation in the city was not much better. *Angela's Ashes*, Frank McCourt's celebrated memoir of a Limerick childhood, offers a harrowing portrayal of urban poverty. As for sport, McCourt later recalled that his native city was one characterised by sharp divides and overlapping loyalties. He wrote: 'In the Limerick City of my youth there was no shortage of sports. There were Catholic sports and Protestant sports and some we couldn't place. Nationalists, patriots, Catholics played the native games.' Despite this, McCourt recalled how, when the international Irish rugby team won the Triple Crown in 1948 and the Grand Slam in 1949, 'we never asked if the scorers were Protestant or Catholic, and we knew Gaelic football players and hurlers cheered as loudly as we did.'

The Limerick of the early twenty-first century bears little resemblance to that which shaped McCourt's youth. The changes, social and sporting, have been profound. Although rugby and hurling retain the largest support bases, the professionalisation of the former and the creation of a powerful brand around the successful Munster team has created a new audience for rugby in the city and county. The rise of rugby could have been a matter of bigger consequence had the response from the local GAA been to remain static. It has not, however. Despite an absence of senior inter-county success – their 1973 All-Ireland hurling victory is their only senior title since 1940 – and a revival of the culture of internal feuding in the 1990s and 2000s between players and managers, and managers and county board officials, the GAA in Limerick took important steps to secure its future. For a start, it focused on games and infrastructure. Participation rates in city schools, previously low, increased significantly and facilities at club and county levels were improved. This was all necessary groundwork, but given the strength of sporting competition within the county, more was required. As Mike O'Riordan, Limerick's first full-time secretary, commented after his appointment in 2009: 'With the success of Munster rugby and all the young guys wearing the Munster jersey it is essential that, in the not too distant future, we will get to an All-Ireland.'

J. J. Flanagan prepares to swing the hammer, *c.* 1908. From Kilmallock, Flanagan established several world records in the 16 lb hammer in the late nineteenth and early twentieth centuries. On moving to America, where he worked in the New York Police Department, he became the first man to win three successive Olympic gold medals in a track and field event. He returned to farm in Limerick in 1911. *(Getty Images)*

The Limerick team, then All-Ireland champions, parade around the Cork Athletic Grounds prior to the 1937 Munster final against Tipperary. Although this game ended in defeat, the decade marked a highpoint for Limerick hurling: alongside their three All-Ireland titles (won in 1934, 1936 and 1940), they won five National Hurling League titles. From October 1933 until April 1938, indeed, the Shannonsiders would play a total of sixty-five games against opposition from Ireland, England and America; they won fifty-eight, drew four and lost only three. *(Patsy Coffey)*

Mick Mackey instructs his charges as Limerick team trainer in 1955. Known as 'Mackey's young greyhounds', this Limerick team surprised many by winning the Munster championship that year. Mackey was by then already recognised as one of hurling's greatest ever players and he would later be recognised as centre-forward on the GAA's Teams of the Century and Millennium. *(Fr Liam Ryan)*

The Limerick Gaelic Grounds are lit up for the International
Rules match between Australia and Ireland, October 2010.
These grounds were opened in 1934 (although they had been in
use since 1926) having been purchased and developed by the
Limerick City Board with the help of subscriptions from members
and local businesses. The Gaelic Grounds have been updated on
an ongoing basis since and, with a capacity of 50,000, remain
the largest sporting venue in Limerick. *(Inpho)*

John Galvin from Croom attacks the Kerry defence in the 2010 Munster football final at Fitzgerald Stadium, Killarney. Galvin came to prominence as part of Limerick's first ever Munster Under-21 championship winning team in 2000, but he would be on the losing side for Limerick in four senior provincial finals in the decade that followed. *(Sportsfile)*

'A young fella might be no good at the Under-12, but if he got matches he could turn out to be the best hurler in Ireland. I remember one time ... I was involved in an Under-16 team ... they were playing a county semi-final — South Liberties in hurling, Under-16 — and there was a fella playing corner-forward and we took him off at half-time, in case he'd fall asleep and get a belt of a hurley down on the head ... he was a complete mope ... And a couple of weeks after he got transferred onto a neighbouring club ... He won an All-Ireland junior with Limerick five years after; he was a great hurler ... The bad fellas turn out to be great hurlers — if they get games and are encouraged along.'

Harry Greensmyth, b. 1936.

'It was a sad thing; when the steamer would be leaving Queenstown that time, they'd be playing "The Last Glimpse of Ireland" ... but they kept the people at home going, they'd a pile of money coming from America to the Mountcollins parish — a small parish with big families.'

John Lenihan, b. 1911.

'You had members of the GAA suspended that time for attending dances that were organised by soccer or rugby clubs, you know, like, which is a very harsh rule. But now that has all changed — they'd nearly get a medal now for going to rugby or soccer dances, or rugby or soccer matches.'

Rory Kiely, b. 1934.

'[Jack] Behan-O'Brien used tell them go away after a training session and have one pint, or maybe a pint and a half because, he said, "You come back tomorrow night you'll have to have something to sweat out of you." He said "You train without having a drink, you'll have nothing to sweat out of yourself and you'll find it very weak."'

Leo Morrison, b. 1937.

'A huge honour but a huge psychological strain ... the sheer pain of the anxiety before a match was enormous, the fear of not playing well and all that kind of thing. I suppose while you were at it you enjoyed it but the anticipation in the build-up to it was fearsome, 'twas just awful. Looking back on it I sometimes felt it was hardly worth it.'

Fr Ronnie Neville, b. 1933.

Local heroes: sods of blazing turf lead the way as Mostrim are paraded through the streets of Edgeworthstown on winning the 1974 Longford county championship. *(GAA Oral History Project/John Mc Gerr)*

Longford

The question posed in late 1892 by the Ballymahon reporter of the *Roscommon Leader* newspaper was simple and direct: what has become of the 'Gaels of Longford County'? The answer provided was as short and straightforward as the question. The GAA was all but defunct. The so-called 'Gaels of Longford', mostly men from farming backgrounds, had moved on, fleeing the Association as quickly as they had joined it. In keeping with the rest of nationalist Ireland, Longford had split over the issue of support for Charles Stewart Parnell and the fallout for the GAA had been disastrous: an organisation that boasted twenty-five clubs and over a thousand members in 1890 collapsed to the point where it barely existed for most of the following decade.

In many ways, the GAA in Longford had begun as it was destined to continue – locked in an ongoing struggle with adversity. What splenetic politics did to it in the final decade of the nineteenth century, emigration threatened to do for much of the twentieth century. The vulnerability of this small inland county to wider social and economic circumstances ensured that it often lagged behind that of other GAA units. In 1946, for example, as Ireland emerged from its wartime isolation, Longford stood as the most depleted of GAA counties, with fewer clubs than any other county in Ireland. For all that, however, the story of the Association in Longford has been about more than mere survival. Despite the relative paucity of trophies won, Gaelic games, or more specifically Gaelic football, became as deeply embedded in the social and sporting fabric of Longford as it did in any other county. This was a point made implicit in a county development plan, prepared in the year of the GAA's 125th anniversary – 2009 – in an endeavour to secure and develop the future of the Association in Longford. When it came to mapping a path for Longford over the following decade, local GAA administrators declared confidently that they would be building from a position of strength, not one of weakness. Their logic was irrefutable: having established itself in every parish, school and community, the Association's planners considered themselves well positioned to expand Gaelic games and culture. The essential infrastructure was already in place; the challenge now was to use that infrastructure to maximum effect.

The modern sporting landscape of Longford is essentially that which took shape in the late nineteenth century. Yet the roots of popular pastimes in the county ran much deeper than the wave of codification that defined the Victorian sports revolution. Gaelic games, no more than soccer and rugby, were able to build upon a long tradition of folk football. In the mid 1730s, for example, teams from Longford and Westmeath met at Aghamore for an all-in, cross-country game of football. An account of the event left by Dudley Bradstreet, a Tipperary-born spy and fortune-seeker, spoke more of war than leisure. 'I never observed between hostile armies ... greater animosities than between those two neighbouring counties', Bradstreet wrote in his popular memoir. Riotousness on this scale was not quite the stuff of early GAA activity in Longford, but disputes and concerns over discipline certainly were. Indeed, problems of this sort were sufficiently serious to impel the county committee of the GAA – which had only been formed in October 1889, five years after the Association's birth in Thurles and a year after the establishment of Granard Healy's, the first Longford-based club – to set about introducing bye-laws to impose an order on local Gaelic games. These new rules, adopted in November 1890, made clear that discipline was not simply a matter for the field of play, but extended to all aspects of the organisation and the reportage of games. Included, for instance, was a prohibition on the serving of 'refreshments' at matches, a stricture born of a fear, and some experience, that drink and sport made for a disorderly mix. Politics too was covered. Clubs in Longford, in common with elsewhere, were already prone to adopting names that honoured a heroic Irish nationalist past, yet the bye-laws insisted that their members also be affiliated to the Irish National League. This League campaigned for the introduction of Home Rule for Ireland.

These trappings of politics, significant as they were, should not deflect from the fact that the primary attraction of the GAA was sport and social opportunity. Those who joined clubs or attended games benefited from enhanced lifestyles, entry into a broader social network and access to organised leisure and entertainment. A day out at GAA events in Longford did not begin or end with the action on the pitch. It spilled onto the streets and involved music and pageantry and often, for the players at least, a post-match meal and drinks. Gaelic games certainly offered a break from the humdrum of the everyday, but they could also summon moments of unalloyed joy. When the Colmcille's club won the first Longford football championship in 1890, it sparked scenes of wild celebrations: supporters 'leaped about like children' and 'old men hugged one another like young lovers'. This kind of sporting enthusiasm did not dampen just because political dissension brought GAA activity to an effective stop; it simply found an outlet elsewhere. In Longford town and other places, the vacuum left by the GAA at the turn of the twentieth century was filled mostly by soccer and GAA members were among those who assisted in the spectacular growth of what had previously been seen as a rival code. The ceding of ground to soccer was nowhere more apparent than in the shifting sporting preoccupations of J. P. Farrell, the GAA's first county president. In 1898, shortly after he had been elected as an anti-Parnellite MP and subsequent to his establishment of the *Longford Leader* newspaper, Farrell was appointed as president of the Longford Wanderers, a soccer club that established its headquarters in Great Water Street in Longford town.

These developments were vital to soccer assuming a firm and lasting foothold in the county's principal urban centre during this period, yet the new century also brought with it the beginnings of a GAA revival. What facilitated the resurgence was the healing of political divisions and the rise of cultural nationalism. In the early 1900s, it was notable that new hurling and camogie clubs sprang from the ranks of the Gaelic League. One such club was Leo Caseys, which was linked to the Longford town branch of the Gaelic League and which, in 1904, won the first ever county hurling championship. Almost everything that needs to be said about the fortunes of hurling in Longford can be discerned from the fact that three clubs entered the original championship, yet by 2009, the number of hurling clubs still stood at only four. The simple truth was that hurling, and indeed camogie, flirted incessantly with extinction in Longford, its place within the local GAA entirely eclipsed by the popularity of Gaelic football.

This preference for football was as apparent in the schools and colleges as it was in the clubs. In St Mel's, where cricket, handball and soccer held sway until the early twentieth century, Gaelic football became one of the principal drivers of the college's reputation. St Mel's won the first ever Leinster colleges competition in 1928 and, in the sixteen years from 1933 to 1948, added a further fourteen titles, a run of success that established it as the foremost Gaelic football college in the province. The vast majority of these titles were won under the tutelage of Fr Seán Manning, a proponent of the Kerry style of catch-and-kick and himself a past pupil of St Mel's. Manning, who also occupied the role of county board chairman, imposed upon his young students a strict regime of training and was wary of indulging their sporting fantasies where he thought them unworthy. In 1948, he began the season by telling his bright-eyed charges: 'You are not too good but I'll try to make the best of it.' They ended up adding yet another provincial title and a first Hogan Cup, which was awarded for the then newly instituted All-Ireland colleges competition.

For those emerging from St Mel's, no less than those in the wider community, there was no escaping the prospect that many would be forced to leave their home-place to make a living. Emigration hit Longford hard. In the immediate post-war years, indeed, the rate of departures from Longford ran at twice the national average, the process of decline most obvious in the falling number of small farms, which tended to predominate in the north of the county. As a measure of the social cost of this exodus, the GAA served as a useful barometer. Club after club was affected. In places, teams were decimated as those in Britain and the United

States filled up. In March 1954, for example, the *Longford Leader* reported that the Cricklewood club in London then included among its number two senior county footballers from Longford and eight former students of St Mel's. What is remarkable is that this haemorrhaging of talent did not damage Longford GAA for a generation or more. Instead, the 1960s delivered unprecedented success. The improved performances of the county's footballers coincided with a period of local dominance for the Clonguish club, which in the early years of the decade had successfully appealed to exiled players to return from England and America. Clonguish players provided the core of a county team which, under the stewardship of Fr Phil McGee and former Cavan player Mick Higgins, shed the burdens of the past to win a first National Football League title in 1966 and a first Leinster title in 1968. Victory in both these competitions was remarkable in the context of the disappointments that had preceded them.

The 1960s were undoubtedly the high point of Longford's achievement in inter-county senior football, even if regrets lingered at the failure to add an All-Ireland title. In the years that followed, the county did not come remotely close to repeating these achievements, the scale of their challenge at senior level growing with the introduction of the back-door system for the All-Ireland championships. This revamp of the inter-county championships coincided with the expansion of sponsorship and television coverage of Gaelic games, as well as the redevelopment of Croke Park. These changes, spearheaded by the then GAA Director General, Longford man Liam Mulvihill, were intended to equip the GAA to withstand the challenges of massive socio-economic and cultural change that left no county untouched. Longford saw its economy become less reliant on agriculture and its people more urban-based. Up to the time of Ireland's economic collapse in the late 2000s, it even saw its population grow. Despite this, Longford remained one of the least populated counties and it was in acknowledgement of this fact that the local GAA channelled its energies into maximising limited resources. From the early 1990s, a system of development squads was established to ensure that no underage potential went untapped. It worked. By the end of the following decade, the policy had delivered two Leinster minor football championships – in 2002 and 2010. This was a stunning achievement and a triumph of perseverance and wise administration. For all their historical travails and demographic difficulties, the question as to the whereabouts of the 'Gaels of County Longford' is no longer one open for discussion.

Two young hurlers, pictured at a field in Longford, *c.* 1917. Although hurling was played in Longford in the pre-GAA period, the county played its first inter-county hurling match in 1902, when the Leo Caseys club took on Roscommon Gaels at Longford Park. When a return match was organised, a special marching song, 'The Longford Hurling Men', was composed for the occasion. *(McGuinness Collection)*

A day out at the hurling in Longford town, *c.* 1917. As this photograph demonstrates, the attractions of the GAA were often as much social as sporting. Pictured at the front of this group is Margaret (Maggie) McGuinness. She would later marry Richard Callanan, who joined the National Army on its foundation and became its Assistant Chief of Staff. *(McGuinness Collection)*

This action photograph from a club football game in 1979 shows Liam Mulvihill (second from right) playing for his local Kenagh club. That same year, Mulvihill was appointed Director General of the GAA, a position he would hold until his retirement in 2008. Mulvihill would navigate the GAA through an era of enormous social, economic and cultural change. In doing so, he oversaw the overhaul of the GAA's competitive structures, the expansion of live television and team sponsorship, and the redevelopment of Croke Park. Mulvihill is the second longest serving Director General of the Association. *(GAA Oral History Project/Paddy Egan)*

A refurbished Pearse Park, full to capacity for the Leinster senior championship meeting of Longford and Dublin in June 2006. Acquired by the GAA in 1930, the establishment of this ground – previously a barracks – as a major venue for games brought a new vigour to Longford town. In 1938, the venue played host to an All-Ireland minor and junior semi-final and an attendance of 5,000 people. The *Longford Leader* reported: 'From early on Sunday hundreds of cyclists poured into the town and a special train brought over 500 Leitrim enthusiasts. Catering establishments were severely taxed and there was little to complain of with regard to the patronage extended to the various trading establishments.' *(Sportsfile)*

The spirit of youth: Longford minors celebrate victory over Kildare in a Leinster championship game at Pearse Park, July 2010. The county would go on to win its second provincial title of the decade at this grade, a significant achievement given the small size of its player base. *(Ray Donlon Photography)*

'The Association is made up of groups of people — you have the players, you have the administrators, you have referees — and at any one time any of those groups, their position within the GAA is far more important than anybody else's insofar as you can't have a game if you don't have referees, you can't have a game if you don't have players. So I don't buy into the argument where players say "Well, we put all this money into Croke Park."'

Albert Fallon, b. 1947.

'I went to see Longford Town play and I was seen. Fr McGee, he was a good man in Longford here. I got twelve months anyway. So I wasn't gonna be out of football so we started a team in the town here, a soccer team — "Spartak" was the name of the team. We got all the players, played it … but the Ban was on at that time, so … we enjoyed ourselves playing it now, I'll tell ya.'

Jody Sheridan, b. 1946.

'Everyone on the executive was smoking. We used to have our meetings in a little room in the Longford Arms … and eleven fags or a couple of pipes all puffing, and you would not see your hand if you put it up in the air. And you'd come out and your eyes, water running out of your eyes and still we couldn't see. There was a little double door at the back at the wall; we used to open the doors every now and again to let out a wave of smoke. I'm sure if there was people passing or if they could see the window they'd think the damn place was on fire.'

Jimmy Fox, b. 1940.

'Before the GAA started it was all soccer football they played, prior to 1884 … they learned that because the army crowd used play it in the sports field, the British army.'

Pearse Daly, b. 1916.

'Victory is sweet when you're used to defeat,
all the more so when champions tumble.
On the league '66 in your name is affixed,
though the critics all said we'd be humbled …
you weak counties take heart, for though now we're apart,
though the steps of the ladder divide us.
The weak will prevail, and the strong sometimes fail,
there's nothing to beat honest trying.'

Johnny Creegan, b. 1933.

'When we won that championship over there sure they went absolutely mad. Absolutely mad … there was no other word for it. My wife came out along with me that night for the celebrations and she says "Never again". She says, "Ye should be all locked up."'

Seamus Flynn, b. 1939.

WELL DONE LOUTH

A welcome home: Louth return to a triumphant reception
in Dundalk after defeating Cork in the 1957 All-Ireland final.
(Paul Kavanagh Collection)

Westmeath Mayo Offaly
Limerick Laois Waterford
Carlow Longford Leitrim
Tipperary Kilkenny Derry
Kerry Cork Wicklow
Kildare Antrim Meath
Tyrone Dublin Galway
Armagh Fermanagh
Donegal Sligo Roscommon
Clare Cavan Monaghan
Louth Wexford Down

Louth

It was the goal that wasn't. It came in the dying seconds of the 2010 Leinster final with Louth on the verge of bridging a 53-year gap to win their ninth senior provincial title. The television pictures, replayed at length over the following days, showed clearly that the Meath forward had thrown rather than kicked the ball over the opposition goal line. A foul had undoubtedly been committed, but the score, which condemned Louth to defeat, stood. Controversies over decisions by referees and umpires are commonplace in hurling and football, but this incident was distinguished both by the context in which it occurred and the scandalous scenes that followed: when the game ended, missiles were fired from the stand and some irate supporters rushed the field. These were the actions of an irresponsible minority; the majority of the vast contingent of Louth supporters who had journeyed to Croke Park looked on, numbed or sickened by what had just transpired. Among them was the Louth county board chairman, Pádraic O'Connor. Some months later, when addressing his county convention, O'Connor recalled the almost surreal mood that hung over Louth supporters following the game's dramatic climax. 'The sense of isolation and being completely on your own, despite the fact you were in a crowd of 40,000 Louth people was astounding,' he remarked. 'Most of us could not speak after that. What was meant to be a joyous occasion was one of shock, disbelief, regret, anger and hurt.'

Why the defeat and the manner of it should cut so deep was not difficult to comprehend. In both the build-up to, and the aftermath of, the Leinster final, much had been made of the huge longing for success in the county and the fact that a gulf of more than half a century separated them from their previous stand-out triumph. That had come in 1957, the historic touchstone of Louth GAA and the reference point to which subsequent generations of players, trainers and officials would, willingly or not, be drawn again and again. In winning a third All-Ireland and an eighth provincial title, Louth's footballers had shown in 1957 just how a county team's success could sway a public mood. Louth defeated Cork in that All-Ireland final and when the victorious team, men mostly in their early to mid twenties, returned home the following night, vast crowds poured onto the streets of towns and villages, the damp air everywhere thickened with smoke from the bonfires that had been lit in celebration. The procession took the team through Drogheda, Dunleer and Castlebellingham before arriving at Dundalk, where almost 60,000 supporters were waiting.

That Dundalk should draw the largest crowd was to be expected. Not only was it the largest town in Ireland's smallest county, it was also the home place of Sean Cunningham, the 23-year-old right-corner-forward who, the day before, had scored the match-winning goal, fisting the ball to the net following a sideline free by Kevin Beahan as the game edged towards its tension-packed end. Dundalk, too, had been the cradle of Gaelic games in the county. It was there in November 1885 that the first Louth club to affiliate to the GAA was based. The 'Dundalk Young Ireland Society Gaelic Athletic Club' was founded by members of the Young Ireland Society, which had emerged in the town the year before with a view to uniting all shades of nationalist opinion in an effort to revive and support Irish language, culture and identity. The club was as much a meeting place and social club as it was a part of a wider cultural and political movement – storytelling nights and music recitals were just some of the entertainments the club laid on for its membership. That a sports club should grow from this particular milieu says much about the early character of the Association. As the sports historian Tom Hunt has acutely observed, the example of Dundalk Young Irelands is a classic case of 'pre-existing social networks providing the focus for GAA club developments'.

As it happened, the club would prove a seminal force within and without the county. Its members were instrumental to the diffusion of knowledge about the rules of Gaelic football and assisted in the establishment of new clubs across Louth and beyond. One was as important as the other, yet the very fact that Dundalk men would travel to act as referees in neighbouring counties such as Armagh, Meath and Monaghan was crucial in ensuring that the rules drawn up for the game by Maurice Davin became more uniformly applied. Familiarity with the rules and proficiency at the game appeared to go hand in glove. Within a year of contesting the first inter-club football match in Louth against Tullyallen in April 1886 – an event sufficiently important to encourage Michael Cusack to travel from Dublin to officiate – Dundalk Young Irelands beat off the opposition of twenty-three other clubs to win the inaugural Louth county championship. It was a championship run that continued up until the very first All-Ireland final where they would eventually succumb by 1 4 to 0 3 to Limerick Commercials.

The disappointment of Dundalk's All-Ireland final defeat took nothing from the lustre of the nascent Association in Louth. And yet this early momentum was not built upon. Instead, the progress that had been achieved was squandered in the destructive relationship the Association forged with radical nationalist politics. By identifying itself with the IRB and support for Charles Stewart Parnell, the GAA in the county weakened to the point of virtual extinction. Secret police reports from that time told of the retreat of a politically influenced GAA: one such report, dated 1890, asserted that the Association in Louth was 'entirely under IRB control'; another at the close of the following year reported that club activity had effectively ground to a stop.

To an extent, what followed was a lost decade. GAA action resumed in the mid 1890s, but the real revival had to wait until the early years of the new century when Louth once again managed to secure a reputation for being among the most progressive of GAA counties. While hurling was played in places – four clubs engaged with the game by 1910 and the county entered a team in the provincial junior championships – it was the 'unbounded' support for Gaelic football that helped the GAA regain ceded ground. Generous coverage in the local press boosted attendances at games, but more important, perhaps, were the simple, effective steps the GAA itself took to stimulate interest and grow participation. In 1905, for instance, Louth became the first county to publish a county annual. Lavishly illustrated and produced by Bernard J. Roe, a veteran journalist with the *Dundalk Democrat*, it was hailed as a model publication, one that other counties bent on similar-styled promotion were advised to follow. Another innovation was the introduction of a schools' league in the north of the county in 1909, the success of which contrasted sharply with the fate of a similar venture in the south of the county, where, with the exception of the Christian Brothers in Drogheda, it was reported that schools were 'singularly inactive'.

In Louth, however, the GAA in the early twentieth century was divided as much between town and country as it was between north and south. Clubs from rural Louth had few of the advantages of their town counterparts: they invariably drew from more dispersed communities, suffered from poorer training facilities and were more prone to losing their players to emigration. A new intermediate grade of competition – pitched between junior and senior levels – was introduced to encourage these rural clubs, but this did little to upset the established power bases of Louth football. As if to underline this point, it was players from clubs in Dundalk and Drogheda who dominated the teams that in 1910 and 1912 delivered the county two All-Ireland titles in three years.

Remarkably, the first of these was achieved without even having to contest a final: Louth received a walkover in the 1910 All-Ireland final when their opponents, Kerry, refused to travel after a dispute with the Great Southern Railway Company, which had been unwilling to accord a special 'excursion' rate to their large party of officials and supporters. When, three years later, the two teams were rematched in the final of a special competition organised to honour Archbishop Croke – a founding patron of the Association – a crowd of more than 32,000 descended on the Jones's Road sports ground in Dublin. Louth, whose teams deployed a ground-based brand of football that owed much to the soccer traditions of its major towns, eventually succumbed to Kerry in a replay, but these games, the first to involve fifteen-a-side teams, were a powerful affirmation of the emergence of Gaelic games as mass spectator sports. The gate receipts alone were enough to enable the GAA to buy the Jones's Road sports ground from Frank Dineen, a prominent GAA journalist and supporter. This, in time, proved a decision of profound significance: the purchase of what became known as Croke Park secured for the Association a permanent home in the heart of the capital and provided it with a focal point for all its showpiece events.

The record of Louth's early teams highlighted the relative unimportance of geographic size to a county's sporting performance. The truth then, as now, is that the success or otherwise of the GAA in any given county depended on a multitude of factors: population, competition from other sports, internal organisation, socio-economic circumstances and politics. All of these factors have played a part in the shaping of the Louth GAA experience. When, for instance, the island was partitioned as part of the political settlement between Ireland and Britain in the early 1920s, Louth found itself recast as a border county, situated on the frontier that divided the newly created Irish Free State from Northern Ireland. The GAA authorities in the county continued to look northwards in search of competition. In the early 1930s, for instance, Louth opted out of the recently established National Leagues for a year in order to concentrate on other competitions, including the Saul Cup which had been instituted to raise funds for an oratory to commemorate St Patrick's landing in Ireland and which involved three other teams from north of the then recently drawn border: Armagh, Down and Antrim. For Louth, the post-partition decades lacked the stunning successes that came before them, but they were not short on achievement. The acquisition of new grounds in Drogheda in 1926 with the support of a Leinster Council grant was truly historic, while on the field of play, the county's minors contested seven provincial finals and three All-Ireland finals between 1934 and 1941. Senior success followed and the county won five provincial titles in the 1940s and 50s, before topping it with an All-Ireland triumph in 1957.

In a sense, the 1957 All-Ireland final signalled the end of one phase of Louth's sporting story and the beginning of another. Speaking in December 1999 at the millennium convention of the Louth GAA, Terry Maher, the incoming chairman, reflected on the century of Gaelic games in Louth that was then passing. He said:

'The first sixty years had seen Louth winning All-Irelands at minor, junior and senior level. In contrast, during the past forty years, only the Under-21s and the hurlers achieved limited success.' The reality is, of course, more complex than such a quick stocktake allowed. It is also more encouraging. For despite the absence of any major titles, Louth has always kept step with wider GAA developments. The expansion of social and sporting activities – evident in the uptake of Scór in the 1970s and the introduction of ladies' Gaelic football – has taken place alongside the acquisition of club grounds and, in the early 2000s, the development of an impressive centre of excellence for county teams at Darver. All of this has been significant in further embedding the GAA in the community life of the county. A major provincial or national trophy is needed only to honour this achievement.

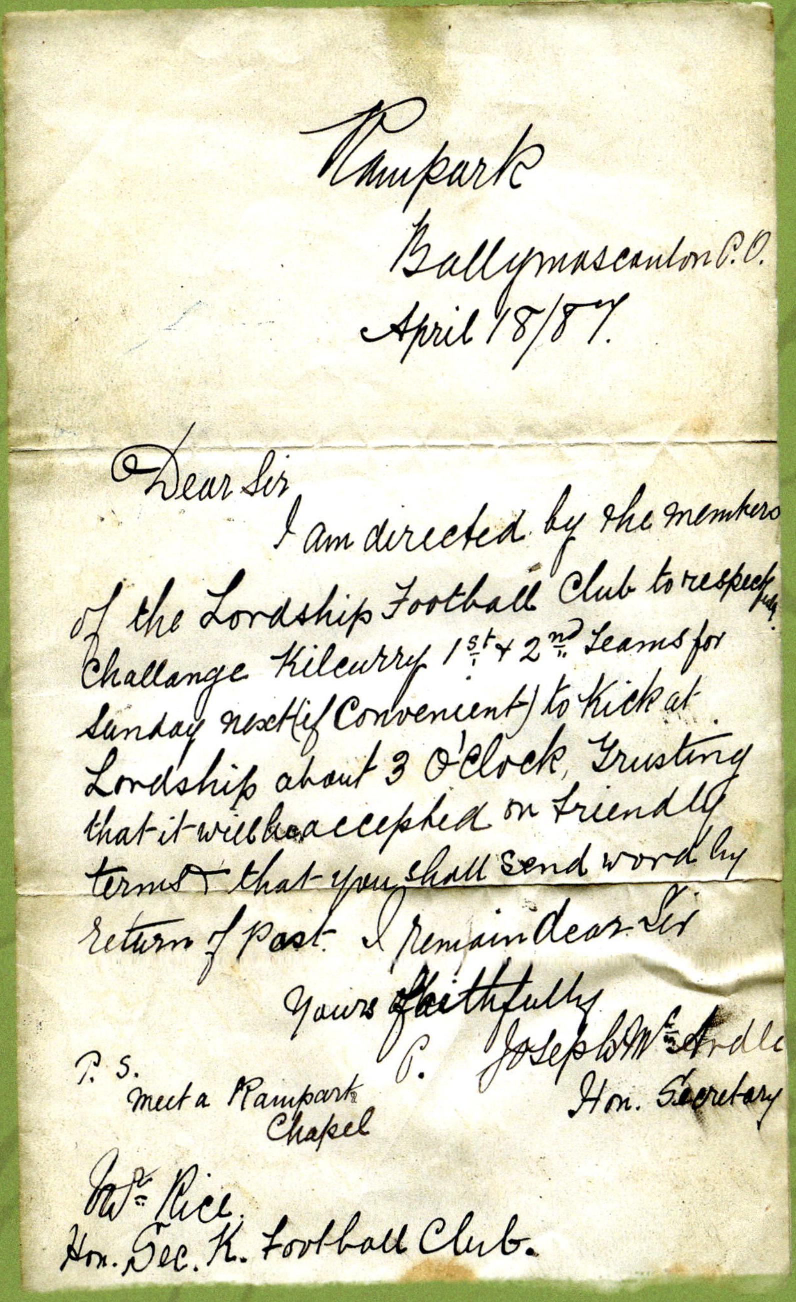

Rampark

Ballymascanlon P.O.

April 18/87

Dear Sir

I am directed by the members
of the Lordship Football Club to respectfully
Challenge Kilcurry 1st & 2nd Teams for
Sunday next (if Convenient) to Kick at
Lordship about 3 O'clock, Trusting
that it will be accepted on friendly
terms & that you shall send word by
return of Post. I remain dear Sir

Yours faithfully
Joseph McArdle
Hon. Secretary

P.S.
meet a Rampark
Chapel

Wm Rice
Hon. Sec. K. Football Club.

Before either county or inter-county competitions became properly established, many GAA games took the form of informally arranged challenge matches. This rare letter from April 1887, part of an exchange between the Lordship and Kilcurry football clubs, shows how such fixtures were made. *(GAA Oral History Project/Jim Burns)*

A Dundalk Young Ireland Society outing to Carlingford in the 1890s. It was out of this Society that the first club to affiliate to the GAA in Louth was sprung. The Dundalk Young Ireland Society Gaelic Athletic Club had a broad social and cultural mission, with outings only one of many activities organised for the benefit of members. The Dundalk club would make an immediate mark in GAA competition, contesting, albeit unsuccessfully, the very first All-Ireland final in 1887. *(Dundalk Young Irelands GFC)*

Louth players train prior to the 1957 All-Ireland final. The team at the time included two Mayo-born Gardaí (Dan O'Neill and Seamie O'Donnell), who had been transferred to work in the county. *(Paul Kavanagh Collection)*

Desolation: The look on the Louth players' faces says it all after Meath are awarded a controversial goal in the dying moments of the 2010 Leinster senior football final. *(Sportsfile)*

'I suppose it'd be fair to say, in former years up until about fifteen years ago, the football clubs treated ladies the same as the Church did; they were good for certain things — making the tea and sandwiches and washing the gear — but they didn't venture into officerships or be part of the decision-making. From the point of view of committees, in the '50s, '60s and '70s — and even into the '80s — it'd be taboo for a lady to be at a football club meeting. Somebody would say, "What the hell is she doing here?" Attitude like, you know? It just wasn't the done thing. But if you wanted tea made, or you wanted jerseys washed, "Oh, what-do-you-call-her's good at that. She'll do that."'

Jim Thornton, b. 1945.

'One thing that I like about what the club has done for the village is there used to be nearly a divide, where there would have been people of the village and then people of the surrounding area. And there was a certain amount of divide, cause there's two schools in the parish here ... in the Omeath part of it, and there was that sort of separation. But it is amazing in five years how close-knit and how everybody's come together and taken part.'

Garrett Mallon, b. 1968.

'Sometimes the fellas that win an All-Ireland are not the same fellas that are trying to win an All-Ireland. Sometimes fellas that you had to persuade they were great footballers to get them going, when they win it they think they are.'

Kevin Beahan, b. 1933.

'If things weren't going right I'd feel it more. I'd feel it, it would get to me. I wouldn't lose my temper but it would hurt me inside ... When you're there from the creation of something it becomes like a family ... It's only a bloody aul' football match and things like that, but it's not — it's more than that. It's all the people, you know all the people are thinking the same way — the players and the mentors and the supporters ... the whole lot.'

Jim Burns, b. 1930.

'Of course the whole thing about the GAA is how to fit in games for clubs; that is really the big, big thing in the GAA, how to give them regular football — because over the years, you'd come along into a fella who'd play soccer, and I asked this umpteen times: "Why do you play soccer? Why?" "Well," he said "look, like I have, I know when there's a game on. And I know they'll take part. And I get a game practically every week. The GAA, I'd be playing with you," he said, "and I'd get stop-start-stop-start. All over inter-county. Which comes first, inter-county or club?" And that is really a big gripe over the years about the club football.'

Mick Matthews, b. 1931.

The opening of the new ball alley in Charlestown in 1931 drew a huge crowd.
The ball alley was built by Michael and Tommy Regan of Barrack Street in Charlestown.
In the 1960s, the deserted ball alley was depicted by John Healy in his book,
No One Shouted Stop!: The Death of an Irish Town, as emblematic of the
way emigration ravaged Charlestown. *(GAA Oral History Project/Cathal Henry)*

Westmeath **Mayo** Offaly
Limerick Laois Waterford
Carlow Longford Leitrim
Tipperary Kilkenny Derry
Kerry Cork Wicklow
Kildare Antrim Meath
Tyrone Dublin Galway
Armagh Fermanagh
Donegal Sligo Roscommon
Clare Cavan Monaghan
Louth Wexford Down

Mayo

The greatest Irish athlete in history is Mayo man Martin Sheridan, who won nine Olympic medals – five gold, three silver, one bronze. Sheridan comes from a time that has been lost to the GAA, a time when athletics were more important to the Association than football or hurling. Sheridan was born in Bohola in 1881 and, like the two main founders of the GAA, Michael Cusack and Maurice Davin, his speciality was weight-throwing. He grew up in a west-of-Ireland tradition that celebrated strength; it was the athletics events which showcased strength that sat at the heart of the sports days organised so brilliantly by the GAA in the nineteenth century. Along with his two brothers – Richard and Andrew – Martin Sheridan emigrated to America in 1897. He joined the Irish-American Athletic Club and became the finest weight-thrower in New York.

In his prime he stood 6 ft 3 in and weighed 13 st 6 lb, and his unique combination of power, speed and agility marked him out as the leading all-round athlete of his generation. He won numerous sprinting and jumping titles, as well as throwing events, and became the dominant figure at three Olympic Games, in all of which he competed under the American flag. The sportswriters of that country acclaimed him as the greatest all-round athlete of all time. At the 1908 Games in London he won gold medals in the discus throw and the Greek-style discus throw, and a bronze in the standing long jump. He was also at the centre of a political controversy at those Games when he supported the refusal of the American flag-bearer at the opening ceremony, Ralph Rose, to dip the US flag to King Edward VII, saying: 'This flag dips to no earthly king.' The incident was part of a dispute between athletes representing America and Britain which was billed as a battle between the old world and the new, and ended in decisive American success. Irish and Irish-American athletes played no small part in this success – and in the dispute between Britain and America. It says much for the passions that flared that, at a reception in New York to celebrate Olympic success, the Irish-American athletics administrator, James Sullivan, arrived with a lion cub on a chain.

After the 1908 Olympics, Sheridan visited Ireland and gave exhibitions at Jones's Road in Dublin and in Dungarvan, Dundalk, and Ballina. Following the exhibition in Ballina, a banquet was held at the local Imperial Hotel and he presented his vaulting pole to his cousin, P. J. Clarke. After retirement from athletics, Martin Sheridan continued to work for the New York Police Department, which he had joined in 1902; he rose to the rank of first-grade detective. In March 1918 he contracted pneumonia while working a double shift to cover for a sick colleague and he died, on 25 March 1918, aged thirty-seven. His memory lives on, however. In 1932 the Mayomen's Association of New York presented a solid silver statue, the Martin Sheridan trophy, for a competition between the Mayo and New York Gaelic football teams. New York won the match, but the trophy rests in the Mayo home of the O'Dwyer family of Lismirrane. In May 1966 a memorial by New York artist Paul Fjelde, costing £13,000 and consisting of a bronze bust on a three-ton limestone pedestal, was unveiled in Bohola. Amongst the entourage who travelled from New York for the occasion were Sheridan's brother Andrew, then aged eighty-four, and US congressman Gene Tunney. The Martin Sheridan Memorial Community Centre was opened in Bohola and includes a fine museum to his memory. His five gold medals will never be seen again, however; they were melted down for the chalice used in a local ordination in Bohola.

Sheridan was part of an extraordinary story of Irish athletic success. Twenty-five Olympic titles were won by Irish athletes (some competing on American teams, others on British) in the years between 1896 and 1924. Many more took silver and bronze medals. This is partly the result of the way in which the GAA tapped into the rural Irish tradition of weight-throwing and jumping following its foundation in 1884. Over time, of course, the GAA unwound its commitment to athletics and eventually abandoned that sport entirely in favour of football and hurling. In respect of Mayo – even as Sheridan's career was reaching its peak – football and hurling had displaced athletics as the focus of local interest. Slowly, inexorably, the lure of Gaelic football in particular shifted the athletics priorities of the very sections of rural society from which Ireland's Olympic champions such as Martin Sheridan were drawn.

The emergence of clubs such as Castlebar Mitchels in 1885 and Ballina Stephenites in 1888 underpinned this process. These clubs had met in the final of the first ever Mayo senior football championship, played in 1888 and won by Castlebar. It was only with the establishment of the Connacht provincial council in 1901 that the GAA laid down the organisational structures in the west of Ireland which have sustained it ever since. In the first Connacht final of this new era, Mayo defeated Galway in the 1901 final played at Claremorris. All told, Mayo remained the dominant county force in Connacht football; of the nine provincial championship finals held between 1901 and 1910, Mayo won eight. The majority of these players belonged to the Ballina Stephenites club, who made the Mayo championship their own. Of the twenty-three championships awarded between 1904 and 1929 Ballina Stephenites claimed twenty-one.

Although Mayo were untouchable in Connacht, they struggled at All-Ireland level. There was, however, success in the Croke Cup – an inter-county competition that ranked just below the All-Ireland championship in prestige. After a series of narrow defeats in finals and semi-finals, Mayo defeated Kerry in the 1908 final played at Jones's Road, courtesy of a crucial goal which was described in the press at the time: 'Fully fourteen men were now in front of the goal, and there was a desperate scrummage for possession. Ryder and [G.] Fitzgerald hovered round the outside, eager as hawks; the ball came out from the scrum towards Fitzgerald; he was on it like a shot, and amidst deafening cheers he landed a beautiful goal, beating the Kerry custodian in hollow style.' After the game, *The Western People* reported that a 'tar barrel was lighted in Crossmolina in honour of their success' and that there had 'been no local event of recent times that has caused at all such a remarkable display of enthusiasm'. The cup was retained the following year; it was to be Mayo's last national success until the 1930s. Good teams continued to represent the county, but All-Ireland finals were lost in 1916 (to Wexford) and in 1921 (to Dublin). Eoghan Corry records, in respect of the 1921 final, that the 'spectators watched a new tactic in operation that day. Mayo point scorer Sean Lavin was one of the first to perfect the hand-to-toe technique and was later to represent Ireland in the sprints at the 1924 Olympics.' The technique does not appear to have helped his team much, however, as Dublin romped to a 1-09 to 0-2 victory.

There seemed to be no change in fortunes when another All-Ireland final was lost to Kerry in 1932 (giving that county a four-in-a-row of titles). And yet the ultimate success was just around the corner. Indeed, the 1930s brought extraordinary success at all levels. Firstly, on 8 October 1933, 'under a blazing Autumn sun at Croke Park', Mayo hammered Donegal by a huge score to win the All-Ireland junior title. Secondly, Mayo won the All-Ireland minor title in 1935. That championship had been inaugurated in 1929 and Mayo had been prominent from the start, losing the 1930 and 1933 finals. Thirdly, Mayo senior footballers went on an extraordinary run of success in the National Football League. They won their first National Football League title in 1934 when they defeated Dublin. Mayo were captained on that day by Gerald Courell who later recalled: 'I can still remember the cold feel of the Cup in my hands as I took it and the feeling it sent through me. It was the first time a Mayo Captain had ever held the trophy in the history of the game; it was the first time the title went to Connacht, and it brought Mayo out of the football wilderness on a record-breaking run of six National League titles in a row.' Such was Mayo's dominance that they went fifty-seven games without defeat in league football.

In the midst of league success came the greatest triumph of all. By 1936 Mayo

– as Terry Reilly and Ivan Neill wrote in their fine book *The Green Above the Red* – 'had formed the nucleus of a fine side, bringing together at midfield for the first time the powerhouse partnership of Henry Kenny and Patsy Flannelly, which was to give the team the platform to attain the highest rewards'. In Connacht they defeated Galway, the reigning All-Ireland champions; in the All-Ireland semi-final they beat Kerry; and then in the All-Ireland final, 50,160 people turned up to see a one-sided game with Laois, which finished with Mayo eighteen points clear, 4-11 to 0-5. It is worth noting that this victory confirmed the dominance of Connacht in the second half of the 1930s. As well as Mayo's hegemony on the National Football League and their All-Ireland success, Galway won two All-Ireland senior football titles and Connacht won the Railway Cup four times.

A reminder that success in sport is almost always cyclical came with the emergence of Roscommon as the dominant power in Connacht in the 1940s – winning two All-Irelands in the process. Mayo had rebuilt a team by the end of the 1940s, however, which saw them lose only narrowly to Cavan in the 1948 All-Ireland final, before going on to win back-to-back titles in 1950 and 1951. The backdrop to these victories was the demand by the players on the team that the standards of preparation be improved. Collective training was redesigned. For example, former players Gerald Courell and Jackie Carney had the team in great shape following a 'very methodical yet relaxing routine in Ballina'. More than that, however, the Mayo team was filled with great footballers who offered fine leadership. From the captain Seán Flanagan in the backline, to Pádraig Carney and Éamonn Mongey in midfield, and on to Tom Langan at full-forward, these were footballers of the highest calibre. Langan was described by the brilliant Galway footballer, Jack Mahon, as 'one of the greatest of all full-forwards. There is and always will be only one Langan.' Such was the appeal of these players that just short of 80,000 spectators turned out to see them defeat Meath in the 1951 All-Ireland final.

Mayo's victories in 1950 and 1951 are all the more notable for the fact that they were achieved against the backdrop of economic disaster. This is most obviously seen in the population of the county. In 1841 a scarcely credible 388,887 people lived in the county of Mayo; by 1901 this had fallen to 199,166; by 1951 it had fallen again to reach 141,867; and the decline continued all the way to 1971 when it reached 109,019. All told, these were years of poverty, hardship and persistent decline. Most people were still reliant on agriculture; income was low and families were often dependent for their survival on money remitted by relatives living abroad, or from seasonal work. Emigration destroyed the life of the county. This is most memorably chronicled by the journalist John Healy in his extraordinary 1968 book, *No One Shouted Stop!: The Death of an Irish Town*. The book detailed Healy's early years growing up in Charlestown, and graphically portrayed the economic and social decimation of the town's population over those years. Healy researched what became of his senior class of 1944 after they left Lowpark National School and how this affected the town's ability to sustain itself. Of the twenty-three students, only three remained in Charlestown, while twelve had left the country completely. Healy laid bare the impact on the next generation: 'Out of a random class of 23, three remain in the town itself and have given it a renewal of four children. That class has renewed North America with the gift of 24 children; it has renewed Britain with 10 children and Dublin with seven. In any permutation, Ireland loses heavily. Ten of the 23 got some sort of post-primary education: not one of the class, as far as I am aware, attended any of the universities of Ireland.' Healy's book was a powerful, emotional, overwhelming tirade against the failures of Ireland and the impact of those failures on the lives of the ordinary citizens of the new republic.

The story of Mayo football in the decades that passed after the 1950s has been wonderfully described by Keith Duggan in his book *House of Pain: Through the Rooms of Mayo Football*. Duggan chronicles the failure to win even a Connacht title in the 1970s. He rummages through the ruins of defeat in five All-Ireland finals, stretching from the 1980s through to the new millennium. The memories of 1951 are fading by the year – and yet there is a magnificence to the style of Mayo football that is indisputable. The quality of its club football is equally undeniable. It is a quality that has seen both Crossmolina and Ballina Stephenites crowned All-Ireland club champions since the year 2000. The yearning for another senior All-Ireland title is immense. It is a yearning rooted not simply in a desire for success in itself, but to push back against the cruelty of more than a half century of defeat.

As Duggan wrote: 'The fascinating and sometimes tortured relationship that Mayo has had with the All-Ireland football championship has made for a sometimes uncomfortable and voyeuristic spectacle. Several Mayo teams and many thousands of Mayo people have had their morale crushed on big days in

Croke Park. They have dealt with those defeats with eloquence and dignity. And most importantly, they have always returned, with big-hearted, open, skilful teams and behind them the Mayo public – a chorus that is, when it comes down to it, incapable of true cynicism. It seems true to say that the next time Mayo qualify for an All-Ireland final, fear will grip the county as much as excitement. But they will turn up and they will honour the fixture. And some year they will win it all.'

Returned Olympic champion Martin Sheridan judges the height to be jumped in the pole vault competition during his appearance at a Sports Day in aid of the Ballina Stephenites in 1905. Also in the picture are T. S. Moclair, Tom Boshell, Michael Padden, Pakie Farmer, Dinny 'Kerry' O'Connell and John Hanlon. *(Terry Reilly)*

During the 1950s, Pádraig Carney flew back and forth from America to play for Mayo in championship football. It earned him the sobriquet, 'The Flying Doctor.' Here, he rests after his journey by plane from New York. *(National Library of Ireland, Irish Independent Collection)*

Club football in Mayo stirs ancient passions in generation after generation. Here, Ger Feeney skips past Michael Kenny when Ballintubber played Aghamore in the 1970 Mayo intermediate football semi-final in Ballinrobe. *(The Western People)*

A group of young boys kick football
on Achill Island in the early 1990s.
(Corbis)

'My hero is ... my dad, because he helped me to learn Gaelic.'

Maggie, b. 1999, St Aidan's N.S., Kiltimagh.

'Always something to prepare, look forward to, and look back on afterwards.'

James Reddiough, b. 1968.

'I was in Thailand recently, and watched a game out in a barn streamed over the web from Mullingar. Amazing stuff.'

Adrian Hession, b. 1978.

'We used to travel to Castlebar and Tuam. My uncle brought me to my first match in Croke Park in the early 1970s to see Galway playing Offaly. We would ask questions about our team and ate Tayto crisps. We would stop for a cup of tea halfway to the game and have a bit to eat. We used to stop at "Harry's" in Kinnegad ... I played in the 1989 All-Ireland final when nearly 80,000 people attended the match. It was a great match but we lost by a few points. I always wanted to win an All-Ireland senior medal, but it wasn't meant to be. There was terrible disappointment for days and weeks after.'

Kevin McStay, b. 1962.

'Our National School teacher was a footballer himself and always played with us at lunch time and sometimes got carried away and went on longer.'

Martin Forkan, b. 1940.

'They used to kill pigs, and there would be a big pig market in Bonniconlon and they killed the pigs and the refuse would be thrown ... back in the fields and the local lads would go out getting the pigs bladders and blow them up and it might last them, it would surprise you how tough they were ... There'd be no goalposts, just two jackets one either side for goalposts and sometimes you couldn't so well leave your jacket because the owner of the land might come and you had to be quick, whoever's jacket was there for the goalposts, to have it gone and run. People didn't like to see their bit of land tramped, I don't know was it any harm ... At that time then was a lot of migration, and round this area they'd go to England on the twentieth of June, what they'd call the hay farmers, they go into Lancashire ... and once that would come you'd hardly have a team left. Most of the young men would go and even before that I remember some of them were afraid to play football in case they'd get hurt.'

Paddy Weir, b. 1923.

As the population of Meath has expanded, many clubs have been forced to upgrade their facilities to cater for the extra demand and to serve their members' interests better. This photograph shows some of the splendid facilities opened in December 2007 by the Donaghmore/Ashbourne GAA Club. *(Fred Reilly)*

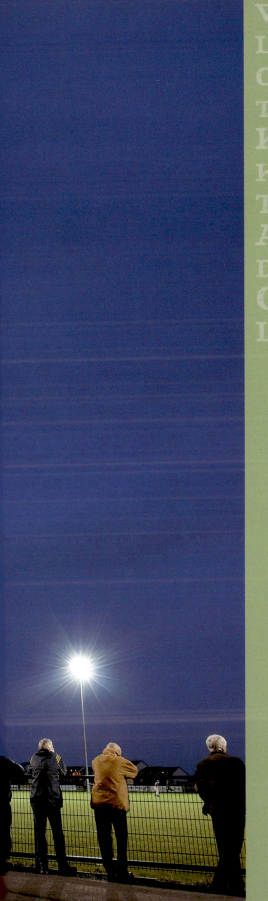

Westmeath Mayo Offaly
Limerick Laois Waterford
Carlow Longford Leitrim
Tipperary Kilkenny Derry
Kerry Cork Wicklow
Kildare Antrim **Meath**
Tyrone Dublin Galway
Armagh Fermanagh
Donegal Sligo Roscommon
Clare Cavan Monaghan
Louth Wexford Down

Meath

In the summer of 1897, John P. Timmons rose to address a meeting of the Meath GAA county committee in Navan. He had a lot to get off his chest. Looking ahead to the following year's centenary commemoration of the 1798 Rebellion, Timmons, the county committee's chairman, spoke passionately of the need for the GAA to concentrate its energies exclusively on the promotion of sport and to cast itself explicitly as non-political and non-sectarian. 'Sport and politics,' he said, 'are incompatible, and it would be most inconsistent and unwise to associate them – it is like driving a hearse to a wedding, or launching a pleasure boat on waters that have already wrecked a life-boat.' Timmons had good reason to decry the enmeshing of the GAA in political affairs. Over the previous decade, the GAA in his own county, initially among the best organised, had plunged into disrepair. Club numbers collapsed, the frequency of games slowed to a trickle and membership fell away as quickly as it had been built up.

None of this, of course, marked Meath out as anything peculiar or different from other counties. The experience of decline was mirrored across the country, as were its causes. The fact that the county found itself the object of Fenian design and clerical opprobrium merely made it typical of the late-nineteenth-century GAA experience. A simple interplay was at work: the more influence the IRB gained within the Association, the more hostile the Catholic Church became towards it. In Meath, a campaign of opposition to the fledgling GAA was led by the local Bishop (Bishop Nulty) and supported by his priests, one of whom went so far as to suggest that the British government had been involved in bribing Gaelic players to enrol Fenians in order to strengthen the argument against the granting of Home Rule for Ireland. This was a charge that had to be refuted on the floor of the House of Commons. Clerical opposition only hardened when the revelations broke of Charles Stewart Parnell's affair with Katherine O'Shea and the GAA weighed in with support for their patron, who had previously been an MP for the Meath constituency.

It was against this backdrop of division that the remarks of John P. Timmons in 1897 are best understood. However, it was a forerunner of Timmons as chairman of Meath's county committee who led the GAA's change in direction and the shift in emphasis back towards the playing fields. Richard T. Blake, a well-known referee from Navan, had been elected to the post of chairman in April 1894 and immediately set about delivering on two core objectives: the revival of competition and the reform of Gaelic football. A Meath county football championship was promptly organised and Gaelic football, a code only invented by the GAA in early 1885, was refined with the introduction of new rules covering such matters as the standardisation of the size of footballs, the introduction of linesmen to assist referees and the abolition of the practice of 'going for the man' rather than the ball.

Blake's influence extended well beyond his home county. A figure of national importance, he became Secretary of the GAA in 1895 where his undimmed zeal for reform saw the prohibition of political discussions at GAA meetings and the abolition of a ban on the playing of foreign games. It was the muted nature of

Blake's nationalism that ultimately saw him ousted as GAA Secretary, yet his short tenure had far-reaching consequences. He left the GAA in a far healthier state than he found it and though some of his reforms were reversed, others stuck. His revamping of Gaelic football, for instance, made it safer to play and better to watch. In time, it would also prove a vital step in the evolution of the modern game. Ultimately, the moderation of Blake's nationalism saw him removed from the GAA by a new cohort of GAA activists who rose through the Association in the aftermath of the centenary celebrations of the 1798 Rebellion. This new cohort were determined that the GAA would fulfil a broader cultural mission – a mission which would be directed towards the achievement of political independence for Ireland. Games would matter, but not as much as the ideal of the construction of an Irish-Ireland.

Blake was so outraged by his treatment by the men who deposed him in 1898 that he published a pamphlet, *How the GAA was Grabbed,* in which he outlined the nature of his treatment. In many respects, the great disappointment is that the man who was central to reinventing Gaelic football should have been ostracised even as his work was in progress; one wonders where eventually Blake would have brought the game of football. It is perhaps not surprising that the sport that Blake did so much to shape was the one most favoured in his home county. From the very inception of the GAA, Meath was committed to football. Dowdstown, winners of the first county title, were one of only twelve clubs to contest the first All-Ireland championships in 1887 and in 1896 the Navan-based Pierce O'Mahony's club became the first Meath side to reach an All-Ireland final. Hurling, in contrast, was virtually non-existent during this time. Indeed, it was not until the early 1900s that hurling began to be organised in anything like the same way as football. Eight clubs participated in the inaugural county hurling championship in 1904, the same year as two teams of pioneering women, members of the Keatings and Cúchulainns clubs from Dublin, played in the very first recorded camogie match at the Meath Agricultural Society Grounds (later redeveloped as Páirc Tailteann). Hurling, however, has remained a marginal interest and over the course of the following century, in spite of some notable successes at junior inter-county grades, the game was inclined to be more agonised over than played. There have been some outstanding hurlers produced and some fine club matches played, but meaningful inroads at inter-county level have remained elusive.

Within Meath's GAA clubs, there was simply no supplanting Gaelic football. And yet, for all the game's evident popular appeal, success was slow in coming. In the early decades of the twentieth century the county's ambitions were thwarted by local rivalries, disputes over county team selection and the strength of its provincial opposition. In fact, it was not until the post-Second World War years that a Meath team finally won an All-Ireland senior title. And not just one: after winning the Sam Maguire cup for the first time in 1949, they returned again to claim it for a second time in 1954, losing another final in between. The two victories were striking for the contrast in preparations that underpinned them: prior to the 1949 All-Ireland final, for instance, the Meath team retreated into camp where, under the direction of Fr Pat Tully, then chairman of the county board, they were subjected to an 'almost military regimentation schedule of training'. The players' days were organised from start to finish, with time for morning Mass and evening prayers factored in. No such approach was possible in 1954, the GAA having moved earlier that year to ban the practice of collective training for reasons of cost and for fear of a creeping professionalism. In its place, Meath, and their opponents Kerry, resorted to playing trial matches amongst themselves, the frequent match-play helping, *The Irish Times* GAA correspondent believed, to hone fitness and develop 'team-ship and understanding'.

A central figure in Meath's emergence as a major football force during this period was Peter McDermott, a man of restless energy and multiple roles: in 1954, the slightly built Donaghmore man had the remarkable distinction of combining his duties as player and captain with that of team selector and county secretary. McDermott afterwards acted as an adviser to the great Down team of the early 1960s before assisting his own county to further All-Ireland glory later that same decade. But perhaps McDermott's most remarkable endeavour concerned his contribution, alongside Australian entrepreneur Harry Beitzel, to the forging of a competitive international outlet for Gaelic football. The visit of an Australian Rules team to Ireland in 1967 and a return trip by the Meath footballers the following year effectively laid the basis for a full-scale international exchange, which the governing bodies of the two sports established in the mid 1980s. The 'hybrid' code that eventually evolved was a compromise not only between two distinct games, but between two different sporting cultures. The impact of this sporting experiment was ultimately mixed. But for all its obvious flaws, it not only led to rule changes that enhanced Gaelic football as a spectacle, it also afforded leading players a unique opportunity to represent their country in an international sport.

As it happened, the revival of GAA links with Australia in the mid 1980s coincided with a resurgence in the fortunes of Meath football. After a decade or more in the doldrums, the county's re-emergence was largely attributable to the appointment as county manager of a herbalist from Dunboyne with a background in hurling. If Seán Boylan was a most unlikely Meath football manager, he was also a charismatic and hugely successful one. His career spanned two decades and yielded four All-Ireland titles, two each in the 1980s and 1990s. Outside their own county, Boylan's teams became more admired than loved, their reputation being built as much upon their toughness and resilience as their unquestionable craft and flair. This uncompromising image was forged in the course of intense, and occasionally thrilling, rivalries with Cork in the 1980s and Mayo in the 1990s, but mostly with Dublin, against whom they would famously require four matches to decide the outcome of a first-round Leinster championship match in 1991. Meath eventually prevailed in these matches and, in a campaign remarkable for being something of an emotional rollercoaster, ended with a narrow loss to Down in the All-Ireland football final.

Meath's proximity to the capital city brought challenges beyond the playing field, however. When the Irish economy temporarily boomed in the late 1990s and early 2000s, the population expanded at a rapid rate. The figures were startling: in the fifteen years from 1991 to 2006, the number of people residing in the county increased by more than 50 per cent. Such an influx might reasonably have been expected to weaken community cohesion and undermine identity, yet evidence emerged to suggest that in many of these enlarged areas, the GAA acted as a valuable social glue. In places like Ratoath, where the population increased tenfold in under twenty years, the involvement of parents and their children in the local GAA club was recognised by sociologists as a significant factor in the high levels of social and place attachment that were found. While getting people into the GAA clubs was one challenge, catering effectively for their needs was another. In Meath, as elsewhere, the raising of the profile of the county team, in tandem with the expansion of the inter-county scene from the mid 1990s, led to an increased squeezing of club activity and a growing disenchantment among club players. Their grievances were well founded. A survey of club players in Meath in 2010 revealed, for instance, the extent to which the poor planning of fixtures – manifest in the inadequate notice of games, their concentration into short time-frames and long periods of idleness – impacted detrimentally not only upon their enjoyment of the games, but their wider lives. More than a century after John P. Timmons' plea for less politics and more play in the GAA, then, it appears that there is still much work to be done. Politics may no longer intrude into GAA business as once it did, but the grievances of the rank and file of club members suggest that problems around the provision of play have yet to be adequately resolved.

C.º MEATH AGRICULTURAL SHOW. 1906.

High fashion at the County Meath Agricultural Show in 1906, held at the Navan Showgrounds, now the site of Páirc Tailteann. In the early decades of the twentieth century, the GAA rented these grounds for matches from the Meath Agricultural Society, but at a rate which the local Association claimed was far greater than that charged to the Meath Cricket Club. In September 1913, an editorial in *The Gaelic Athlete* raged that 'the Gaels of Meath are subsidising the Agricultural Society in order that the Agricultural Society may subsidise the cricketers. What a farce!' *(Michael O'Brien)*

A place of their own: members Seán Nolan and Peter Landy of Syddan GFC look out over their playing field at Ludlow Park. The land which the club now calls home was donated to them free of charge in the 1960s by Tommy Ludlow. Since then, the grounds have been subject to ongoing improvement. Ludlow Park was officially opened in 1971 and a pavilion with dressing rooms was added in the 1980s. The following decade, the entire grounds were completely refurbished. *(Syddan GFC)*

Meath players (l–r) Peter McDermott, Brian Smyth, Frankie Byrne and Paddy Meegan (kneeling) prepare for a relaxing game of tennis at their training camp in the Gaeltacht Hostel, Gibbstown, prior to the 1949 All-Ireland final. A journalist who visited the camp described the players' routine as 'rigorous but not severe.' Each day began and ended with prayers. *(Irish Independent)*

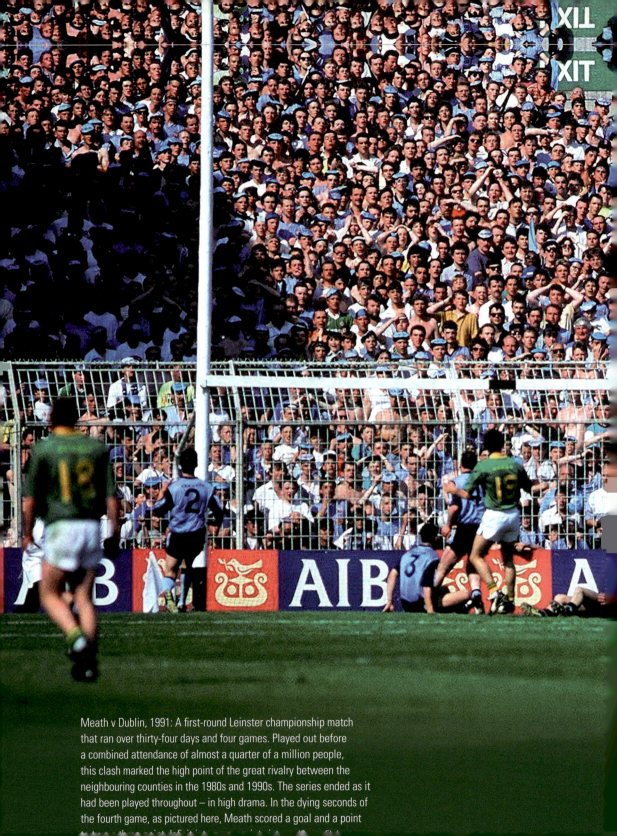

Meath v Dublin, 1991: A first-round Leinster championship match
that ran over thirty-four days and four games. Played out before
a combined attendance of almost a quarter of a million people,
this clash marked the high point of the great rivalry between the
neighbouring counties in the 1980s and 1990s. The series ended as it
had been played throughout – in high drama. In the dying seconds of
the fourth game, as pictured here, Meath scored a goal and a point

Peter McDermott (with cap) is assisted by teammates Matty McDonnell and Brian Smyth in preventing Cavan from breaking out of their defence in the 1949 All-Ireland final. The game, which ended in a scoreline of 1-10 to 1-6, saw Meath claim their first ever All-Ireland title. *(Hogan Stand)*

'My aunt lived in Gardiner Street, which is where we'd park the car, have a bit of grub with her. And this went on Sunday after Sunday because Meath were having a great run, but my aunt told me many years later ... I can't remember, it was some time between 1949 and 1954, we went out in an early round and she said "I'm sure my prayers were answered, because I prayed that Meath would get beaten in the first round, I had enough of you".'

Ollie Mulligan, b. 1946.

'There was no phones even ... to ring and find out if the meeting was on or off or on. You'd only find out after riding the bike to Navan that there was none. Still fellas kept coming. They'd be back again the following week just the same.'

Patsy Duff, b. 1929.

'With the Meath colours, and as a farmer, I recall being opportunistic and making Meath flags from green and yellow fertiliser bags. We could mass produce them and wrap them around telephone poles up and down the roads.'

Francis Ludlow, b. 1980.

'I'm in Ratoath parish as well, but I did play my juvenile football with Ratoath and won a minor championship with them but I always had Dunshaughlin in mind ... We lived, slept and done everything we wanted to do; shopping and church and all, we always went to Dunshaughlin and that's just the way it was. Strange as it seems, the next generation has come along now and I'm in a position where my son actually plays with Ratoath, having played from juvenile level up under the parish rule, so I couldn't break his neck to come to Dunshaughlin.'

Jim Smith, b. 1961.

'I ran a camp in Gormanstown college over the Easter holidays and we brought in all the lads that we had on the panel and they all paid a tenner each out of their own pockets ... And ran things in Gormanstown college and we played matches as well. That was in '75. At about the same time, we used to play matches in what we used to call the North East minor league and that involved Louth, Meath, Down and Armagh and we used to play matches with them and that used to get Meath ready because prior to that, what used to happen in Meath was, you'd have a trial or two on the two Saturdays before you played the first round of the Leinster minor and then you go out and run into some good team.'

Pat O'Neill, b. 1938.

Monaghan players are carried from the field following
their victory over Kildare in the 1956 All-Ireland junior
football championship 'home' final at Carrickmacross.
(Rose O'Rourke and family)

Westmeath Mayo Offaly
Limerick Laois Waterford
Carlow Longford Leitrim
Tipperary Kilkenny Derry
Kerry Cork Wicklow
Kildare Antrim Meath
Tyrone Dublin Galway
Armagh Fermanagh
Donegal Sligo Roscommon
Clare Cavan Monaghan
Louth Wexford Down

Monaghan

'The life of the game not only in Monaghan, but all of Ulster.' This was how *The Gaelic Athlete* newspaper described the contribution of Eoin O'Duffy to the development of the GAA in the second decade of the twentieth century. All told, O'Duffy was an extraordinary man – loved and loathed, respected and derided – who was a member of the Supreme Council of the IRB and an IRA commander during the War of Independence. Later, O'Duffy was a central figure in the creation of modern Ireland in his role as the first commissioner of An Garda Síochána, before leaving a much more dubious legacy as the founder of the quasi-fascist Blueshirt movement and as the leader of a brigade of men who fought for General Franco during the Spanish Civil War in the 1930s. Through all of this, O'Duffy was a committed GAA man. He served as secretary and then vice-chairman of the Ulster Council of the GAA from 1912 to 1922, and was a member of the central executive of the GAA until 1934. And yet Eoin O'Duffy never played a Gaelic football or a hurling match in his life. He had been born on a farm near Castleblayney in 1890 and – after the early death of his mother and the emigration of his older brothers and sisters – joined Monaghan County Council as a clerk in 1910. He worked around the Clones area as a surveyor, engineer and architect. Later, inspired by the 1916 Rising, he joined the Volunteers and fought in the War of Independence.

In many respects, O'Duffy is the epitome of the men who came to politics through culture. While in his teens, he had been drawn to the Irish-Ireland campaign and to the Gaelic League. His next step was to take membership of the Harps GAA club in 1910. While most men joined the GAA for love of playing the game, O'Duffy was drawn to its social and cultural aspects; the GAA, he said, 'seeks to aid Irish youth in playing national games in preference to games which because of their alien origin and atmosphere tend to injure their proper sense of nationality'. This ideology saw O'Duffy make some extravagant claims, not least in respect of rugby. William Webb Ellis is credited with the invention of rugby when in 1823 he was supposed to have picked up the ball and run with it in a game at his school when such an act was previously unheard of. Irish rugby aficionados saw an opportunity to claim credit for the invention of the game of rugby by saying that William Webb Ellis was a son of Tipperary, born when his father was stationed there. Seeing the potential to underline the supremacy of Gaelic football over any other kind of football, O'Duffy claimed Ellis for the GAA: 'My theory is that the Tipperary lad was consciously emulating Gaelic footballers he had seen in his homelands and that rugby, like soccer, is thus another anglicised form of an Irish game.' The difficulty with O'Duffy's thesis is that even had Ellis been born in Ireland, his father was stationed here for only twelve months.

Nonetheless, O'Duffy's talent for organisation saw him quickly flourish in an association where such skills were vital. He quickly moved beyond Harps to serve the wider GAA in Ulster. It was a perfect match. The GAA in Ulster was ripe for expansion and O'Duffy saw that potential. He travelled through the province promoting the games, helping clubs to organise and affiliate, and doing the groundwork essential to the prosperity of the Association. Even as his life became consumed with national politics, he retained this devotion to the GAA and to Monaghan; his final house on the southside of Dublin was known simply as 'Farney', an ancient name associated with the southern area of the county.

The GAA, of course, had made considerable strides in Monaghan before O'Duffy had become involved. There is some dispute as to which club was first established in the county. It has been claimed, variously, that a club was established in Inniskeen in 1883 even before the GAA was founded, that the Clones Red Hands were born in 1884 and that Currin Sons of St Patrick was actually the first-established club. All of this remains disputed. Either way, it was not until 27 December 1887 that a county board was established in Monaghan at a meeting in a hotel in Carrickmacross. Within a year, it was recorded that there were actually thirty-two clubs operating in the county; this was second in Ulster only to Cavan's thirty-eight clubs.

That same year – 1888 – saw Monaghan hold its first ever county championship. This ended with the final between Inniskeen Grattans and Clones played in a field in Donaghmoyne parish, and Grattans emerged victorious. The Grattans went on to represent Monaghan in the Ulster senior football championship final against Maghera MacFinns from Cavan. A final, and then a replay, were played in Drogheda and Grattans were crowned the first champions of Ulster. That year's All-Ireland championship was left unfinished due to a tour of America by GAA representatives, so the opportunity to pit themselves against the champions of the other provinces was lost to the Monaghan men.

The GAA in Monaghan declined in line with much of the country in the 1890s, but the nature of its rebirth was underlined in the names of the county's clubs. Whereas in the 1880s the clubs of Monaghan went by names such as Castleblayney Gladstonians, Carrickmacross Sextons amd Magheracloone Parnells, the years after 1900 saw the adoption of names which owed more to the revolutionary tradition than the parliamentary one. One by one the old names disappeared and were replaced by clubs such as the Carrickmacross Emmets. Indeed, the Emmets quickly established themselves as a significant force, winning seven senior football titles between 1908 and 1919.

This was the period when O'Duffy was in his pomp, but another administrator, Patrick Whelan from Newbliss, was also vital to the spread of the GAA in

Monaghan. Whelan became a central presence in the Monaghan county board after its re-establishment in May 1904. With Whelan as chairman, a vibrant club scene was forged in the county. In part, this revolved around taking players from soccer and bringing them into the GAA. Castleblayney, for example, was a town where soccer had a formidable presence and the town's soccer team had been good enough to beat Belfast Celtic. The formation of the Castleblayney Faughs GAA club in December 1905 changed all this and, through a determined campaign, Faughs emerged as the predominant club in the town. Soccer retained a presence, of course, but in the most unlikely of ways: contemporary newspaper reports note how the Faughs' players continued to use 'Association Football tactics', seldom making an effort to catch the ball.

A breakthrough on the inter-county scene was no straightforward matter. A second Ulster title was won in 1906 but Monaghan struggled to compete against Cavan and Antrim in the years before the First World War. A third title was won in 1914 and this victory was made all the more illustrious by virtue of the Monaghan hurlers also winning that year's Ulster senior hurling title. The hurlers won their second (and last) Ulster championship when they retained the title the following year, but the chances of a 'double double' were scuppered through narrow defeat to Cavan in the football final. Whelan and O'Duffy were not willing merely to accept defeat, however. At an Ulster Council meeting they complained of crowd encroachments and a disallowed goal and asked that the match be replayed. No Cavan representative attended the meeting and the Ulster Council deemed a replay necessary. Cavan were not for lying down on the matter, however, and an appeal to the Central Council of the GAA saw the decision of the Ulster Council overturned and the title awarded to Cavan.

This controversy gave added impetus to the inevitable rivalry of neighbours. The following year – 1916 – Monaghan hammered Cavan in the Ulster semi-final before beating Antrim in the final at Clones before a record crowd. They retained the crown in 1917, beating Cavan along the way, but provoking the Cavan men into lodging an objection that Monaghan should be stripped of the match because they 'were late fielding'. The spiralling bitterness of the rivalry saw Cavan attempt to escape what they considered the smothering hands of O'Duffy and Whelan by proposing the establishment of a fifth GAA province, which would be known as Tara and would include Cavan, Meath, Westmeath, Louth and Longford.

The proposal was rejected, but it served to emphasise the perceived power of Monaghan within Ulster football at the time.

In the early years of the Irish Free State, Monaghan football was dominated by Castleblayney Faughs who won ten county championships in the years from 1922 to 1941. The championship was keenly contested, however, and although the Faughs were the most successful club, they were also beaten in championships by teams from Carrickmacross, Inniskeen, Donaghmoyne and Kileevan. The competitive nature of the football championship helped produce players which brought Monaghan one of the greatest periods of success in their history. Ulster championships were won in 1927, 1929 and 1930. Again, there was controversy. Some Cavan players refused to travel to Carrickmacross because of the way they believed they were treated on a previous visit; the tradition of ill-feeling remained.

There was no great expectation of Monaghan enjoying success beyond Ulster, but the 1930 victory over Kildare was considered at the time to be 'one of the most sensational upsets in football history'. Monaghan's tactic of driving the ball along the ground was perceived to be crucial in a 1-6 to 1-4 victory and it left Kerry nervous of their 'soccer style'. Their nerves were quickly dispelled on match day. In a rout, Kerry won by 3-11 to 0-2. The following day the *Irish Independent* referred to the match as the poorest final on record. There was certainly no let-up by the Kerry team and folk memory records that the anti-Treaty men on the Kerry team were determined to drive home a message to the Monaghan men who, because of the activities of Eoin O'Duffy, were perceived to be pro-Treaty. In the popular mind, this was 'the last battle of the civil war'.

In the years that followed, the GAA in Monaghan struggled. The border narrowed the hinterland upon which towns such as Clones depended. The depression in agricultural prices meant general economic depression in a region where farming dominated. In the years immediately after the Second World War emigration reached new heights. Emigration from Monaghan had been higher than from any other Irish county in the 1880s and this process seemed to reach a climax in the 1950s when the population fell by 10 per cent alone in the years between 1956 and 1961. This was a flood from the land. In the 1950s, as Peadar Livingstone has shown, the number of farmers in the county fell by 14.4 per cent, the number of farmers' relatives living on the land fell by 43.9 per cent and the number of farm labourers fell by 42.5 per cent. A generation of Monaghan footballers headed for England and America. Those who stayed at home bore witness to Clontibret O'Neills and Pearse Brothers of Ballybay dominating the local senior football championship. Remarkably, Monaghan still managed to put together a team good enough to win the All-Ireland junior championship for the only time in its history. So dominant were they over Kildare in the All-Ireland final that their goalkeeper, Tommy McArdle, said that his position in goal felt somewhat like 'working on a job scheme'. And yet for all the strength of club football and for all that the junior success was a huge boost, there was nothing but disappointment at senior level. Year after year, Monaghan toiled with such little effect that between 1945 and 1978, they reached only one Ulster senior football final, and that was lost to Cavan in 1952.

Through the 1970s and 1980s, the number of people working on the land continued to fall, but the economy of Monaghan was buoyed by new factories, some based in the agricultural sector, but others in textiles and furniture. There was a slow transformation of living standards; emigration remained a constant and not everyone prospered, but more people had more money than ever before. Castleblayney Faughs dominated the local championship, winning eleven senior football titles between 1963 and 1976. Scotstown also emerged in the 1970s and reached the 1978 All-Ireland club final before losing to Nemo Rangers. Such was the intensity of competition in the county that it was later written: "'Sure, they'd ate you without salt" was the oft expressed sentiment about Monaghan club football.' The challenge was to bring this intensity to the inter-county stage. Ultimately, a modernisation of organisation of the county board, the improvement of club facilities and a general overhaul of preparation saw Sean McCague installed as county football manager in 1978. The following year Monaghan won the Ulster senior football championship for the first time in over forty years. Two more Ulster championships followed in the 1980s, including one in 1985, the year which must rank as the finest in Monaghan's history because it also saw victory in the final of the National Football League. Players from that team such as Ciaran Murray and Eugene 'Nudie' Hughes won All-Stars and became household names. No senior All-Ireland title followed, however, until the Monaghan ladies' football teams shot to the fore in the 1990s, winning three minor, one junior and two senior All-Ireland championships. The county's hurlers, too, won an All-Ireland junior title in 1997, but the men's senior football team could not make the breakthrough and such has been the strength of competition in the province that even an Ulster title has proved beyond their reach. The qualifiers brought glimpses of glory, not least when Kerry were almost defeated in Croke Park in 2007 and again in 2008, but on both occasions Monaghan people left Croke Park suffused with pride and regret.

General Eoin O'Duffy was key in developing the GAA in Monaghan. An IRA commander and the first commissioner of An Garda Síochána, this is O'Duffy sitting at his desk in July 1922. *(National Library of Ireland, Hogan Collection)*

The great poet and one-time Inniskeen goalkeeper, Partick Kavanagh, once wrote: 'O stony grey soil of Monaghan, The laugh from my love you thieved; You took the gay child of my passion, And gave me your clod-conceived.' Here, in the early 1980s, members of the Toome GAA club gather stones from the grey soil as they labour to create a new pitch for their club. That pitch, named St Victors Park, now stands as a monument to the voluntary endeavours of the people of Toome. *(Toome GAA Club)*

Members of the Monaghan ladies' football team celebrate in August 2008. Monaghan have reached seven All-Ireland ladies' football finals, winning two of them. *(Sportsfile)*

These are the magnificent Cremartin Shamrocks grounds. A revolution in the facilities available to GAA members has taken place over the decades. Back in 1933, a local man P. J. Duffy wrote of a field belonging to John McGuiness of Lismagunshion, where himself and the young men of the area played football: 'This field was too small for playing matches and so our football was confined to playing into the one solitary goal. When night fell we used sit or lie on the hay in a little shed inside McGuiness's gate and talk football until it was time to go home.' *(GAA Oral History Project/ Emmett Flanagan)*

In 1984 the GAA staged a special knockout Centenary Cup competition to celebrate the anniversary of the founding of the GAA. Monaghan made it all the way to the final of the competition. Here, future GAA President Sean McCague issues instructions to his players, while Ciaran Murray takes a long drink. *(John McAviney)*

[Favourite memory:] 'When the Sam Maguire cup visited my house.'

Eoghan, b. 2000, Edenmore N.S.

'There were five brothers on the team. And if you hit one you hit them all.'

Martan Quinn, b. 1963.

'My brothers and myself would get lifts to football matches with a man called Joe McMahon. All of us would jump into the back of his Ford Anglia. We all learned the reg. number so we'd know when he was coming. I still remember it. It is CID 616. Joe smoked a cigarette at the tip of his lips and every so often he would say: "All right in the back?"'

Philip Duffy, b. 1960.

'As a child, I remember dozens of hurleys around our house, in various conditions. Some needed banding, some were being "prepared" and more were kept in storage as spares for matches or teams. Sliotars for hurling and camogie were often found "drying out" in the house.'

Marianne Lynch, b. 1959.

'When the wireless arrived a bunch of men and young lads would come to gather outside a local's house, Terry Reilly's, on a Sunday to hear Michael O'Hehir report on games. Then a game of football would take place also a game of toss-the-penny and skittles.'

Jimmy Leonard, b. 1927.

'My mother washed his shorts and when he was going to the matches he would drag them in the dirt before getting to the match as it was bad luck to play in clean shorts.'

Teresa Duffy, b. 1968.

'We used to follow the senior players around like pied pipers. It was unbelievable; they couldn't go anywhere and we'd be behind them, everywhere they went ... Once you were on the senior team you were the men, it was unreal.'

Brian McCarthy, b. 1941.

'My memories of supporting the county are good ones. Remember going to Clones and taking a packed lunch and hot tea and I also remember cycling to matches in Clones with friends when I was old enough.'

Enda Murphy, b. 1979.

In 1939 Offaly shocked Laois in the Leinster senior football championship. Evelyn McCloskey was a young girl from Laois who stopped outside a newsagents to read the bad news of Offaly's defeat of Laois in the 1939 Leinster football championship. Offaly did not win its first Leinster senior football championship until 1960. *(Irish Picture Library/Fr F. M. Browne S.J. Collection)*

Westmeath Mayo Offaly
Limerick Laois Waterford
Carlow Longford Leitrim
Tipperary Kilkenny Derry
Kerry Cork Wicklow
Kildare Antrim Meath
Tyrone Dublin Galway
Armagh Fermanagh
Donegal Sligo Roscommon
Clare Cavan Monaghan
Louth Wexford Down

Offaly

When Offaly played Galway in the final of the 1971 All-Ireland football championship, the match was anything but a classic. Played on a wet and windy day, it was characterised by 'merciless and remorseless tackling' and 'shattering' shoulder-charges. Offaly won a narrow victory and, in the words of the journalist Con Houlihan, 'all heaven broke loose and its colours were green-white-and-gold'. It was the county's first senior All-Ireland success. The rain fell in sheets as Offaly people sang and danced out on the field. Up in the Hogan Stand, with the light fading fast, the Offaly captain, Willie Bryan, lifted the Sam Maguire cup. He proclaimed to the crowd: 'This is the happiest moment of my life.' It was the start of a week (and then many more weeks) of considerable mayhem. When Willie Bryan brought the Sam Maguire back to his home village of Walsh Island, there were hundreds of people waiting: 'We got to Walsh Island in the middle of the week. It was still spilling rain. They had a marquee up in the place – for the first time and possibly the last. That was an incredible night and the water still falling down. Not until then did it hit me.' The victory over Galway was the catalyst for an extraordinary period of success in both football and hurling. Over the three decades that followed Offaly won six more senior All-Irelands (two in football and four in hurling). Two out of every three years brought provincial success at either senior or underage level. By the time this era ended in 2000, Offaly was the first county to be awarded an All-Star in every position on the field in both football and hurling. It is the most striking example of a county overturning the great traditional powers of Gaelic games. As the full-back on the 1971 All-Ireland winning team, Paddy McCormack, said: 'To hell with tradition. Tradition alone is no substitute if you haven't the team.'

The key questions that stand are: how did Offaly get the team to win an All-Ireland championship? And, then, how did it keep getting teams good enough to win All-Irelands in both football and hurling? In answer to those questions, it is immediately apparent that the success of the period between 1970 and 2000 was the product of a long gestation. Offaly, then known as King's County, was involved in the GAA immediately from its inception. Indeed, it was a King's County club – Clara – which was the third club in Ireland to affiliate to the GAA, beaten only by Michael Cusack's own Metropolitan Hurling Club and by Nenagh GAA club.

While it was inevitable that not all towns and parishes in the county would respond with such alacrity, it was equally the case that some simply did not respond at all. Indeed, it was not until 1896 that King's County successfully completed hurling and football county championships. That is not to say that there were no games played in the county before then. In fact, the first All-Ireland hurling final was staged in Birr between Meelick of Galway and Thurles of Tipperary on 1 April 1888. This staging, however, was a consequence of the strategic location of Birr between the finalists, rather than any native genius for organisation. Nonetheless, the crowds who attended that match and the fact that even bigger crowds had attended the semi-finals of the King's County senior hurling championship played at the same venue on a previous weekend, offer eloquent testimony to the love of hurling in the south of the county.

When the GAA clubs of King's County successfully established a county board and their championships in the 1890s, the GAA began to prosper. The number of affiliated clubs in the county increased generation after generation. By 1907, there were twenty-five affiliated clubs; in 1937, there were fifty-two; in 1945, there were sixty; and by 1970, there were seventy-four clubs. This was not just a matter of quantity, however. It was an indication of the quality of the clubs of Offaly that, when the Leinster club championships were first staged in 1970-71, both titles were claimed by Offaly teams, with St Rynagh's winning the hurling and Gracefield winning the football. That neither club managed to go on and win the All-Ireland was a disappointment. In the case of St Rynagh's it was the first of several disappointments at that level. Three times they reached the All-Ireland club hurling final but three times they were defeated. The fact that defeat in an All-Ireland final constitutes disappointment, of course, is a testimony to the strength of the club. In the end, it was St Rynagh's great rivals, Birr, who have emerged as Offaly's only All-Ireland winning club by taking the All-Ireland senior club hurling championship four times in the 1990s and 2000s.

For all that the Offaly club scene was fiercely competitive, success on the inter-county stage remained stubbornly elusive. In some respects, this reflects the fact that Offaly is a small county of fewer than 60,000 inhabitants. It also reflects the fact that the county was divided unto itself. Crudely drawn, this divide sees the north of Offaly as a football area and the south as a hurling one. There is concrete evidence of this: of the 113 Offaly hurling championships played up to 2010, exactly 100 have been won by clubs from within a ten-mile radius of Birr. By contrast, only once has one of the clubs – Banagher – from this 'hurling area' won a senior football championship, and that was in 1910.

Despite this divide, it is somewhat ironic that without Gaelic games, there is nothing that unites Offaly. The county boundaries were first laid out in 1557 during the Plantation of Leix-Offaly. Crucially, the idea of Offaly as a county was largely ignored by the people who lived there. For example, five Catholic dioceses run across the county and also included are the ancient fiefdoms of a host of Gaelic chieftains. Even under the Anglo-Irish families, there was no autonomous unifying force. The traditions of the Pale-influenced east of the county varied greatly from those of the more Gaelic-influenced western areas. All told, before the GAA was established, there was nothing to bind together the disparate parishes in either history or geography.

The GAA changed all that and the idea of an Offaly county team brought a unity which defied the geographical divide between hurling and football. Success came neither easily nor in torrents. Two All-Ireland junior hurling championships were won in the 1920s. In that same decade, three Leinster senior hurling finals were reached but all were lost. Newspaper reports from the time underline the quality of the hurling played by the Offaly men, but lack of strength in depth remained a huge problem. The trail of emigration brought many talented hurlers to New York and Offaly won numerous hurling championships in that city during the 1920s and 1930s.

If there was at least success of a type in hurling, there was none at all in football. By the 1930s, Offaly was the only Leinster county without a provincial football final at any grade. Two things happened to undo this damning statistic. The first was a decision to concentrate on developing the game at underage level. This was exemplified by Offaly's involvement in 1928 in the first ever minor football match organised by the GAA. Crucially, as new generations of footballers and hurlers were developed, more and more of them were retained in Offaly. This brings us to the second critical development: the expansion of the operations of Bord na Móna and the ESB after the Second World War. Turf-fuelled fire stations were built by the ESB in Rhode, Ferbane, Shannonbridge and Portarlington. By 1968, one-fifth of Ireland's electricity was generated in Offaly and a significant proportion of the ESB's 10,000 employees were based in the county. The turf to fuel the fire stations was taken from the bogs of Offaly. By 1970, almost 2 million tons of turf was being harvested in Offaly, with obvious implications for employment in the county. The construction of housing estates and the provision of a transport infrastructure brought further employment.

With prodigious talent now remaining at home, Offaly rose and rose in the football firmament. A first Leinster senior title was won in 1960. A second was added the following year, before a one-point loss to Down in front of 91,550 people in the 1961 All-Ireland final. Several of the key men from this team were still playing when Offaly won that first All-Ireland in 1971. They were joined by a new generation who had enjoyed underage success. Four Leinster minor titles were won between 1960 and 1965, and an All-Ireland minor title was claimed in

1964. From that team came such outstanding players as Martin Furlong and Tony McTeague. As McTeague said, winning brought a momentum all of its own: 'The 1964 win was the best ever for me. But all that came from 1960 and 1961 when we were kids. No doubt 1960–61 created 1964, and 1964 created 1971–72.'

The Offaly hurlers had to wait a further decade for their own success. The club scene in Offaly had been revitalised in the 1960s and Offaly had almost made a breakthrough in that decade. In 1969 they beat defending All-Ireland champions Wexford in the semi-final, before losing to Kilkenny by one point in a Leinster final. Just as with the footballers, fewer hurlers were now being lost to emigration. The arrival of Br Dennis to teach at the Presentation College in Birr and the later arrival of Dermot Healy as coach to the senior hurling team brought further impetus.

The impact was decisive. In 1980, Offaly stunned Kilkenny to win the Leinster hurling championship. It was the first time that Offaly had ever defeated Kilkenny in championship hurling. There were extraordinary scenes: 'The Offaly followers flooded onto the field like a tidal wave. For former players and long-time followers this was a time of great emotion. They had known years of effort and hope and disappointment.' That night bonfires blazed in many parts of the county, with the biggest burning in the square in Birr. The fires were lit again the following year when a first ever All-Ireland hurling title was won. Norman Freeman had no doubt of the significance of the victory: 'Offaly's victory was one for the disadvantaged, for the good hurlers who had never played in an All-Ireland final, let alone won one, for teams from countles that were always championship fodder – Clare, Westmeath, Roscommon, Antrim, Down, Dublin, Kildare, Kerry, Waterford, Carlow.'

Through the 1980s and 1990s, Offaly enjoyed unprecedented success in hurling. They repeatedly beat Kilkenny in championship hurling in Leinster and won a total of four senior All-Irelands. The new millennium has brought disappointment, however. Offaly has slipped from centre-stage in hurling and in football. The last Leinster football final success in 1997 now seems a long time past. There have been fleeting glimpses of success in subsequent years, but none has been realised. Instead, it is the Offaly camogie team that has stepped into the limelight. The scenes which accompanied All-Ireland success in football and hurling in previous decades have been repeated (on a smaller scale) for camogie All-Irelands in recent years.

In 1957, at a match in Tuam between Galway and Louth, the crossbar broke in two in the second half. The umpires on the day were Noel Clancy and Jim Fox from Tullamore. The referee was another Tullamore man, John Dowling, who later refereed a total of five All-Ireland finals, three in hurling and two in football. Dowling was the secretary of the county board when Offaly won its first senior hurling All-Ireland in 1981 and the senior football All-Ireland in 1982. He later became the president of the GAA. *(Paddy Cotter/ Aidan Claffey)*

Hurlers from Offaly and Kilkenny line up before a match at Gaelic Park in New York in the 1950s. The Offaly club in New York has traditionally been strong. Many of the players who won All-Ireland junior championships with Offaly in 1923 and 1929 emigrated and won several championships in New York in the 1930s. Offaly also won the 2010 New York senior hurling championship; it was their fourth victory in succession in that competition. *(Pickow Collection, James Hardiman Library, NUIG)*

More than 90,000 people crowded into Croke Park to see Offaly lose narrowly to Down in the 1961 All-Ireland football final. Another 30,000 people were said to have been locked out of the game. They missed a brilliant match in which four goals were scored in the first fifteen minutes alone. Offaly were unlucky to lose, but the turnout at the homecoming in Tullamore spoke volumes for the esteem in which this pioneering generation of players was held. *(Paddy Cotter/Aidan Claffey)*

Seamus Darby has just scored a goal to win the 1982 All-Ireland football final and deny Kerry a five-in-a-row of All-Ireland titles. As the umpire waves the green flag, Offaly supporters invade the pitch in ecstasy. Never was a one-in-a-row more cherished. *(Sportsfile)*

Amongst the Birr players celebrating their club's victory over Ballyboden St Enda's in the 2007 Leinster senior hurling final was Brian Whelehan (far right), one of the greatest players in the history of hurling. Whelehan won every honour in the game: two All-Ireland senior titles, three Leinster senior titles, one National Hurling League title and two Railway Cups. He also won four All-Ireland club titles, seven Leinster club titles and twelve Offaly senior county titles. Twice named Hurler of the Year, he was the only then current player to be picked on the Team of the Millennium. *(Sportsfile)*

'She wanted to know, "How is it going to happen? How are you going to be on television? Sure, that's not right at all. Are you sure they're not codding ye?" And I said, "It's the first time ever, Mother. And I'll tell you one thing now; on Sunday when this game is on, when you're not praying for me, make sure you keep back out of the way in case you get a boot of the ball!" And she said, "Lord save us!"'

Paddy Molloy, b. 1934.

'When I was about ten years of age, my father brought me to a hurling match in Clareen. As the crow flies across the fields, it would've been about four mile. And he brought me to there. And we had to cross a big river and he took off his boots and crossed the river and he put me up on his back. That was the first official match I went to.'

Mick Spain, b. 1933.

'Our local field was nicknamed "The Lawn". Every evening after school we headed for The Lawn and played for hours and hours. Our trainer was a very kind man named Dinny Kelly. After games he bought ice cream for us all. He had a huge positive influence on all the players.'

Jerry Leen, b. 1958.

'It is one of the best organisations in Ireland 'cos I love the matches and it joins counties together.'

Cian, b. 1997, Gaelscoil an Eiscir Riada, Cluain Calga.

'When camogie started in '73, hurling wasn't strong in Tullamore. It was on a very weak point. And I recall some boys of our age group, who didn't have a team to play with and they'd be hanging around when we were playing camogie, and it dawned on me one day, I said, "Lads, do ye want to play?" because they'd nobody else to play with. And do you know, they were delighted!'

Miriam O'Callaghan, b. 1955.

'The most vivid memory I have was just of a local match, where my dad and two uncles played for a senior team in a village fete match against the then current village team. It was great to see the older team use their skill to score and pick off points whilst the younger guy rushed about chasing every ball. The older guys knew by instinct where the play was going to take place and showed no hurry in getting there in time. Dad saved two penalties and stopped two very clear goal chances — I was very proud of him.'

Ian Deering, b. 1968.

Roscommon played Kerry in the 1962 All-Ireland football final; it was the first All-Ireland football final to be shown live on television. RTÉ was a mere nine months in existence at that stage, but the decision by the GAA to allow for the televising of the All-Ireland finals and semi-finals, as well as the Railway Cup, brought a whole new dimension to the profile of Gaelic games. Roscommon lost that 1962 final by 1-12 to 1-6. *(Kennelly Archive)*

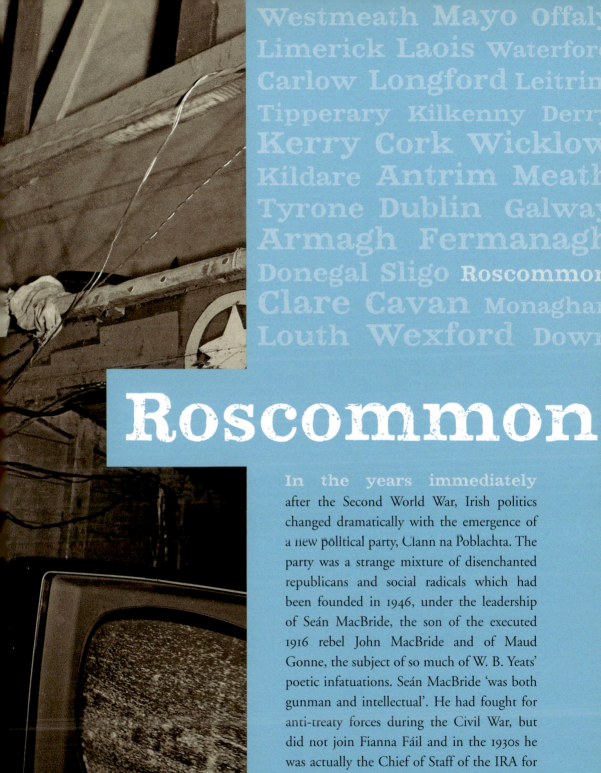

Westmeath Mayo Offaly
Limerick Laois Waterford
Carlow Longford Leitrim
Tipperary Kilkenny Derry
Kerry Cork Wicklow
Kildare Antrim Meath
Tyrone Dublin Galway
Armagh Fermanagh
Donegal Sligo Roscommon
Clare Cavan Monaghan
Louth Wexford Down

Roscommon

In the years immediately after the Second World War, Irish politics changed dramatically with the emergence of a new political party, Clann na Poblachta. The party was a strange mixture of disenchanted republicans and social radicals which had been founded in 1946, under the leadership of Seán MacBride, the son of the executed 1916 rebel John MacBride and of Maud Gonne, the subject of so much of W. B. Yeats' poetic infatuations. Seán MacBride 'was both gunman and intellectual'. He had fought for anti-treaty forces during the Civil War, but did not join Fianna Fáil and in the 1930s he was actually the Chief of Staff of the IRA for a couple of years. Even while he was leading the IRA, MacBride was studying law and he qualified as a barrister in 1937, before establishing Clann na Poblachta. Alongside MacBride in the party were social radicals such as Noel Hartnett and Noël Browne, men who helped construct an election manifesto for Clann na Poblachta, which promised dramatic social and economic reform. This included increased spending on housing, on health, and on rural electrification. This manifesto was sufficiently successful to win for Clann na Poblachta ten seats in the 1948 General Election: one of those seats was won by the Roscommon footballer, Jack McQuillan.

McQuillan had risen to fame as a star on the greatest team in Roscommon's history. Although just 5 ft 9 in tall, he developed his power by lifting weights and was considered one of the strongest players in the game. He scored a goal in the 1943 final and was one of the stars of the 1944 final: Roscommon won both matches. For four years after he was elected as a TD, McQuillan continued to play for Roscommon; his last game was in 1952 as a substitute in the All-Ireland semi-final against Meath. By then, McQuillan was considered one of the most left-wing TDs in Dáil Éireann. When Noël Browne, Minister for Health, resigned from government after it declined to support his plan to introduce free natal care for Irish women and free medical care for every child born in the country until they reached the age of sixteen (the Mother and Child Scheme), McQuillan followed him into opposition. Together, the two men formed the National Progressive Democrats and pushed a popular left-wing platform of rural concerns (fisheries, forestry, land reclamation, etc) combined with anti-Vietnam War protest. In the early 1960s, their profile was such that Seán Lemass referred to Browne and McQuillan as 'the real opposition' in the Dáil. Ultimately, he retained a seat until 1965; it was lost in that year amidst allegations of communism.

The Roscommon team of which McQuillan was a central figure changed Gaelic football in the 1940s. In his fine book, *Ros Comáin: 101 Years of Gaelic Games in County Roscommon 1889 to 1990*, Tony Conboy rooted the rise of Roscommon football in the 1940s as being related to the arrival of new administrators such as Dan O'Rourke and J. J. Fahey, the growth of Roscommon CBS as a successful GAA school that provided Roscommon with hugely talented young players into the 1940s, the experience of seeing Galway and Mayo bring All-Irelands to Connacht and the winning of two minor All-Irelands in 1939 and 1941 and a Junior All-Ireland in 1940. All this transformed Roscommon's senior football panel, which now had numerous talents who had already experienced victory, not just over their rivals in Connacht, but also at national level.

When Roscommon played Galway in the 1943 Connacht final, they were well equipped to claim a first title since the outbreak of the First World War. The team was rooted in a brilliant half-back line of Brendan Lynch, Bill Carlos and Owensie Hoare; Carlos was once memorably described as 'the lion with the velvet paws'. A two-goal victory led to the players being chaired from the field by the rejoicing crowds. Roscommon's provincial victory was followed by even more celebrations after a dramatic and high-quality All-Ireland semi-final with Louth. At half-time the score read Louth 3-3, Roscommon 2-5. The key moment came with a Roscommon break towards the end of the game as Louth were desperately pressing for an equalising point. Roscommon broke from defence and a lightning attack ended in a goal; the final score in a magnificent game was Roscommon 3-10, Louth 3-6.

Despite the severe travel restrictions because of 'The Emergency', a record crowd of 68,023 turned up at Croke Park for the 1943 final against Cavan. As Tony Conboy recalled: 'The ingenuity with which people travelled to those games by bicycle, train, turf lorry, has provided a legion of stories. It is a point seldom mentioned but this team with fresh new names lifted Gaelic football finals onto a new level from which it has rarely slipped.' The 1943 final was, as Eoghan Corry has written, 'one of the great occasions of wartime Ireland,' and it ended in a draw. The replay was famously ill tempered and ended in the referee, Paddy Mythen, having to be escorted from the pitch by gardaí for his own protection. The great controversy in the match was recalled by one of the Roscommon players, Brendan Lynch: 'What I remember most was the mayhem at the end. First Cavan's Joe Stafford was sent off after having a go at Owensie Hoare. We got a point, but Barney Culley didn't agree and put the umpire into the net with a box. Big Tom O'Reilly, the captain of Cavan, came in to remonstrate and TP O'Reilly threw the referee in the air.' Either way, Roscommon had won and, as the train brought the players back to the west, huge crowds gathered at every station to celebrate. On arrival in Roscommon town, the 'team was paraded from the station to the Square, escorted by the Knockcroghery band, where they were lauded to the delight of the huge enthusiastic crowd. This was only the beginning of a series of receptions in the towns throughout the county ending in Castlerea in January. The win meant an awful lot to the people of the county.'

The following year confirmed the greatness of the Roscommon team. The Connacht title was retained, Cavan were beaten again in the All-Ireland semi-final and Kerry were their opponents for the final. For the second year running the attendance record was broken as 79,245 crowded into Croke Park. Many more were locked outside the ground and had to listen to a radio broadcast. Back in Roscommon, those who didn't travel also tuned in to the radio broadcast. Four decades later, one woman who listened to the match recalled: 'That time there was no television to watch the game and as for going to Croke Park – well, that was well beyond our meagre means. The local pub boasted a fair-sized wireless set, which kept the whole village up with the times and especially the matches. We were very happy to be let sit on the ground outside under the window and there we could hear Michael O'Hehir at his best coming over loud and clear. I remember having my rosary beads in my pocket during some of those years as I silently and unseen prayed for victory.' Whether inspired by prayer or otherwise, Donal Keenan drove Roscommon to victory for the second year running. Two years later in 1946 Roscommon and Kerry met again in an All-Ireland final that was delayed until the end of October as rural Ireland fought to save a late harvest. Roscommon lost after a replay – all talk was of one that definitely got away. Two All-Irelands in a decade was fair return, however, for a county that, before then, had won none.

That is not to say there was not a long tradition of Gaelic games in the county. While there was GAA activity in Roscommon in the nineteenth century, it was in the early twentieth century that Roscommon GAA first made inroads on a representative level when they won the 1905 Connacht championship. The final of that competition was not actually played until late May 1906 when they defeated Mayo at Tuam by 0-7 to 0-5. Amongst their players was Jack Brennan who was known by press and public as 'The Electric Shock'. Roscommon were ultimately defeated in the All-Ireland semi-final by Kerry, but the GAA in the county took another giant leap forwards with the opening of dedicated grounds on 28 April 1912. The local press reported that 'to celebrate the occasion four championship matches were played. The field is particularly suited to hurling and football and accommodated 3,000 people. The day's receipts of £42 will pay for a year's rent and clear all expenses connected with the preliminary arrangements of the ground.'

With the new grounds came renewed success. Two more Connacht senior football titles were won in 1912 and 1914, though defeat at All-Ireland semi-final stage followed on both occasions. Sandwiched between the two football successes was Roscommon's only Connacht senior hurling championship. In that 1913 Connacht hurling championship, Roscommon were represented by the county champions Athleague, while other players were drawn in from Four Roads, Ballyforan and Dysart. The tradition of hurling in the area pre-dated the founding of the GAA. In a hugely surprising result, Roscommon defeated Galway by 3-4 to 3-2. In the All-Ireland semi-final, the Roscommon men received a drubbing at the hands of Wedger Meagher and his Toomevara Greyhounds from Tipperary. The final scoreline was 0-1 to 10-0. The match was played in Jones's Road in October 1913, shortly before the GAA purchased the ground and renamed it Croke Memorial Park. Roscommon have never since won a Connacht senior hurling championship and football came to dominate in the county.

Hurling, though, has its passionate adherents, not least in the Four Roads club, down near the Galway border. The quality of the hurlers produced by the club is such that they have twice won the Connacht senior championship. The first time, in 1977, was when the Galway club champions were suspended, but the second came on Sunday, 20 November 1988, when Galway champions Abbeyknockmoy were the opponents. Three late goals from the Roscommon champions, recalled one club member, 'shocked Abbeyknockmoy and the hurling world. The final whistle brought an explosion of emotion and celebration, which had to be seen to be believed. It was a source of great pride for Four Roads people all over the world and will always be a cherished memory for those of us who were lucky to be there.'

The success of Four Roads was achieved despite the number of players lost to emigration. Like every county in rural Ireland – and particularly those in the west of the country – Roscommon endured catastrophic and chronic economic failure. The county has always been primarily a rural agricultural society; as late as 1967 it was noted that 'almost 70% of the total labour force are engaged in agricultural occupations'. Initiatives had been put in place from at least the 1960s to try and draw new enterprise and employment to the county. These initiatives were rooted in the desperation of ongoing population decline. As the agricultural economy collapsed, people flooded off the land and into the cities of Britain and America. The scale of the numbers leaving was stunning. The total population of Roscommon on the eve of the Great Famine was 253,591. By 1851, this had fallen to 173,436, but even in 1911, 93,956 people lived in Roscommon. The decline continued – some decades were worse than others – and by 1996 there were fewer than 52,000 people living in the county. The boom of the new millennium brought a rate of increase in population in Roscommon that at 9.3 per cent actually surpassed the national growth rate of 8.2 per cent. All told, by 2011, the population of the county touched 60,000. This still left Roscommon as the fifth least populous county in Ireland. The great fear is that the collapse of the Irish economy will once again denude the county of its people and that a new generation of Roscommon players will be lost to their clubs and their county.

Through all of this, Roscommon has failed to recapture the glory of the 1940s. It has come close, however. The central point about the 1940s is that it imbued a certain lustre into Roscommon football, not that the years following the 1940s have brought a constant flow of success. Nonetheless, no decade has passed since then without at least a Connacht championship being won. Indeed, the provincial success of 2010 marked Roscommon's twentieth Connacht senior football title. Twice since the 1940s, the county have managed to reach the All-Ireland final. In 1962 they lost by six points to Kerry and then, in 1980, they were involved in a tense, tough struggle with the greatest Gaelic football team of all time – Kerry's four-in-a-row team. For all that they were playing a formidable team, Roscommon entered that match full of belief. They were led by the brilliant Dermot Earley (who later became chief of staff of the army and was awarded with the Distinguished Service Medal with Honour for his lifetime service to the state) and throughout the field they had outstanding footballers. They also had a recent tradition of success. In 1978 they won the All-Ireland Under-21 championship and then in 1979 they won the National Football League – defeating Kerry along the way. When Roscommon netted a goal after thirty-five seconds, they had secured the perfect start. Slowly, but surely, they were reeled in by Kerry, however. As the match disintegrated, Roscommon conceded too many frees and missed too many chances; Kerry won by three points. The men of 1943 and 1944 – including their TD Jack McQuillan – remain the only Roscommon teams to have taken All-Ireland senior titles.

Pictured in the passenger seat of a car with the Sam Maguire cup is the Roscommon captain, Jimmy Murray. Roscommon had just defeated Kerry by two points in the 1944 All-Ireland football final before a crowd of almost 80,000. *(GAA Oral History Project/John Murray)*

Roscommon goalkeeper Gay Sheerin dives but can only watch the ball pass between the posts as Armagh score a goal in the 1980 All-Ireland senior football semi-final. Roscommon won the match, but lost a tense All-Ireland final to Kerry the following month. *(National Library of Ireland, Colman Doyle Collection)*

Jimmy Murray's Pub in Knockcroghery was, for many years, an iconic staging post for GAA people. Here it displays the Sam Maguire cup and other memorabilia. In October 2006 the Roscommon minor football team stopped at Murray's pub when they brought the All-Ireland minor trophy back to the county, having defeated Kerry in a replay. Jimmy Murray passed away four months later, aged eighty-nine. *(GAA Oral History Project/John Murray)*

One of the greatest all-round footballers in the history of Gaelic football, Dermot Earley takes a free in a Connacht championship match in July 1985. In the week after his death, Liam Horan wrote: 'Meet any Roscommon person this week, and expect to find a tear in the eye. This death shakes the county to its core. It wasn't just that he was their greatest player for half a century or more: it was that Dermot Earley was a rare type of hero. Jet black hair, he stood tall and erect, an impossibly handsome Hollywood film star transported into our two-channel world. There was never anything mediocre about Dermot Earley: he did everything the way it should be done.' *(Sportsfile)*

Clann na nGael is situated in the southern end of Roscommon. The area is comprised of the two half-parishes of Drum and Clonow. Between 1983 and 1990 Clann na nGael reached five All-Ireland senior football club finals: all were lost, but along the way they won seven Connacht titles in eight years. Clann na nGael have not won a senior county championship since 1996, but, as can be seen from this presentation to Under-6 and Under-8 boys and girls at a prize-giving on the club field, they are rebuilding from the ground up. Indeed, the club now has one of the biggest numbers of underage players in the county. *(Thomas Lennon, Clann na nGael GAA Club)*

'The story got around now that ... there was a couple of us going to this match and Dr Gibbons came in anyway and the meeting started and everything was going grand, and the next thing he said he heard that there was a few fellas thinking of going to see Sligo Rovers on Sunday. He says, "If you go to see Sligo Rovers on Sunday, you won't be playing next Sunday in the first round of the championship." So that settled Sligo Rovers. That was probably the most disappointing thing I can remember about football. If you think about the ban now ... I thought it was an awful loss; I would have loved to have played soccer and rugby.'

Micheál Killoran, b. 1937.

'As long back as 1905, there's a famous photograph of a team called the Maith-Go-Leors. And maith go leor would imply that you had few drinks before you started because maith go leor means "not exactly drunk, but merry".'

Phonsie Tully, b. 1934.

'It has improved greatly over the years but there needs to be more recognition and promotion for ladies' GAA. If it wasn't for TG4 there would be none at all.'

Lisa Walsh, b. 1992.

'They were boggy pitches and so obviously in the winter ... everyday you'd come in you'd be covered in muck, there was no showers, there was a cold tap. And I had one pair of socks and one pair of togs and one jersey. And you laid your gear out on the pipes and the following day then you sort of had to beat them against the wall to soften them up to put them on again. So it was harsh. In fact, it prepared me very well for the army afterwards, for the cadet school. I found the cadet school quite easy after Nathy's.'

Sean Kilbride, b. 1950.

'The Irish culture is the GAA in my opinion. Worldwide, if you mention your involvement in the GAA you are welcomed anywhere.'

Aoife Fitzmaurice, b. 1989.

'There's as many balls at one training session now, than there was in a whole parish. New rules are changing the game too much. The rules were good enough as they were if they were just left alone.'

Joseph Donoghue Senior, b. 1930.

[GAA Hero:] 'My godfather ... he was a great sportsman and played the game very fairly ... I like playing matches and meeting new people.'

Caoimhe, b. 1997,
Scoil Mhuire, Newtown.

Victory over Mayo in the 1975 Connacht senior football final unleashed scenes of delirium in keeping with a county starved of success for five decades. *(Connacht Tribune)*

Westmeath Mayo Offaly
Limerick Laois Waterford
Carlow Longford Leitrim
Tipperary Kilkenny Derry
Kerry Cork Wicklow
Kildare Antrim Meath
Tyrone Dublin Galway
Armagh Fermanagh
Donegal Sligo Roscommon
Clare Cavan Monaghan
Louth Wexford Down

Sligo

In the midst of the worst economic crisis in modern Irish history, Sligo GAA has turned convention on its head and embarked on the most ambitious development in its history. President of the GAA Christy Cooney turned the sod on the site of the new Sligo GAA Centre of Excellence in April 2011. Phase one will hold three full-size sand-based pitches, plus all underground works, bases for floodlights and dugouts, and perimeter fencing. Phase two will see the construction of a 15,000 sq ft building which will house four dressing rooms, physio rooms, meeting rooms, a gymnasium and – eventually – the Sligo county board's administration office. Embarking on a project valued at €3.2 million in the middle of a brutal recession might seem dangerous, even reckless. To the contrary, however, the timing is a tribute to the prudence and planning of the Sligo county board. The project had actually been mooted in the mid 2000s as part of Sligo GAA's strategic plan, published in 2005, 'Moving forward with Sligo'. The explosion in land and development prices during the Celtic Tiger era persuaded the county board to delay the project. Buying land to build the proposed Centre of Excellence would then have cost several millions. As it was, the board bided its time and bought their 22-acre site at Scarden, about 5 km outside Sligo town on the Strandhill Road in 2010 for a little more than half a million euro.

The chairman of the Sligo county board Cyril Feehily says: 'It's ours now. We had some money ring-fenced in our accounts to put us in a position to start the project. We have people from various professions on our committee, both development and finance, which has given us great professional advice. We're full of enthusiasm about it, have no qualms at all about driving ahead, and feel now is the opportune time to do it. It's a fantastic site, very scenic, and a very good ambience for a place of excellence. We hope to centralise all administration and everything to do with training there, to make a complete academy for GAA in the county, including football and hurling and handball. Crucial to developing the project has been the support of the people of Sligo – those living in the county, across Ireland and overseas.' According to Feehily, this is not simply a matter of money, it is also one of sentiment: 'Most of all there has been a lot of goodwill towards this. You can have all the money in the world available to you, but if people don't see the benefit and have the goodwill towards the project then it's a lot harder to get things off the ground.'

The Centre for Excellence is emblematic of the changed fortunes of the GAA in Sligo. For decades Sligo teams were lost in the shadows of their Connacht neighbours, Galway and Mayo. In history, too, Roscommon's tradition of success was undeniable. It is too much to suggest that recent years have brought a changing of the guard that will see Sligo displace its storied rivals. What is apparent, however, is that Sligo should now be competitive on a regular basis in Connacht, and that dreams of All-Ireland glory are more realistic that ever before. There will, of course, be setbacks, and disappointments, but on foot of the work being carried out at underage level, the new development at Scarden is emblematic of a sea change in attitude.

Indeed, it says much for the change in fortunes in Sligo that the development should take place in the wake of the acute disappointment of losing the 2010 Connacht senior football final against Roscommon. Uniquely in its history Sligo had actually entered the game as favourites, but did not live up to their burgeoning reputation on the day and were unable to add to the existing total of three Connacht championships. This is a record of success that pales beside those of their neighbours: as of 2011, Mayo lead the way with forty-three Connacht senior football titles, Galway have forty, while Roscommon have twenty to their name.

For all that Sligo have not enjoyed such a sustained record of success, it should not be considered that the county does not have a long and extensive involvement with Gaelic games. Indeed, the first GAA club in Sligo was formed at Collooney in January 1885. This was instigated by leading nationalists in the county and, in keeping with the priority of the GAA at the time, it was dedicated to fostering athletics in the area. They also bought a football from Murrays of Cork, which was inscribed with the legend 'GAA match'. Over the two years that followed, clubs were established across the county, including at Ballyrush, Ballintogher, Ballisodare, Ballymore and Bunninadden. A club was also formed in Sligo town and, in January 1886, a contest was arranged between Sligo and Collooney on the banks of the River Arrow. The day's festivities consisted of ten athletics events and a football match. A county board was formed in 1887 and the first county football championship was run in 1888. In keeping with almost every other county in Ireland this initial progress was lost in the 1890s in a welter of political recrimination as moderate and radical nationalists cleaved in the wake of the Parnell split. The GAA did not disappear from Sligo; matches were still recorded in the press, but the momentum of the 1880s had quickly dissipated.

A revival after 1900 saw hurling come to the fore. The first inter-club hurling match in the county was played in Dromard in January 1903, when Sligo Wanderers came out from the city to play the home team. The growth of hurling was associated with the spread of the Gaelic League, but football remained the dominant game, with thirteen clubs entering the 1906 Sligo football championship (four competed for a hurling championship). Over the following two decades the GAA in Sligo made steady progress, endured difficult patches, but by 1923 had produced the best team in its history. That team – which competed in the delayed 1922 Connacht senior championship – defeated Roscommon, Mayo and

Galway to claim the Connacht title. In the All-Ireland semi-final they defeated Tipperary and were set fair for the All-Ireland final when an objection lodged by Galway, 'based on a flimsy technicality', was upheld and Sligo were stripped of the Connacht title. By appalling symmetry, Sligo were also denied a place in the 1927 League final when a defeated Laois team lodged an objection that, on the official team sheet, the name of a Sligo player had been misspelled. A replay was ordered and Sligo were defeated.

The following year brought redemption. Captained by the outstanding 'Click' Brennan, Sligo defeated Leitrim in the Connacht semi-final. In the final, played in Tuam, Sligo played well enough in the first half to lead by 1-4 to 0-4. In the second they failed to score, but a tremendous rearguard action restricted Mayo to just two points, and Sligo ran out winners by the narrowest of margins. Indeed, it is a singular fact that each of Sligo's championship victories has been taken by just one point. The relative failure of Sligo football in the ensuing decades – notwithstanding an All-Ireland junior victory in the 1930s – to make inroads on the inter-county scene was partly related to the strength of soccer in the county. In *Sligo GAA: a Centenary History* reference was made to 'the apathy and indifference of a sizeable section of the population of Sligo town towards Gaelic games, and an unexplained preference for another code'. This stood in contrast to the 'patriotic idealism and parochial pride of a handful of enthusiasts in every corner of Sligo' who had ensured the 'continuation of a tradition that with the passage of time has become part and parcel of the folklore of the county'. It was noted with pride that, although Sligo did not often win competitions, there was more to the GAA than the mere winning of titles. Yet it was in the context of spreading the games and becoming more competitive that in 1929 Sligo passed a motion at its annual congress proposing that the GAA's 'ban on foreign games' be removed. This motion was rejected at central level within the GAA. Up until the 1960s, the issue of the ban surfaced regularly in Sligo GAA circles and a view was formed that in certain quarters that its presence was restricting the development of the GAA in the county. The truth of this argument is impossible to prove or disprove; what is certain is that it was not until after the 'ban' was removed in 1971 that Sligo again won a Connacht championship.

That success came in 1975. In that year's semi-final an ageing Galway team were put to the sword in Markievicz Park. Galway had been beaten All-Ireland finalists for the previous two years and were hammered by Sligo by 1-13 to 0-6. By neat symmetry, it was the first Connacht final between the two counties since 1928. Indeed, the surviving members of both 1928 games were invited to the match in Markievicz Park. Mickey Kearins – then playing in his fifteenth consecutive Connacht campaign – was the star of the Sligo team. Kearins had been good enough to be picked on the 1971 All-Star football team, despite the lowly status of the Sligo footballers. On a sweltering day, a tremendous match ended in a draw. The replay was fixed for McHale Park in Castlebar and another classic ensued. Kearins had been relatively quiet by his standards in the drawn game but in the replay he excelled and scored 1-4. Sligo won by a single point, 2-10 to 0-15. The length of time which had passed since the 1928 success ensured that the celebrations were suitably outrageous; it was, noted the *Sligo Champion*, the day when 'unbearable tension mellowed to uncontrollable emotion, followers jumped on and embraced each other, and Mickey Kearins was carried shoulder-high from the pitch.' Ballads were immediately written, including one that ended: 'This is just the beginning, with Kerry next in line; With their courage and their will-to-win, at Croke Park they will shine.' The All-Ireland semi-final against a young Kerry team provided a rude awakening, however. Sligo were thoroughly outclassed as the blossoming talents of Kerry tore them asunder: John Egan scored 2-2 and Pat Spillane scored 1-1 in a 3-13 to 0-5 result.

The scale of that defeat set Sligo back. In truth, though, the structures in the county were not adequate to build on the potential displayed in that victory. The county championship in the years that followed was dominated by St Mary's and Tubbercurry. Indeed, the clubs played each other in five successive county finals between 1983 and 1987. Their rivalry was a tense one and St Mary's were the most powerful club in the county – good enough to win three Connacht club championships between 1977 and 1983. Nonetheless, club football in the county was not of a high enough standard to produce sufficient players for the county side, nor did Sligo possess educational establishments with a footballing pedigree to match those in other counties. With Sligo town – the largest urban area in the county – dominated by soccer, the GAA faced challenges it usually struggled to overcome. The consequence was that Sligo retreated towards the margins of the Connacht championship.

Perhaps the most notable feature of the 1990s was the extraordinary spread of ladies' football in the county. Gaelic football was first organised for the women of the county in 1993 and, as the excellent *Sligo GAA 125 History* records, since then 'it has flourished all over the county'. The extent of the success in spreading the game was evidenced when Sligo women won the All-Ireland junior football title for the first time in 2006. There were also moves to progress hurling once more, with new clubs initiated, money invested in coaching and the willingness of some existing clubs to make greater efforts to foster the game. Indeed, these moves eventually led to victory in the Nicky Rackard Cup, which Sligo won in 2008.

Football remained the main game in the county, however, and much as the modern rise of Sligo football is rooted in the dedication of the volunteers who run the clubs and county board with great expertise, it has also been facilitated by the introduction in 2001 of a new format for the All-Ireland championship. Sligo is a classic example of a county liberated from the shackles of repeated defeat in its home province. The moment when the cycle of defeat was broken is easily discernible. In 2002 Sligo were unfortunate to lose to Galway in the Connacht football final. Instead of a long year of regret, the introduction of the 'back-door' saw Sligo go on a run in which they defeated Tyrone (overturning a seven-point deficit in the process), before losing by two points after a replay to Armagh at the All-Ireland quarter-final stage. As the Sligo team left the pitch at Páirc Tailteann that August evening, there was something profoundly moving about the emotional scenes shared by players and supporters; amidst the disappointment and the exhaustion there remained the sense of a new beginning.

There was no immediate dividend from the moment, however. Instead, a decade of steady progress through the National Football League was eventually rewarded with championship success. Sligo were significant outsiders when they played Galway in the Connacht final on 8 July 2007. Tradition was with the Galway men but, on the day, Sligo's determination and belief was enough to see them home by a single point. That evening the RTÉ broadcaster Marty Morrissey took the bus with the Sligo players as they travelled home from Hyde Park, and filmed footage later shown on *The Sunday Game*. When the players passed across the border into Sligo there were more emotional scenes; this time, however, there was silverware to accompany the tears. Now the challenge for Sligo is to repeat that success and to do so on a basis regular enough to allow them to emerge as serious contenders for All-Ireland honours.

'The story got around now that ... there was a couple of us going to this match and Dr Gibbons came in anyway and the meeting started and everything was going grand, and the next thing he said he heard that there was a few fellas thinking of going to see Sligo Rovers on Sunday. He says, "If you go to see Sligo Rovers on Sunday, you won't be playing next Sunday in the first round of the championship." So that settled Sligo Rovers. That was probably the most disappointing thing I can remember about football. If you think about the ban now ... I thought it was an awful loss; I would have loved to have played soccer and rugby.'

Micheál Killoran, b. 1937.

'As long back as 1905, there's a famous photograph of a team called the Maith-Go-Leors. And maith go leor would imply that you had few drinks before you started because maith go leor means "not exactly drunk, but merry".'

Phonsie Tully, b. 1934.

'It has improved greatly over the years but there needs to be more recognition and promotion for ladies' GAA. If it wasn't for TG4 there would be none at all.'

Lisa Walsh, b. 1992.

'They were boggy pitches and so obviously in the winter ... everyday you'd come in you'd be covered in muck, there was no showers, there was a cold tap. And I had one pair of socks and one pair of togs and one jersey. And you laid your gear out on the pipes and the following day then you sort of had to beat them against the wall to soften them up to put them on again. So it was harsh. In fact, it prepared me very well for the army afterwards, for the cadet school. I found the cadet school quite easy after Nathy's.'

Sean Kilbride, b. 1950.

'The Irish culture is the GAA in my opinion. Worldwide, if you mention your involvement in the GAA you are welcomed anywhere.'

Aoife Fitzmaurice, b. 1989.

'There's as many balls at one training session now, than there was in a whole parish. New rules are changing the game too much. The rules were good enough as they were if they were just left alone.'

Joseph Donoghue Senior, b. 1930.

[GAA Hero:] 'My godfather ... he was a great sportsman and played the game very fairly ... I like playing matches and meeting new people.'

Caoimhe, b. 1997, Scoil Mhuire, Newtown.

Victory over Mayo in the 1975 Connacht senior football final unleashed scenes of delirium in keeping with a county starved of success for five decades. *(Connacht Tribune)*

GAELIC ATHLETIC ASSOCIATION

FIRST TIES
FOR THE COUNTY SLIGO FOOTBALL CHAMPIONSHIP.

THREE GREAT MEETINGS ARRANGED.

Feb. 6, March 4, and March 11.

The County Council of the GAA has arranged, according to Rule, that the First Ties between Affiliated Branches entered for the County Sligo Football Championship will be played off under the New Rules of the Association, as agreed to by his Grace the Archbishop of Cashel.

In Sligo, on Sunday 4th March, Ballintogher v Knocknarea, at 1.30 o'clock: Drumcliffe v Sooey, at 2.30 o'clock.

In Collooney, on Sunday, 11th March, Calry v Ballymote, at 1.30 o'clock; Collooney v Ballygawley, at 2.30 o'clock; Easkey r St John's, at 3.30 o'clock.

A Match between the Templeboy and Dromore West Branches will also take place on Sunday, 11th March, on the grounds of the former Club.

Admission to Field Threepence.

By order of County Committee,

P. A. M'HUGH,
Mayor, Chairman.

Sligo was one of the counties west of the River Shannon which best organised itself in the 1880s. This advertisement shows the arrangements for the early stages of the 1888 senior football championship, the first ever held in Sligo. *(Sligo Champion, Sligo County Library)*

This 1928 match between Sligo and Louth at Croke Park illustrates the extent to which the headquarters of the GAA have been developed. The shot is taken in front of Hill 16 and looks back across to the recently dedicated Hogan Stand. At that point a row of houses still stood behind the stand. The Nally Stand was only so named in the 1950s. *(GAA Museum)*

Eamonn O'Hara scored a goal which won the Connacht senior football championship final for Sligo against Galway in 2007. Writing in the *Irish Independent*, Eugene McGee said: 'It was worth going to Hyde Park yesterday to see at first-hand what will simply have to be the Goal of the Year. It was an absolute classic effort, involving three simple plays that brought the ball from 100 yards out to the back of the Galway net in the 25th minute. It was the sort of goal young players dream about but hardly ever see nowadays and I hope it is shown at every Cúl summer camp in Ireland this year.' *(Inpho)*

It took two enthralling matches to separate Sligo from Mayo in the 1975 Connacht football final. In the end, Sligo claimed just their second Connacht title. Star of the team was the midfielder Mickey Kearins. It is a tribute to his brilliance that Kearins had actually been named on the All-Star team in 1971. He was the first of four Sligo men to receive the accolade. The others are: Barnes Murphy in 1974; Eamonn O'Hara in 2002; and Charlie Harrison in 2010. *(Connacht Tribune)*

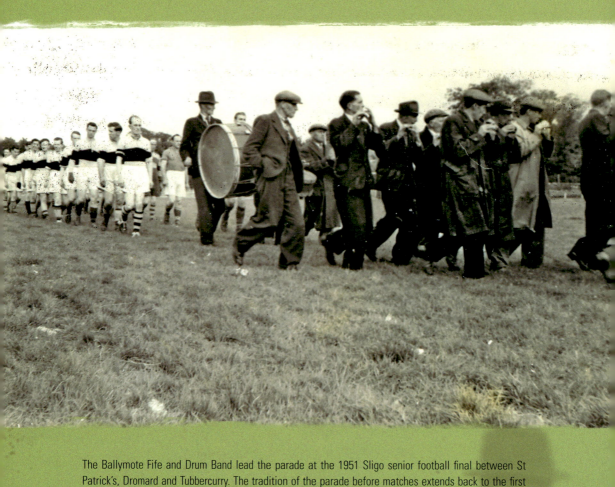

The Ballymote Fife and Drum Band lead the parade at the 1951 Sligo senior football final between St Patrick's, Dromard and Tubbercurry. The tradition of the parade before matches extends back to the first years of the GAA when teams paraded through towns, all the better to attract spectators to the events run by the new organisation. *(Christina Murphy)*

'It's great to get into a habit, I think, of giving of your time'.

Mick Burke, b. 1935.

'One promising player that we have missed out on is Shane Filan of Westlife. Shane was a very promising footballer. I was talking to a man today who was a mentor in his club, St John's, when Shane was a young footballer. Shane was training with the Under-12s, but one weekend an important game was coming up and Shane said to this mentor: "I'm afraid I won't be able to play today – I'm doing some music with my friends." And the mentor said back to him: "Now you forget about the music; if you stick with me you'll be playing for Sligo before too long."

Tommy Kilcoyne, b. 1945.

'There was a vigilance committee appointed, and they were sent into matches at the Showgrounds – the soccer matches – to see who was there. And of course they never reported anyone. They saw nothing! Never reported.'

Peter Cooney, b. 1932.

'It's more difficult to motivate people from the town … The country people would be more Gaelic-minded where the town people would be playing other sports … My views would have changed a lot in the last number of years from, I suppose, competitive at an earlier stage to now; involvement, I'd say, is more important with underage kids. Because if they enjoy it at underage they'll stick at it; if they're too competitive they can lose hope … It's important that they enjoy the games and end up as friends.'

Brian Maguire, b. 1948.

'The war years took some of the best people away from Ireland. I remember going over on the boat – it was the next evening after an All-Ireland football final – and somebody organised a sing-song. Well, do you know there was hardly a county in Ireland but somebody got up and sung a song. It was the best night I ever put in. Lovely. I can see some of the lovely girls singing. And them going off, back to London working.'

Mary Tuffy, b. 1917.

'We used to go down to play Mayo – you know, Sligo. Sligo's colours is black and white, and the Mayo says: "Oh, the magpies is landed".'

Thomas Brennan, b. 1918.

Tipperary players celebrate in the dressing room after the 2010 All-Ireland hurling final. In one of the greatest ever finals, Tipperary denied Kilkenny a historic fifth All-Ireland in a row by a scoreline of 4-17 to 1-18. *(Sportsfile)*

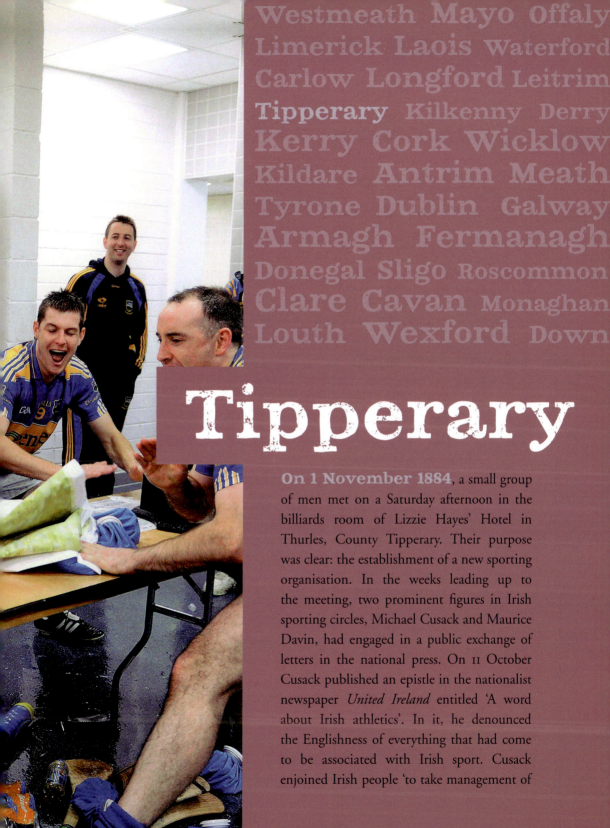

Westmeath Mayo Offaly
Limerick Laois Waterford
Carlow Longford Leitrim
Tipperary Kilkenny Derry
Kerry Cork Wicklow
Kildare Antrim Meath
Tyrone Dublin Galway
Armagh Fermanagh
Donegal Sligo Roscommon
Clare Cavan Monaghan
Louth Wexford Down

Tipperary

On 1 November 1884, a small group of men met on a Saturday afternoon in the billiards room of Lizzie Hayes' Hotel in Thurles, County Tipperary. Their purpose was clear: the establishment of a new sporting organisation. In the weeks leading up to the meeting, two prominent figures in Irish sporting circles, Michael Cusack and Maurice Davin, had engaged in a public exchange of letters in the national press. On 11 October Cusack published an epistle in the nationalist newspaper *United Ireland* entitled 'A word about Irish athletics'. In it, he denounced the Englishness of everything that had come to be associated with Irish sport. Cusack enjoined Irish people 'to take management of their games into their own hands, to encourage and to promote in every way every form of athletics which is peculiarly Irish, and to remove with one sweep everything foreign and iniquitous in the present system.' Responding in print, Davin weighed in with his support, advocating the establishment of an association to draw up proper rules for athletics, hurling and Irish football.

That such a call should come from Davin was significant. His name carried weight. The Carrick-on-Suir farmer and businessman was then a recently retired champion athlete, having dominated for years the power events of lifting and throwing at competitions across Ireland and England, his successes built on a meticulousness of preparation that included the building of a mini-gymnasium at his home at Deerpark. Cusack recognised Davin as the foremost Irish authority on sport, but he also understood that Davin's popularity would be crucial in winning support for a new athletics venture. On 22 October 1884, the two men combined to issue a circular, announcing that the meeting being called for Hayes' Hotel was intended 'to take steps for the formation of a Gaelic Association for the preservation and cultivation of our national pastimes and for providing rational amusements for the Irish people during their leisure hours.'

For all the notice that preceded it, the attendance at Thurles was small. Exact numbers are unclear, but reports put the number at anything between seven and fourteen; seven is by far the most likely number. What is known for certain is that Maurice Davin took the chair and that he told the gathering of the intention of the new sporting body to provide recreation for all Irish people, but most especially the Irish working man, who, he claimed, had been born to 'no inheritance other than an everlasting round of labour'. Davin, who abhorred the tendency towards elitism in British athletics, would be a central figure in the struggle to realise this vision. As the first President of the GAA, he was no mere figurehead. An innovative administrator, he was instrumental in both devising rules for hurling and Gaelic football and drafting the constitution that organised the Association into parish and county units. These decisions, taken in 1885 and 1886, effectively shaped the character of the Association that has passed down through the generations, but their most immediate effect was to lead to the creation of county boards and the establishment of proper inter-county competition. A pattern of unofficial games involving clubs from different counties had already become popular and had shown the potential for just such an initiative. In August 1886, for example, five teams from Tipperary journeyed by train to Cork Park to play a series of matches against the best Cork clubs, attracting a crowd of 20,000 spectators.

Informal challenge games remained a feature of Gaelic games, but they were soon superseded in importance by the introduction of All-Ireland championships for football and hurling in 1887. Tippeary were one of the few counties to be immediately represented in both: Templemore were its standard-bearers in the football, Thurles in the hurling. For the latter, the championship would end with meeting Galway representatives Meelick in the final. Delayed as a result of the political divisions which convulsed the Association in 1887, the game was eventually played on Easter Sunday 1888, the venue a field outside Parsonstown in King's County (later known as Birr in County Offaly). In that final, despite being weakened by the defection of a number of key players in a row over the non-payment of travel expenses, Thurles duly defeated Meelick by 1-2 to no score. In the moment of victory, all thoughts of the pre-match controversies were suddenly dispelled. 'The enthusiasm of the Tips seemed to be unbounded when play was declared,' one newspaper reported. 'They took the plucky captain, James Stapleton, on their shoulders and carried him though the field.'

The row over expenses that blighted the Thurles preparations pointed to the costs of participation and raised questions as to how far the GAA afforded entry to those of humble means, as Davin had insisted it would. Membership of clubs required the payment of subscriptions, which were needed to fund, amongst other things, the purchase of playing equipment and gear. They were also used to cover the costs of transport and post-match meals, though it was not unusual, as the Thurles case had shown, for this burden to be borne directly by players themselves. The ability to cover such costs depended, of course, on the incomes of those who played. So who were the hurlers and footballers of Tipperary? In a brilliant and detailed examination of this very issue, the historian Tom Hunt revealed that they came from a broad base of socio-economic backgrounds. They included all classes of rural society, but the overwhelming majority were farmers or farmers' sons, single men between the ages of nineteen and thirty. Despite the predominance of those from prosperous farming families, it was significant that participation extended to encompass the landless labourer. An under-represented class they may have been, but excluded they were not. The result was that the GAA opened up a recreational outlet to those who had been previously untouched by Ireland's growing wave of sporting organisation.

The players profiled by Hunt were those involved during a period of unrivalled sporting achievement for Tipperary. Between 1895 and 1900, the county embarked on an extraordinary run of success that yielded five All-Ireland hurling and two All-Ireland football titles. They were won by teams drawn from, and selected by, the county's champion club. In hurling, three of the victories were achieved by the Tubberadora club (1895, 1896 and 1898), with the other two being shared between Horse and Jockey (1899) and Two Mile Borris (1900) selections. In football, meanwhile, Arravale Rovers captured the 1895 title and Clonmel Shamrocks that for 1900. The catchment of these clubs did not necessarily conform to the strict idea of a parish unit, their membership being drawn from smaller, more informal, territorial-based social networks. In the case of the successful Tubberadora club, for example, the players who delivered three All-Ireland titles during the dying years of the nineteenth century all came from a small pastoral townland, three miles from the village of Holycross.

Both townland and village were located at the centre of a county that in 1901, for administrative purposes, was carved up between north and south. This territorial division reflected that introduced with the Local Government (Ireland) Act 1898, yet the GAA opted to add a third region – mid Tipperary – in 1907. Much later, in 1930, a fourth region was added to govern the west of the county. Geography would prove crucial to the shaping of sporting preference. While hurling dominated the north and mid districts, Gaelic football prospered in the south and the west. It was from Grangemockler in the south of the county that Michael Hogan came. On 21 November 1920, Hogan was a member of a Tipperary football team that played Dublin in a challenge match in Croke Park when British military forces entered the ground and opened fire. The atrocity, coming after the assassination of fourteen British intelligence officers in Dublin earlier in the day, resulted in the killing of fourteen civilians, including Hogan, who was crawling to safety when a bullet struck him in the mouth. Three days after 'Bloody Sunday', Hogan was buried in his football jersey at home in Grangemockler, his coffin draped in the Irish tricolour. Four years later his memory would be preserved in the naming of a stand in Croke Park in his honour, but perhaps the most poignant memorial came from his former teammates who, after defeating Dublin in the All-Ireland final of 1920 (played at Croke Park in June 1922), gathered at the spot where he had been slain to hear a musical tribute played by the C. J. Kickham band from Tipperary.

That All-Ireland final would be the last won by a Tipperary senior football team, but there would be no retreat from the sporting limelight for the county. Tipperary's hurlers won an All-Ireland in 1925 and over the following two years they would be in the vanguard of the GAA's efforts to expand Gaelic games among the Irish diaspora in Britain and the United States. Indeed, to hurl for Tipperary at this time was to be afforded opportunities to experience a world far beyond Irish shores. The 1926 tour to the United States was particularly special: over two months, the Tipperary team played a series of games, attended various functions and crossed the broad expanse of the American continent. A diary kept by one of the players, Thomas J. Kenny, captured the general sense of amazement at the size and bustle of the cities and the vast, uninhabited spaces of open country. Hurtling westward on a train through the state of Wyoming and beyond the canyons of the great Rocky Mountains, Kenny wrote. 'No fences at all to be seen now and habitations of any kind [have] not [been] seen for hundreds of miles, except at little stations. Hundreds of miles of seemingly unowned or at least uncultivated land.'

The promise of America was enough to seduce six of the travelling party to stay on when the tour ended. Thomas Kenny was not one of them, but he felt moved to wonder ruefully whether there would ever be a day 'when there will be room and work for every Gael in his own country'. On the evidence of the decades that immediately followed, it certainly appeared not. The drain of people from the Irish countryside – Tipperary included – was steady and prolonged. This was no fatalistic acceptance of the reality, however. By the early 1930s, the social and economic forces that had driven population decline now began to give rise to a movement of voluntary resistance, manifested most obviously in the emergence of the Tipperary-based Muintir na Tíre (People of the Land). Founded by Canon John Hayes, Muintir na Tíre aimed at the resuscitation of the rural community by involving people in the creation of guilds or parish councils and using them as vehicles to engender great civic values. In adopting the parish unit as the focus of its activity, Hayes sought not only to build on the example of the GAA, but to make common purpose with them. Closer cooperation between the two organisations would, he believed, help build up a rural Ireland 'strong in body and soul, bright in its social life, secure in its economic life, and faithful in its religious life'.

An alliance of voluntary bodies may not have been equipped to stem the emigrant tide, yet it could definitely add to the attractiveness of rural life for those who remained. Hurling and football and all that went with them provided recreation for young and old and as the fortunes of their county hurlers rose in the middle decades of the century, thousands of Tipperary people would be drawn from their homes to support them. The late 1940s and early 1950s saw a thrilling rivalry develop with Munster neighbours Cork and, notwithstanding the fact that it yielded three All-Ireland titles in a row for Tipperary, it provided a mere prelude to Tipperary's most successful sporting era since the turn of the century. The hurling decade that ran from 1958 to 1968 was dominated by Tipperary, who contested eight All-Ireland finals, winning five of them. Victory in the 1965 final brought to eight the number of All-Ireland medals won by John Doyle from Holycross, who for much of his playing days with Tipperary formed part of a full-back line that became known as 'Hell's Kitchen', a reference to their tough and uncompromising defensive style. For all the accolades that came his way, Doyle would later recall that it was the 'sheer enjoyment' he got out of playing that meant the most.

The decline of the great Tipperary team of which Doyle was a part coincided with a lowering of Tipperary's ranking in the hurling hierarchy. The county still managed to win at least one All-Ireland in each of the subsequent decades, but for long periods, particularly in the 1980s and 1990s, it appeared as if Tipperary was being pushed to the periphery of the sport by a combination of the strongholds of Cork and Kilkenny and the newly emergent powers of Offaly, Galway and Clare. It said much for how this affected the Tipperary mindset that, on defeating Cork in an epic Munster final in 1987, their captain Richie Stakelum felt it necessary to declare that 'The Famine is Over'. An All-Ireland title, a first since 1971, followed in 1989, with another in 1991. A further ten years would then pass until the Liam MacCarthy cup returned to the self-proclaimed 'home of hurling' in 2001 and this was followed by yet another hiatus of nine years. Of the five All-Ireland titles won by Tipperary since the mid 1960s, that of 2010 undoubtedly stands out. In one of the greatest finals of the modern era and with a performance of unbridled intensity, Tipperary denied Kilkenny a record-seeking fifth All-Ireland in a row. As *The Irish Times* reported, Kilkenny had 'stood at the gates of history and found them padlocked against them. Tipp leapfrogged into the record books with a passionate and joyous performance.' In that moment, the county of the GAA's birth was once again the centre of the Irish sporting world.

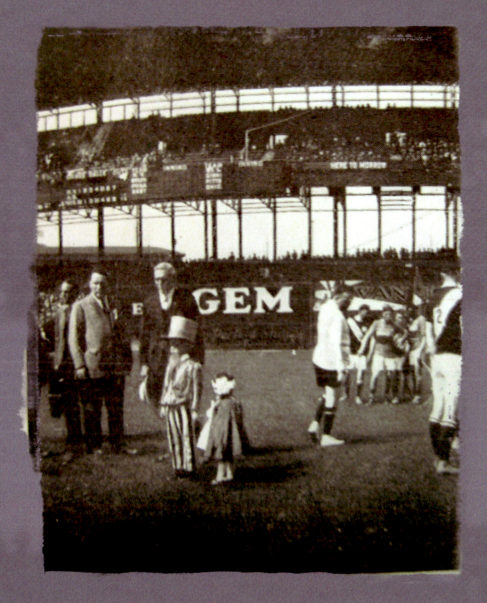

The scene at the New York Polo Grounds at the start of Tipperary's 1926 American tour. Prior to departure from Tipperary in May that year, the players selected to travel were contacted by letter, requesting that they start training and pack the following: '4 good hurleys, 1 pair of hurling boots, 1 spare suit clothes, 1 small handbag, 1 attaché case'. The aim of the trip, as one of the players later noted in his diary, was to revive the GAA in America and help make hurling international. *(GAA Oral History Project)*

The face of determination: Tipperary players walk from the dressing room to the field in Limerick in advance of their Munster final meeting with Cork, July 1954. The rivalry between Tipperary and Cork lay at the core of the Munster championship's appeal, particularly in the early 1950s. Although Cork would emerge triumphant in 1954, the period spanning 1949 to 1968 was a golden age for Tipperary hurling. All-Ireland titles were won on eight occasions. *(Kennelly Archive)*

ABOVE: Kilruane MacDonaghs waste no time in celebrating victory in the North Tipperary senior hurling final in 1940. This photograph shows the players and supporters sharing a barrel of stout, a crate of beer and a bottle of whiskey among them. This was the club's first time to win the competition since 1908, when they were known as Loharna De Wets, the name a reference to a South African general who had fought the British army in the Boer War. The picture features players Jim Spain, Mick Heffernan, Jackie Dunne, Mick O'Meara, Jim Ronan, Jack Reddan, Din Bevans, Rodge Dwan and Jack O'Meara (captain) and supporters Jackie O'Meara, Mick Spain, Mick Rohan, Niall O'Meara, Ned Kelly, Paul Spain, Steve Reddan, Biddy Moylan, Nora O'Meara and Maggie Kemple. *(GAA Oral History Project/Paddy Williams)*

RIGHT: Nicky English wins possession in the 1989 All-Ireland hurling final against Antrim, a game in which he scored a remarkable 2-12. Shortly after this performance, Raymond Smith wrote that Nicholas English 'stood on a pedestal as a born artist of the camán, putting scores against his name that were written in bold letters across the sky'. English was part of two All-Ireland winning Tipperary teams – in 1989 and 1991 – and, despite moving to live and work in Dublin, he would return to coach his native county to a further All-Ireland in 2001. *(Inpho)*

Tipperary players Stephen O'Brien and Gearóid Slattery (right) celebrate victory in the Munster minor football final at Killarney's Fitzgerald Stadium as Cork's Stephen O'Mahony (left) shows his disappointment, July 2011. Despite its reputation as a 'premier' hurling county, Tipperary has embarked on a programme of underage development in football that has begun to yield rewards at provincial level. The 2011 Munster minor title followed under-21 provincial success in 2010. *(Sportsfile)*

'My memory of Tom Semple is that Tom was of fine stature, great carriage and a lovely character ... I always classed Moycarkey and Boherlahan as being real natural Tipperary hurlers, pulling on the ball, in the air, and wherever, it was real hurling. Hurling was the thing and when that went out, these teams went down because it wasn't their natural way of hurling.'

Mícheál Maher, b. 1922.

'I remember ... 'twas a Munster final ... was it Cork and Tipperary were playing? And the priest came down off of the altar anyway and shook hands with Cork people that he picked out, the jerseys on them, in the aisles — a Tipperary man, he came down and shook hands with them.'

John Donovan, b. 1931.

'Cork v Tipperary Munster hurling final, 1987 ... one of my first memories of anything ever. The pageantry, the rivalry, the history, the sheer heaving passion of the crowd, the fear of loss — it was for some people the only release from a year of hard work — no holidays or any such thing just this feeling of exhilaration liberated. Primal. Unique.'

Noel Howley b. 1981.

'My Dad watched matches on TV; we had to be very quiet when they were on.'

Catherine Houlihan, b. 1964.

'It played a very important part growing up. My family were happy to support me as it filled a void in my life as there were few other activities available at that time 1940s/1950s.'

Pat Burke, b. 1939.

'I grew up listening to great stories about past matches and heard all about the legend that is Tony Reddin who is from my own club in Lorrha. This is what inspired me to try and emulate the achievements of all those great people ... Hurling was our first love and we lived, ate and drank the GAA in our household, all our childhood memories are going to matches on a Sunday and coming home to milk the cows at night. The weather always seemed hot, the dust was flying and all the memories seemed to be of great matches and days, my mother making the picnic and eating the sandwiches out of the boot of the car.'

Ken Hogan, b. 1963.

Peter Canavan has just scored one of the greatest goals ever scored in an All-Ireland football final against Kerry in 2005. Canavan told the GAA Oral History Project: 'I can firmly recall as a youngster gathering around the television … to watch All-Ireland finals. Bearing in mind then we didn't get to watch too many live games; the only live games that were on television back then were the All-Ireland semi-finals and the All-Ireland finals, so it was a big thing just to get watching Gaelic games live … That was a great family gathering, everybody got around and watching, you know, eleven, twelve of us sitting around watching a small television, watching the All-Ireland semi-finals and All-Ireland finals and the amount of debate that that generated, them talking about the game after and listening to my father and brothers. And neighbours inevitably would be in as well.' *(Sportsfile)*

Tyrone

In 1984 Tyrone county board published a history of the GAA in the county, written by Joe Martin. It is an outstanding book, comprehensive, enlightened and fair. In the course of his book, Martin acknowledged the heroic endeavours of generations of Tyrone GAA people. Unusually for a history book, however, it offers not simply a wonderful insight into the past, but also a map of the future. Martin understood 'the long road to glory' which was the story of Tyrone's past and then he offered a clarion call to the future: 'What the county needs most now is a raising of aspiration and a belief in its own ability to reach ahead of anything that has been achieved before ... Tyrone GAA, proud of its past and inspired by an awareness of its present potential and a total belief in itself, can aspire to and attain the ultimate success – the winning of the Sam Maguire cup.'

When a second edition of Joe Martin's book was printed in 2004, Tyrone were reigning All-Ireland senior champions for the first time. More than that, they were in the midst of a decade of unprecedented success in which they claimed three All-Ireland senior football titles, two Under-21 titles and five minor titles. In short, Tyrone could no longer be considered a peripheral presence on the inter-county stage; rather, they had begun repeatedly to demonstrate that they were now a major power. It was noted in the book that the 2003 All-Ireland victory was 'a victory not only for the best team ever to leave the county in search of Sam Maguire, but for every player who has ever worn the Tyrone jersey, for every man who has ever managed our county team, for every person who has served on a club committee or in the county committee, for all our supporters and for every boy and girl playing our games at school and club level'.

That second edition of the book was published to mark the centenary of the establishment of a county board in Tyrone in 1904. This is the thing about the GAA in Tyrone: for one hundred years and more, its past was not storied in terms of national honours and it even took many years for the Association to become properly organised in the county, but the fidelity of its GAA people to the 'cherished dream' was enough to sustain it through difficulty for it to flourish all the better in success. There is minimal evidence that the GAA established a presence in Tyrone in the 1880s. This lies almost entirely with the Cookstown Owen Roe O'Neills who are recorded to have lost the 1890 Ulster senior football championship final to Armagh. Even that club seemed to have disappeared within the year, however, and the GAA did not manage to lay down anything approaching a meaningful structure in Tyrone in the nineteenth century. And yet there was a long tradition of play in the county, which suggested that Tyrone should have been ripe for the spread of the GAA. The game of commons or camán – a stick-and-ball game with strong associations to what emerged as hurling – was played in the county through the nineteenth century. There is significant evidence of such a game, similar to that played in Donegal in the same years, being played in Carrickmore and in Strabane until after the 1880s. Indeed, the *Derry Journal* reported in March 1903 that 'the members of the local [Strabane] camán club, who had not allowed the old and popular game to die away, have been compelled to take up another game

– similar in nearly all respects to camán – namely hurley. This step has been taken, not because they were growing tired of the old game, but because they were unable to get any matches.'

The rebirth of the GAA in Tyrone, which culminated in the establishment of a county board, was directly related to the language revival and the general development of cultural nationalism in the years around the turn of the century. Again, as in other counties in Ulster, combating the rise of soccer was an essential element in trying to build the GAA. Even in Cookstown, where the GAA had once enjoyed a fleeting presence, soccer was the game adopted by nationalists who established the Cookstown Celtic club. Instead, it was Strabane that emerged as the hotbed of GAA activity in the county. During 1901 the Gaelic League had promoted Irish language classes and the Strabane Rapparees and Strabane Lámh Dhearg clubs were prominent by 1903.

The first chairman of the county board was the Strabane man Michael O'Nolan. His other claim on history is that he was the father of Brian O'Nolan who wrote under the pseudonyms of Flann O'Brien and Myles na gCopaleen. Under O'Nolan, Tyrone entered the Ulster senior hurling championship in 1903, the Ulster senior football championship in 1904 and ran its own county football championship in 1905. As well as in Strabane, clubs were active in Dungannon, Lisdhu, Coalisland, Donaghmore and Omagh. As well as matches, these clubs promoted the Irish language, Irish dancing and the study of Irish history. This was not simply sport; instead, it was about the promotion of a wider cultural movement.

This brave new dawn did not lengthen into a glorious morning, however. Although the GAA spread through Tyrone in the years between 1904 and 1908, it then almost entirely lost momentum. In Omagh, for example, a soccer club was established in 1909 and its membership included members of the Irish-Ireland movement. The result was the collapse of the GAA in the town. Early enthusiasm for the GAA as part of a wider cultural revival withered all across west Tyrone into 'blighting lethargy' and 'deplorable paralysis'. Indeed, for much of the next two decades the GAA in Tyrone struggled to survive. In fact, the Tyrone county board failed to have a football championship more often than not in the years before 1925. And even to the extent that the Association was represented in Tyrone in these years it was usually restricted to just the eastern half of the county.

When the Ulster Council sought to reorganise itself in 1921 Tyrone was not represented. When the draw was made for an Ulster championship, Tyrone alone of the nine counties in the province was not included. A revival began with a meeting of GAA clubs from the east of the county in January 1923 and this, in turn, led to the relaunch of the Tyrone county board at a convention in June 1923. The new board faced many new challenges, not least those presented by the fallout from the years of war and the establishment of a border across the country, which left Tyrone in Northern Ireland. Men who sought to travel to Clones in County Monaghan for matches were stopped and searched by police; this was reported by the *Ulster Herald,* for example, as something which occurred when Tyrone rejoined the Ulster championship by travelling to Clones to play Monaghan in August 1923.

Through the 1920s the GAA in Tyrone struggled along without gathering much in the way of momentum. However, the 1930s brought evidence that work in expanding the playing numbers through clubs and schools was paying dividends. In 1931 the Tyrone county board had officially adopted the white jersey adorned with the red hand of the O'Neills as the county colours. That jersey saw action in an Ulster senior final when Tyrone beat Antrim (after a second replay) and Fermanagh (by a point) to reach the 1931 Ulster final, where they faced Cavan. The final brought unmitigated disaster. An hour before throw-in a dispute in the camp with the Dungannon players on one side and all others on the opposite side ended with the Dungannon players leaving the Railway Hotel in Cavan where the players were based. All appeals to take part in the game were lost. Tyrone were forced to round up players to make up a team and in the end they were savaged by Cavan who won by 6-13 to 1-2. Cavan went on to win the All-Ireland title.

When Tyrone returned to the Ulster final in 1941, Cavan were again the opponents. The Tyrone players headed to Armagh for a two-week training camp before the game, under the direction of Belfast trainer, Joe Devlin. Again, Cavan proved too strong, as they were to prove on several other occasions in the 1940s. There was no mistaking the progress being made by Tyrone, however. A new emphasis was placed on the development of minor football and minor leagues were established across the county. These brought new forces to the fore with Omagh emerging as a serious power in club football. To add to the sense of progress, excellent grounds were developed at Dungannon, Pomeroy and Coalisland.

The burgeoning number of young players in the county saw Tyrone send out extremely talented minor teams in the 1940s. In the process they produced two of the outstanding players of that – or any – era: Eddie Devlin and Iggy Jones. Those players had first come to national attention as members of the St Patrick's, Armagh school team who enjoyed a memorable victory over St Jarlath's of Tuam to win the Hogan Cup in 1946. Jones was actually over age for the Tyrone minor team that reached the All-Ireland final in 1947. On the same day that Cavan defeated Kerry in New York in the senior final, Tyrone defeated Mayo in a remarkable minor match by just one point in Croke Park. As if to prove that that success was no fluke, they came back and won it again the following year.

Several of the players from those two teams (only five survivors from 1947 were underage for the 1948 triumph) were key to Tyrone eventually making the breakthrough at senior level when they won their first Ulster senior championship title in 1956. Many were lost along the way, however. For some it was a simple matter of not managing to fulfil the promise shown at minor level, others fell away from injury, a couple joined the priesthood and many emigrated. The core of survivors who broke the mould in the 1940s did so again against the odds in 1956. As if to emphasise the challenge facing Tyrone, they were pitted against Cavan in the Ulster final. Cavan were playing in their eighteenth consecutive Ulster final and had never been beaten by Tyrone in the entire history of the Ulster championship. On a wet and windy day, an outstanding second half performance saw Tyrone claim victory. The celebrations were suitably raucous. The following year – 1957 – Tyrone came back and retained the trophy; it was a mark of the quality of the team; yet they failed to push ahead on the All-Ireland stage.

The 1960s and 1970s brought more disappointment than success, despite the continued attempts to develop games in the schools. In all of this, outstanding footballers were produced, though never enough made their way through to the senior team to bring regular success. A third Ulster title was claimed in 1973, but it was not until the 1980s that Tyrone produced another top-quality team. That team won three Ulster titles – 1984, 1986 and 1989. The All-Ireland final was reached in 1986 and early in the second half Tyrone were leading Kerry by 1-7 to 0-4. A shock victory seemed on the cards, until Kerry went on the rampage and went on to win comfortably. The backdrop to the success of Tyrone in this era was, of course, provided by the Troubles. Through the 1970s and 1980s, life in Tyrone was stained by violence and vendetta. Even into the 1990s, the threat to the lives of GAA people was a very real one. In January 1993, for example, the UDA placed GAA members within a 'pan-nationalist' grouping which it considered as legitimate targets for attack. The claim was that 'GAA members were at the cutting edge of IRA violence'. The 1990s and 2000s, of course, brought dramatic change. That dissident republicans, by 2011, should themselves be issuing threats to the membership of the GAA, claiming they were legitimate targets, lent eloquent testimony to the metamorphosis of life in Northern Ireland.

By then Tyrone was well established in the very front rank of GAA counties. The recent surge of success leaves the county third – behind Cavan and Monaghan – in the roll of honour of Ulster senior football championship success with thirteen titles to their credit, as well as the three senior All-Ireland titles. It is a success rooted in planning, commitment, desire and vision. Critically, though, even had Tyrone never won an All-Ireland, or even an Ulster title, the triumph of the GAA in the county has been its central position in the lives of so many people. This was most potently revealed in a series of tragedies that occurred even as Tyrone's success seemed at its greatest. The loss in the prime of life of Paul McGirr, Cormac McAnallen, Michaela Harte and Ronan Kerr – all in different and distressing ways – was a tragedy firstly for their families, and secondly for the wider GAA community. The response to the loss of such young members demonstrated in the most profound way the place of the GAA in the lives of so many people in Tyrone. More so even than the All-Ireland success, the manner in which the GAA is embedded in community and the fact that some fifty clubs are engaged in playing football, hurling, camogie, handball and other social and cultural initiatives is perhaps the greatest testament to the success of the Association in the county.

It seems apt to leave the last word to Joe Martin, who offers the following synopsis of the history of the GAA in Tyrone: 'A difficult beginning, near collapse, revival, consolidation, breakthrough, setback, more breakthroughs, more setbacks, false dawns, small and big steps forwards and backwards – and one very long wait. Then, the ultimate achievement ...'

The Brantry GAA sports day in County Tyrone in the 1930s. While Gaelic games were the centrepiece of such sports days, the inclusion of athletics and other events was a throwback to the nineteenth-century activities of the GAA. *(Clare and Anthony Daly)*

Iggy Jones playing for Tyrone against Galway in the All-Ireland senior football semi-final in 1956. The *Connacht Tribune* report on the match noted that Jones was the best forward Tyrone had and that 'while Galway won by a narrow margin, the result could just as easily have been reversed'. Jones had first shot to national prominence in the first ever Hogan Cup final, when playing for St Patrick's, Armagh, against St Jarlath's, Tuam. He scored 3-4, as St Patrick's claimed a four-point victory. *(Dungannon Thomas Clarke GFC)*

In the aftermath of the Second World War, members of the Coalisland Na Fianna club put up goalposts in what was then McCrory Park. The pitch is now called Fr Peter Campbell Park, having been named in his honour in 1988, the year after his death. Fr Campbell had played on a championship winning team for Na Fianna in 1946; he also played county football for Tyrone and Railway Cup football for Ulster. *(GAA Oral History Project/Oliver Corr)*

On 29 September 2003, the Sam Maguire was brought to Tyrone. The homecoming in Omagh was one of the great emotional occasions in the history of the GAA. Local musicians, including Philomena Begley, entertained the crowds before the players were introduced to the vast crowd who turned out. *(Inpho)*

In the early hours of Saturday morning, 7 November 2008, the clubhouse of St Malachy's GAA Club in Edendork, County Tyrone, was destroyed by fire. The following day – even as the fire continued to smoulder – St Malachy's played a league match against Pomeroy. *(Sportsfile)*

'My father was then dispatched to Dungannon to buy a football and a copy of *How to Play Gaelic Football* by Dick Fitzgerald … The book was still in the house when I was growing up and I remember looking at the picture demonstrating the 'screw kick' and photographs of teams, which in the 1940s, looked strange, since many of the players sported moustaches … My mother, when we were younger, did not understand football and could not appreciate our interest in it. My father, however, complained about us tramping the grass when playing football, and felt that the wireless battery should not be wasted, listening to commentaries on matches that didn't concern us, especially hurling.

Felix A. Hagan, b. 1940.

'Me ma, to be honest, was never mad about me playing football, she just thought it was too rough for girls and all that sort of thing you know, pure traditionalist and that I should be at home and have part in the kitchen instead of running around after a ball but I was quite determined, I just went anyway. When we would have started out and that, we would have nearly have been laughed at, you know, just the thought of … well, probably because I'm from a traditional wee town anyway … As me da used to say, he goes, "Aileen, I'm not going to go to watch that game, it'd be like hens chasing a crust." And he used to say that and we'd just say, "Daddy, behave yourself and just come out and watch us".'

Aileen Breen, b. 1982.

'It means being part of something. It means hard training sessions. It means building friendships and playing with your [fellow] parishioners. It means working hard voluntarily. It means wanting to win to make your club a success and bring glory to the town.'

Aoife McReynolds, b. 1984.

'In the late '70s and early '80s, my club would have been greatly affected by emigration — it is safe to say that at least 75 per cent of the minor team I played on had left the country before they were twenty-one and unfortunately many have never returned … I went to Polytechnic in Wales and ended up working in England for the best part of the next eighteen years. I probably played my last game for my club when I was twenty-two years old and this is something I regret. I miss not being able to join in with friends now when they start reminiscing about past games.'

Damien Colgan, b. 1962.

One the earliest action shots of a hurling match, taken at the Gaelic Field, Dungarvan, in the late 1890s. It shows the old goalposts, which allowed for goals, points and forfeit points. Within a number of years, rule changes introduced by the GAA would see team sizes reduced and the scoring system amended. *(Waterford County Images)*

Waterford

They came on bicycles, by car and on foot. The vast majority, however, arrived by train. Of the 14,000 people who flooded into Dungarvan to witness the Croke Memorial Cup final between Tipperary and Kilkenny on the first Sunday in June 1913, approximately 9,000 were passengers with the Great Southern and Western Railway, with those coming from the Wexford direction availing of the service laid on by the Dublin and South Eastern Railway. But it was not merely the railway companies that had made special provision for the occasion. For the comfort of those who had made the journey to see the game and for the safety of the players, the surroundings of the Gaelic Field, one of the finest playing surfaces in the country, were given a major makeover. New pavilions were erected, sloped banks were built, stands were extended and a row of sideline seats was installed as a frame to the playing field. At the time, there were few grounds or towns as well equipped as Dungarvan to host an event of this size. Over the previous decade, various All-Ireland hurling finals had been staged at the very same venue. There was a simple explanation for why it had become a location of choice: convenience. Waterford was a county bordered by the sea on one side and by the emerging hurling strongholds of Cork, Tipperary and Kilkenny on the other. More crucially, perhaps, it was easily accessible, linked as it was to an extensive regional and national rail network. The importance of the railways to the development of the GAA defies exaggeration. If organised sport was a manifestation of the growing modernity of Irish society in the late nineteenth century, that entire process of modernisation would not have been possible without the improvements in transport, and consequently mobility, that the construction of the railways facilitated.

In Waterford, as with other counties, it was no surprise to find that it was towns situated along these lines of railway track that provided the focus for early GAA activity. In October 1885, for instance, the GAA chose the coastal resort of Tramore as the venue for its first national athletics championships. On a wet, breezy day, under the watchful eye of Maurice Davin, the Association's first President, many of Ireland's best athletes competed across a range of field events – jumping and throwing mostly – that the GAA had considered best suited to the Irish character. Among them was Dan Fraher, a Dungarvan-based draper, who emerged as the winner of the hop, step and jump event. Nobody came close to exercising the influence that Fraher had over the early GAA in Waterford. An indefatigable organiser, he combined family life with Gaelic League activism, the running of a business – he was the proprietor of a 'Gaelic Outfitting Store'– and occupancy of a variety of roles within the GAA. Fraher was a brilliant athlete, a high-profile referee and a long-serving GAA administrator; but he was also responsible for leasing land (from Richard Curran) in Dungarvan in 1885 and developing it as a sports ground. Known initially as Gaelic Field and latterly as Fraher Field, this stretch of ground would not only become the venue for big inter-county hurling matches, it also served as a hub for local GAA activity.

The sports that predominated at Gaelic Field in its early days reflected the bias of GAA interests within the county towards athletics and Gaelic football. From the very beginning, indeed, the preference for Gaelic football over hurling was a particularly striking feature of the Association in Waterford. A county football championship – won by Ballysaggart – was held in 1885 and within months of a county committee being established in December 1886, Waterford would be one of only nine counties to compete in the inaugural All-Ireland football championship. The high point for Waterford football came when the Dungarvan club, Erin's Hope, won through to an All-Ireland final in 1898, only to fall to the Dublin club, Geraldines. Against all this, the progress of hurling appeared sluggish at best. In spite of both a pre-Famine tradition of the game in the county and efforts to excite revival in the years immediately after the GAA's foundation, it was not until 1897 that Waterford got around to running a hurling championship of its own and not until the early 1900s that the competition was organised on anything like a regular basis.

Whether it was athletics, football or hurling, those who engaged in GAA activity were overwhelmingly Catholic and nationalist. This was no more than recognition of local demographic and political realities. By the early twentieth century, over 95 per cent of the Waterford population was Catholic and the majority gave their political allegiance to John Redmond, the leader of the Irish Party in the House of Commons. Events would conspire to scupper Redmond's dream of delivering Home Rule for Ireland and the hardening of nationalist sentiment that followed the 1916 Rising was reflected in the 1918 Westminster election when Waterford returned, amongst others, Cathal Brugha, the Sinn Féiner from Dublin who doubled as chief of staff of the Irish Republican Army. That election was a constitutional prelude to a military campaign that brought fighting and bloodshed to Waterford. In March 1921, for instance, the IRA ambushed a joint police/British army patrol at Burgery, two miles outside Dungarvan. Two policemen and two IRA volunteers died in the initial attack and subsequent skirmishes. Among the latter was Patrick Keating, who had captained Kilrossanty, a rural club based at the foothills of the Comeragh Mountains, to win the Waterford county football championship just two years previously.

When the fighting ended and society was once again calm, the impulses that drove Irish nationalism did not dissipate; from the 1920s onwards, they found alternative expression in, amongst other things, the politics of culture and sport.

In Waterford, for example, the ban on GAA players participating in or attending foreign games was supported with unwavering commitment by officials, if not always by members. As President of the GAA in the mid 1950s, Waterford man Vincent O'Donoghue explained that the ban was a defence against forces – cultural and sporting – which sought, through their promotion of 'imperial' pastimes, to 'blunt the national conscience, weaken the national fibre and sabotage the national revival effort'. For others, like Pat Fanning, a prominent hurler and administrator in the county, the ban was also bound up with a wider sense of service to an Association that took precedence over almost everything else in their lives. In an interview with the GAA Oral History Project shortly before his death in 2010, Fanning spoke unrepentantly of how he had eschewed opportunities for advancement in his professional life for fear it would take from the time he could devote to GAA duties. Like O'Donoghue before him, Fanning rose to the position of GAA President and it was ironic, given his wholehearted backing for the ban, that it fell to him to preside over its ultimate abolition in 1971.

For all that it sought to disadvantage so-called foreign sports, the truth is that the ban contributed little to the growing of participation in Gaelic games. That was essentially the work of schools and clubs and no more so than in Waterford, where the rise of hurling was directly attributable to developments in the city during the 1920s and 1930s. The rivalry that sprang up between two new city-based clubs – Erin's Own, founded in 1923, and Mount Sion, founded in 1932 – helped drive up standards and reverse a chronic cycle of defeat. So uncompetitive had Waterford hurling been in the early twentieth century that a gap of twenty years separated the winning of their first Munster senior championship match – against Kerry in 1903 – and their second. All that changed in the 1930s. The emergence of Mount Sion was critical to this and to the future development of hurling in the county. The club was effectively an outgrowth of the Edmund Rice-established Christian Brothers' school in the heart of the city and was intended to cater for current and past pupils who wished to hurl. It met with stunning success: in the sixty years between 1938 and 1998, the club won thirty senior hurling county titles. Not only did this ensure a pre-eminence for hurling in the most populous part of the county, it also produced a succession of players who would help raise the status of the Waterford team.

In a remarkably competitive decade for hurling in the province, Waterford won their first Munster title in 1938 and a decade later, in 1948, three of that team would return to win a second Munster and a first All-Ireland title, defeating Dublin in the decider. Critical to that victory was the move of the brilliant Mount Sion hurler John Keane from his usual berth at centre-back to centre-forward, where he contributed 2-3 to his side's 6-7 total. When the final whistle blew and the crowds rushed the field, it was, one newspaper reported, towards Keane that many of them headed – 'to congratulate him, hug him, kiss him, cry over him, carry him in wild tribute all around Croke Park'.

John Keane's retirement from inter-county hurling did not mean withdrawal. He returned to train Waterford to two All-Ireland finals in 1957 and 1959, winning the latter. In an age when county hurlers tended towards the big, the strong and the tough, Keane took a group of physically small players and encouraged them to use their speed and skill to overcome what was often more robust opposition. The success enjoyed by Waterford during the middle decades of the century saw them join hurling's hierarchy, but following the county's All-Ireland final defeat to Kilkenny in 1963, its fortunes receded once more. The reason for this was simple enough. As the journalist and writer Damien Tiernan has explained it, most of the Waterford team of the 1950s had started their careers together, had grown old as players together and, in the end, they retired together.

They left behind them a void that would take decades to fill. In fact, it was not until the closing years of the twentieth century that Waterford would regain a national prominence. And it was not just in hurling that they did it. By the 1990s, ladies' football was flourishing, the sport having initially emerged as a form of popular recreation among women in rural west Waterford in the early 1970s. Before a national association for ladies' football had even been founded, and at a time when hurling and camogie in the county lay in a state of decay, Waterford women set about organising themselves into a county board and began to run their own championship, the first being sponsored by the rural community development group, Muintir na Tíre. These were the modest beginnings of a sport that would grow rapidly in the 1990s, a decade during which Waterford would develop into a powerhouse, winning five All-Ireland titles. Remarkable as it was, this success had a limited impact on the wider community. Women's sport remained a sideshow, more to be admired than watched or actively encouraged. Indeed, it spoke volumes for the relative spectator appeal of women's and men's Gaelic games that almost four times more people were on hand to view Waterford's defeat to Clare in the Munster hurling final replay of 1998 than were in attendance at the winning by the ladies' footballers of their fifth All-Ireland title later that same year.

For hurling, nevertheless, 1998 was certainly a turning point. It signalled Waterford's re-emergence as a formidable force in senior hurling, the consequence of an increasingly vibrant club scene, underage county success and the installation of the first in a sequence of outside team managers. Over the next decade, the story of Waterford hurling provided compelling drama. Playing a brand of sometimes brilliant, freewheeling hurling, Waterford contested some classic matches, winning four Munster titles in the process, an achievement that mirrored the successes of Ballygunner, Mount Sion and De La Salle at club level. But the Waterford club and county experience was united by a failure to extend dominance beyond the provincial boundary. At inter-county level, the repeated loss of All-Ireland semi-finals in the opening decade of the 2000s suggested that it was not just bad luck or the rise of a great Kilkenny team that prevented them from bridging the gap to All-Ireland success. It appeared as if the generation of Waterford hurlers that came to the fore were as cursed as they were blessed, at times lacking the unity of purpose and self-discipline that defined those teams which achieved the ultimate honours in the game.

And yet the failure to win an All-Ireland clearly rankles. When the county board commissioned Michael Walsh, the City Manager for Waterford Corporation, to map out a plan of development for the local Association, the former county player from Ballyduff Upper wondered aloud about Waterford's entitlement to consider themselves among hurling's best. 'Can a county with a rich tradition genuinely call itself successful if it has failed to win a senior All-Ireland in fifty years and has to go back nearly twenty years for ultimate success at underage level?' he asked. The question was purely rhetorical for, in plotting a path forward, Walsh recommended radical change, including the ending of the long-standing administrative division of the county where separate boards would govern the east and west. For the immediate future, the focus will be on more efficient organisation and fixed objectives. However, what started out as primarily a football county will remain one, first and foremost, in thrall to hurling. On this, policy and public taste are in broad agreement.

A bicycle race at the Gaelic Field in Shandon, Dungarvan, *c.* 1902. The man kneeling with the bowler hat and stick on the right of the photograph is Dan Fraher, the Dungarvan-based draper, athlete and a driver of the GAA's early development in Waterford. It was Fraher who leased this field from Captain Richard Curran in 1885 and transformed it into one of the country's premier sports and entertainment venues. *(Waterford County Images)*

Dan Fraher's Drapery Store, also known as The Gaelic Outfitting Store, based on Grattan Square, Dungarvan, *c.* 1940. Fraher was a member of the Gaelic League and keen promoter of all matters Irish. Alongside his sporting interests, he was a collector of Irish manuscripts, a promoter of the Irish language and a trader in goods of Irish manufacture. Pictured in the centre here is Dan's son, Maurice. *(Waterford County Images)*

Waterford trainer John Keane instructs Dick Roche to return to goal while tending to an injured Tom Cunningham during Waterford's 1957 All-Ireland semi-final against Galway. Keane himself was selected as centre-back on the *Irish Independent's* Team of the Century in 1984. In the course of a senior inter-county career that ran from 1935 to 1952, he became the first Waterford man to captain Munster in inter-provincial competition in 1939. A central figure in the Mount Sion hurling success story – he won eight county championships with the club – Keane's enthusiasm for the game never wavered in retirement. As well as coaching Waterford to All-Ireland finals in 1957 and 1959, he also served for many years as chairman of his club. *(Dick Roche)*

Ger Fitzgerald and Mícheál Walsh from Kilrossanty contest possession with Tom Walsh of the Nire, in the 1989 Waterford senior football county final. Despite being the dominant Gaelic code in the late nineteenth century, football was largely eclipsed by the rise of hurling in the twentieth century. Indeed, football success has been conspicuous only for its rarity. Despite showing promising signs of progress in the 1990s and 2000s – an under-21 Munster Championship was won in 2003 – Waterford footballers continue to live life in the inter-county slow lane, the reality of which was documented by journalist Damien Lawlor in his book on their 2009 season, *Working on a Dream*. *(Dungarvan Observer)*

The day of deliverance, 30 June 2002: Waterford bridge a 39-year gap by winning the Munster senior title, defeating reigning All-Ireland champions Tipperary by a single point. Writing in *The Irish Times* the following day, Seán Moran likened the victory to the other 'great liberations' that hurling had witnessed in the previous years through Clare and Wexford. This photograph shows Waterford players Eoin Kelly and John Mullane celebrating with supporters at Páirc Uí Chaoimh. The decade that followed would bring further provincial honours for the county, but no All-Ireland title. *(Inpho)*

'Had the Christian Brothers not existed, had they not occupied those key positions throughout the country, particularly in urban Ireland, the GAA might not have emerged and certainly would not be the force it is today but the Brothers making an almost incredible contribution to the growth and development of the thing ... It's quite extraordinary today to travel Ireland and to see the church, the school and the GAA ground occupying pride of place in the villages and small towns of Ireland ... To see people immersed in the club, to see people living for the club, is to emphasise for me the significance of the GAA ... I was ever conscious of the distinctiveness, the uniqueness of the Gaelic Athletic Association and from the beginning I never regarded it as just a sporting organisation.'

Pat Fanning, b. 1918.

'But anyway, my team was beaten. And I went home, and I went out in the back and I was crying. And my mother came out to console me, and she said, "Austin, what are you crying about? What good is an aul' medal?" she said. "Your brother Michael is a sub on the other team and he got a medal, and he wasn't even at the match. He went to the pictures instead! So what good is an aul' medal? You played a good match and that's it!" So that always stood to me.'

Austin Flynn, b. 1933.

'As a supporter hurling has enabled me to connect with aunts, uncles and cousins on a level I would have found difficult, if not impossible. Seeing them at that first hurling game was like finding out you share a dirty secret with previously distant neighbours. Outside immediate family, I've managed to completely indoctrinate my girlfriend and routinely attempt to spread the hurling disease to all I meet.'

Damien Murphy, b. 1979.

'... as the final result was known [1959 All-Ireland hurling final] my father and I walked to the Shandon Dairy in Dungarvan where my father worked as a fitter and we found a huge tyre which we wheeled to the pond in Abbeyside, soon other people brought along smaller tyres and with the help of a can of petrol, branches of trees and timber logs we lit a huge bonfire which burned till midnight. We danced and sang around the bonfire and the names of our hurling heroes were echoed and re-echoed against the night sky.'

Seamus Fitzgerald, b. 1949.

The Mullingar Street Leagues in the 1970s were played at Cusack Park and were vital to the success of the GAA in the town. In country towns all across Ireland, Street Leagues were an integral part of GAA life. Players who lined out together for the same club regularly tore into each other with abandon seeking glory for their part of the town. *(GAA Oral History Project/Terry O'Dowd)*

Westmeath Mayo Offaly
Limerick Laois Waterford
Carlow Longford Leitrim
Tipperary Kilkenny Derry
Kerry Cork Wicklow
Kildare Antrim Meath
Tyrone Dublin Galway
Armagh Fermanagh
Donegal Sligo Roscommon
Clare Cavan Monaghan
Louth Wexford Down

Westmeath

As dramatic, innovative stunts go, it must have been the greatest in the history of the Gaelic Athletic Association. On 16 July 1933 the new GAA field in Mullingar – Cusack Park – was officially opened. The first match on the programme was a football match between Cavan and Kildare, but now the main attraction was about to start. It was another football match, this time between Kerry and Dublin in a repeat of the previous year's All-Ireland semi-final. The players assumed their positions when, in a moment of extraordinary pageantry, an aeroplane, hired at a cost of £3 10s, flew above the ground. From the aeroplane, the match ball was thrown between the waiting players. It didn't land in the middle of the field, but the game was on. To put it in context, this spectacle took place before the establishment of Aer Lingus or the opening of Dublin airport. Indeed, newspapers at the time continued to fill columns written by people enthralled at the idea of flight. Many of the people who attended the game would not have seen a plane, let alone have flown in one. It was enough to lead the *Midland Reporter* to describe an aeroplane as 'something not unlike a bird with huge wings'.

As the historian Tom Hunt has shown, festivities had actually begun the night before when the great Kerry team, who had just won four All-Irelands in succession arrived in the town. They were just back from America – where they had been acclaimed as 'world champions' – and were met in Mullingar by the Confraternity Band who led them in torchlit procession through the town for a civic reception. Indeed, the celebrations of the whole weekend were meticulously planned. There were committees established to take charge of catering, entertainment, processions, car parking, decorations and rail excursions. Nothing was left to chance. For example, the GAA in Westmeath published a list of publicans and hoteliers who would serve food and drink at reasonable prices; nobody would leave the town saying that they had been ripped off and thereby providing an excuse for Mullingar not to be given major matches in the future. The entire development had been completed at the cost of £3,284 11s 8d. The money had been raised by the GAA clubs of Westmeath, who had divided the county into twenty-two separate districts and sought subscriptions across each from individuals and from businesses. The largest individual subscriptions came from two publicans with pubs close to Cusack Park: James Corcoran and Martin McGreevey contributed £25 and £10, respectively. Other notable subscriptions came from the Guinness brewery in Dublin, which contributed £5, and from others outside the traditional GAA community, including Lord Longford and Lady Chapman. The events of the spectacular opening ceremonies were brought to a close with a monster céilí, organised by the Mullingar branch of the Gaelic League, in Mullingar Town Hall.

In a sense, the opening of the GAA field marked a coming of age for the GAA in Westmeath. Even in the 1880s when counties across Ireland were rallying to the cause of the newly founded Gaelic Athletic Association, Westmeath was slow to heed the call. This is partly because of the prior existence of a highly developed sporting culture in the county, which encompassed everything from hunting and polo to rugby and cricket; this world has been brilliantly described by Tom Hunt in his book, *Sport and Society in Victorian Ireland: The Case of Westmeath*. The most active football clubs were in the east of the county, notably at Killucan and Kinnegad. At the Kinnegad Slashers club in 1887, newspaper reports tell of a game played between two sets of players in the club who divided themselves into Tories and Liberals in order to play.

Despite the formation of various clubs in the county, it was not until March 1891 that a county board was established. Indeed, Westmeath somewhat bucked the trend of decline across the rest of Ireland when it actually experienced a growth of clubs in the first half of the 1890s. The Westmeath county championship was hotly contested and, interestingly, there is evidence of Gaelic football enjoying a strong relationship with cricket – at least in certain parts. For example, the captain of the Moate team in the 1890 Westmeath county final was Frank Doran, who was also the professional at the Moate Cricket Club. In Killucan, meanwhile, a pattern developed where players played football in the winter and cricket in the summer.

The development of the GAA in Westmeath was stunted by the inability of the county board to garner the support of all the clubs of the county. Bitter dispute followed bitter dispute as clubs in the county refused to accept decisions given against them. The end result was the disbandment of the Mullingar Shamrocks club and the decision of the Athlone GAA club to abandon Gaelic games in favour of soccer. The story of the second half of the 1890s is the story of the decline of the GAA in Westmeath. A broader nationalist revival culminated in the rebirth of the GAA in the county after 1900. Clubs were re-formed across the county and a county board was re-established in 1904. A Leinster junior football title was won in 1905 and another followed in 1915; a Leinster junior hurling title was also won in 1912.

The reality was that Westmeath continued to struggle in senior championships. Renewed endeavour in the late 1920s saw a change of fortune. In 1929 Westmeath went on a run that saw them claim the Leinster junior final by defeating Laois in Tullamore in September of that year. Emboldened by that victory they then overcame Roscommon in the All-Ireland semi-final and Limerick in the 'Home' final. That final was played three days before Christmas 1929. Westmeath could not be crowned All-Ireland champions, however. They had still to defeat London in the All-Ireland final proper. This duly happened when London were beaten by 0-9 to 1-2 in Croke Park in February 1930. One of the players, Dinny Breen, remembered the quality of that team: 'We had a fine side and no team really came close to beating us. Winning the junior All-Ireland was a big thing back then, only second to winning the senior All-Ireland.'

Following victory in the All-Ireland junior championship in 1929, Westmeath entered the Leinster senior championship in 1930. In the first round they defeated Dublin in Tullamore and went on to reach the Leinster final against Kildare. After a creditable performance they lost by just six points to a team that was on the way to winning six Leinster championships in a row. A second chance to win a Leinster championship was created in the 1930s, but it was in hurling rather than football. While Gaelic football has always been the priority of the clubs of Westmeath, hurling has also had its adherents. Indeed, Westmeath played a part in the spread of the game during the 1930s, the great democratic decade of that game. It was in that decade, after all, that five different counties won Munster championships. And of that five, Cork, Tipperary and Limerick duly won All-Irelands, while Waterford and Clare were both narrowly beaten in finals. Kilkenny were the strongest team in Leinster, winning four All-Irelands, but Dublin, too, won an All-Ireland championship in 1938 and were beaten in two more finals. On top of that, Galway won the National Hurling League in 1932 and were unlucky in a series of All-Ireland semi-finals. For their part, London won the All-Ireland junior hurling championship – and so did Westmeath when they defeated Waterford in the 1936 final. That 1936 season showed the prowess of the hurlers of the county who chalked up ten straight wins, four in the Leinster league and six in the junior championship. Victory in the junior championship brought entry to the Leinster senior championship in 1937. Sustaining the momentum of 1936, they defeated Meath, Offaly and Laois to qualify for the final. Westmeath played defending champions, Kilkenny, in the final. They believed they would win and seemed set to do so as they led going into the last fifteen minutes. Kilkenny escaped courtesy of two late goals, however, on a score line of 5-3 to 2-4. This is the closest Westmeath have ever come to winning the Leinster championship. The wing-back on that team was Tod Nugent from Clonkill, who lived into his nineties. In his latter days he recalled: 'That was a lost opportunity. To this day, I don't think we ever managed to fulfil our potential.' Over the years, Westmeath have continued to produce brilliant hurlers and in areas such as Clonkill and Castletown-Geoghegan the passion for the game is as forceful as in any part of Ireland. The great regret is that the playing base has never been wide enough to triumph at senior level and victories have been restricted to the Christy Ring Cup.

Across the decades the clubs of Westmeath laboured to promote Gaelic games. The local championships produced matches that were as keenly fought as anywhere in the country. Sometimes too keenly. When Mullingar Shamrocks played the Mental Hospital Club in the second round of the 1945 senior football championship, the match disintegrated into mayhem. As melee followed melee, the referee had to abandon the game, which the local press described as having been played in a spirit 'which must have disgusted every real Gael and sportsman in the large crowd present'. However, poor behaviour was something that was known to extend to the supporters. The *Westmeath Examiner* reported on another match involving Mullingar when the behaviour of the spectators was 'nothing short of scandalous ... The epithets and abuse hurled at the players was a disgrace. It was not fair to the players listening to this every Sunday. Another incident which the referee did not see was a spectator rushing in and striking one of the players.'

Properly harnessed, this passion for play saw Westmeath produce minor teams that won the Leinster championship in 1939, 1952 and 1963. This was never replicated at senior level, not least because of the manner in which Westmeath was denuded of players through emigration in generation after generation. In 1985, for example, fourteen members of the Castletown-Geoghegan senior hurling panel emigrated to America. Already in the US at that stage was one of the great players in the history of Westmeath: Willie Lowery. Lowery was one of four brothers – Tommy, Martin and Mick (also an outstanding dual player for the county) were the others – who drove Castletown-Geoghegan to three senior hurling championships and St Malachy's to victory in the 1981 Westmeath senior football championship. For several years in the early 1980s Willie flew home from America to play for club and county. His performances were such that he was chosen as dual replacement All-Star in 1982. Even after he settled in America, Willie remained involved in Gaelic games. He helped refound the Westmeath club in New York and in 1996 Willie was part of the teams that won the senior hurling and football championships. He was by then in his forties.

Back in Ireland, Westmeath was then producing the finest generation of footballers in its history. This generation – including outstanding talents such as Damien Gavin and Tom Cleary – became involved in an extraordinary trilogy of matches with Laois at the Leinster final stage in 1995. It was a first look at the two coming teams of Leinster football. Eventually, Westmeath won out in a series of matches that, at their peak, drew 15,000 spectators to Tullamore. Victory propelled them all the way to the All-Ireland final where they defeated a hugely fancied Derry team. As Damien Gavin recalled: 'I don't think the importance of the win hit us until we arrived back in Mullingar where thousands of fans turned out to greet us. You could see in people's faces what an All-Ireland victory meant to them – it really was the ending of a famine.' More All-Ireland success followed at Under-21 level in 1999. The stars of the 1995 minor team were joined by other talents such as Aidan Canning and Dessie Dolan, with Luke Dempsey managing. Old rivals Laois were defeated in a Leinster final and Westmeath went on to meet Kerry in the All-Ireland final in Limerick. What ensued was, wrote Gerry Buckley, 'unquestionably the greatest day in the history of Westmeath GAA'. An enormous Westmeath crowd saw Kerry outplayed, although it still required a brilliant penalty save from Cathal Mullin to deny the Munster men. Aidan Canning remembered the emotion of it all: 'When the final whistle sounded it was the greatest moment of my life. To see thousands of Westmeath fans invading the pitch was a sight to behold.'

The challenge now was to replicate underage success at senior level. The heartbreak of narrow losses against Meath suggested that Westmeath would never overcome the psychological hurdle of winning a senior provincial title. That theory was disproved in 2004. Under the guidance of the former Kerry footballer Páidí Ó Sé, Westmeath went on an extraordinary run through Leinster, defeating Dublin, Wexford and Offaly before overcoming Laois by two points in a thrilling replayed final held on a warm July Saturday afternoon in Croke Park. Later that night, when the Westmeath footballers were welcomed back to an ecstatic Mullingar, the scenes in the town were reminiscent of the opening of Cusack Park in the 1930s. Amidst the throng it was acknowledged as the coming of age of the GAA in Westmeath.

The ability of the GAA to promote itself has sometimes been criticised. And yet the Association has been engaged in some of the most innovative events in modern Irish history. Few were more spectacular than this stunt in July 1933, represented in this apparently mocked-up photograph, when an aeroplane was used to drop a ball to start a challenge match between Kerry and Dublin to mark the official opening of Cusack Park in Mullingar. *(GAA Museum)*

Part of the success of the GAA is its ability to cultivate other sports, such as handball. For a time, tug-of-war was also very popular with GAA men, as Seamus Downes told the GAA Oral History Project: 'There were footballers but they kinda retired from the football ... you'd be 35, 40, up to 50 you'd be pulling tug-of-war. Big men. Strong men, 14 to 15, 16 stone weight. Big strong men, big strong hands and arms. Because your legs and your feet were in the ground. And you had to dig holes in the ground. And you wouldn't be allowed dig them before you start; you had to dig them when you were pulling.' *(Westmeath Examiner)*

Camogie and ladies' football have enjoyed a relatively high profile in Westmeath. Westmeath native Geraldine Giles became president of the Ladies' Gaelic Football Association. She recalled the influence that her father's garage had on her love of Gaelic games: 'It was a meeting place for the locals after a match. Every match was orally replayed ... Because we were on the main thoroughfare to Croke Park for all the western teams ... the same people came in, time in, time out. The TV was up in the corner and they could see it ... The place would be packed, people would come in and out, and the banter was fantastic.'
(Westmeath Examiner)

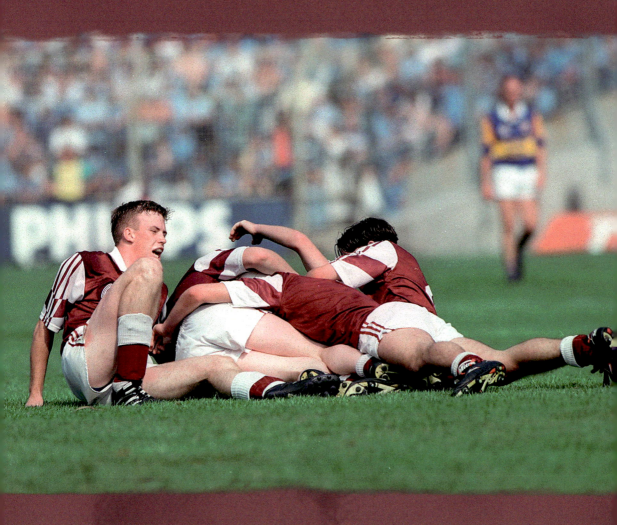

Westmeath minors celebrate their victory over Tipperary in the 1995 All-Ireland minor semi-final. The following month Westmeath claimed the All-Ireland minor title for the first time in their history. In an interview with the GAA Oral History Project, Séamus Ó Faoláin said: 'When we won our minor All-Ireland, the number of letters of congratulations from abroad. Touching – that's all I'll say. And how much it meant to them. It's a vital part of their lives abroad still – what's happening at home, who's winning championships, all of that. It's very important to the people abroad.' *(Inpho)*

'A football didn't come into the school until our school teacher — she was Ms Naughton, she was in Spittle — asked Frank Fitzgerald, who was an out-and-out Gael, to buy a football because she wanted to give us a present before she left ... That was back around '51 or that, you know, '52 ... and I remember Frank Fitzgerald getting out of the car and kicking this ball high up in the air into the schoolyard and saying: "Now lads — kick the lard out of it."'

George Hatton, b. 1937.

'Facilities at club grounds have improved beyond all recognition. I remember lads wading into the Brosna after matches for a wash.'

David Gavin, b. 1953.

'My first memory of GAA was when I was about three years old, or four ... I'd a twin brother, and my father, Lord have mercy on him, he went to a fair, and he bought us a football. But he was afraid that the football would be kicked away — the two of us so small — and he got a rope and tied the football to the rope ... The rope was big — he bought a rope as well — and tied the ball up and we kicked the ball up and down, in and out, all day long.'

Johnny Hannify, b. 1947.

'GAA is important to me because it is all about getting a place on the team and to be a team player.'

David, b. 1998, St Baoithín's N.S., Loughanaghvally.

'If I was asked would I like to get paid, when I was playing, of course I'd say, you're getting a hundred a week or something like that for doing something you love doing — you're not going to say no. If you don't get it, what about it? You'll be still out training and playing just as hard. And I know when we were out in Australia that time, if we were offered a thousand pounds a man to win that match, we would not have played any better than we did. We didn't need to be paid.'

Michael 'Spike' Fagan, b. 1960.

'You'd get an ash tree in the banks with a little crook on it, bring it home — you'd nearly always end up with some fella you know that was an ancient hurler or something like that, he'd cut out the hurl for you ... but then we used to be in a terrible state when we'd break one because it was so hard to get another one.'

Ned Mann, b. 1920.

Enthusiastic crowds throng the streets of Enniscorthy to greet the Wexford hurlers on their return home from defeating Cork in the 1956 All-Ireland final.
(Denis O'Connor Archive, Wexford)

Wexford

Less than three years after the GAA was founded, the first All-Ireland championships were held. It was a national competition in name only. The championships were open to such counties as had established county committees, a stipulation that ensured limited participation because, by early 1887, only twelve counties had county committees and, for various reasons, not all of these participated in the championships. In the end, only five counties contested the hurling championships and nine the football. It was a matter of some surprise that Wexford featured in both. From the foundation of the GAA, the county was one mostly identified with football: many of the earliest GAA clubs were formed exclusively for the purpose of football and games between them, as well as against clubs from neighbouring Wicklow, were reported to have attracted crowds in excess of 15,000. Such, indeed, was the pace at which Gaelic football spread that twenty-four clubs entered into the inaugural Wexford football championship, which opened with the meeting of Taghmon and Kilmannon in February 1887, the first championship match played anywhere in Ireland.

Hurling, in contrast, held nothing like this appeal. In March 1887, Michael Cusack lamented the failure of Wexford to develop beyond the 'football stage'. It was an assessment that was as fair as it was critical. No hurling championship was held in 1887, although Castlebridge, the county football champions, did volunteer to meet Meelick of Galway in the opening fixture of the All-Ireland hurling championship in the summer of that year, a match they duly lost. The challenge to establish Gaelic games in Wexford was at once helped and hindered by the complexity of the local sporting landscape. Put simply, the GAA did not have the sporting field to itself. As with elsewhere, the people of Wexford could choose from a wide variety of sporting attractions. The late nineteenth century had witnessed a proliferation of sporting activity within the county, though involvement in one sport did not preclude participation in another. Sporting ecumenism was not unusual: for instance, M. J. Whelan, a founding member of the GAA in Enniscorthy, was also a keen huntsman and a leading player in the Wexford County Polo Club. In Whelan's home town of Enniscorthy, indeed, the growth of sporting choice proved no barrier to the rise of the GAA. Despite the availability of a wide array of sports clubs, by the early twentieth century three GAA clubs had emerged to serve the one town. The rise of the GAA in Enniscorthy mirrored the impressive health of the Association in the wider county and the standards reached were on a par with any county in the country.

In fact, they were frequently better. In the second decade of the twentieth century, Wexford enjoyed stunning success, winning five All-Ireland titles, one in hurling in 1910 and four successive titles in football between 1915 and 1918. A central personality in all of these victories was Seán O'Kennedy from New Ross. A GAA administrator as much as a player, an Irish nationalist as much as a sportsman, O'Kennedy helped shape the character of the GAA in Wexford during one of its most turbulent, if successful, eras. He was one of a number of prominent Wexford GAA men – another was journalist Seán Etchingham, later an MP and President of the county board – who joined the Irish Volunteers and ended up temporarily interned in England during the War of the Independence. The disruption of war was detrimental to local GAA activity in Wexford, but it did nothing to stop the progress of its county footballers, who were led, unsurprisingly, by the powerfully built and inspirational O'Kennedy. A model of commitment and tactical intelligence, O'Kennedy captained Wexford to a run of All-Ireland success that has since been equalled, but never eclipsed.

At a national level, the demise of the great team of 1915–1918 ushered in a period of relative obscurity for the Wexford teams. Yet the immediate post-independence decades were not without accomplishment. Statistics alone tell of a steady progression: club numbers, which stood at a mere 14 in 1897 and had climbed to 20 by 1907, rocketed to 85 by 1930 and to more than 150 by 1953. More clubs meant more players and more games. It also meant more of a demand for pitches and this was something the county took significant steps to address. Within a twenty-year period, the county board acquired two pitches to serve as county grounds. Wexford Park, a venue for Gaelic games in the heart of Wexford town over the previous thirty years, was finally purchased in 1932 and subsequently revamped, though the cost of this redevelopment was a source of later regret to a board which came to regard it as 'over-elaborate'. Remorse at the overspend did not deter further investment and a second county ground in New Ross was added in the early 1950s when the board purchased Barrett's Park, promptly renaming it in honour of the then deceased Seán O'Kennedy. The acquisition of grounds was a big financial outlay, but these facilities – and others – also served as a crucial means of income generation for the county board. Local club championship and inter-county National League games generated money from gate receipts which was used to fund, amongst other things, contributions to teams' expenses, an accident fund for players and payments to referees.

While the development of county grounds in the early to mid twentieth century stand out as significant achievements of administration, it is important to point out that there were limits to the enlightenment of local GAA officials. On the issue of the ban on foreign games, the Wexford county board's stance was inclined to be hard line. Despite objections on the part of some clubs, the board staunchly defended the decision of the GAA's Central Council in 1938 to invoke the ban against its own patron, Dr Douglas Hyde, after he had attended an international soccer match in Dublin. Not that this was an isolated invocation of GAA dogma – the Wexford county board proved itself equally discriminating towards Hyde's successor as President, Seán T. O'Kelly. In advance of a planned visit by O'Kelly to open a feis in Wexford in June 1946, the board voted by a large majority – seventeen to six – not to attend the official welcome or allow the President to throw in the ball at the specially organised feis match. When one delegate pointed out that a few weeks previously, the county board had done nothing when a 'rugby official' had thrown in the ball to start an inter-county game in Enniscorthy, he was met with the retort: 'That man gave £150 to help pay the expenses of that match to help the Christian Brothers build a school in Enniscorthy for training of boys of the town who will be playing Gaelic games only.'

Notwithstanding the somewhat arbitrary zeal with which the ban was enforced, the attitudes of GAA officials were consistent with the general atmosphere of nationalism that came to pervade the games in the county. As if to underline the link between the two, the local celebrations which attended the 150th anniversary of the 1798 Rebellion saw the Battle of New Ross re-enacted on the GAA field in New Ross. And when a few years later – in 1955 – the Wexford hurlers won their first All-Ireland title since 1910, the frenetic celebrations included the parading of the team through the streets of the county's main towns behind a legion of pike men and pipe bands. The historian Tom Dunne, a child in Wexford at the time, recalled that for many of his fellow county men and women, the 1798 rebels and the county's hurling heroes were perceived as 'part of the same culture and continuum'. Yet, in pure sporting terms, the Wexford hurlers of the 1950s did not so much mimic history as create it. The personality and style of their play, wedded to the fact that they were challenging hurling's long-established powers, brought to their sport a fresh excitement and unprecedented glamour. From the goalkeeper to the full-forward line, the team was filled with names that, through radio and newspapers, quickly became household; among them were Art Foley, Nick O'Donnell and, most famously of all, the three Rackard brothers from Killane, Nicky, Billy and Bobby.

The triumphs of Wexford hurlers in the 1950s – they won All-Irelands in 1955 and 1956, defeating Galway and Cork in successive finals – transformed the GAA culture within the county. Most obviously, it led to the supplanting of Gaelic football as the sport of choice, the shift towards hurling being copper-fastened by developments in the 1960s and 1970s. St Peter's College, based in Wexford town, won its first All-Ireland colleges title in 1962, adding two more before the decade ended, and another in 1973. Several of the players who played on these St Peter's teams progressed to play on successful county minor, Under-21 and senior sides, among them the Quigley brothers from Rathnure. Dan Quigley captained Wexford to a senior All-Ireland title in 1968 and, two years later, he lined out in a final alongside three of his brothers (Martin, John and Pat), a game they lost to Cork. Alongside Kilkenny in Leinster, Cork provided the principal opposition to Wexford throughout the 1970s. The two counties met in three All-Ireland finals – 1970, 1976 and 1977 – and on each occasion the Wexford men found themselves on the end of a defeat.

Whatever the results, All-Ireland final appearances brought national profile, yet throughout this period, the plight of the GAA in Wexford was one of local difficulty. To their credit, this was something that Wexford GAA administrators were willing to acknowledge. In a brave and unprecedented move, they commissioned a report into the structures of the Association in the county by An Foras Talúntais, a state body involved in agricultural and rural research. Published in 1980, the report exposed a litany of problems and reinforced concerns – raised by a national GAA Commission a decade before – about the impact of urbanisation, competition from soccer and other sports and the level and quality of media treatment of Gaelic games. The image that emerged from the report was of an Association dominated by men (women accounted for only 7 per cent of all GAA members), where amenities at club level were poor (fewer than half of all clubs had dressing rooms) and where attitudes to coaching and games development fell far short of the Association's ideal.

The message was not all downbeat, however. There were encouraging stirrings of change, not least the huge increase in the acquisition of club playing pitches in the previous five years and the erection of floodlights for winter training sessions in Enniscorthy. For all its obvious merits, the publication of the report did not result in an appreciable reversal of fortune and the thirty years since have seen only an intensification of the pressures on the GAA identified by An Foras Talúntais. The economic boom of the 1990s and early 2000s saw a spillover of population from Dublin into Wexford, turning the county into one that was largely urban-based. This, allied to growing competition from soccer and rugby, placed an added pressure on Wexford county teams to maintain a high profile. This they have done with only limited success. Taking advantage of a new back-door championship route, the Wexford footballers revived memories of a more glorious past when they reached the semi-final of the 2008 All-Ireland championship. However, it is the plight of hurling that has given cause for most concern. Since the 1980s, Wexford's role as the principal opposition to Kilkenny in Leinster has been largely lost, first to Offaly and, more recently, to Dublin and Galway, the latter having joined the province in 2009 to provide more games for the westerners and more competition for the increasingly dominant Kilkenny.

There was nothing inevitable about this loss of place. In the mid 1990s, indeed, Wexford were part of a wonderful hurling renaissance, managing to add another All-Ireland hurling title under the guidance of local hotelier Liam Griffin. The public response to the 1996 All-Ireland victory was comparable to anything that greeted the great Wexford team of the 1950s. Bonfires were lit and crowds flocked the streets. A week after the 1996 final, team manager Liam Griffin and captain Martin Storey brought the Liam MacCarthy Cup to the grave of one of Wexford's greatest ever players, Nicky Rackard. There, the two men knelt and said a prayer. As so often in Wexford, past and present united under the umbrella of the GAA.

An action shot from the 1916 Leinster final between Wexford and Kildare at Croke Park. The photograph shows Tom Doyle of Ballyhogue fielding a high ball. Facing him is the Wexford captain John Kennedy with John Wall of Bunclody (with cap) in the centre. This Wexford team would win four successive All-Ireland titles between 1915 and 1918. *(Billy Kielthy Collection, County Wexford in the Rare Oul' Times, Vol. 1, by Furlong and Hayes (1985))*

The collective experience: a crowd gathers around the window of Kenny's of Campile, County Wexford, to listen to an All-Ireland final commentary in the 1930s. There were only two radios in the parish at the time. Scenes like this would have been repeated across rural Ireland during the 1930s, 1940s and 1950s, yet the tradition of radio broadcasting of Gaelic games began a decade earlier: the first sports broadcast on the national airwaves, and the first open-air sports broadcast anywhere in Europe, took place in 1926 when journalist P.D. Mehigan commentated on the All-Ireland semi-final meeting of Kilkenny and Galway. *(Thomas Grennan)*

Delegates gather at the Wexford GAA's Annual Convention in 1970, held in Enniscorthy. Less than a decade later, Wexford's GAA administrators commissioned a special report into their structures and operations. That report, published by An Foras Talúntais in 1980, began by setting out the broad challenges facing the GAA. 'The difficult problem for the Association in the 1980s will be to maintain its broad base across the increasing variety of social groups in Irish society ... In the relatively homogenous agrarian society of the past the GAA's appeal could be very much taken for granted. In the future this will have to be earned.' *(P. J. Browne Photography)*

A crowd gathers for a GAA lotto night in O'Brien's pub in New Ross, County Wexford, 1996. In many towns and villages across Wexford and beyond, GAA match days, as well as club and county social activities, have helped bring people together and sustain local business. *(P. J. Browne Photography)*

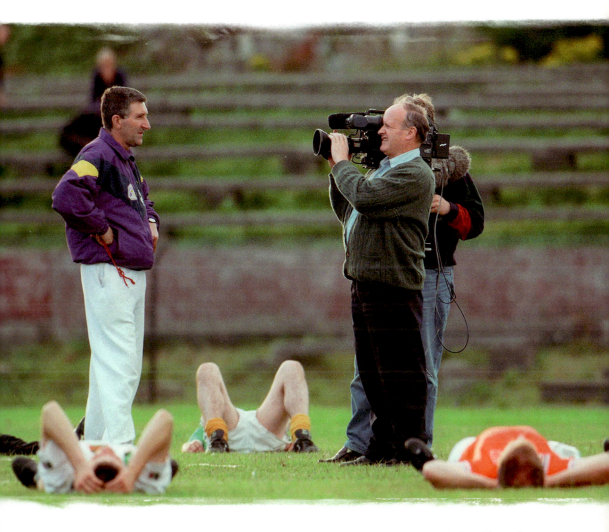

Wexford trainer Liam Griffin conducts a television interview while his players stretch about him on the grass. The summer of 1996 brought Wexford on an extraordinary journey that saw them claim their first All-Ireland title since 1968. *(Inpho)*

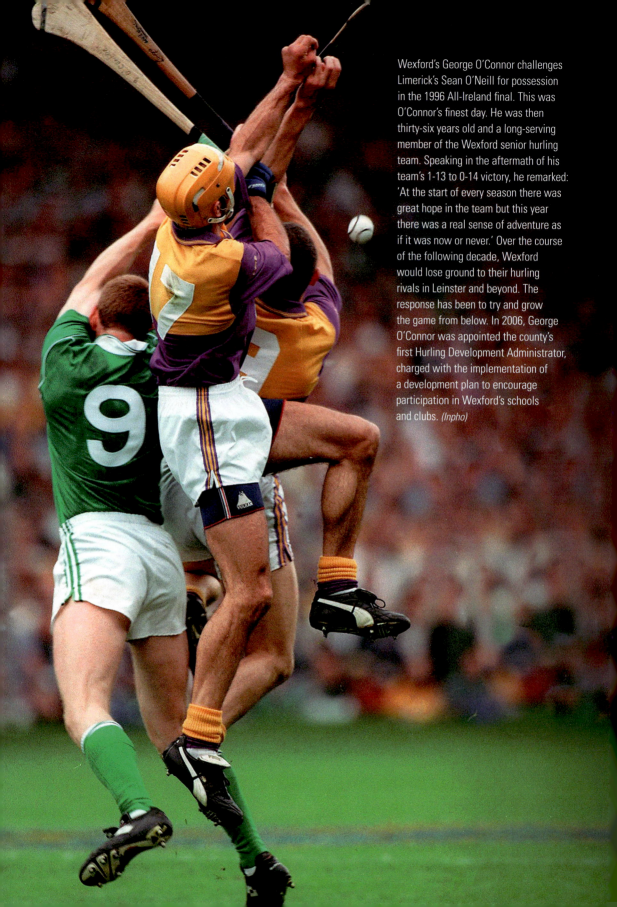

Wexford's George O'Connor challenges Limerick's Sean O'Neill for possession in the 1996 All-Ireland final. This was O'Connor's finest day. He was then thirty-six years old and a long-serving member of the Wexford senior hurling team. Speaking in the aftermath of his team's 1-13 to 0-14 victory, he remarked: 'At the start of every season there was great hope in the team but this year there was a real sense of adventure as if it was now or never.' Over the course of the following decade, Wexford would lose ground to their hurling rivals in Leinster and beyond. The response has been to try and grow the game from below. In 2006, George O'Connor was appointed the county's first Hurling Development Administrator, charged with the implementation of a development plan to encourage participation in Wexford's schools and clubs. *(Inpho)*

'Hurling — as I saw it — in the '40s, was savagery. And now, great players like Henry Shefflin and those can run through a defence, and they're protected by the rules — and rightly so. But in those days, the great Jim Langton, Christy Ring and Mick Mackey were targets for serious injury. And if they didn't protect themselves one hundred per cent, they wouldn't have survived.'

Nick O'Callaghan, b. 1936.

'Emigration would have really hit the club very hard because it's so close to Rosslare, it was very easy to get on the boat and go across. When I was a child in the '60s I thought that everybody, when they reached the age of sixteen or eighteen, that emigration said you had to do it ... The club was just barely able to field a team at that stage. I can remember actually playing on a team with men in their fifties just to make up the number at that stage.'

Bobby Goff, b. 1956.

'I tied a rag ball to the bough of a tree, hit it with the hurley, left and right, overhead ... I hit it overhead hours upon hours, that's how I became fairly proficient in the overhead strike.'

Ned Wheeler, b. 1932.

'I think camogie was frowned upon in secondary school. It was not ladylike — or so the nuns said. We tried to get them to form a team but it was not to be ... I suppose the greatest disappointments would have to be the lack of support to the camogie over the years. It has taken a lot of people in the GAA a long time to realise that women can produce as good a game as the men and have great skills.'

Eileen Dillon (née Kehoe), b. 1959.

'When the Rapparees/Starlights or Wexford were playing it would be the talk for the entire week beforehand — everything would centre around the game and we would be planning how we would get to the venue, planning the food, sandwiches etc., rooting out the flags and hats from the previous game or indeed the previous year. Afterwards we would really be delighted to get to the celebrations. Sure it was almost always back to the clubhouse — sure we stopped in pubs along the way home — that was all part of it — as we travelled home through other townlands we stopped so that others could join in our celebrations and it sounds a strange thing to say but our victory could often have a financial spin-off for some of these smaller communities on our way home. As a child I accepted that the pub was the place to celebrate, it was never questioned back then and I am not really so sure that it had an adverse effect on us children.'

Maria Nolan, b. 1957.

The Wicklow way: the county's senior footballers bathe their limbs after a training session in Shillelagh, March 2007. Under the management of former Kerry, Kildare and Laois manager, Mick O'Dwyer, Wicklow would enjoy a limited measure of success. Although still playing their league football in the lowest division, the county enjoyed one of its longest ever championship runs in 2009, playing six games over a summer campaign that took them into the month of August. Writing at the time, the journalist P. J. Cunningham remarked that 'Wicklow had finally arisen and taken its place among the nations of the Gaelic world'. For all that, Wicklow remains one of only two counties – Fermanagh being the other – not to have won a senior provincial title. *(Dave Barrett)*

Westmeath Mayo Offaly
Limerick Laois Waterford
Carlow Longford Leitrim
Tipperary Kilkenny Derry
Kerry Cork **Wicklow**
Kildare Antrim Meath
Tyrone Dublin Galway
Armagh Fermanagh
Donegal Sligo Roscommon
Clare Cavan Monaghan
Louth Wexford Down

Wicklow

On the last Sunday in October 1886, six teams from Wicklow and six from Wexford met on the grounds of the Avondale estate, home to the Irish nationalist MP and GAA patron, Charles Stewart Parnell. The occasion, billed as the first ever 'grand' inter-county contest, was a model of sound organisation and careful planning. A programme of events was printed in advance setting out the schedule for the six games – to be played at forty-five minute intervals – and listing the names of the pre-appointed referees, umpires and timekeepers, as well as the times of the special trains that had been laid on to take players and supporters to and from Wexford and Dublin for the event. The day lived up to the effort that went into its preparation. 'Never for a century had contests of such magnitude taken place in Ireland', one newspaper reported excitedly in its aftermath. The scale of the event was undoubtedly impressive. As well as the games, there was plenty of pageantry on display, with six bands – including one comprising boys from the nearby Rathdrum Industrial School – on hand to provide musical entertainment for an attendance that swelled to 12,000 spectators, among them Parnell's mother and brother, and GAA founders Michael Cusack and John Wyse Power.

If the presence of so many prominent GAA figures spoke of the historic nature of the Avondale games, the choice of participating counties was an acknowledgement of the speed and enthusiasm with which they had responded to a sporting body still at its embryonic stage. When, for instance, Wicklow held its first county convention on St Stephen's Day in 1886, representatives attended from more than thirty clubs, the levels of participation having mushroomed since the summer of 1885 when clubs first sprang up in Ashford and Roundwood. Their emergence was assisted by Dublin-based locals Jack Byrne and Larry Murphy, the former a pupil at Terenure College – the first school to align itself to the GAA – and the latter a student at Cusack's Academy, a special preparatory school intended for those taking civil service and other public examinations.

In Wicklow, however, the popular response to the GAA's founding failed to ensure its trouble-free development. The county entered into the first All-Ireland football championship in 1887, but refused to turn out for its match with Clare when it became clear that players would be expected to play midweek and be away from home for up to three days. And while the level of local activity was expanded greatly at this time, concerns were expressed at the occasional disorder that accompanied it. In May 1887, for instance, a series of Wicklow championship matches, held once again at Avondale and this time beneath Parnell's own gaze, descended into chaos. Michael Cusack, who had travelled from Dublin for the games, professed himself sickened by what he saw: 'I saw the spectators … steadily advancing on the field of play, and squatting on the ground as the day advanced. I saw a few ill-conditioned youths running round with a pole … I saw stewards and spectators freely using ash saplings on one another's heads, in a manner worthy of the halcyon days of faction-fighting.'

Such scenes were neither isolated nor singular to Wicklow, yet they became totemic of specific teething problems faced by the fledgling sporting organisation. Later that same year, when reporting on the convention of the Wicklow County Committee, Cusack's *Celtic Times* newspaper lamented the failure of delegates to spend more time on the 'best means of stamping out the bad features which have shown their ugly heads at our contests for the past year, notably in Avondale, where an attempt was made to revive the long-faded glories of the Donnybrook fair.'

The breakdown in GAA discipline and unity was not confined to the playing fields, however. It was also apparent at administrative levels where the cracks that opened up between the IRB and constitutional wings of Irish nationalism were mirrored across many county boards. So severely was Wicklow affected that its board temporarily sundered, with some clubs opting to affiliate to the Association and others not. Worse followed. For much of the 1890s, in the wake of the scandal that engulfed Parnell and his Irish Parliamentary Party, the GAA in the charismatic leader's native county was rendered effectively moribund – club numbers plummeted and county conventions and club championships were as often abandoned as held.

Meaningful revival came only with the new century. However, while Wicklow joined in the general GAA resurgence that followed the election of Tinahely native Luke O'Toole as Secretary of the Association in 1901, many of its distinctive local features remained unchanged. To a large extent, Wicklow was still a county that was football focused and eastern dominated. The reasons for this were many, but principal among them was the natural physical boundary that divided east from west. The large mountain range that runs on a north/south axis through the centre of the county ensured that in developmental terms, sporting and otherwise, regional variations were more inclined to be accentuated rather than minimised. And that is exactly how it turned out. Although the county saw its overall population fall by half in the sixty years that followed the Famine of the mid nineteenth century, there was nothing uniform or even about that experience. Against a wider backdrop of decline, the stories of particular villages and towns were characterised by many of the traditional markers of progress: physical development and population growth. Greystones, Wicklow town and Arklow were prime examples, each of them located along the east coast and each of them, from the 1850s onwards, served by a new railway line, the creation of the entrepreneurial William Dargan. Bray was similarly situated and served.

What had once been a small, seaside, fishing village was transformed with the arrival of Wicklow's first rail link to Dublin (in 1853) and the emergence of popular tourism in the second half of the nineteenth century. The popularity of Bray – its population soared from 15,537 in 1841 to 26,216 in 1911 – had everything to do with its proximity to, and connectivity with, Dublin and it was to that city that the local GAA club, founded in 1885, increasingly looked.

Despite being originally affiliated to Wicklow, Bray Emmets were accepted into the Dublin championship in the late 1890s where their impact was almost immediate. Led by Jack Dempsey, a member of a well-known Wexford football family, they won the 1901 Dublin championship after a final not played until late 1902. Victory brought with it the right to select a Dublin team for the 1902 Leinster championship, which they did with an extraordinary lack of self-regard. Only six Bray players were included on the Dublin selection which saw off all provincial opposition – including Wicklow representatives, Rathnew – and whose championship campaign ended with the defeat of London in an All-Ireland final played at the Cork Athletic Grounds in September 1904. In Bray, the celebrations ran on for months. When the players were presented with their winners' medals at a special function in February 1905, *The Wicklow People* went into overdrive with their coverage. Sixteen pages were devoted to an event that the newspaper suggested had captured the popular imagination. 'The citizens of Bray, from the leering denizens of the street corners to the most influential residents, manifested a strong interest in the ceremony, and, in fact ... no other topic was popular.'

The success of Bray Emmets in Dublin competitions – at various levels and in both codes – was confirmation of two essential realities: firstly, the high calibre of player that the club had produced; and secondly, the scale of the loss to Wicklow caused by their affiliation to a neighbouring county. It is noteworthy, for instance, that the great success of Bray in Dublin competitions and beyond occurred almost simultaneously with the designation of Wicklow among Leinster's weaker counties. Alongside Carlow, Longford and Westmeath, Wicklow was included in a newly established 'Second Division' in 1905 and it was with these same counties principally in mind that a new junior championship was introduced in 1908.

Whatever it said about the general quality of Gaelic games in Wicklow, the new grading system unquestionably brought with it fresh opportunity. And promise. Over the following century, many of Wicklow's best days came in the contesting of second-tier competitions. In 1909, they emerged triumphant from a twelve-county Leinster junior football championship, an achievement that brought with it promotion to the senior ranks. It was a status that was soon enough surrendered. According to the county's GAA historian Jim Brophy, 'local differences' were to blame for the failure of Wicklow to maintain senior status and by the end of the war years, the county was back competing at junior level, a situation that continued up until 1936 when they not only added a second Leinster junior championship, but a first All-Ireland junior title. The improvement in football standards in the county had been helped by the return to Wicklow – after several unsuccessful attempts, yet without unanimous support – of Bray Emmets two years previously, the club immediately winning back-to-back senior club titles (their last senior football championship win) and contributing several players to the Wicklow history-making junior winning side.

As it did for football, it would later do for hurling. Junior competition afforded Wicklow the opportunity not alone to be competitive at inter-county level, but to harbour genuine ambitions that their efforts might meet with some tangible reward. None of which is to suggest that success came either quickly or often. It didn't. On the contrary, for many years, Wicklow's record in hurling was dismal; such victories as there were being notable mostly for their scarcity. To an extent, the slow pace of progress reflected the late development of the game in the county. A local hurling championship had only been introduced in 1903 (the game had been described as 'defunct' in the county five years before), long after football had become entrenched as the Gaelic code of choice. The development of the game was undoubtedly helped in places by the influx of talent from outside the county. For instance, the establishment of a forestry school at Avondale at the beginning of the twentieth century led to a small, if influential, supply of hurlers to the local club, which, alongside Rathnew, was one of the early strongholds of the game. The tradition of settlers in the county assisting home-grown talent became a feature of Wicklow's hurling development and would ultimately make a contribution to the county winning All-Ireland junior titles in 1967 and 1971. This period marked a particular high point for Wicklow hurling, the relative local strength of the game being further underlined by the fact that in 1971 they also came close to winning an All-Ireland intermediate title and held a strong Galway side to a draw in a National League game in Portumna.

The make-up of these Wicklow teams reflected the hurling bias towards clubs in the east of the county; only one player from the west, John Doyle from Donard, figured on the 1971 All-Ireland junior winning team. This statistic alone reinforced the idea of Wicklow as little more than an amalgam of disparate regions, each with their own unique personality and sporting traditions. The GAA acknowledged as much when, from 1911 to 1979, they divided the county administratively into different district boards. From the very beginning of the GAA, the simple truth was that territories in the west of the county had more in common with neighbouring counties Carlow, Dublin and Kildare than with the coastal areas to the east, an identification that the construction of the Great Southern and Western Railway in the 1880s (linking Sallins and Tullow) served only to strengthen. That such an important development in public transport provision ran with, rather than against, the natural geography presented very practical problems for teams from the west of the county. Interviewed as part of the GAA Oral History Project, a Kiltegan clubman and former Wicklow GAA Chairman, Peter Keogh, reflected on how playing matches in the late nineteenth century often meant crossing the mountains: '... we're on the west-hand side of them here and most of the county is on the far side; administration and all is on the far side of the county. So we had to get a team across the mountains, or around them ... Now you could go around them today, because you've a motor car. You had no motor cars at that time and getting the teams to the far side of the county was next thing to impossible.'

No club did more to break the dominance of the east than Baltinglass. The club came to real prominence in the late 1950s when winning its first senior football championship. It would be the first of many. Four more county titles followed in the 1960s, another four in the 1970s, six in the 1980s and five in the 1990s. This was a phenomenal run of local success and it came garlanded with national honours. In 1990, Baltinglass reached the summit of club football, securing a first All-Ireland senior title for Wicklow with a talented team that included among its ranks the star forward Kevin O'Brien, subsequently an All-Star, an All-Ireland 'B' medal winner with Wicklow (in 1992) and an Irish International Rules player. Where Baltinglass left off in the mid 1990s, Rathnew continued into the latter years of the decade and into the early 2000s. Winning eight championships in a row, the 'village' club assumed a similar dominance on the local club scene and, though they failed to emulate their western rivals by winning an All-Ireland, they did manage to claim a Leinster club title in 2001.

The successes of Baltinglass and Rathnew are modern high points of Wicklow achievement, yet the very intensity of the local inter-club competition – in football and hurling – has been criticised for detracting from the performance of county teams. Writing in a centenary history of the Association in the county, Jim Brophy speculated that 'If GAA people in Wicklow can give the same commitment to the county that they give to the club, we will win All-Irelands'. In part, it was the perception of a continued primacy of club over county loyalties that led the county board to appoint the legendary Kerry man Mick O'Dwyer as county senior football manager in 2006. Although the results of his tenure were mixed – the county remained mired in the lowest division of the National Football League, but won both a Tommy Murphy cup and a first ever senior championship game at Croke Park – the mania that greeted O'Dwyer's arrival was likened to a 'tsumani' breaking over the county. In truth, O'Dwyer was tapping into something that was always there – a deep passion for the GAA and an enthusiasm for football. In a personal essay written in 1935 as part of an early history of the Association in the county, C. M. Byrne remarked on how a reader might well ask just what Wicklow's achievements were or whether they had done anything worth recalling. 'And I reply', he wrote, 'we have no great achievements, but we have kept the Gaelic flag flying to the mast for 50 years.' It is a flag that flies with even greater vigour today.

AVONDALE . Co . WICKLOW 581. W. L.

A view of Avondale house and estate, *c.* 1900. Once home to the Irish nationalist MP and GAA patron, Charles Stewart Parnell, a forestry school was opened here in the early twentieth century. The grounds of Avondale were a popular location for early Gaelic games in Wicklow: the first official inter-county games were held on this site in October 1886, when twelve teams from Wicklow and Wexford contested a series of six games across one action-packed afternoon. The event attracted an attendance of 12,000 spectators. *(National Library of Ireland, Lawrence Collection)*

Wicklow footballers, pictured at the Bel-Air Hotel in Ashford, 1936. This photograph was taken as the players were engaged in collective training prior to their All-Ireland junior football final with Mayo. It was a game that the Garden County won in dramatic fashion, overturning a seven-point deficit to claim a first ever All-Ireland junior title. *(Wicklow GAA County Board)*

Ronan Coffey in action for Rathnew in the 2001 Leinster club final replay against Na Fianna, December 2001. In defeating the Dublin champions, Rathnew became the first Wicklow club since Baltinglass to win a senior provincial title. However, where the west Wicklow club went in 1990 – they won an All-Ireland club title – the Rathnew men would ultimately come up short. Even so, the two clubs have essentially dominated the local club football scene since the late 1950s. *(Sportsfile)*

Bray Emmets player Mikey Lee chooses a new hurley during the Wicklow Under-16 hurling final in 2009. Hurling only became organised in the county in the early twentieth century, with Wicklow town winning the first county championship in 1903. Although the game has largely retained a secondary status within the county, club competition continues to be fought out with great intensity. Since their arrival on the scene in the mid 1960s, Carnew Emmets have become the most successful Wicklow club, their main challengers being Arklow Rock Parnells in the 1970s, Kiltegan in 1990s, and Glenealy in the 2000s. Despite making major strides at underage level in recent times, Bray Emmets' one and only senior title was won in 1952. *(Dave Barrett)*

A bonfire is lit in the village of Donard to mark the victory of Donard/Glen in the 2009 Wicklow senior camogie final. The game had been introduced into the county shortly before the outbreak of the First World War and its subsequent development was greatly helped by Lucy Byrne, wife of long-serving GAA administrator, C. M. Byrne. Despite occasional strains in the relationship between Wicklow and the Camogie Association – they were expelled for participating in the 1924 Tailteann Games – the game survived. A first Leinster junior title was won in 1964. *(Dave Barrett)*

'I live in Kilcoole but Bray Emmets is my club and always will be although I've lived here for thirty-eight years in Kilcoole. Rivalries can be difficult at times; it can split families on certain occasions.'

Jack Napier, b. 1942.

'For local matches I remember the whole area having flags and bunting up and having teddies dressed up in the club colours sitting on the gate posts. The whole village would then travel in convoy to Aughrim to the game. If we won the convoy would return with all horns blowing. Victorious teams would be greeted with bonfires at the crossroads and tea, sandwiches or maybe dinner, prepared by the ladies.'

Ann Lennon, b. 1978.

'It is a strange county. It's kind of a county of two halves; you've the west away up in the mountains, dividing us. And I think that's a lot to do with it because how could we — we'd never ever see one of the footballers from the west to have a chat with them or anything else. And they're the same with us. And it's like as if, when you meet then, you're enemies ... But I do think as the world has got smaller and the people have got cars and all that sort of thing, I do think it's not as it used to be.'

Betty Doyle, b. 1936.

'My brother Hugh and I, at one stage, we had a field down below the house ... the top part was kind of rushy — sparsely grown — and then it levelled out to a beautiful ... just enough for a pitch. And we called it the hairy field because of the rushes that grew there. But Hugh and I cut ... birch trees and made two goalposts and marked out the pitch, flew the tricolour from an old sceach thorn at the side of the field and many's the battle that was there between neighbours.'

Donal Cooney, b. 1928.

'When you form a club in a country place, players don't come like apples; apples come every year, players have to develop and train.'

Cathal Friel, b. 1939.

'The same effort that goes on in Kilkenny goes on in Wicklow. We put in as much of an effort, and maybe more, than happens in Kilkenny, because it's natural in Kilkenny, it's natural in Kerry for them to win. They believe they're going to win. We go out sometimes feeling that "Well, we'll have to put up a good show here", but that mentality is moving away from the new lads that are there and that has been helped quite a lot by Mick O'Dwyer who is instilling in them, to believe in themselves, believe that you're as good as the other guy.'

Jimmy Dunne, b. 1938.

GAA matches played by touring and visiting county sides have been a regular attraction for Irish people living in the United States. In October 1954, Cork travelled to the Polo Grounds (scene of the famous 1947 All-Ireland football final) to play New York in hurling. Cork won out by 7-8 to 3-10, but the value of such high-profile visitors to the diaspora was immense. *(Getty Images)*

Westmeath Mayo Offaly
Limerick Laois Waterford
Carlow Longford Leitrim
Tipperary Kilkenny Derry
Kerry Cork Wicklow
Kildare Antrim Meath
Tyrone Dublin Galway
Armagh Fermanagh
Donegal Sligo Roscommon
Clare Cavan Monaghan
Louth Wexford Down

Overseas

In the summer of 2008, as the full extent of Ireland's financial problems were beginning to become apparent, the commentator David McWilliams wrote in the *Irish Independent* that 'one of the most fascinating barometers of the Irish economy is published not by the ESRI, the Central Bank or any of the many stockbrokers paid to monitor the state of things. If you want to understand what is happening on the ground, go to www. gaa.ie'. McWilliams was highlighting trends revealed by the figures produced every month by the GAA detailing which players had requested a transfer to a new club. During the boom years, most requests to move club had been within Ireland, and related to players relocating in order to take up a new job. By August 2008, it was clear that an increasing number of moves were being made overseas, with thirty-four of the sixty players who made a request that month heading out of the country. Emigration, one of the most constant themes in Irish history, had returned as a fact of life for a new generation of Irish men and women. And it returned with a vengeance. In 2010 the GAA received 960 official applications for transfers to overseas clubs, and it was estimated that 250 club players were emigrating every month. Reflecting on the departure of so many players from the county in 2011, Westmeath county board chairman, Tom Farrell noted, 'Unfortunately, people have to go where the work is, and it's going to have an impact on the GAA, and other sporting bodies, too. Thankfully, the GAA has close-knit communities throughout the world, and they look after each other, but unfortunately this trend of players leaving for pastures new shows no sign of stopping at the moment.'

The GAA's communities across the globe are an essential entry point for many Irish men and women when they arrive in a new country. The fact that GAA clubs are found in Asia, Australasia, Europe and North America reflects the importance of the Association and its games to Irish emigrants. The spread of those clubs and their respective histories reveal much about the history of Irish emigration. Where once Britain and the United States were the most common destinations for Irish emigrants, during the Celtic Tiger years and the halt in emigration, many clubs there struggled to maintain an active membership. While the size of the GAA may have retracted in cities such as Boston or New York in the 1990s and for much of the 2000s, the growth of the financial sectors in the Middle and Far East at the same time saw the opening of clubs in cities such as Dubai and Hong Kong, as Irish graduates took well-paid jobs in the booming markets. Most recently, the current wave of emigrants have favoured Australia and New Zealand over more traditional emigrant destinations, because of their growing economies and the relative ease of legal entry compared with the complexities of getting an entry visa for the United States.

Prior to the establishment of the GAA in 1884, Gaelic games, particularly hurling, were recorded as having been played periodically in Argentina, Australia and the United States. After the establishment of the GAA, the ongoing flow of emigrants from Ireland and the export of Irish newspapers to the diaspora took the news of Ireland's newest sporting body across the world. The first game to be played under GAA rules outside Ireland took place on Boston Common in 1886, between Galway and Kerry. As noted by Paul Darby, such matches 'served to heighten interest and increase awareness of opportunities to engage in sports which offered the émigré a sense of the familiar in strange surroundings'.

In the late nineteenth and early twentieth centuries, the games of the GAA spread quickly to those areas where the Irish had settled in large numbers, particularly Australia, Britain, Canada and the United States, and there were also smaller pockets in less settled nations such as Argentina, New Zealand and South Africa. Argentina is illustrative of more general patterns. While the number of Irish settlers there was small in comparison to other places, perhaps 40,000 by the late 1920s, they were drawn from specific counties, notably Westmeath (which accounted for over 40 per cent of the total), Wexford and Longford. Elsewhere in the world, it was common for immigrants from specific counties to move en masse to specific nations, cities and neighbourhoods, and once these patterns were established, such local concentrations were reinforced by later arrivals, such as the high concentration of Donegal immigrants to Glasgow, or those from Connemara to South Boston. In Argentina, where hurling held sway amongst the Irish, it was the force of energy provided by one man which did much to sustain the GAA there, namely Offaly man William Bulfin. As editor of the *Southern Cross* newspaper in Argentina he relentlessly promoted the game, and in August 1900 he published the rules of hurling, a month after organising the first formal game in Buenos Aires. By the 1920s, hurling in Argentina had its own grounds and clubhouse, and support for the game regularly came from home such as the gift, in the 1930s from the Cork county board, of 100 hurleys and 6 sliotars. The Second World War all but ended Irish emigration to Argentina, and that – and other factors – meant that the game went into steep decline.

The power of the organising individual, which has been an important asset to the GAA since the enthusiastic drive of Michael Cusack, is particularly evident in the GAA overseas. In Argentina there was Bulfin; in the first decades of twentieth-century London the Association there was driven along by Sam Maguire; in New York from the 1950s it was John Kerry O'Donnell; and in Scotland, during the difficult years of the 1970s and 1980s, it was priests Dominic Towey and James Sheils who kept the GAA alive. As emigration rates have ebbed and flowed over the years, and as the choice of favoured destination has changed in time, the GAA abroad does not necessarily have a next generation to take over the running of a club in the same way as happens at home. Given that, and acknowledging that many second and third generation Irish abroad may turn away from the GAA and opt for sporting assimilation with their new home, clubs have often struggled to stay alive. For all those to survive and prosper, the newspapers that have served the Irish diaspora are full of countless teams that flared like a beacon, only to be extinguished a few short years later.

That first game under GAA rules in Boston in 1886 is also instructive in understanding the GAA overseas. The teams that day did not play under the names of Boston's Irish suburbs. It was not Roxbury against Dorchester, but rather Galway against Kerry. As with county associations across the world that have brought Irish people from a specific locale together to socialise and network, so the GAA overseas has often replicated county identities. This is less common nowadays, but throughout the nineteenth and into the twentieth centuries, Gaels overseas saw themselves, in sporting terms, not as a homogenous Irish diaspora, but rather as being from their home county or region. Even today, a glance at the list of affiliated overseas teams reveals the legacy of this trend: in Auckland, the Connemara Gaels; in London, the Kingdom Kerry Gaels; in New York, the Armagh, Cavan, Cork, Donegal, Dublin, Galway, Kerry, Kildare, Leitrim, Mayo, Monaghan, Offaly, Roscommon, Sligo, Tipperary and Tyrone clubs. County allegiances run deep, and even when stranges in a foreign land, the members of the GAA bond and organise around their home identities. There is, nonetheless, a certain fluidity around this – there are those who step readily across the county border in America who would never imagine such an act at home.

While there is a wealth of GAA clubs across the world, it is London and New York that have the most revered status: they both have the right to enter the All-Ireland championship, competing in the Connacht championship in football (London also competes in hurling's Nicky Rackard Cup). London was particularly important in the All-Ireland championship in the first decade of the twentieth century. Back then the format of the competition was such that the All-Ireland championship ended with a 'Home' final, being followed by the actual final played against the champions of England. As such, London teams competed in the football final in 1900, 1901, 1902, 1903 and 1909 (losing all of them), and in every hurling final between 1900 and 1904. London, famously, became All-Ireland hurling champions in 1901 when they beat Cork in the final. The pivotal role of two early GAA organisers in London, Liam MacCarthy and Sam Maguire, both of whom served on the London county board, is remembered to this day in the form of the All-Ireland trophies for hurling and football respectively.

That MacCarthy and Maguire served on the London county board in the late 1890s and early 1900s is evidence of how much a part the GAA overseas has been of the GAA administratively. Indeed, New York and London are the two oldest overseas county boards, but have been joined in more recent times by ones that cover Europe, North America, Australasia and Asia. The North American board, in addition to attending the GAA Annual Congress, works within the United States to support over 110 clubs, while the Canadian board works with sixteen clubs. In North America alone, the map of GAA clubs stretches from sunny San José in California to the colder climes of Red Deer, Alberta, in central Canada.

From the 1980s, the geographical spread of the GAA broadened. While the Irish emigrated during the 1980s depression to traditional destinations such as the United States and Britain, Ireland's close relationship with the European Union meant that greater numbers of Gaels were located across the continent and new clubs sprang up. The process was hastened at the start of the new century as Irish companies and individuals set up businesses in an array of countries. The European county board now administers clubs in thirteen different countries, from Gothenburg GAA (founded in 2004), Luxembourg Gaelic Sports Club (1978), Den Haag GAA club (1993) to Naomh Fermin Pamplona (2007). A further shift in the scope of the GAA overseas took place from the 1990s when the Asian Tiger roared and the Irish moved to the Far and Middle East to work in the booming construction, financial and business service sectors. The Asian county board now supports twenty-four clubs ranging from the Abu Dhabi Na Fianna (1994), Hong Kong GAA (1996), Jakarta Dragonflies (2008) and the Viet Celts (2007).

The impact of the GAA in such a distant land as Thailand, with no history of large-scale emigration, is evidenced by the story of one player there, John Campbell, who wrote that it was 'good to know that if you do travel within the region, whether for business or leisure, that most countries now have clubs and people you can contact for a run-around or even just local advice. Having now spent half of my life outside Ireland, GAA in Asia has allowed me to get back in touch with my Irish identity and culture.'

One of the most profound problems for the GAA overseas is that it effectively relies on a continuing tide of emigration to sustain itself. During the Celtic Tiger years, when outward emigration to the United States all but stopped, the GAA in New York saw nine clubs close due to lack of members. In Boston, it was a similar story, with the problem of lack of legal status also leading many Irish in the city to head for home. The *Boston Globe* noted, 'Another telling barometer of change in the Irish community is in its beloved diversions. Several teams that play the Gaelic games of hurling and football have folded or consolidated for want of players.' The problem of renewal, of the next wave of young emigrants who want to sustain their GAA culture overseas, is that it relies on a moribund Irish economy. The difficulty for the GAA overseas, when numbers of emigrants decline because of economics, destination trends or visa regulations, is how to keep the games going. The challenge for the GAA overseas is how to encourage locals with no Irish connection, or else those with an Irish heritage, to come to a GAA club and try out the games. This challenge is being confronted. In Boston, at the Irish Cultural Centre in Canton, across the Warwickshire GAA, in Scotland and elsewhere, local GAA clubs have worked tirelessly to attract non-immigrants into the club, with notable success. In Scotland, for example, the focus has been on the descendants of immigrants, so that 'since the mid 1990s thousands of primary level schoolchildren (including many hundreds from outside the Irish diasporic community) have participated in Gaelic games in the west of Scotland'.

Whatever the future of the GAA overseas, its many clubs in a range of countries have provided an entry point for Irish emigrants into their new home. It has allowed them to play, to socialise and provided them with networks to find jobs and homes. Ultimately, the GAA club overseas provides a 'venue within which Ireland can be invoked – Ireland as a copy of the original – on a weekly basis'.

A photograph of a hurling match in London, which was reproduced in the G. R. Sims series of books 'Living London', *c.* 1902. During the early twentieth century, two of the principal GAA organisers in London were Liam MacCarthy and Sam Maguire, both of whom served on the London County Board and both of whom later lent their names to All-Ireland trophies. *(Museum of London)*

Aonach Tailteann, the Irish Olympiad, was staged in 1924, 1928 and 1932. It was a massive undertaking that brought athletes of Irish heritage from across the world to compete in a variety of events. Here, at Croke Park, the teams from America and Ireland compete for the hurling title in 1928. Aonach Tailteann was a most spectacular attempt by the Irish Free State to reconnect with the Irish sporting diaspora after the years of revolution. *(National Library of Ireland, Irish Independent Collection)*

Dick 'The Boiler' Conroy (far right), from Rhode, County Offaly, shakes hands with an unnamed man who used to drive GAA players out to the New Eltham Grounds in London in the early 1960s in a fifteen-seater minibus. Trading as Richard Conroy Contractor, 'The Boiler' employed many footballers who played for the Round Towers club in London, including Tony Kilmurray (Offaly), Mick Rouse (Offaly), Seamus Dolan (Offaly), Jody Hickey (Offaly) and Donal Fox (Offaly). Another Offaly man, Dermot O'Brien from Tullamore, was the driving force behind the Round Towers club and has given more than fifty years of dedicated service to the club as a player and an administrator. *(GAA Oral History Project/Paul Rouse)*

Members of the Meath football team enjoy the sights of Sydney during their historic tour of Australia in 1968. Travelling as All-Ireland champions and engaging in a series of test matches against Australian rules opposition, the Meath men began a relationship that would blossom into a full-scale international exchange in the 1980s. In more recent times, as the Irish economy has stagnated, there has been a marked increase in the numbers of young Irish people emigrating to Australia and these have helped swell the ranks of GAA clubs in the major cities of Brisbane, Melbourne, Perth and Sydney. *(Peter McDermott)*

The GAA has, since its foundation, planted seeds far from home. The end of the twentieth century saw the games transplanted to the Far East. The games were embraced not only by emigrant Irish men and women, but also by many of their local hosts. The 2006 Asian games were played in Shanghai, and as well as the Irish ladies' footballers, there were many locals displaying their skills. *(Tom Coyner)*

'The history of Gaelic games in Canada, before the founding of the GAA in Ireland in 1884 and in the years since, proves a determination by Irish immigrants who have arrived on these shores of Canada. Through their dedication the flag of Irish sports has flown strong, and will continue to fly in the years to come.'

John O'Flynn, Vancouver, b. 1964.

'In New Zealand, it has been a struggle to stay alive as we are very much a minority code. In the '50s immigrants came and stayed; now they come and stay a short period. The (Irish) priests have always been in both administration and playing since 1950. Now fewer priests are coming from Ireland and we miss their help and enthusiasm.'

Patrick Somers,
Carlow and Auckland, b. 1923.

'For the young Irish coming to America, nobody does more for them than the GAA. Because they give them apartments, they give them jobs, they pick them up at the airport, they take them everywhere. There's no organisation, I think, in America as good to the young Irish as the GAA is.'

John McDevitt,
Donegal and Boston, b. 1945.

'It wasn't set up but Paddy Sullivan picked me up at the boat – I came on the SS America – and it was more or less understood that I'd play with Cork. There was no work here in 1955 either, so things were tough and he got you a job in the warehouse – a tough, hard job. That's what all the fellas done, unless you had a trade – if you had a trade you were all right.'

Joe Carey, Tipperary and New York, b. 1934.

'I got an email about six months ago from a Czech guy, I think he must have found us online; at the beginning our website was just one page with my email address at the bottom if you wanted to contact us. The guy had lived in Dublin for three years – he had moved there with a company – and he moved back, and basically his kids were GAA fanatics.'

Enda Gorman,
Kildare and Prague, b. 1978.

'The English people never get to know that side of our life; we lead, if you like, a double life … It's a strange way of life that the Irish in Britain have that I suppose no one can understand unless they were involved.' Frank Shovlin, Donegal and Liverpool, b. 1970.

Bibliographical Note

The research upon which this book is based is rooted in the GAA Oral History Project: in the interviews recorded, the questionnaires submitted, the documents donated and the photographs presented. Underpinning this oral history are the written words of several generations of GAA journalists and historians. Each chapter draws from histories of club, county and province. The histories of club and county used are listed below, while provincial histories of the GAA that were consulted comprise the following: Con Short, *The Ulster G.A.A. Story* (1984), Thomas Moran, *Stair CLG Chonnacht: History of Connacht GAA 1902–2002* (2002) and Jim Cronin, *Munster GAA Story* (1984).

Recent years have also seen a great increase in the academic attention given to the history of Gaelic games. The 125th anniversary of the establishment of the GAA saw the publication of a number of books that have been vital to the completion of this book. These include Dónal McAnallen, David Hassan and Roddy Hegarty (eds.), *The Evolution of the GAA: Ulaidh, Éire agus Eile* (2009), Mike Cronin, Mark Duncan and Paul Rouse, *The GAA: A People's History* (2009), and Mike Cronin, William Murphy and Paul Rouse (eds.), *The Gaelic Athletic Association: 1884–2009* (2009). Particular tribute must be paid to the work of Tom Hunt and Dónal McAnallen whose pioneering work has changed the way that people think and write about the GAA.

Of course, all historians owe a debt to those who have gone before and this book, like those mentioned above, has necessarily drawn on the vast range of books that have been produced over many years on various aspects of the history of the GAA. These include Desmond Fahy, *How the GAA Survived the Troubles* (2001), Marcus de Búrca, *Michael Cusack and the GAA* (1989), Marcus de Búrca, *The GAA: A History (1980)*, Pádraig Puirséal, *The GAA in its Time* (1984), Séamus McRory, *The Voice from the Sideline: Famous GAA Managers* (1997), Jerome Quinn, *Ulster Football & Hurling: The Path of Champions* (1993), Eamonn Rafferty, *Talking Gaelic: Leading Personalities on the GAA* (1997), John Scally, *100 GAA Greats: From Christy Ring to Joe Canning* (2010), W. F. Mandle, *The GAA and Irish Nationalist Politics* (1987), Padraig Griffin, *The Politics of Irish athletics, 1850–1990* (1990), Joe Lennon, *The Playing Rules of Football and Hurling, 1884–1995* (1997), Art Ó Maolfabhail, *Camán: Two Thousand Years of Hurling in Ireland* (1973), Seamus J. King, *A History of Hurling* (1998), Marcus de Búrca, *The GAA: A History* (1984), Liam Ó Caithnia, *Scéal na hIomána* (1980), Breandán Ó hÉithir, *Over the Bar* (1991), Seamus Ó Riain, *Maurice Davin, 1842–1927* (1998), J. J. Barrett, *In the Name of the Game* (1997), Tom McElligott, *The Story of Handball* (1990), Eoghan Corry, *The History of Gaelic Football* (2009), Tom Humphries, *Green Fields: Gaelic Sport in Ireland* (1996), Brendan Fullam, *Lest We Forget: Gems of Gaelic Games and Those Who Made Them* (2009) and various titles by Raymond Smith, *Decades of Glory: A Comprehensive History of the National Game* (1966), *The Football Immortals: A Comprehensive History of Gaelic Football* (1968), *Players No. 6 Book of Hurling: A Popular History of the National Game 1884–1974* (1974), *The Greatest Hurlers of Our Time* (1990).

Equally, the fact that the GAA is entwined with so many aspects of the life of the country has rendered the wider histories of various counties useful. Of great assistance in writing this book has been the great array of local history journals and, in particular, the brilliant *History and Society* series published by Geography Publications. It should also be noted that local newspapers were used extensively in providing the material included in these pages.

Finally, online sources now offer a wealth of information to anyone with even a passing interest in the GAA. Excellent historical articles and current material – as well as statistics and other details – can be found on websites run by various GAA clubs, county boards, provincial boards and at central level, and by other websites such as anfearrua.com and hoganstand.com. While one might despair at some of the anonymous bile spilled onto the noticeboards of some sites, a full acknowledgement should be made of the manner in which they have both enhanced coverage of the GAA through a new medium and provided a forum for public discussion on all GAA-related matters. A degree of caution must be maintained in accepting the accuracy of some of this material, but a similar caution is also useful when dealing with newspapers, periodicals and books! Websites run by the Central Statistics Office, the Houses of the Oireachtas and various government departments were also invaluable in providing information for this book, not least in respect of population change.

All of the above sources were used across the thirty-three chapters of this book and were complemented by the books listed below which relate to the individual chapters in the book.

Introduction

The single best source for studying the development of Irish counties is Mary E. Daly (ed.) *County & Town. One Hundred Years of Local Government in Ireland* (2001), in particular the opening chapter by Mary E. Daly, 'The County in Irish History'. Other valuable information was gleaned from John Morrissey, 'Contours of Colonialism: Gaelic Ireland and the early colonial subject', *Irish Geography*, 37, 1 (2004) and Gillian Smith, 'An eye on the survey: perceptions of the Ordnance Survey in Ireland, 1824–1842', *History Ireland*, 9, 2 (2001).

Antrim

There is no history of the GAA in Antrim, but – as well as the general histories listed above – this chapter has relied on books such as Marnie Hay, *Bulmer Hobson and the Nationalist Movement in Twentieth-Century Ireland* (2009), Eamon Phoenix, Pádraic Ó Cléireacháin, Eileen McAuley and Nuala McSparran (eds.), *Feis na nGleann: A Century of Gaelic Culture in the Antrim Glens* (2005) and Ja Walshe, *From Clonard to Croke: A History of St. Gall's GAC, 1910–2010* (2010).

Armagh

The principle text used for this chapter was Con Short, *Árd Mhacha 1884–1984: A Century of GAA Progress* (1985). Short's books make for fascinating reading; they are insightful, invariably well written and convince in a way that not every GAA publication succeeds in doing. This aura of authority is rooted in the obvious depth of research that is evident in almost every page. Amongst the club histories used were Phil McGinn, *Armagh Harps GFC 1888–2008: Celebrating 120 Years* (2008) and Con Short, *The Crossmaglen G.A.A. Story*, Crossmaglen Rangers G.A.C. (1987).

Carlow

The earliest published history of the GAA across Carlow is *Cumman Lút-cleas Co. Ceatarloca: 1886–1927* (1929). This and subsequent phases of the GAA's development – and that of the wider society – have also been covered in articles published in *Carloviana*, the journal of the Carlow Historical and Archaeological Society. These provided a bedrock of research for this chapter as did Leo McGough (ed.), *Carlow Hurling Memories. Inné agus Inniu* (1978) and various club histories, principally Eamonn Ryan, *Tinryland G.F.C. 100 Years History 1888–1988* (c. 1988), *Baile na mBrannach 1890–1990: A Centenary Celebration* (c. 1990) and Willie D. White, *Kildavin GAA Club (A Local History): Footprints to the Future* (n.d.).

Cavan

The basic research for this chapter is taken from Rev. Daniel Gallogly, *Cavan's Football Story* (1979). It was also assisted by A. F. McEntee, *Memories of the Lifetime in Journalism in Cavan of A. F. McEntee* (1991). *Breffni Blue – the Cavan GAA Yearbook* was a useful source as were club histories such as Hugh O'Brien's *The Celtics 1894–1994: A Centenary History of the G.A.A. in Cootehill* (2000). Raymond Gillespie's edited collection, *Cavan: Essays on the History of an Irish County* (2004) was most enjoyable and informative reading.

Clare

As the birthplace of the GAA's founder and for other reasons, the county features prominently in many of the general GAA histories listed above. Many of these helped underpin this chapter as did Seamus O'Reilly, *Clare GAA: The Club Scene 1887–2010* (2010) and Ollie Byrnes, *Against the Wind: Memories of Clare Hurling* (1996). There is an excellent club history by Sean Kierse, *A History of Smith O'Brien's GAA Club 1886–1987 (1991)*, while essays by Daniel McCarthy ('Citizen Cusack and Clare's Gaelic Games') and Jimmy Smyth ('A Lifetime in Hurling'), both broad-ranging in scope, were published in Matthew Lynch and Patrick Nugent (eds.), *Clare: History & Society* (2008).

Cork

This chapter is underpinned by a vast array of published work that is both general to the GAA and specific to Cork. Of the latter, important starting points were John Joe Brosnan and Diarmuid O Murchadha (eds.) [compiled by James Cronin], *Cork GAA: A History 1886–1986* (1987); Jim Cronin, *Making Connections – A Cork GAA Miscellany* (2005), Donal O'Sullivan, *Sport in Cork: A History* (2010) and Mary Moran, *Cork's Camogie Story 1904–2000* (2004). John A. Murphy has written compellingly on the role of the GAA in the forging of Cork identity in 'Cork: Anatomy and Essence', published in Patrick O'Flanagan & Cornelius Buttimer (eds.), *Cork History and Society* (1994) and 'Cork GAA: Windows on History', *The Cork GAA Strategic Vision and Action Plan 2010–2015* (2010). J. J. Walsh left behind a valuable memoir in *Recollections of a Rebel* (1944), while the genius of Christy Ring has been documented by many writers, among them Val Dorgan, *Christy Ring: A Personal Portrait* (1980) and Tim Horgan, *Christy Ring: Hurling's Greatest* (2007). The latter also authored *Cork's Hurling Story* (1977). As well as club histories and a spate of player memoirs, the recent decades in Cork GAA's history were covered by Michael Moynihan in *Blood Brothers: the Inside Story of the Cork Hurlers, 1996–2008* (2008) and *Rebels: Cork GAA Since 1950* (2010).

Derry

Derry still awaits a comprehensive history of the GAA in the county. This chapter relied heavily on Eoghan Corry's book, *Oakboys: Derry's Football Dream Come True* (1993). It also used Aidan Hegarty's, *Kevin Lynch and the Irish Hunger Strike* (2006), Sean McMahon's *A History of County Derry* (2004), Gerard O'Brien and William Nolan (eds.), *Derry and Londonderry: History & Society; Interdisciplinary Essays on the History of an Irish County* (1999).

Donegal

Just as with Derry, Donegal awaits a full county history. There are some excellent club histories, however, including the outstanding D. Campbell, D. Dowds, and D. Mullan's *Against the Grain: A History of Burt, its People and the GAA* (2000) and Seán MacConaill (ed.), *Idir Peil agus Pobail. A History of the GAA in the Parish of Ardara 1921–2003* (2004). Donegal's GAA Yearbooks from the 1980s were useful sources of information on the GAA in the county, as was Sean Ó Gallchóir's *Book of Donegal GAA Facts*. Most useful of all is Conor Curran's *A History of Sport in Donegal* (2010), which is a model of scholarship, writing and analysis. It is one of the best pieces of historical writing on sport ever published in Ireland.

Down

The key book in writing this chapter was Síghle Nic an Ultaigh, *An Dún – The GAA Story* (1984); it is comprehensive, illuminating and entertaining. The range of publications produced by Joe Lennon was invaluable, as was Jim McCartan's 2010 autobiography, *The King of Down Football*, which is a fascinating book. Interesting background reading on the history of the county can be found in Lindsay Proudfoot and William Nolan (eds.), *Down: History & Society; Interdisciplinary Essays on the History of an Irish County* (1997).

Dublin

This chapter relied heavily on the phenomenal three-volume history of the GAA in Dublin, William Nolan (ed.), *The Gaelic Athletic Association in Dublin 1884–2000* (2005). David Gorry was also involved in that epic undertaking and his unpublished thesis, 'The Gaelic Athletic Association in Dublin 1884–2000:

a geographic analysis' (M. Litt thesis, UCD, 2001), also proved a valuable resource. In addition, it also drew from Seán Óg Ó Ceallacháin, *The Dubs: Dublin GAA since the 1940s* (2006), Tom Humphries, *Dublin V. Kerry: the Story of the Epic Rivalry that Changed Irish Sport* (2007) and the Paddy Donnelly compiled *Cumann Iomáine agus Peile Naomh Uinsionn: 1931–1981: Na Blianta Órga* (c. 1981). Given the importance of the capital as the biggest centre of population, major investigations into the future of the GAA have all focused particular attention on the issue of Dublin. The reports of two such investigations assisted this chapter: *The Report of the Commission on the GAA* (1971) and *Strategic Review: Enhancing Community Identity* (2002).

Fermanagh

The single most important text used in writing this chapter is the recent – and very fine – history of the GAA in Fermanagh published in 2009. The book was compiled by the Fermanagh County Committee CLG Centenary Committee and is entitled *A Gaelic Graduation: A History of Fermanagh GAA* (2009). The other vital source of information used in writing this chapter was the Fermanagh County Committee's development plan – *Forbairt Fhearmanach 2007–2012* – which is beautifully written and offers a great insight into the GAA in Fermanagh, past and present. A wider sense of the county was also provided by Eileen M. Murphy and William J. Roulston (eds.), *Fermanagh: History & Society; Interdisciplinary Essays on the History of an Irish County* (2004).

Galway

The principle works used in this chapter were Pádraic Ó Laoi, *Annals of the GAA in Galway, volume one, 1884–1901* (1983) and *Annals of the GAA in Galway, volume two, 1901–34* (1992). Further to those books, Jack Mahon and John Scally's books were particularly insightful on the history of the GAA in Galway. The fact that Mahon was an integral part of Galway GAA for an extended period lends a wonderful insight into the story of the GAA – particularly that of Gaelic football – during the middle decades of the twentieth century. Galway is also particularly well served by club histories. Most notably, club histories of Mullagh, Meelick, Killimor and Kiltormer carry excellent detail on the hurling traditions of the eastern area of the county, particularly the land that stretches along the River Shannon.

Kerry

Although no modern, single-volume history exists of the GAA in Kerry, the county is well served by club and county historians, as well as the broader literary community. For the early development of the GAA in Kerry, this chapter drew on a variety of sources: "P. F.", *Kerry's Football Story* (1945), John Barry and Eamon Horan, *Years of Glory: The Story of Kerry's All-Ireland Senior Victories* (1977), Richard McElligott's paper '"Degenerating, from sterling Irishmen into contemptible West Britons": The GAA and Rugby Football in Kerry, 1885–1905', delivered to the *Sports History Ireland* Conference at the Mater Dei Institute, September 2010, Eamonn Fitzgerald (ed.), *Dr. Crokes: A Gaelic Century 1886–1986* (1986), Dick Fitzgerald, *How to Play Gaelic Football* (1914), Thomas B. Looney, *King in a Kingdom of Kings: Dick Fitzgerald and Kerry Football* (2008), as well as a number of articles published in the *Journal of the Kerry Archaeological & Historical Society*. A number of these publications covered longer time frames than others, but the Kerry-specific works that were consulted for the period from the War of Independence onwards included: J. J. Barrett, *In the Name of the Game* (1997), Eamonn O'Sullivan, *The Art and Science of Gaelic Football* (1958), Weeshie Fogarty, *Dr. Eamonn O'Sullivan: A Man Before His Time* (2007), Pádraig Ó Concubhair, *Sixty Years A-growing, The North Kerry Board 1924–1984. The Story of the Clubs of North Kerry* (c. 1984), Joe Ó Muircheartaigh and T. J. Flynn, *Princes of Pigskin: A Century of Kerry Footballers* (2007), Owen McCrohan, *Mick O'Dwyer: The Authorised Biography* (1990), Jack O'Connor (written with Tom Humphries), *Keys to the Kingdom* (2008), Gabriel Fitzmaurice (ed.), *The Kerry Anthology* (2000), and Gabriel Fitzmaurice, *In Praise of Football* (2011).

Kildare

The principle work upon which the chapter draws is Eoghan Corry, *Kildare GAA: A Centenary History* (1984). Important developments at the beginning of the twentieth century were also documented in 'Progress of the G.A.A. in Kildare. From 1900 to 1907', *The Gaelic Athletic Annual and County Directory 1907–8*, while wider developments in the county across the nineteenth and twentieth centuries are well covered in Willam Nolan and Thomas McGrath (eds.), *Kildare History and Society* (2006). Of particular importance here is the essay by David Gorry, 'Population in County Kildare – Change, Contrast and Challenges'. The response of the GAA to the massive expansion to the Dublin commuter belt during the 1990s and early 2000s is discussed in the chapter by Mary P. Corcoran, Jane Gray and Michel Peillon, 'Ties that Bind? The Social Fabric of Daily Life in New Suburbs', in Tony Fahey, Helen Russell and Christopher Whelan (eds.), *Best of Times? The Social Impact of the Celtic Tiger* (2007). In 1998, Kildare won their first Leinster championship since 1956, the background to which was well documented in the newspapers of the time, but also in Mick O'Dwyer (with Martin Breheny), *Blessed and Obsessed* (2007).

Kilkenny

This chapter draws from a wealth of local sources. Apart from newspapers and the academic works on the early GAA listed above, the development of the Association in Kilkenny, and the game of hurling in particular, is documented in Tom Ryall's, *Kilkenny: The GAA Story, 1884–1984* (1984) and a range of club histories, including Denis Kinsella (ed.), *The Mooncoin Story* (1990), Antóin Ó Dúill, *Famous Tullaroan 1884–1984* (1984), Anon., *Up the 'Boro: Dicksboro GAA Club 1909–2009* (2009), Senan Cooke, *A History of the GAA in Kilmacow 1884–2010* (2010) and Michael O'Dwyer, *The History of Cricket in County Kilkenny – the Forgotten Game* (2006). Among the other works consulted for this chapter are: Phil O'Neill, *A History of the GAA 1910–1930: A History and Reference Book for Gaels* (1931), Cill Chainnigh, *Caoga Blian Óg: A History of Kilkenny Primary Schools' Board, 1939–1989* (1989), Fearghus Ó Fearghail, *St. Kieran's College, Kilkenny 1782–1982* (1982), Marilyn Silverman, *An Irish Working Class. Explorations in Political Economy and Hegemony, 1800–1950* (2001); William Nolan, Kevin Whelan (ed.), *Kilkenny: History and Society* (1990), Brian Cody (with Martin Breheny), *Cody. The Autobiography* (2009), *Kilkenny GAA Strategic Vision and Action Plan, 2010–2015*.

Laois

Two commemorative GAA publications, Teddy Fennelly, *100 Years of the GAA in Laois: A Centenary Yearbook* (1984) and *125 Laois GAA: Club and County History* (2009) provided a starting point for the research underpinning this chapter. However, the analysis of the early development of the GAA in the county was also informed by material held in the John J. Higgins Collection, a substantial archive of documents detailing how the Laois County Board prepared for the 1914 and 1915 All-Ireland hurling finals, which is held by the GAA Museum. It was also helped by recent scholarly research, some unpublished and some soon to be published. This includes an article by Ross O'Carroll and Paul Rouse, *Sport and War: The 1915 All-Ireland Hurling Championship*, forthcoming 2011, Ross O'Carroll, *The Gaelic Athletic Association, 1914–1918*, unpublished MA thesis, UCD, 2010, and Arnold Mahon, *An Analysis of the Development of Sport in Laois/Queen's County Within the Context of the Period 1910–1920*, unpublished MA thesis, UCD, 2007. The wider social and political context to the GAA story in the county is explored in a number of essays in Padraig G. Lane and William Nolan (eds.), *Laois: History & Society (1999)*.

Leitrim

The history of the GAA in Leitrim is expertly served by Seán Ó Suilleabháin (ed.) in two books, *Scéal Liatroma: Leitrim GAA story 1886–1984* (1984) and *Leitrim GAA Millenium book: Scéal Liatroma sa Mhílaois, Foilsithe ag Coiste Chontae Liatroma Cumann Lúth-Chleas Gael* (2000). Ó Suilleabháin's work sits at the heart of this chapter, while amongst the various club histories that were insightful on the GAA in Leitrim were Pádraig Leyden's *Fenagh: the GAA Story, Fenagh GAA Club* (1985) and Pádraic Ó

Cléirigh's, *Scéal Gortleitreach: The Gortletteragh GAA Story: 1889–1991* (1992). The collected works of John McGahern, particularly his *Memoir* (2005) provided much of the context to this chapter.

Limerick

As with any research on the history of the GAA in Limerick, the starting point for this chapter was Séamus P. Ó Ceallaigh, *History of the Limerick G.A.A. From the Earliest Times to the Present Day* (1937), Seamus Ó Ceallaigh and Sean Murphy, *One Hundred Years of Glory. A History of Limerick GAA* (1987). Seamus Ó Ceallaigh and Sean Murphy also collaborated on *The Mackey Story* (1982), a subject also well covered by Sean Murphy in his Ahane club history, *Come on Ahane: 'The Spuds are Boiling': A History of GAA Affairs in the Parish of Ahane-Castleconnell 1884–2002* (2001), as well as all of the major works on the history of hurling by, *inter alia*, Raymond Smith, Brendan Fullam and Seamus King. A short history of Limerick Commercials, written by P. J. Corbett, a player and secretary with the club when they won the 1887 All-Ireland football championship, was published in *The Gaelic Athletic Annual and County Directory, No. 3, 1910–11*. The contents of the extensive Seamus O'Ceallaigh collection, much of it focused on local GAA affairs, was consulted online via the excellent Limerick City Library website. For portrayals of urban and rural social life and conditions, Jeremiah Newman (ed.) *The Limerick Rural Survey, 1958–1964* (1964) and the writings of Frank McCourt, most notably *Angela's Ashes: A Memoir of a Childhood* (1996), were valuable sources, while the Limerick rugby experience – examined to counterpoint that of the GAA – was explored through Charlie Mulqueen, *Limerick's Rugby History* (1978) and Michael O'Flaherty, *The Story of Young Munster Rugby Football Club, 1895/96–1995/96* (1996). For more recent GAA developments in the county, the chapter was helped by reference to Henry Martin's *Unlimited Heartbreak: The Inside Story of Limerick Hurling* (2009).

Longford

As well as Seán Ó Corcora, *C.L.C.G. Chontae Longfoirt 1887–1987* (1987), various club histories were consulted in the preparation of this chapter, including Mel Clarke (ed.), *Cluain Geis: Clonguish GAA Club 1889–1984, Official Opening of Park and Complex 3 June 1984*, and Paddy Egan, Tommy Flanagan and William Mulvihill, *The GAA in Kenagh: 100 Years of History 1889–1989 (1989).* Other valuable works were Des Guckian, *The Life and Times of Fr Sean Manning* (1979) and Eugene McGee, *St Mel's of Longford* (1996), while Tom Hunt contributed a typically detailed and insightful essay entitled 'County Longford: Sport & Society, 1850–1905', which was published in Martin Morris and Fergus O'Ferrall (eds.) *Longford: History & Society* (2010). The account provided in the chapter of pre-GAA football in Longford was taken from Dudley Bradstreet, *The Life and Uncommon Adventures of Captain Dudley Bradstreet* (1755). Liam Mulvihill contributed an article entitled 'The GAA Story' to *75 Years of Longford – The Longford Leader 1897–1972*, while the *County Longford Yearbook* was also consulted, along with an assortment of material held by the GAA Oral History Archive, including an 'Unpublished history of Mostrim GAA, Dromard GAA club, *A Souvenir Programme from opening of James J. Donoghue Memorial Park, 16 May 1976*, and Colmcille GAA Club, *Programme for Official Opening of Fr McGee Park,* 1982. For wider historical developments in the county, the chapter drew on the work of Raymond Gillespie and Gerard Moran (eds.), *Longford: Essays in County History* (1991) and Marie Coleman, *County Longford and the Irish Revolution, 1913–21* (2003).

Louth

In addition to those major publications listed above, the principle texts that underpin this chapter are those by Fr John Mulligan, author of *The G.A.A. in Louth: An Historical Record* (1984) and *Dundalk Young Irelands GFC. An Historical Record of the Green and Blacks* (2005). The early development of the GAA in the county was also informed by an article on 'The work of the GAA in Louth', published in *The Gaelic Athletic Annual and County Directory,* No. 3, 1910–11, and Marcus Bourke's, 'Early GAA in South Ulster', published in the *Cloger Record, 1969*. The story of soccer in Dundalk was researched with the help of Jim Murphy, *The History of Dundalk F.C.: The First 100 Years* (2003), while Louth's last All-Ireland title success in 1957 has been recalled in two books – Eunan Whyte, *Heroes of '57. The Complete Story of Louth's All-Ireland Victory* (1997) and Dan O'Neill, *Divided Loyalties: The Life and Times of a Mayo man who won an All-Ireland title with Louth in 1957* (2008). In advance of the millennium year, Fr Mulligan updated his GAA history of the county and the result – *The G.A.A. in Louth: An Historical Record: The Centenary – The Millennium* (2000) – offers an excellent overview of developments in the years since the GAA's centenary year. The current condition and future plans of the GAA in Louth are set out in the *Louth GAA: Strategic Vision and Action Plan 2010–2015.*

Mayo

Terry Reilly and Ivan Neill's book *The Green Above the Red: A Compilation of Mayo's All-Ireland Triumphs at All Levels* (1985) was the essential text used in writing this chapter. Also of huge assistance was the entry on Martin Sheridan, published in the Royal Irish Academy's *Dictionary of Irish Biography*. General information on Mayo (as well as GAA-related material) was taken from John Healy's masterpiece, *No One Shouted Stop!: The Death of an Irish Town* (1988) and from Rosa Meehan's *The Story of Mayo* (2003). Amongst the many club histories from Mayo, the histories of Ballina, Ballinrobe and Garrymore were helpful, while Keith Duggan's *House of Pain* (2007) is simply one of the best books published in Ireland over the last decade.

Meath

Newspapers and general histories (see above) yielded a wealth of material on Meath, but another core text underpinning this chapter is Michael O'Brien, *Royal and Loyal: Meath GAA's History, Part 1 – 1884–1940* (2002). Much that is general to the history of the Association in Meath is also contained within another O'Brien book, *Perseverance Brings Success, 1887–1987: The GAA in Johnstown/Walterstown* (1987). The story of the Meath relationship with Australian Rules football is documented and discussed in Peter McDermott, *Gaels in the Sun. A Detailed Account of Meath's Historic Trip to Australia* (1970) and Mike Cronin, 'When the World Cup is Played on Roller Skates': The Attempt to Make Gaelic Games International: The Meath–Australia Matches of 1967–68', in *Immigrants & Minorities*, Vol. 17, No. 1, March 1998. Useful sources for more recent sporting developments in the county were Liam Hayes, *Out of Our Skins* (1992) and Liam Hayes (ed.) *The Boylan Years: One Man, One Team, Twenty Years* (2002). As for the exploration of the impact of population overspill from Dublin on the county, this was done with reference to Michel Peillon, *A Tale of Four Suburbs: Social Resources at the Periphery*, a paper delivered to the Symposium on Civic and Social Life in the Suburbs, 8 April 2005, and Mary P. Corcoran, Jane Gray and Michel Peillon, *Ties that Bind? The Social Fabric of Daily Life in New Suburbs*, in Tony Fahey, Helen Russell and Christopher Whelan (eds.), *Best of Times? The Social Impact of the Celtic Tiger* (2007), as well as Mary P. Corcoran's contribution to the round table discussion at the GAA 125 Sports History Conference at Croke Park, 25 April 2009.

Monaghan

The principle books used in writing this piece were John P. Graham (ed.), *Torthaí 125 Bliain: A Book of Monaghan GAA Facts–1884 to 2009* (2009), Séamus McCluskey, *The G.A.A in Co. Monaghan … A History* (1984) and Séamus McCluskey, *The Monaghan Gael: Eighty Years A Growing 1887 to 1967* (1967). Fearghal McGarry's biography *Eoin O'Duffy: A Self-Made Hero* (2005) was also used to provide context to the history of the GAA in Monaghan and to the career of Duffy who was such a vital presence in the establishment of the GAA in the county.

Offaly

This chapter drew from P. J. Cunningham and Ricey Scully, *History Of Offaly GAA* (1984) and Paul Rouse, 'Sport and the Offaly tradition: The Gaelic Athletic Association,' in Timothy P. O'Neill and William Nolan (eds.), *Offaly: History & Society; Interdisciplinary Essays on the History of an Irish County*

(1997). On a broader note, the *Journal of the Offaly Archaeological and Historical Society* is a mine of information. Indeed, the county is very well served by that society and by its libraries, whose local studies collections are of the very highest order.

Roscommon

The principal source for this chapter was Tony Conboy, *Ros Comáin: 101 Years of Gaelic Games in County Roscommon 1889 to 1990* (1990). In this chapter – as in most of the chapters written about the counties of Connacht – the work of John Scally and Jack Mahon was extremely helpful. In this instance, Scally's books, *The Earley Years* (1992) and *The Best of the West: GAA Greats of Connacht* (2008) were of great assistance. Roscommon GAA yearbooks from 1983 to 1995 were interesting to read, as were a range of club histories, from Michael Cassidy's *Roscommon Town G.A.A: A History 1889–1983* (1983) to John Hunt (ed.), *History of Kilbride G.A.A. Club 1887–1992* (n.d.). Use was also made of two plans published by Roscommon County Council, *Development Plan for County Roscommon* (1967) and *County Roscommon: Development Plan 1981 – Plan Forbatha 1981* (1981). Also useful was Eithne MacDermott's book, *Clann Na Poblachta* (1998) and the *Dictionary of Irish Biography* entry on Jack McQuillan.

Sligo

This chapter is heavily reliant on Tommy Kilcoyne (ed.), *Sligo GAA 125 History, 1884–2009, Incorporating A Centenary History, 1884–1984* (2009). The chapter also used a range of club histories, including Christina Murphy, *Tubbercurry GAA Club: A History* (1996) and Rory O'Beirne, *Dromore West and Templeboy G.A.A. Clubs 1888–1963, St. Farnan's G.A.A. Club 1964–2000: A History* (2001). The Sligo GAA Strategic Plan of 2005 was insightful reading, as was the *Club Sligo Brochure* (2011). Background information came from John C. McTernan's books, *A Sligo Miscellany: A Chronicle of People, Places & Events of Other Days* (2000) and *Historic Sligo; A Bibliographical Introduction to the Antiquities and History, Maps and Surveys, MSS. and Newspapers, Historical Families and Notable Individuals of County Sligo* (1965).

Tipperary

This chapter drew from different sources for different periods. For the early decades of the GAA, the principal works were Philip Fogarty, *Tipperary's GAA Story* (1960), Seamus Ó Riain, *Maurice Davin (1842–1927): First President of the GAA (1994)*, Tom Hunt, 'Tipperary hurlers, 1895–1900, a socio-economic profile', published in *Tipperary Historical Journal* (2009), and Nancy Murphy, 'Joseph K. Bracken, GAA founder, fenian and politician', in William Nolan and Thomas G. McGrath, *Tipperary: History & Society* (1997). The events of Bloody Sunday are covered in a multitude of publications, including Anne Dolan, 'Killing and Bloody Sunday, November 1920', *Historical Journal*, Vol. 49.3, 2006 and Miceál Ó Meára (ed.), *Bloody Sunday 1920–1995: A Commemorative Booklet* (1995). The overlap in interests on rural issues between the GAA and Muintir na Tíre from the 1930s onwards was traced through newspapers, but also drew on Mark Tierney, *The Story of Muintir na Tíre 1931–2001 – the First Seventy Years* (2004) and John Hayes, 'Preface' to J. J. Meagher, *Conventions, Or a Dozen Years with the Gaels of Tipperary* (1939). The Tipperary hurling tour to the United States in 1926 is excellently documented in Thomas J. Kenny, *Tour of the Tipperary Hurling Team in America 1926* (1928), while the publication of Tony Wall's *Hurling* (1965) still stands as a vital moment in the history of Gaelic games coaching. Many of the great days enjoyed by Tipperary hurling in the middle decades of the twentieth century onwards are recalled in, *inter alia*, Raymond Smith, *Players No. 6 Book of Hurling : A Popular History of the National Game 1884–1974* (1974), Raymond Smith, *The Greatest Hurlers of Our Time* (1990), Brendan Fullam, *Giants of the Ash* (1991), Seamus King, *A History of Hurling* (1996), and Seamus King, Liam Ó Donnchú and Jimmy Smyth, *Tipperary's GAA Ballads: A Millennium Production* (2000).

Tyrone

This chapter relies heavily on Joseph Martin, *The GAA in Tyrone: The Long Road to Glory* (2003) which

– as is noted in the text of the chapter – is an excellent book, possibly the finest county history yet produced. Various books cited at the start of this note were also extremely useful in the writing of the chapter, as was H. Jefferies (ed.) *Tyrone: History and Society* (2000), which provided interested background material, particularly on the development of nationalist politics.

Waterford

The closest that Waterford has to a county GAA history is the commemorative publication *Portláirge '84 – Comóradh an Chéid 1884–1984 (1985)*. This, together with articles contained in the pages of the journal *An Déiseach* in the early 1970s, provide some insight into the early development of the GAA in Waterford, but in the course of preparing this chapter, it was necessary to supplement this work with research through local sources (including those made available online by the Waterford County Museum) and more general histories of the GAA, among them Phil O'Neill, *A History of the GAA 1910–1930: A History and Reference Book for Gaels* (1931). Since the late 1990s, however, there has been a proliferation of publications focusing on Waterford GAA and these have covered a broad time span, from the emergence of Waterford hurling in 1930s up to the present. The authors and titles include: Tom Keith, *The Colours Blue & White. Waterford's Successes in Hurling and Football, 1938–1948* (1998), Conor Power, *My Father A Hurling Revolutionary. The Life and Times of Ned Power* (2009), Damian Lawlor, *Working On A Dream. A Year on the Road with Waterford's Footballers* (2009), David Smith, *The Unconquerable Keane, John Keane and the Rise of Waterford Hurling* (2010) and Damien Tiernan, *The Ecstasy and the Agony* (2010).

Westmeath

The research in this chapter is drawn from Tom Hunt, *Sport and Society in Victorian Ireland: the Case of Westmeath* (2008) and from Tom Hunt, 'Cusack Park, Mullingar: the conception, difficult gestation and spectacular delivery of a GAA venue', *Ríocht na Mídhe XVII* (2006), pp. 271–291. Tom Hunt also provided a considerable amount of currently unpublished material that was invaluable in the completion of the chapter. Of further note is Gerry Buckley's *The Millennium Handbook of Westmeath Gaelic Games* (2000), which is a fine resource for anyone seeking to understand the GAA in the county.

Wexford

There is no full-scale history of the GAA in Wexford, yet the county has been well served by its local writers and historians. Sources for the early development of the GAA in Wexford include Séan Ó Faoláin, *With the Gaels of Wexford* (1955), Paul Rouse, 'Empires of Sport: Enniscorthy, 1880–1920', in Colm Toibín (ed.), *Enniscorthy: A History* (2010), Sean Whelan, *The Ghosts of Bygone Days: An Enniscorthy GAA History* (1998) and Dominic Williams, *The Wexford Hurling and Football Bible, 1887–2008. A Complete Statistical History of Wexford GAA* (2008). The story of the Wexford footballers' four-in-a-row between 1915 and 1918 is recounted in all major histories of Gaelic football and among those consulted was Eoghan Corry, *Catch and Kick* (1989). The GAA Oral History Project Archive holds an assortment of material on Wexford, including reports of County Conventions, and these, supplemented by newspapers, were widely consulted in the preparation of this chapter. So too were many of the books that chart the rise of Wexford hurling in the 1950s, among them Nicholas Furlong, *The Greatest Hurling Decade: Wexford and the Epic Teams of the '50s* (1993), Billy Rackard, *No Hurling at the Dairy Door* (1996), and Tom Williams, *Cúchullain's Son: The Story of Nickey Rackard* (2006). Impressions on the societal impact of that glamorous Wexford team are also provided in the award-winning book by Tom Dunne, *Rebellions: Memoir, Memory and 1798* (2004). A fascinating, and comprehensive study of the GAA in Wexford at a critical moment in its development was provided by Patricia O'Hara and Carmel Kelleher, An Foras Talúntais, *The GAA in County Wexford: A Report on Organisational Structure* (1980). Denis Walsh, *Hurling: the Revolution Years* (2005) contains an excellent chapter on the background to Wexford's 1996 All-Ireland victory, but the most comprehensive account of this period was provided by Tom Williams, *With Heart and Hand: the Inside Story of Wexford's Hurling Resurgence* (1996).

Wicklow

The starting points in researching this chapter were two histories of the GAA in Wicklow, written almost fifty years apart: C. M. Byrne and P. J. Noonan, *50 years of the GAA in Wicklow* (1935), and Jim Brophy, *The Leathers Echo. A Story of Hurling, Football, Handball and Camogie in Co. Wicklow from 1884 to 1984* (1984). These texts were supplemented by newspapers and by such club histories as Jim Brophy, *By the Banks of the River Dargle: A History of Bray Emmets 1885–1985* (1985) and David Hallahan, *The Path to the Pinnacle: A History of Baltinglass GAA* (1984).

Overseas

The literature that focuses on the GAA overseas has grown steadily in recent years, and there now exists a considerable body of work on which this chapter draws. Among the earliest to cover this subject matter is Seamus King, *The Clash of the Ash in Foreign Fields: Hurling Abroad* (1998). Of the more recent publications, Paul Darby's *Gaelic Games, Nationalism and the Irish Diaspora in the United States* (2009) affords the most comprehensive treatment of the GAA in that particular part of the world. For the GAA in the context of Irish American sport see, Ralph Wilcox, 'Irish Americans in Sports: The Nineteenth Century' and Larry McCarthy, 'Irish Americans in Sports: The Twentieth Century', both of which appear in J. J. Lee and Marion R. Casey (eds.), *Making the Irish American: History and Heritage of the Irish in the United States* (2006). For London, see Tom Griffin, *Gaelic Hearts: History of the London GAA* (2011) and for Scotland, the wide range of work by Joseph Bradley, including his *The Gaelic Athletic Association in Scotland: History, Ethnicity, Politics, Culture, Identity* (2007). A good reflection on the spread of the GAA in recent years to new parts of the world can be found in Aaron Dunne, *Around the World in GAA Days* (2009), while Robert Mulhern's *A Very Different County* (2011) is an excellent portrayal of the GAA in London.

Index

Glen Rovers 81
golf 134, 215
Gothenburg 445
Graiguecullen 216
Grealy, Joe 167
Great War 80, 242
Greene, Henry 156
Gribben, Roddy 95
Griffin, Liam 418, 423
Guinness brewery 135, 402
Guthrie, Karen 115

H

Hamilton, Canon Michael 67–8
handball
    Armagh 32
    Limerick 241
    Longford 256
    Mayo 276
    Tyrone 378
    Westmeath 408
Hanlon, John F. 52
Harrison, Charlie 354
Hartnett, Noel 332
Hayden, Brendan 48
Hayes, Canon John 363
Hayes, Maurice 120
Healy, Cahir 149
Healy, Dermot 323
Healy, Diarmuid 204–5
Healy, John 276, 282
Heffernan, Kevin 137, 142, 178
Heffernan, Mick 368
Henderson, John 7–8
Hennessy, Paddy 67
Hickey, Jody 450
Higgins, Mick 56, 257
Hoare, Owensie 333
Hobson, Bulmer 15
Hogan Cup (All-Ireland inter-colleges competition) 29, 96–7, 123–4, 256, 377
Hogan, Michael 136, 362–3
Holmes, Rev. Samuel 122
Hong Kong 442, 445
Horan, Liam 341
Houlihan, Con 319
Hughes, Eugene 'Nudie' 310
Hughes, Fred 15
Hunt, Tom 267, 361–2, 402, 403
hurling 79, 360
    Antrim 14–17, 20
    Carlow 43–4, 47
    Cavan 52

    Clare 64, 66–7, 68, 69–70, 71, 72, 74
    Cork 4–5, 16, 20, 79, 80, 81–2, 88, 440
    Derry 93–4, 97
    Donegal 106, 107, 108
    Down 122, 123, 124, 127
    Dublin 134, 136, 137, 139, 141
    Fermanagh 148, 150
    first All-Ireland final 5–6, 163, 361
    Galway 5–6, 162, 163–5, 166, 169, 170
    Kerry 174–5, 182
    Kildare 190, 194
    Kilkenny 6, 198, 200–2, 203–5, 206, 207, 208, 209
    Laois 213–14, 215–16, 217, 219, 221
    Leitrim 227, 231
    Limerick 238, 240, 241–3, 244, 246, 247
    Longford 256, 258, 259
    Louth 268, 270
    Mayo 279
    Meath 293
    Monaghan 308, 310
    Offaly 16, 320–2, 323, 324, 325, 328
    overseas 322, 325, 440, 442, 443, 444–5, 446, 447, 449
    Roscommon 334, 335
    rules 18, 106, 162, 360, 386, 443
    Sligo 347, 350
    Tipperary 4–6, 16, 358, 361, 362, 363, 364, 365, 367, 368
    Tyrone 374–5, 378
    Waterford 386, 388, 389, 390–2, 396, 398
    Westmeath 403, 404–5
    Wexford 412, 413, 414, 416–17, 418, 424
    Wicklow 431–2, 433, 437
Hyde, Dr Douglas 415–16

I

Inishkeen Grattans 53
instructional manuals 177
    first 176, 180
Irish Amateur Athletics Association (IAAA) 78, 173–4
Irish National League 174, 255
Irish Republican Army (IRA) 30, 81, 151, 305, 331–2, 389
Irish Republican Brotherhood (IRB) 26, 53, 78, 80, 93, 149, 161, 162, 174, 190, 202, 214, 240, 267, 292, 305, 429
Irish Volunteers 98, 176, 202, 306, 415
Irish-Ireland movement 293, 306, 375

J

Jakarta 445
Jones, Iggy 377, 380
Jordan, Jeremiah 150

hurling 268, 270
ladies' football 270
Lowery brothers 405
Lowery, Willie 405
Ludlow, Tommy 298
Luxembourg 445
Lynch, Brendan 333
Lynch, Jack 16, 82
Lynch, Kevin 97

M

McAleese, Mary 119–20
McAnallen, Dónal 14, 15
McArdle, Tommy 310
MacBride, Seán 331–2
McCague, Sean 310, 316
MacCarthy, Liam 80, 445
McCarthy, Seán 81
McCloskey, Evelyn 318
McCormack, Paddy 320
McCourt, Frank 243
McCullough, 'Big' Jim 28–9
McCullough, Dennis 15
McDermott, Peter 294, 299, 302
McDonagh, Joe 164
McDonagh, Mattie 166
McDonnell, Matty 302
McElligott, Richard 175
McEniff, Brian 109, 110, 227–8
McEntee, Andy 54
McFadden, Canon James 107–8
McGahern, John 225–6
McGarty, Packie 229
McGee, Eugene 353
McGee, Fr Phil 257
McGettigan, Sean 21
McGinnity, Peter 152
McGoldrick, Johnny 229
McGovern, Vincent 55
McGrath, Marty 153
McGrath, Peter 121
McGreevey, Martin 402
McGreevy, Frank 95
McGuinness, John 229
McGuinness, Margaret (Maggie) 259
McGuinness, Philip 230–1
McHugh, Martin 110
McInerney, Gerry 164
McIniff, Eddie 225–6
McKay, John 77–8
McKeever, Jim 95, 96, 100
Mackey, John 'Tyler' 241–2, 243
Mackey, Michael 243

Mackey, Mick 243, 247
McMahon, Bryan 71
MacMahon, Con 67
MacManus, Seumas 107, 108
McMonagle, Yvonne 115
MacOrristin, Magnus 105–6
McQuillan, Jack 332
McTeague, Tony 323
McWilliams, David 441
Madden, Paul 78
Mageean, Dr (Bishop of Down and Connor) 20
Maghera MacFinns 52–3
Maguire, Sam 80, 190, 443, 445
Maher, Fr Tommy 204
Maher, Terry 269–70
Mahony, Johnny 180
Mangan, Jack 166
Manning, Fr Seán 256
mapping 3
Marcus, Louis 82
Martin, Joe 373–4, 378
Masterson, Packie 54
Mayo 277–89
athletics 277–9, 280, 284
football 279–81, 282–3, 285, 286, 288
handball 276
hurling 279
Meagher, Henry J. 201
Meagher, Lory 203
Meath 291–303
camogie 293
football 292, 293, 294–6, 299, 300, 302, 451
hurling 293
soccer 308
Meegan, Paddy 299
Mehigan, P. D. 55, 76, 216, 243, 420
Metropolitans 134, 141, 162, 320
military teams 190
Molloy, Anthony 110
Molohan, Paddy 194
Monaghan 305–17
football 304, 307, 308–11, 315, 316
hurling 308, 310
ladies' football 310, 314
Monaghan, Danny 154
Monaghan, Johnny 154
Mongey, Éamonn 281
Mooncoin 6, 200, 206
Moran, Denis (Massey) 183
Moran, Mickey 231
Moran, Seán 398
Morrissey, Jody 48
Morrissey, Marty 146, 350

New York 1–2, 56, 62, 67, 224, 229, 278, 322, 325, 405, 440, 442, 443, 444, 446
  see also emigration
Owens, Barry 153

P
parade before matches 356
Parnell, Charles Stewart 27, 42, 51, 66, 149, 188, 201, 240–1, 253–4, 267, 292, 347, 429, 434
  football at Avondale 5, 427–8
Pathé newsreel 193
Patterson, Frank and Robert 122
Peace Process 124
polo 42, 403, 414
Poor Law Unions 3
Portlaoise 217–18
Portumna 170
Power, John Wyse 189, 428
professionalism 176, 177, 180, 202–3, 215, 242, 294
Protestants 124, 149, 150
Purcell, Sean 165–6

Q
Quigley brothers 417
Quinn, Mickey 230, 236

R
Rackard brothers 416
Rackard, Nicky 204, 416, 418
radio 420
Radley, Dick 188
railways 7, 80, 172, 177, 232, 268, 388, 429–30, 432
Ramsbottom, Fr (Thigeen Roe) 189
Rankins, Dick 220
Rathnew 432–3, 436
Ratoath 295
Reddan, Jack 368
Reddan, Steve 368
Redmond, John 389
Rees, Merlyn 30
Regan, Michael and Tommy 276
Reid, Dinny 154
Reid, Donal 110
Reilly, Jason 57
Reilly, Terry 281
Ribbonism 26, 53
Rice, Brother 123
Ring, Christy 16, 76, 81–2
Roche, Lawrence 242
Rochfort, Horace 41–2
Roe, Bernard J. 268
Roe, Thigeen (Fr Ramsbottom) 189
Rohan, Mick 368

Ronan, Jim 368
Roscommon 331–43
  football 330, 332–5, 336, 337, 338, 341, 342
  hurling 334, 335
Rose, Ralph 278
Rouse, Mick 450
Royal Irish Constabulary 3
Ruane, Paddy 167
rugby 4, 28, 79, 94, 134, 189, 306, 418
  Carlow 42
  Kerry 175–6
  Kilkenny 203–4, 208
  Limerick 241, 243, 244
  Westmeath 403
rules
  All-Ireland championship 5–6
  Australian 294–5
  first All-Round athletic championships under GAA 241
  first football match under GAA 200
  football 176, 177, 267, 293, 360
  foreign games 40–1, 67–8, 92, 94, 150, 175, 201, 292, 348, 390, 415–16
  hurling 18, 106, 162, 360, 386, 443
  Longford 255
  security forces 124
  whole-time collective training 177
Russell, Paul 95
Ryall, Tom 201
Ryan, Thomas 41

S
St Colman's College, Newry 121, 123–4
St Flannan's College 68
St Gall's, Antrim 14, 17, 22
St John's, Antrim 14, 16, 17
St Joseph's, Ballycran 124
St Kieran's College 203–4, 208
St Malachy's, Tyrone 384
St Mary's, Sligo 349
St Mel's College 256, 257
St Patrick's College, Armagh 29, 32, 377, 380
St Patrick's College, Cavan 50
St Peter's College, Wexford 417
St Rynagh's, Offaly 17, 321
St Vincents, Dublin 137
Savage, J. L. 122
Scór 227, 270
Scotland 107, 443, 446
Shanahan, Dan 241
Shannon Airport 68–9
Sheehy, Fr Eugene 240
Sheehy, John Joe 177